RECOVERING
PRAGMATISM'S
VOICE

SUNY SERIES IN THE PHILOSOPHY
OF THE SOCIAL SCIENCES

LENORE LANGSDORF, EDITOR

RECOVERING PRAGMATISM'S VOICE

⬳⬳

The Classical Tradition, Rorty, and the Philosophy of Communication

EDITED BY

Lenore Langsdorf and Andrew R. Smith

STATE UNIVERSITY OF NEW YORK PRESS

Published by
State University of New York Press, Albany

© 1995 State University of New York

For information, address State University of New York
Press, State University Plaza, Albany, N.Y., 12246

Production by Diane Ganeles
Marketing by Theresa Abad Swierzowski

Library of Congress Cataloging-in-Publication Data

Recovering pragmatism's voice : the classical tradition, Rorty, and
  the philosophy of communication / edited by Lenore Langsdorf and
  Andrew R. Smith.
      p.   cm. — (SUNY series in the philosophy of the social sciences)
      Includes index.
      ISBN 0-7914-2213-5 (alk. paper). — ISBN 0-7914-2214-3 (pbk. :
  alk. paper)
      1. Pragmatism.   2. Rorty, Richard.   3. Communication.
  I. Langsdorf, Lenore, 1943–   .   II. Smith, Andrew R.,   1953–
  III. Series.
  B832.R39   1995   94-1571
  144′ .3—dc20   CIP

10 9 8 7 6 5 4 3 2 1

For Our Teachers

A.R.S. especially thanks John Angus Campbell,
Richard L. Lanigan, and Thomas Pace

L.L. especially thanks Charles Hartshorne, Thelma Z. Lavine,
John J. McDermott, and Richard M. Zaner

Contents

I

Introduction

1

The Voice of Pragmatism
in Contemporary Philosophy
of Communication

<∙≥∙ ∙≤∙>

Lenore Langsdorf and Andrew R. Smith

The upheaval in the practice of philosophy in America during this last quarter of the century is, at the very least, a reaction against a narrow conception of philosophy as analysis of decontextualized (formal) problems, carried out by a distinct professional class that minimized (even denied) the relevance of history, literature, and sociopolitical institutions to those problems. Nothing more than the inevitable exhaustion of possibilities within such a delimited field may be responsible for postanalytic philosophy's emergence. The very limited audience for mainstream analytic, linguistic, and logical-positivistic philosophy is now overshadowed by scholars who speak in a variety of cultural and disciplinary voices, about topics once relegated to the margins of philosophical discourse. We are in the midst of a protracted revolution (in the Kuhnian sense) in philosophy. Two aspects of that upheaval provide the impetus for this book.

First, scholars' current rejection of the hegemony of analysis as the method (form) and goal of philosophy in mid-century America almost necessitates thinking anew about the subject-matter (content) in close conjunction with the methods (forms) of philosophy. We need no longer ignore issues that are not amenable to analytic procedures and ideals developed in admiration of certain formal, physical, and social sciences that dominated late nineteenth-century scholarship. Our subject-matter in *Recovering Pragmatism's Voice* exemplifies this broadening of interests, for the philosophy of communication was overlooked or misconstrued by mainstream philosophy and the philosophy of science that it inspired. Some linguistic results of communication— claims,

1

statements, proofs—were appropriate to analytic methods and goals. But these products were taken up in reified form, without attention to the communicative practices necessary to their formation or to the communicative forms of their presence. Insofar as philosophy understood itself as offering what Rorty calls a "mirror of nature," it focused upon correct representation of things and events presumed resident in "nature." Correlatively, it ignored the ongoing discourse in which a community of inquirers (in Peirce's sense) forms, presents, and implements its understanding of "nature." Our change of orientation toward that discursive activity, however, is a refocusing on "culture" in Dewey's sense (*Later Works* 1: 361–364)—and more particularly, on how communication functions in the formation and reformation of cultural institutions.

It is this radical shift in subject matter, rather than a dominant interest in methodology, that motivates us to identify or develop alternative methods and goals for the philosophy of communication. Pragmatism's central interest in the communal formation of knowledge and of the knowing subject (the emergent self), as well as in the efficacy of fallible knowledge, informs our understanding of how communication expands human inquiry rather than contracting or reducing inquiry to arguments for or against proposed foundational representations. William James's reliance upon concrete justification of belief in natural processes of encounter with phenomena as they inform interactive knowing suggests one direction for that expansion: communicative justification is a pervasive feature of alternatives to the statistical and stipulative empirical methods that still dominate communication research. George Herbert Mead's reconception of the knowing subject as emergent in communicative interaction—rather than as functioning as the cause of such interaction—provides another dimension for developing the philosophy of communication. Insofar as the philosophy of communication relies upon communicative assessment of knowledge claims and conceptualizes the knowing subject as emergent in those communication-based processes of inquiry and assessment, pragmatic philosophy of communication does not simply concur with contemporary rejection of the Cartesian self and its claims to universal and apodictic knowledge. It goes beyond critique to reconstruction, by developing an alternative conceptualization of human beings as communicative agents who formulate conjectures, test them against experience, and use the results.

A further contribution of the classical pragmatism of Peirce, Dewey, James, and Mead to a more encompassing conception of communication should be mentioned. Ideals of assent within communicative communities, and perhaps even of generalized adherence across institutional and cultural domains, can function as standards against which the value of actual communicative events may be assessed. Thus the philosophy of communication is able to reach beyond empirical research, and also beyond Rortyean "edification," into axiological and even normative inquiry. This expansion (together with other aspects of classical pragmatism) is resisted by many communication researchers as well as by Rortyean neopragmatism. Thus, a diversity of views is evident in the chapters of this book, all of which are original essays written for this volume. Most of the contributors focus upon the implications of classical pragmatism for the philosophy of communication within a postanalytic, postempirical, postmodern era of inquiry quite different from the intellectual climate in which Peirce, Dewey, James, and Mead wrote. Only some of the contributors understand the significance of that difference as Rorty does. That seems to us an appropriate breadth of perspectives in a volume unified by its contributors' appreciation of the pragmatic tradition as itself in process, responding to a universal need for localized knowledge that may be used by particular historical and sociopolitical communities—rather than responding to a particular intellectual culture's need for foundational principles, static objects of knowledge, or algorithmic proofs.

Classical Pragmatism

Pragmatism has come to mean so many things that any endeavor aimed at recovering a singular voice of pragmatism may seem audacious, at the very least, to readers who prefer a polyphony to an oration. But polyphony, despite its poetic pleasure in the arts and its rhetorical reality in a democracy, can easily turn into cacophony when we engage in conceptualization. That danger is especially present when we attempt to understand and apply a philosophy such as pragmatism, which eschews theory in favor of practice. For in the absence of clear or unified self-definition, the many ends to which the term pragmatism is put may endanger its original force as a way of formulating and testing radically new ways of thinking that might work to advance the welfare and future sustenance of a community.

The essays in this volume explore what we (the editors) understand as the intension of pragmatism; the persistent themes that can be identified as present in one after another of the tradition's classical extensions, and commend pragmatism as a methodology for social change and human development. Our interest in recovering a singular voice of pragmatism thus begins with appreciating the extent to which certain themes are not present in it—for that very absence documents pragmatism's contrast to other modern philosophies. Pragmatism fosters inquiry and pluralism by eschewing strategies for closure (including essentialism), questioning prevailing metanarratives, and encouraging the development of new habits of conduct through a critical practice that is fundamentally self-reflective, to the extent of reconceptualizing the very concept of the self.

Moreover, pragmatism to some extent assumes, and to some extent proposes, a philosophy of communication that has scarcely been articulated, despite the wealth of commentary on other aspects of pragmatism. We suggested earlier that the impetus for this philosophical development may be an exhaustion of earlier conceptualizations of communication as reduced to its linguistic products, conceived as providing (at least ideally) a mirror of nature. For such a philosophy of language, communication simply is a means for expressing preconceived ideas and truths about an antecedent reality. From early through late empiricism—from Locke through Carnap and the early Wittgenstein and extending into Austin and Searle—there was a good deal of philosophical analysis focused on how that transmission can lead us astray in our thinking, and so, on how transmission might be accomplished more clearly and distinctly. The basic prescription was to minimize transmission interference through strategies such as conceptual (logical and linguistic) analysis and the development of normed languages that would eliminate, insofar as possible, the plurivocity intrinsic to natural language.

Beginning with the recognition of linguistic performativity in the work of the later empiricists, however, this conception of language as merely reportorial, at best, or as a barrier to inquiry (by virtue of multiple meanings), at worst, expanded to include a conception of linguistic activity as a social process of discerning how things are, what language users believe about how things are, and how we would have them otherwise. In effect, this is a new domain for philosophical investigation. It begins in recognizing communication as a process encompassing the use of language by someone to inform someone. Insofar as all communication is concerned with informing, it is concerned with ways of inquiring and goals of inquiry; with assumptions about inquiring and with objects of inquiry. As traditional philosophical endeavors (such as metaphysics, epistemology, and axiology) are pursued in relation to communication, the particular value of pragmatism for the philosophy of communication can be articulated in terms of pragmatism's understanding of inquiry as intrinsically fallible and oriented toward its consequences, and of the self—the instigator and assessor of inquiry—as emergent from and effectively reflective on communicative practice. We hope that the essays in this volume initiate that articulation, and so contribute to what we see as a philosophical turn—a reconceptualization of the field—within contemporary communication studies, as well as to what may be a communicative turn within contemporary philosophical thinking.

Perhaps we can best begin that articulation by looking briefly at both classical and Rortyean pragmatism. In speaking of the "classical tradition" in American pragmatism, we mean a body of philosophical thinking and social theory formulated by John Dewey, William James, George Herbert Mead, and Charles Sanders Peirce. The work of Ralph Waldo Emerson, Josiah Royce, George Santayana, Henry David Thoreau, and Alfred North Whitehead exhibits strong affinities with that core of work, and often is identified in commentaries as pragmatic. However, we are concerned in these essays only with the work of Dewey, James, Mead, and Peirce, because their work demonstrates explicit and sustained interest in the phenomenon of communication.

Metaphysically, classical pragmatism rejects certain dualisms that have marked mainstream modern philosophy: mind and matter; nature and culture; belief and knowledge; thought and action; facts and values; individual and community. This is not to say that pragmatism ignores the powerful effects of these oppositional modes of thinking. Rather, by rejecting them as metaphysical categories intrinsic to reality, pragmatism is able to respecify them as functional distinctions that we use and find useful in developing practices that respond to acculturated experiences in which reality is present for us. This respecification enables and even requires investigating both the genesis of these dichotomies and the interests they may serve. In other words, by abandoning unquestioned acceptance of these categories, pragmatism encourages our reflection on how and to what end they are instituted. That line of inquiry may then extend to reconstructing categories so that they might serve alternative ends.

In pursuing epistemological and axiological questions, classical pragmatism replaces "the quest for certainty" with a quest for testable answers that make a difference within specific domains of culture (experience). Thus, pragmatism does not base inquiry on conscious subjects' knowledge claims about values and objects understood as either directly perceived or deduced from observation. Rather, it advocates persisting inquiry by communities of inquirers, who acknowledge their own complicity in constituting those values and objects in relation to particular exigencies and anticipated consequences.

Researchers are thus constrained to reflect on that constitutive process as a complex of axiological, cultural, physical, psychological, and social conditions. For pragmatism, in other words, the very conditions for inquiry are also topics for inquiry.

Furthermore, classical pragmatism displays a marked meliorative determination that contrasts with the distanciated ideal of other philosophical orientations. Thought is to be used—put into practice—so as to improve the human condition. Thus, in its practice of philosophy, pragmatism rejects both the "analytic" and "descriptive/interpretive" models, insofar as those traditions have understood philosophy as the posing and solving (or dissolving) of theoretical "problems" about facts or values. That rejection follows from pragmatism's recognition of those problems as products of the very search for abstract values, certain knowledge, eternal truth, or unchanging reality that preoccupied philosophy for several centuries. This is not to say that pragmatism is not concerned with knowing. Rather, it conceives its epistemic and evaluative tasks as practical and critical; as pursued by inquirers who are intrinsically social, and who discern and delineate values and concepts in actual situations, and test them by their consequences—rather than by reducing them to facts or propositions about a presumed antecedent reality.

Rortyean Pragmatism

Richard Rorty's considerable influence on contemporary American intellectual life may well be due to his advocacy of many of these reconstructed philosophical interests. That advocacy identifies, and even goes some distance toward justifying, his self-classification as a pragmatist. That affiliation also is substantiated by his adoption of Dewey's notion of "warranted assertibility": what warrants an assertion is neither confirmation by accepted doctrine nor fit with empirical evidence, but appropriateness when tested by the habits and practices of daily life. Thus, Rorty retains a fundamental feature of classical pragmatism: he emphasizes consequent possibilities rather than antecedent certainties. That emphasis does not mean that we exercise a deliberate or consistent focus on setting goals or postulating particular ends, and then delineating the means to achieve them. Rather, Rorty's (and Dewey's) emphasis on the consequent employs the art of imagining possible results of conceptions as they become engrained in a community as habits of conduct; as habitual ways of acting, thinking, feeling, believing, and knowing.

The idea that conduct should be oriented to future meaning, rather than toward past doctrine or present perception, is as much Darwinian as mainstream philosophy has been Cartesian. Beliefs evolve as they are put into practice by a community. Some aspects of a belief are shed when they no longer cohere with social experience, while other aspects may be retained. Hence pragmatism is evolutionary rather than revolutionary, in either the Kuhnian or Marxian senses. Rorty's work furthers our understanding and appreciation of this "naturalistic" dimension of pragmatism. Moreover, Rorty demonstrates that evolution in thinking, acting, and speaking is a function of how a particular community uses communicative strategies to link and justify habits of conduct. In this sense he follows James more than Peirce or Dewey, since he draws on the precepts of individualism to justify ethnocentrism. Our beliefs are true, he argues, to the extent that they can be justified according to procedures for justification extant in a community that is defined by a particular time, place, and accepted linguistic and communicative conventions.

Finally, Rorty follows Peirce as a fallibilist in that he recognizes that a belief may be justified within a particular set of conditions, but later turn out (under other conditions) to be wrong. Accordingly, communication is vital for the development and flourishing of new belief, and may even engender a (polyphonous) conversation of humankind.

Once we go beyond these decidedly brief notations of the affinities and continuity that we discern between Rortyean and classical pragmatism, conversation must give way to argumentation. For contemporary discussion among philosophers who identify themselves with the pragmatic tradition does divide rather sharply on the legitimacy of Rorty's claim to membership in the tradition. The postmodern context of Rorty's pragmatism surely supports, and perhaps even necessitates, his replacement of classical pragmatism's reliance upon the subject (however construed) as agent for reflection on and reconstruction of institutions (including philosophy). But our changed historical situation does not in itself ratify replacing the subject of modernity with an ethnocentric solidarity that uncritically conserves a long and limited conversation.

To many contemporary pragmatists, Rorty's disinterest in the practical consequences of intellectual discourse—his valuing of a discourse that makes no difference—disqualifies his claim to membership. To others, however, the affiliations we have noted are sufficient; insisting upon complete allegiance to a philosophy marked by issues of an earlier day would be nothing less than essentialism. Since several of our contributors address this issue as part of the general question of prag-

matism's contribution to the philosophy of communication, we turn
now to a preview of the positions developed in the following chapters.

Contemporary Voices of Pragmatism

C. S. Peirce's theory of signs is often conceived as a logic of classification bent on bringing all depictions of phenomena within its
explanatory grasp. This foundational conception invites modernists
such as Morris to appropriate Peirce's *semiotics* as a way of marking all
communication practices as representational. Vincent Colapietro's
essay, "Immediacy, Opposition, and Mediation: Peirce on the
Irreducible Aspects of the Communicative Process" (chap. 2), takes
issue with this distorted interpretation of Peirce's philosophy, and
especially with Richard Rorty's attempt to "bury" Peirce because of it.

Colapietro argues that Peirce's theory of signs and his "pragmaticism" go hand in hand as a heuristic for critical inquiry rather than as
a system for explanation. Peirce radicalizes the notion of the "practical"
to encompass the possible consequences of our conceptions—a notion
that hinges on imagination rather than rationalization. He thus pushes
beyond the limits of what we think we know about a phenomenon by
virtue of the circumstances of its emergence. The significance of any
expression (gesture, word, phrase, proposition, argument, or belief)
understood as a form of conduct is, for Peirce, ill-conceived if practice
is thought of as limited to nominal or atomistic formulations. To reach
the intricacies and excesses of meaning necessary for gaining insight
and developing an evolutionary approach to communication, pragmaticists should be critically self-conscious, according to Colapietro,
which means they should be capable of working through otherness in
radically different ways. Pragmaticism thus conceived is an imaginative and collaborative semiotics of consequence.

Colapietro presents Peirce's phenomenological categories of
immediacy ("firstness"), opposition ("secondness") and mediation
("thirdness") as communication concepts that edify the self-other relationship. His discussion of otherness reveals how the radical conception of practice in fact hinges on a primordial tension and intercession
of self and other. Indeed, it is only through a consideration of otherness
that consequences of practice for oneself can be worked through. The
other is radically other in that she or he is never a terminal point in
which communication ends, but a condition of fluctuating significance
through which "ever higher levels of self-consciousness, self-criticism,
and self-control" become accessible. Colapietro draws a parallel

between Peirce and Derrida along these lines, especially with regard to speech, writing, and the process of codification. In the end the reader should see how Peirce, pace Rorty, is no more a metaphysician of presence than is Derrida.

In "From Enthymeme to Abduction: The Classical Law of Logic and the Postmodern Rule of Rhetoric" (chap. 3), Richard Lanigan depicts the semiotics of consequence operating as a rhetoric of communication practice that engenders both power and desire. Modernity is marked, argues Lanigan, by the power of the few to exclude the many by demarcating "correct" thought and translating this thought into symbolic discourse that abides by the laws of identity and noncontradiction. Postmodernity is marked, on the other hand, by the desire of the many to be included in discourse(s), and to transgress the laws of noncontradiction and identity through practices that reveal how something can, through signs, both be and not be at the same time. Lanigan shows how Peirce was pivotal in reconceptualizing the communicative import of "symbol" and "sign" from the "classical law of logic to the postmodern rule of rhetoric," respectively. Hence it would appear that Rorty's "conversation of [hu]mankind" is actually a debt paid to Peirce.

The notion of abduction and its corollary, "retroduction" or "adduction," are the pivots through which the radicalization of discourse—as practice—takes place. Since discourse in conversation functions rhetorically, the best way to grasp how abduction operates is, according to Lanigan, through a reconsideration of the enthymeme. He proceeds by criticizing the traditional approach to the enthymeme as a "logic of rhetoric"—an approach characteristic of modernity in which the enthymeme is thought to be formally valid but materially deficient. Since the definition is given in such a scheme, all that is required of the addressee is to fill in the deficiency with what is the correct, albeit suppressed, material. The postmodern conception of the enthymeme, on the other hand, is a "rhetoric of logic" in which the syllogism is both materially uncertain and formally deficient. The addressee fills in the gaps of discourse through a "formal (not material!)" process that coheres with "Peirce's notion of tone."

Abduction operates in communication, argues Lanigan, as "the embodied intentionality of speech," which is materially uncertain, "while the enthymeme is abduction's articulation as formal deficiency." Uncertainty and deficiency are in fact the sufficient conditions for insight and reciprocity. Lanigan shows how abduction (hypothesis formation) and adduction (hypothesis testing) are tropological acts practiced by speakers and listeners in everyday communication. This poetic conception contributes, in turn, to an appreciation of communication as an art of rhetoric and a science of living in which self and other, and the same and the different, are continually actualized anew.

Newness, however, is not always pleasant, especially when injustices occur as a result of conflicting versions of the truth of some matter. Andrew Smith and Leonard Shyles take up the issue of "Ethnocentric Truth and Pragmatic Justice" (chap. 4), as a way of examining how the classical pragmatism of Peirce (pragmaticism) and Dewey (instrumentalism) contribute to the modern-postmodern debate on the possibility of truth and justice. They address the semiotics of consequence in both Peirce and Dewey by first reviewing how this logic has been appropriated by Rorty in philosophy and Richard Shweder in cultural psychology. Both Rorty and Shweder accept the principles of fallibilism laid out by Peirce, and the idea that truth is manifested and pluralized through processes of communication. But whereas Rorty eschews much of Peirce's system formations and conceptions of "ideal ends," Shweder recognizes the significance of transcendental realities, and discusses how such realities are accessed abductively through communication. Smith and Shyles argue that such imaginative access is crucial for intercultural understanding—however tentative and fallible that understanding may be—and consider how problems of truth and justice can be addressed across cultural realities through idioms formed by communicative and metacommunicative engagement of differences—for example, race, gender, class, age, role, rank, discipline, and so on.

Abductive processes, Smith and Shyles suggest, operate in intercultural communication in much the same way that Peirce and Dewey conceived the operations of critical inquiry. They argue that developing the capability of imagining how something might be the case from another cultural point of view is part and parcel of recognizing its truth. The creation of this newness requires an ongoing collaborative recognition and rearrangement of cultural instruments. Smith and Shyles thus advance Dewey's critique of custom and his advocation of thinking progressively even though one may not be familiar with the ends one seeks. The discussion of ends in Peirce and Dewey is then reconceptualized as an imaginative process that is not determinate for insight and understanding, but conditional for organizing a progressive—that is, evolutionary—axiology through communication practice.

This collaborative project of negotiating ends-in-view imaginatively among a plurality of perspectives, according to Charleen Haddock Seigfried in "Devising Ends Worth Striving For: William James and the Reconstruction of Philosophy" (chap. 6), was James's principal interest throughout in his life's work. James' contribution to the philosophy of communication is articulated most clearly in his struggle to work through the subjective-objective problematic. Seigfried shows how the notion of ends-in-view is developed as an evolving thematic in a struggle that began with a critique of the rationalist program of gaining insight into being.

Early in his career James believed that the encompassing ends that guide our proximate choices could be conceived as objective postulates to be invoked for deciding disputes among various subjectivities. But he later abandoned this idea (Seigfried points out) at the risk of becoming nihilistic, since such a conception could easily place subjective insight and belief in the hands of established religious and mystical doctrines. The purposeful nature of human conduct was one universal condition of truth that James was able to accept, but the complement to this condition was that human experience is inherently ambiguous or vague, and thus personal and singular. Any meaningful action is performed according to the purposes of that action as we define it for ourselves. This means, Seigfried argues, that the significance or "nature of an event can only be determined within a horizon of enacted meanings . . . [that] are both cultural and personal, that is, bounded by socially constructed and individually appropriated ends-in-view."

For James, then, the definition of truth hinges on a phenomenological orientation to the world; on a way of describing events and the "living" processes of reasoning about events in as concrete a manner as possible. We should be concerned with emphasis and selection, with signifying and edifying, with the plurality of perspectives and partial truths that coordinate around an event, and with the human purposes brought to bear on description and interpretation. Seigfried argues that these concerns do not define or otherwise determine an epistemological problematic, but realign descriptions according to "intimacy" instead of "transparency." This intimacy involves an ethical dimension insofar as it assumes a cooperative association of people working, and it involves an aesthetic dimension insofar as that association conceives of some unity of purpose for their interpretations that is worth striving for.

One purpose worth rethinking for communication philosophy and pedagogy, according to Isaac Catt in "The 'Cash Value' of Communication: An Interpretation of William James" (chap. 5), is the notion of competence. The modern concern with "communication competence" is associated too readily and perhaps unwittingly, argues Catt, with an "ideological allegiance to careerism/consumerism in higher education." The "cash-value" of communication under this paradigm is determined according to dominant economic interests, and this is definitely not what James had in mind when he invented the phrase. The original conception is actually more postmodern in that it focuses on the concrete singularity of an event and the interpretations developed out of an engagement with that event.

Catt contends that, in pushing back toward the original conception of "cash-value," we might also rethink the purposes of the human sciences, and the role of communication education in the university. Competency researchers are committed implicitly to an integrative approach to the human sciences which tends toward abstraction and hypostatization. James's approach is, indeed, more phenomenological. To study the concrete lived-experience of human conduct as communication phenomena requires that we push beyond the representationalist insistence on deliberate speech and eloquence, and toward a critical analysis of the social conditions and cultural myths out of which competency education is conceived. In this way we might radicalize the so-called empirical givens. These are the moves to make, Catt argues, if communication pedagogy is to contribute to an understanding of and negotiation within the postmodern world. The philosophy of communication, as conceived through a recovery of the semiotic and phenomenological emphases of classical pragmatism as espoused by James, is one way to radicalize the idea of competence and thus enrich human conscious experience. Such enrichment is, after all, the pragmatic—as opposed to conventionally practical—heart of a liberal arts education.

This radical notion of competency—the heart of a truly liberal and artful education—generates the kind of communication a democratic society is built on, according to Thomas Alexander in "John Dewey and the Roots of Democratic Imagination" (chap. 7). Rationality need not be abandoned in such a society, but pluralized in such a way that "diversity of outlooks, the cultivation of social imagination, and a pervasive context of mutual care are intrinsic features." Alexander develops these fundamental notions of pluralistic rationality in a defense of "community" conceived as a sustained and imaginatively coordinated democratic life. He discusses how Dewey was concerned with the process of communication as a pivotal and transformative force that ensures the evolution of such a community.

In developing a theory of democratic communication out of Dewey's philosophy, Alexander offers a critique of Enlightenment models of rationality—in which communication is conceived mechanically—and of postmodern conceptions of communication—in which the tendency toward anarchy predominates. Dewey's conception is aligned with neither of these extremes, Alexander argues, but offers a "reconstruction of reason" as a form of "social intelligence" in which an organism and its environment impact one another dynamically and integratively. Learning is defined by this dynamic process, through which the "identification of `facts' and formation of `values' become functionally related phases of organizing the meaning of the situation." Rationality, argues Alexander, should be conceived as this type of learning, which is characterized by its communicative features.

One of the principal features of communication for both Dewey and Mead was the capability of individuals to see themselves from the "social standpoint." Alexander reviews how such a standpoint is embodied so that a situation can be conceived "in terms of its possibilities as well as its actualities." To do so, one must look to the connections of things and events—and this perception is made possible by a shared narrative, rather than by propositional communication. Narrative is progressive both temporally and socially, and it is only through this movement, Alexander argues, that selfhood makes sense and a pluralistic intelligence is possible.

It should be evident thus far that one voice of pragmatism worth recovering is the concern with consequences in inquiry. Consequences, as Rorty has pointed out, may never be actually known when a theory is conceived. Peirce, for example, probably had no idea that some day a group of philosophers and communication theorists would define a field of study by using his work as a primary inspiration. But this kind of specific result is not what the classical pragmatists were concerned with. Rather they were interested in how meanings took hold for the conceivable future of a social community, how art and aesthetic experience contributed to insight in critical inquiry, and how communication should be conceived if we hoped to pull ourselves out of the debilitating conditions that plague humankind. Frank Macke, in "Pragmatism Reconsidered: John Dewey and Michel Foucault on the Consequences of Inquiry" (chap. 8), poignantly focuses on these concerns.

Macke argues that "precisely because it is concerned with the consequences of critical and reflective activity, pragmatism cannot assume a neutral philosophical stance." We work for something; some interest, result, obligation, condition, and so on. And our work becomes something that can be perceived both as process and product—at times, self-consciously and critically. The pragmatic dimension of our work (as reflexive noun and verb) enters precisely at such a reflective moment, when we realize both what has already been accomplished as historical facticity, and what will have been done if we stay the course. Work then requires an imaginative element that is consistent with artistic endeavor. This, Macke argues, is a theme to which Dewey devoted a good deal of his work.

Macke links Dewey's phenomenology of artistic experience with the phenomenology of Merleau-Ponty and Foucault by showing that pragmatism is a philosophy of the body par excellence: "The sensation and vitality of the body within the space and movement of a gesture," he proposes, "finds its energy in artistic form." Conceived as a feeling manifest in its own expression as gesture or tone, this artistic form is irreducible to any other elemental functions of human experience. It is passionate and eminently coherent experience. Thus to postulate consequences is not a matter of conceiving a grid of possibilities, but of orienting action to artistic experience. The ends are in the body of thought.

This sense of aesthetic life, Macke argues, is consistent with Foucault's reflection on the works of Michel Leiris and Raymond Roussel. Here and elsewhere one comes face to face with "existential limits (as opposed to uses) of language." When the limits of language are conceived in terms of "presence, finitude, and capacity of its forms," we might imagine a sense of what is possible beyond conventional ways of conceiving, much as the surrealists are able to transfigure the customary perception of art and the world through their experimental play. Macke suggests that the experimental heart of Deweyian pragmatism encourages similar artistic orientations to critical inquiry and to the formation of everyday life. Hence the human scientist becomes a creative artist (and vice versa) through transgressive practices of communication.

Imagining the possible consequences of conduct through feeling is more a function of poiesis than praxis. Peirce continually returns to feeling in the large sense as that which orients the kinds of questions we ask about what should or could be the case. He also challenges our self-control in following those questions out. Along these lines Lenore Langsdorf takes issue with the neopragmatic emphasis on language as praxis and directs attention to the pioneering efforts of the classical pragmatists toward enunciating the creative productive forces of communicative poiesis in social life. Her essay (chap. 10) focuses particularly on Dewey's and Mead's developments of this voice of pragmatism as integral to a philosophy of communication concerned with the pushing and pulling of issues in political and pedagogical life. It may appear that an overarching concern with poiesis would mean that either action is avoided or ethical concerns are abrogated. Langsdorf proposes that this was not the case for Dewey and Mead. They neither restricted their philosophies to "the good" nor advocated practical action at any cost; their concern was in doing the good without imposing ethical systems on policy development or taking action purely for action's sake.

Langsdorf provides an overview of traditional philosophical investigations of language as the part of the intellectual context in which classical pragmatism worked. She argues that the pragmatists' contribution forms around both implicit and explicit concern with communication. Hence instead of working through structures of action displayed by language—a concern of praxis—Dewey and Mead were interested in the communicative functions that transform social life—a concern with poiesis. The historical antagonism between philosophy and rhetoric, Langsdorf proposes, is the larger context of this bifurcation of linguistic product and communicative practice. She shows how classical pragmatism's orientation toward the creative productivity of communication allows the "flux of mundane experience" to be addressed contextually, and without divorcing philosophical theory from communicative practice. As an exemplar of this change of view, Langsdorf reflects upon her writing as both an invention and discovery of the event she is describing. The process and product of empirical work is thus made problematic, and an experimental attitude is fostered that conceives the art of communication as a "blend of poetic and praxial functions," through which thought emerges.

This blend reconfigures the idea of progress as a "an essential feature of emancipatory discourse," as Mitchell Aboulafia discusses in "Mead and the Many Voices of Universality" (chap. 9). He engages the modern-postmodern debate by offering a view of progress that does not succumb to metanarrative explanation, and a conception of local and individual experience that recommends itself as a universal concern of pragmatism, especially of the pragmatism of George Herbert Mead.

Aboulafia reviews Mead's conception of the intimate relation between science and social progress, and probes the common progressive assumption that science exploits whatever it touches. Science, Mead argued, should be meliorative but not determinative. Once it becomes teleological, it loses its capacity as a instrument of human choice in a democratic society. Perhaps its greatest contribution to the world is its capacity to transcend particular interest and foster an international and cosmopolitan life. Notwithstanding the romantic and enlightened sound of these views, Aboulafia argues that "in Mead we have a secularized (left) Hegelian alternative to postmodernism. It tells us that difference and novelty can be respected while some form of historical continuity is maintained." The ironic turn in this orientation, for Mead and Aboulafia, is that the singularity of an event or particular case cannot be seen or understood unless a more generalized sense of the other and "an ensuing denunciation of prejudice" is developed.

Mead's philosophy of communication hinges on the notion of global interdependence that promotes the welfare of workers. However, his examples for this possibility come from everyday communication situations, particularly those in which gestures are transformed into symbols with normative content. In addressing Mead's view of communication out of which the "generalized other" takes form, Aboulafia takes issue with Habermas's critical appropriation of Mead's philosophy. He develops the relation between self, roles, social groups, and the evolutionary potential of human experience that attempts to live by thinking according to others. Moving toward the singularity of the other creates the conditions for "more inclusive, universalistic, selves (or self)," which is, in turn, "intimately bound up with [Mead's] vision of ethical progress." Aboulafia extends this notion of universality to a study of texts in which the "deconstructivist paradigm" is inverted while the plurality of operative textual voices is still recognized, albeit demarcated heuristically.

Throughout his discussion Aboulafia emphasizes the primacy of oral communication in Mead's thinking. Recognizing the orality of written texts, he holds, is an extension of pragmatic theory that actually coheres with some voices of neopragmatism. The essays in the final portion of this volume, in taking up the expressly rhetorical dimensions of scientific practice and relating Richard Rorty's views to a consideration of speech communication and textual criticism, demonstrate that extension.

In "Talking-With as a Model for Writing-About: Implications of Rortian Pragmatism" (chap. 11), Arthur Bochner and Joanne Waugh take issue with traditional assumptions about communication as a research object and contemporary appropriations of writing as a model for speaking. They review Rorty's criticism of the "scientist as moral exemplar" and show how this exemplary status hinges on how writing fixes language into an object out of which meaning can be found. The authors trace this tendency of finding truth to Plato and show how philosophical speech became parasitic on writing that claimed a power external to ourselves. Nature can be known because this power provides ways of inscribing itself as an object, and the history of philosophy became a debate on the veracity (truth/falsity), modality (subjective/objective), and valences (strength/weakness) of various inscriptions. Bochner and Waugh propose that the linkages between language, experience, and the world developed by philosophers of science such as Sellars, Quine, and Kuhn have influenced Rorty's conceptions of communication practice. They adopt the Davidsonian notion of a "passing theory" in explicating how interpretation works with "a particular utterance on a particular occasion." The "construction of a pass-ing theory entails just those aspects of the communication situation," they argue, "that are lost or ignored when it is assumed that writing can preserve the communicative act by transmitting 'meanings' or a propo-sitional core in an unmediated manner."

In the final section of their essay Bochner and Waugh "formulate some goals for a human science of communication that takes talking-with as the model for writing-about, and provide a few exemplars that blur the narrative genres dividing literature and social science." These exemplars are practical, not ontological, and demonstrate how the con-versational rather than the causal can become primary. The significance of the conversational is not to be taken lightly, since researchers in the formal, physical, and social/human sciences situate their subject mat-ters through rhetorical dimensions of communication. Thus "talking-with" should become a conscious model of "writing-about," in which the distinctions between customary genres are blurred and stories are told that reach into the heart of communication in unexpected and edi-fying ways.

Janet Horne would agree with this orientation to human science research since it upholds her basic thesis about language and rhetorical theory. In "Changing the Subject: Rorty and Contemporary Rhetorical Theory" (chap. 12), Horne discusses the influence of "rhetoric of inquiry," "epistemic rhetoric," and "critical rhetoric" on thinking about research in the human sciences. She argues that the rhetorical turn enables a shift away from epistemology toward more edifying ways of thinking about inquiry.

Horne offers a cogent account of Rorty's influence on rhetorical theory, his suggestions for redefining inquiry as a rhetorical enterprise, and the disdain Rorty has encountered with regard to his political views. Is it inconsistent with the tenets of critical rhetoric, for example, to hold liberal bourgeois views and advocate mixing in the "bazaar" during the day but retiring to the comforts of one's club at night? We should not be distracted by these more or less personal preferences, argues Horne, when taking into account Rorty's considerable contribu-tions to the theorizing of inquiry. With regard to the classical pragmat-ic tradition, it is clear that Rorty selectively and painstakingly develops Dewey's work. As a corollary Horne offers an account of Rorty's con-tributions to communication inquiry as linked in an evolutionary man-ner to James's work, and especially to the view "that the purpose of inquiry is production of a means of determining conduct." The means of production for this effort should be based principally on a guarantee, above all else, of "free and open encounter."

Horne goes on to depict Rorty's influence in relation to recent advances in rhetorical theory. She argues that Rorty's views on contingency, for example, are actually more radical than those that most rhetorical theorists, and especially advocates of epistemic rhetoric still tied to the notion of consensus, are prepared to adopt. Rorty, in the end, would appear to be a collaborator in the project of developing a critical rhetoric "without foundations," concerned with demystifying discourses of power. Demystification is, of course, a traditional province of rhetorical criticism—but with important qualifications, as Mick Presnell discusses in the final chapter of the volume.

In "Icons, Fragments, and Ironists: Richard Rorty and Contemporary Rhetorical Criticism" (chap. 13), Presnell invokes the oral tradition of interest to so much of postmodern philosophy. Although "public address" would seem to be quite an odd form of communication in which to work if one is a postmodernist, he points out that the meaning of "public address" has changed significantly as a result of contemporary theorizing. It now includes not only mass media and other forms of popular culture, but also the deceptively mute presences of architecture, clothing, food, and other forms of semiotic expression. Hence in the past decade concern with what, exactly, constitutes a text has become a topic of debate among scholars in philosophy and literature. Presnell shows how the debate concerning textuality has developed and seemingly come to fruition for rhetorical critics around the differences between public address conceived as text, and as event.

Rorty, argues Presnell, contributes to this debate in ways that might get us beyond the tendency toward dichotomous distinctions. The nub of the debate concerns how an event becomes textualized, and how a text becomes eventful. Presnell reviews Michael Leff and Andrew Sach's discussion of the tension between content and form (*res* and *verba*) in relation to the latter concern. Content and form, they argue, should be thought of in light of their "iconic" relations. In contrast, Michael Calvin McGee holds that events take on textual form as fragments that should be linked indexically to larger historical and ideological contexts. Fragmentation is definitive of the human condition: the "apparent coherence" of nations, for example, should not distract us from their actual patchwork constitution. The same is true of public discourse; it is a fragment in itself, and it consists of fragments of other discourses.

Presnell sees this contrast between McGee on fragmentation, and Leff and Sachs on iconic relations, as a precursor to Rorty's changing the topic of conversation in order to keep it (the conversation) going.

This debate of text and event is really a language game, says Rorty, whose stakes are not very clear. In his comparisons of Rorty and Leff on one hand, and Rorty and McGee on the other, Presnell defines these stakes in terms of the communicative conditions for creating a just and equitable society—a concern that has actually motivated the study of public address since antiquity. It should be no surprise, then, that communication theorists are interested in the consequences of discourse, its poetic forms and praxial conditions, its ways of situating inquiry as well as our perceptions of the significance of events and texts, and the prospects discourse offers for a society in which people speaking and writing do so with hope for and charity toward others.

The philosophy of communication develops those interests as basic questions of the nature and function of communication. At the core of that inquiry are questions concerning the conditions for, and consequences of, diverse communicative activity. Argumentation and conversation, debate and dialogue, demonstration and interpretation, proof and performance—all give their distinctive tones to the evolution of society and self, as well as to our inquiry into that evolution. The voice of pragmatism sings in these tones. And this, the contributors to this book believe, is a song worth recovering.

II

The Logic of Communication

2

Immediacy, Opposition, and Mediation: Peirce on Irreducible Aspects of the Communicative Process

❖ ❖

Vincent M. Colapietro

Reclaiming the Relevance of Peirce

In "Pragmatism, Relativism, and Irrationalism," Richard Rorty suggests that pragmatism is more radical than we ordinarily suppose. He contends that it is not another attempt "to make philosophy into a foundational discipline.[1] Rather it is a radical critique of the foundationalist drive so characteristic of Western philosophy, especially during the modern epoch. For Rorty, then, the pragmatist perspective is not one more transcendental attempt to escape the contingencies of human history, but rather a candid confession of a historicist faith in the possibilities inherent in this thoroughly contingent process.[2] Just as there is no need to go beyond nature in order to explain nature, there is no need to go beyond history in order to interpret the complex array of human practices in and through which identities are forged, solidarity is achieved, and strategies of coping have actually evolved and are effectively evaluated.[3] Somehow the contingencies of *our* history, of the communities we have *shaped* rather than *found*,[4] make possible not only "amused condescension"[5] toward our ancestors but also the moral passions requisite for sustaining the humanizing conversation of Western liberalism. In short, these contingencies make possible solidarity as well as irony.

According to Rorty, one symptom of this failure to recognize pragmatism for what it is—a truly radical critique of the foundationalist impulse—"is a tendency to overpraise Peirce" in comparison to James and Dewey.[6] He proposes that "the main reason for Peirce's undeserved apotheosis is that his talk about a general theory of signs looks like an early discovery of the importance of language."[7] But this apparent anticipation of the linguistic turn diverts our attention from the predominant concern of Peircean pragmatism. To illuminate this concern, we must recognize that what is most distinctive about Peirce is not the ways he anticipates contemporary innovations but the fact that he perpetuates traditional preoccupations. Rorty goes so far as to allege that Peirce's "contribution to pragmatism was merely to have given it a name, and to have stimulated James. Peirce himself remained the most Kantian of thinkers—the most convinced that philosophy gave us an all-embracing ahistorical context in which every other species of discourse could be assigned its proper place and rank."[8] Whereas James and Dewey help us overcome the Western philosophical tradition, Peirce tries to repair a structure that it would be better to raze than to renovate.[9]

In recent years, Rorty has come to praise pragmatism *and* to bury Peirce, at least the Peirce who (allegedly) sought to secure a foundational status for philosophical discourse, to sketch a comprehensive and timeless framework "in which every other species of discourse could be assigned its proper place and rank."[10] For him, Peirce was a hopelessly muddled philosopher as well as an obsessively foundationalist one. "For all his genius . . . Peirce never made up his mind what he wanted a general theory of signs *for,* nor what it might look like, nor what its relation to either logic or epistemology was supposed to be."[11] Leveled against a pragmatist, this charge is especially serious and, if valid, thoroughly damning.

But, in my judgment, this charge against Peirce hardly seems fair. Just as the proof of the pudding is in the eating, so the proof of pragmatism is in the applications of this doctrine to questions arising out of our frustrations and failures as agents-in-the-world. Moreover, Peirce's general theory of signs and his distinctive conception of pragmatism cannot be separated from one another. On the one hand, pragmatism is itself a semeiotic doctrine; on the other, Peirce's attempts to render clear(er) our conception of semiosis (or sign-action) *and* to classify the types of signs are, at bottom, the work of a pragmatist or, better, a pragmaticist.[12] From Rorty's perspective, however, Peirce's semeiotic is a transcendental gesture, an attempt to define the conditions for the possibility of all discourse, or *the* conditions for discourse as such.

Such a gesture is, in Rorty's judgment, over ambitious. It is also inescapably arrogant; for it entails the attempt to determine, not only *once and for all* but also *for all* participants in the conversation of humankind, the specific rhetorical strategies to be employed and the overarching, extraconversational objective to be espoused. In reference to not Peirce but Jean-François Lyotard, Rorty characterizes "the *défaillance* of modernity" as "a loss of faith in our ability to come up with a single set of criteria which everybody in all times and places can accept, [in our capacity to] invent a single language-game which can somehow take over all the jobs previously done by all the language-games ever played."[13] For Rorty, this loss is, of course, a gain. Also for him, Peirce's pragmatism represents, first and foremost, an expression of the very faith that Jamesian and Deweyan forms of pragmatism encourage us to shed. This faith is expressed in numerous ways and contexts, not least of all in Peirce's untiring efforts to articulate a truly comprehensive theory of signs.

From Peirce's own viewpoint, his theory of signs is a series of generalizations (CP 1.82)[14] derived by an *abstractive* process from our communicative practices.[15] These generalizations have been made and integrated for the purpose of illuminating not only these communicative practices but also the various contexts in which these practices have emerged and continue to evolve (e.g., the historical, institutional, and ultimately cosmological contexts of anthroposemiosis). Put alternatively, this theory is part of Peirce's quest of quests, his inquiry into the nature and varieties of inquiries, undertaken for the purpose of facilitating inquiry. Pace Rorty, semeiotic is *for* inquiry: its function is heuristic. It is concerned with fostering *intelligence*, pragmatically understood. In this sense, "intelligence does not consist in feeling intelligently but in acting so that one's deeds are concentrated upon a result" (CP 7.559). But in acting intelligently, the goals we espouse no less than the means we employ become objects of self-criticism (see, e.g., CP 1.574). We never fully or even adequately know what we are doing; in some manner and measure, the conditions and consequences of our conduct always escape our consciousness and theories. The drive to bring into sharper focus the conditions and consequences of human conduct, inclusively conceived, originates in our frustrations as agents-in-the-world. It aims at the overcoming of these frustrations and, thereby, a fuller realization of human autonomy. The trajectory of this drive, however, points *beyond* the immediate circumstances in which our most urgent frustrations occur; it points *to* an ever wider and deeper comprehension of our agency-in-the-world.[16]

At least two points need to be stressed here. One concerns Peirce's approach to semeiotic, the other his conception of the practical. If these points are accorded the status and importance they deserve, then we are in the position to see more fully the purpose informing Peirce's work in semeiotic. In other words, we thereby attain a more adequate perspective from which to glimpse what Peirce wanted his general theory of signs *for.*

In a letter to Lady Victoria Welby, dated December 23, 1908, Peirce disclosed that "being a convinced Pragmaticist in Semeiotic, naturally and necessarily nothing can appear to me sillier than rationalism" (SS 1977, 78). One way to interpret this self-disclosure is that, in his investigations of signs, Peirce was especially careful to avoid falling back on the a priori method (i.e., the method of fixing beliefs because of their agreeableness to an individual and, at least in effect, deracinated consciousness). For this method is, of all those Peirce examines, the one most appropriately designated as *rationalistic;* indeed, his own tendency to associate this method with *modern metaphysicians* such as Descartes, Spinoza, and Leibniz helps secure the plausibility of this explication of *rationalism.* Abstract definitions, the rationalists' stock in trade, are invaluable but insufficient tools: for the sake of clarity, even (should we say "especially"?) our most abstract words must be translated into habits of action, not just other abstract terms.[17]

In another letter (this one to F. C. S. Schiller and dated Sept. 10, 1906, Peirce announced that "by 'practical' I mean apt to affect conduct; and by conduct, voluntary[,] that is[,] self-controlled, i.e., controlled by adequate deliberation" (CP 8.322). The meaning of concepts, including the concepts of sign and of semiosis (or sign-action), "lies in their conceivable practical bearings" (CP 8.322). Thus, being a convinced pragmaticist in sign theory does not mean subordinating theory to practical consequences but rather conceiving theory itself as a consequential practice,[18] a form of conduct in which the very meaning of concepts is most adequately clarified in terms of their "conceivable practical bearings." Peirce goes so far as to contend that "man is so completely hemmed in by the bounds of his possible practical experience, his mind is so restricted to being the instrument of his needs, that he cannot, in the least, *mean* anything that transcends those limits" (CP 5.536). But this stress on the finitude of human intelligence does not preclude recognizing the transcendence of such intelligence, in particular, the capacity of humans to transcend the limits of their actual or historical practical experience. This much should be clear from Peirce's own words, in particular, the expression "*possible* practical experience." The *conceivable* or *possible* practical bearings of our concepts are wider than their *actual* practical bearings. Since virtually all of our conceptions have been framed in severely circumscribed or narrow circumstances, their actual bearings upon human conduct often offer only the barest hint of their full meaning.

What Peirce says about the indubitable beliefs of common sense (a topic to which we shall return in the next section) is relevant here. Such "beliefs refer to a somewhat primitive mode of life, and . . . while they never become dubitable in so far as our mode of life remains that of somewhat primitive man, yet as we develop *degrees of self-control* unknown to that man, occasions of action arise in relation to which the original beliefs, if stretched to cover them, have no sufficient authority" (CP 5.511). In its most primitive form, the practical is that which bears upon conduct in such a way that even the most resistant agents cannot, in practice, deny this bearing. In its more sophisticated forms, the practical is that which might possibly bear upon our agency (i.e., our self-control), especially in unfamiliar and even highly unlikely circumstances (e.g., humans traveling near the speed of light). The discovery of what might possibly bear upon human autonomy in unfamiliar situations (circumstances other than the somewhat primitive one to which our commonsensical beliefs most directly and satisfactorily apply) is made through the mediation of self-consciousness and thereby of self-criticism.

Theoretical accounts of signs grow out of the unreflective use of signs. Here as elsewhere, practice precedes theory; more precisely, unreflexive and uncriticized usages and practices are superceded by more self-conscious and self-directed reliance on these usages and engagements in these practices.[19] Just as Peirce's semeiotic drives toward a pragmatic theory of meaning, so does his pragmaticism drive toward a systematic investigation of signs. For such processes as inference,[20] utterance, interpretation, and inquiry are, at bottom, modes of conduct susceptible to higher degrees of self-control than we have yet attained. In other words, such processes are practices: they are more or less controllable forms of human conduct. They are part and parcel of the ways we as agents comport ourselves in the world, exposing ourselves to injury or worse, and the world to damage and possibly even destruction. The practical is what indirectly no less than directly bears upon our conduct as agents-in-the-world. Signs or, better, the actions of signs (*semiosis*) are the means by which we discover the bearings of our engagements in the world. Just as we become aware of ourselves through the experience of ignorance and error (see, e.g., CP 5.225–37),[21] we become formally conscious of signs as such through mistakes in interpretation (e.g., taking the appearance of this surface to be a reliable or trustworthy sign of its capacity to support one's weight). Moreover, semiosis makes possible the most distinctively human forms of engagement—for example, participation in a community of self-critical inquirers, in a community of self-legislating citizens, or in a community of self-interpreting agents.

If we are to recover pragmatism's voice in the conversation of humankind, we would do well to be faithful to the pluralism characteristic of classical American pragmatism—to the fact that the pragmatists frequently do not speak with one voice.[22] Thus, our task in this volume of essays *might be* best described as recovering the voices of pragmatism. This should not be taken to mean that there are no overarching themes or shared concerns among pragmatists. Such themes and concerns—for example, the emphasis on practice rather than theory, or the construal of theory itself as a form of practice—count in favor of using the singular rather than voices. But the distinctive features of the Peircean idiolect merit attention in their own right. So, despite Rorty's disclaimers and criticisms, the utterances of Peirce deserve a hearing from anyone desirous of approaching our communicative practices from a pragmatic perspective.

For this and other reasons, I am just as suspicious of Rorty's pragmatism as he is Philosophy: pragmatism in its Rortyean sense needs to be contested as much as philosophy in its Platonic sense. One way to do so is by suggesting that Rorty's wholesale rejection of Peirce's general theory of signs amounts to nothing less than leaving unopened a box of tools whose value is inestimable for research into communication. My objective is to sketch a distinctively Peircean approach to human communication and, in doing so, to go some way toward showing *by the way* that Rorty's rejection of Peirce's semeiotic entails this consequence.[23] One consequence of Pragmatism in the Rortyean sense is, then, a diminishment of pragmatism in its full power. But my essay is *not* primarily concerned with any further consequences of Rorty's incapacitating score; nor is it even primarily concerned with answering Rorty's dismissal of Peirce's theory. If my application of several distinctively Peircean doctrines to the specific field of communication is illuminating, then Rorty's doubts about the fecundity of Peirce's theory would have been defanged.

Preparing the Canvas

The resources of Peirce's semeiotic for an understanding of communication have not been explored to the depth they deserve. This is understandable but unfortunate. It is understandable because Peirce's general theory of signs is so difficult to comprehend on its own terms, let alone in terms of its applicability to a domain of inquiry to which Peirce did not primarily devote his attention.[24] While he was engaged in formulating a truly general or inclusive theory of signs,[25] his engagement in this task was deeply informed by both his logical and, more generally, scientific interests. Accordingly, the implicit model[26] of the sign process is the investigation of a startling phenomenon, not the interpretation of a puzzling text. But one of the virtues of Peirce's semeiotic is the ability of this theory to exhume the common root of our investigative and our interpretive practices, without blurring the fundamental differences between inquiry and interpretation.[27] This root is abduction; the differences reside, above all, in the different ways of testing hypotheses and the different fields of experience to which appeals are made in such testing. The neglect of Peirce's semeiotic for an understanding of communication is regrettable since this theory has, in my judgment, the power to illuminate the communicative process in its full complexity.[28]

Peirce's theory of signs both presupposes and exemplifies his doctrine of categories.[29] These categories are—at least for our purposes—best viewed as recursive heuristic conceptions. To describe them as *heuristic* implies that they are first and foremost guides and goads to inquiry (see, e.g., CP 1.351). They are instruments of investigation; but this characterization does not, of itself, entail a purely instrumentalist interpretation of the most general categories. That these categories empower us to cope with reality does not preclude the possibility that they also provide a means of revealing reality. The question of their revelatory power must itself be couched in terms of the categories themselves, otherwise these conceptions would be less than truly general (i.e., undeserving of categoreal status).[30] To describe the categories as *recursive* brings into focus their dialectical and self-generative nature.

In Peirce's hands, phenomenology is primarily a doctrine of categories (see, e.g., CP 1.280)—that is, a branch of inquiry devoted to discovering whether there are any ubiquitous features or facets of whatever is, in whatever way.[31] But the value of this doctrine resides not so much in the abstract articulation of purely formal conceptions as in the concrete applications of these conceptions to virtually every context of investigation. (Pace Rorty, these applications do not need to be construed in terms of securing a foundation for the edifice of knowledge; they might be construed, to adapt one of Peirce's own metaphors, as the marks of a trailblazer to help us orient ourselves along some bewildering stretch of an ongoing inquiry.) To repeat, the principal function of the Peircean categories is heuristic, to guide and goad investigators to describe phenomena in the most nuanced and inclusive manner and, then, to dream of explanations of the most powerful and penetrating character. Identified in purely abstract terms, the categories are firstness, secondness, and thirdness; they are, in phenomenological terms, qualitative immediacy, brute opposition, and indeliminable mediation.

The relevance of these considerations to our investigation of communication is that a semeiotic account of communication presupposes a phenomenological description of the phenomenon or range of phenomena that we as agents-in-the-world subsume under the heading of *communication*. The Peircean categories are not procrustean beds; they are not a priori molds into which the *facts* must be poured. They are universally relevant guidelines for phenomenologically fruitful description.

The whole of our self-critical and self-controlled interpretations and inquiries (including the articulation and application of the categories) presupposes a largely unarticulated body of indubitable beliefs. We should take *beliefs* here to designate dispositions to action. This body of beliefs is, vis-à-vis even the most secure discoveries of controlled investigation, unshakable (see, e.g., 5.60): it is what the actual course of our communal experience, over countless generations, has forced upon not so much our consciousness as our very being. This *being* resides primarily in our capacity to acquire new habits and, as a prerequisite for such acquisition, to lose or at least modify old habits. It involves as well the tendency toward the integration of the complex array of instinctual and acquired habits so indispensable to organisms like ourselves. This array of habits is nothing less than that by which we attain our humanity and, indeed, establish our uniqueness. Peirce's explicit acknowledgment of such habits and his strenuous insistence that they cannot be dismissed lightly (even in—or perhaps especially in—philosophy) point to an important connection, namely, the link between Peircean pragmatism and critical commonsensism. What Paul Weiss says in his own name might be taken as an accurate description of Peirce's philosophical approach: "Any view that wholly abandons common sense is at best a fiction or a fantasy. Any view that refuses to examine it is at best uncritical and dogmatic. Reflection and reason require one to stand somewhere between these two extremes."[32] Peirce's critical commonsensism is just such an attempt to stand between the fantastic and the uncritical.[33] Peirce makes precisely this point. For, on the one hand, he denies that "there can be any *direct* profit in going behind common sense"; but, on the other, he recognizes that, inescapably, there is a difficulty in determining "what really is and what is not the authoritative decision of common sense and what is merely *obiter dictum*" (CP 1.129). Hence, "there is no escape from the need of a critical examination of 'first principles'"—to determine what should count as a "first principle"—that is, an indubitable belief about which further inquiry would be wasted effort.

Thus, even before offering a phenomenological description of human communication, it would be necessary to come to terms with what we, as agents-in-the-world, must mean by *communication*. For Peirce, philosophy is not and, indeed, in principle cannot be presuppositionless. At every turn (though not necessarily in any obvious way), it presupposes the largely unconscious beliefs of embodied agents, agents destined to secure their survival and fulfillment in a more or less precarious world. Just as Peirce did not slight the importance of these beliefs in his own efforts to formulate a vision of our agency-in-the-world, so too we should not overlook them in offering a sketch of a Peircean approach to the communicative process.

Let us return to the level of controlled interpretation and inquiry (what Peirce called *scientific* investigation). One of the principal defects of common sense derives from its vagueness and, beyond this, its dumbness (the fact that the countless beliefs constitutive of common sense are unformulated and, to a significant extent, unformulatable). In the most narrowly practical of circumstances (e.g., that of an onrushing car), the *dumb* certitudes of common sense are not in the least defective; quite the contrary. In the context of theoretical inquiry, however, the drive toward precision and articulation needs to push beyond the limit appropriate to or characteristic of our commonsensical beliefs.

One way to view phenomenology, as it is situated in Peirce's hierarchy of the sciences,[34] is as a deliberate effort to unleash the generalizing capacity of the human mind (see, e.g., CP 5.42). But this is, in itself, not an adequate way to mark the difference between common sense and phenomenological inquiry; for this generalizing ability is already evident in the very formation of the habits and maxims constitutive of common sense. In phenomenology, this omnipresent tendency is given freer *play*.[35] Paradoxically, it is also more rigorously controlled. Phenomenology constitutes that stage in inquiry in which the human mind tries to break beyond what, for the theoretical inquirer, can only feel like cripplingly narrow limits imposed by immediate practical concerns. It does so by suspending consideration of what *ought to be realized* and *what ought to be done*, in order to see what *appears* to you and me and any other observer with whom we would be able to communicate. It also does so by attending carefully to the forms of appearance, especially for the purpose of ascertaining whether there are any ubiquitous forms. That there are such forms, and that Peirce identifies them with the categories, is well known to all students of his thought. So too is the fact that these universal categories, based upon the ubiquitous forms of possible experience, provide the inquirer with an invaluable set of heuristic clues. This applies to the investigator of signs no less than to any other inquirer. So, Peirce's general theory of signs is unintelligible apart from his doctrine of the three universal categories.

Not only does semeiotic have its proximate roots in phenomenology, it has its proximate fruits in the normative sciences (logic, ethics, and esthetics).[36] That is, Peirce's investigations of signs are only properly understood if they are situated in his own classification of the sciences.[37] For our purposes, this means that a truly Peircean account of the communicative process must be one in which phenomenological description and normative reflection play their distinctively Peircean roles. The role of phenomenological description is to bring into focus a phenomenon or range of phenomena in its full complexity. The role of normative reflection is to explicate the norms and ideals *inherent in* our communicative practices.[38] To begin somewhere other than phenomenology is to leave unidentified or, at best, inadequately specified the object of inquiry. To stop short of normative reflection is, in this context, to commit the fallacy of misplaced concreteness, to treat an abstracted result (namely, forms of mediation) as though it were a concrete actuality.[39] For the forms of mediation are historically evolved and evolving processes and practices that, at the level of distinctively human sign-use, result in the enhancement or frustration of the self-consciousness, self-criticism, and self-control of human sign-users. As such, these processes and practices constitute the matrix out of which human agents emerge and the arenas in which they characteristically act. The human organism is transformed into a personal agent by virtue of participating in these processes and practices.[40]

Explicitly normative consideration of what bears upon the acquisition, maintenance, and refinement of such agency (of being a self-conscious, -critical, and -controlling actor) is the terminus ad quem of a distinctively Peircean account of communication. But as a first step toward a controlled inquiry into the phenomenon of communication, it is necessary to recognize formally the indubitable habits (the uncontrollable and, thus, uncriticizable dispositions) that make possible not only such inquiry but also every form of communication. Accordingly, a truly Peircean approach to human communication would marshal the resources of his critical commonsensism no less than those of his phenomenology, semeiotic, and the like.

In what follows, I will sketch in very broad strokes a distinctively Peircean approach to our communicative practices and also in a finer (yet still all too quick) hand some of the most salient ways in which Peirce's category of secondness should inform a truly Peircean approach to communication. In fact, the first strokes of this broad sketch have already been made. What should become apparent as we proceed is that the phenomenological *category* of opposition and its distillate, the formal category of secondness, provide *a* warrant for the normative doctrine of fallibilism, understood precisely as an alternative to cocksureness (phallogocentrism?) and skepticism. Of course, the principal warrant for cultivating a fallibilistic sensibility is the unavoidable and all too frequent experience of being mistaken about both trivial and momentous matters. Even so, Peirce's categories of firstness, secondness, and thirdness help us to see the ways in which immediacy, otherness, and mediation define communicative processes and practices, ways bearing upon (among other topics) his doctrine of fallibilism. In particular, they help us see the way claims regarding truth and even meaning are warranted in the present and, simultaneously, deferrable in the meantime. In turn, this enables us to establish a link—whereby a meaningful contrast can be drawn—between Peircean secondness and Derridean *différance*. For pragmaticists at least, herein lies a difference that truly makes a difference. Unlike Derridean *différance*, Peircean secondness offers more than an undifferentiated or unnuanced conception of *différance* (more than one by which fundamental differences are erased and tenuous connections essentialized). It provides the inquirer with an array of concepts by which to differentiate various modes of difference (e.g., genuine and degenerate instances of secondness).[41]

Sketching the Communicative Process in Light of Common Sense and Uncommon Observation

The first task of inquirers is to bring into focus their specific object of inquiry. For those who devote themselves to semeiotic, this means *first* recalling the familiar or customary meanings of the term *sign*, *then* articulating an abstract and formal definition of this word, and *finally* determining what actual and merely conceivable practical consequences flow from treating objects as *signs* or processes as *significant*. This means exhibiting what the term *sign* means on three distinct yet (ideally) continuous levels of clearness.[42] It is necessary here to assume a familiarity with Peirce's doctrine of how to make our ideas clear *and* (to a less extent) his abstract, formal definition of sign.[43] For our principal concern is not with Peirce's general theory of signs but with a semeiotic account of communication.

For those who are devoted to investigating communication, their task also begins by marking off the field of their investigation. This means defining, though only in a preliminary and provisional way, the phenomenon of communication itself. "The place for an accurate and comprehensive definition of a subject is at the *end* of an inquiry rather than at the beginning, but a brief [provisional] definition will serve to mark out the field."[44]

It may well be, as John Dewey claimed:

> Of all affairs, communication is the most wonderful. That things should be able to pass from the plane of external pushing and pulling to that of revealing themselves to man, and thereby to themselves; and that the fruit of communication should be participation, sharing, is a wonder by the side of which transubstantiation pales.[45]

According communication this status did not deter Dewey from trying to explain what takes place in processes of communication and also how such processes are possible.[46] Nor should it deter inquirers who, even more than Dewey himself, are committed to drawing upon Peirce's general theory of signs for a deeper understanding of communication.

As Winfried Nöth notes, "communication is a key concept in semiotics and many of its neighboring disciplines. Yet, the meaning of this term is extremely diffuse."[47] Beyond this, the very status of this term in semiotic discourse is problematic. On the one hand, the term might be taken as one of the (if not *the*) most basic explanatory terms in semiotic discourse. If it is so construed, then semiosis or sign-activity is defined or explained in terms of communication. On the other, *communication* might be treated as a more or less derivative conception.

Here it is relevant to note that: "The founders of modern semiotics [e.g., Peirce and Morris] . . . rarely used the term *communication*."[48] This suggests that, for Peirce, this term is derivative. *Communication* does not provide the means of explaining sign-action but rather designates a phenomenon or range of phenomena to be explained by means of other, more basic conceptions (e.g., semiosis, interpretants, and the various types of interpretants). There are, however, a number of texts in which Peirce himself defines the sign in terms of communication. For instance, he proposes in MS 339 that "a sign is a species of medium of communication" (1906, p. 271). In MS 793, he suggests that, for the purposes of his inquiry, "a *Sign* may be defined as a Medium for the communication of a Form" (p. 1).

What are we to make of these characterizations of sign? An invaluable hint is provided in MS 283 when Peirce observes that, in considering the question "What is a sign?" "we are not studying lexicography. . . . We all have a ragged-outlined notion of what we call a sign. We wish to replace that by a well-defined concept, which may exclude some things ordinarily called signs, and will almost certainly include some things not ordinarily so called" (p. 105; see CP 8.332). The overriding concern in refining our ordinary conception is to contribute to "the science of logic," the normative science of controlled inquiry. The clarification of our understanding is intended to have *the highest utility* for this science. "As far as this condition will allow, it is to express that which is most essential in the vulgar notion of a sign or representamen. Now a sign as ordinarily [or vulgarly] understood is an implement of intercommunication" (MS 283, p. 106).

What this suggests is that the characterization of a sign as a medium or implement of communication attains nothing more than the first grade of clarity, while the purely abstract and formal definition of a sign (the one in which a sign is defined as that which stands to an other in such a way as to determine how it stands to some third) marks the second level of clearness. We do not move beyond the second grade to the third—we do not transcend abstract definition via pragmatic clarification—until we define a sign in such terms as "something by knowing which we know something more" (CP 8.332) *or* anything "that plays an essential part in the spread of intelligence" (MS 602, p. 8) *or* a form tending to act upon interpreters through their own self-controlled utterances and interpretations (CP 4.538).

In its most customary sense, a sign is an implement of communication, a medium through which one organism addresses another, most frequently perhaps an organism of the same species. In a more refined and abstract sense, it is a process of mediation (see, e.g., MS 318, p. 13) observable even in the absence of what we ordinarily call *minds* (see, e.g., CP 6.199; 6.301; and 6.559). Finally, at the highest level of clarity (that of pragmatic clarification), a sign is defined as a means by which utterers or interpreters of signs might attain fuller control over the processes of utterance and interpretation.

As a first step toward marking off communication as a field of inquiry, let me propose the following. In the most general sense, communication is a semiotic process in which at least formally distinct agents participate and thereby transform themselves and one another, even if only superficially. Two qualifications need to be made immediately. *First*, this definition is as it stands inadequate, because it makes no mention of the reciprocity essential to communication.[49] Communication should not unqualifiedly be identified with any process of signification: in and of itself, the production of signs does not necessarily equal a process of communication. Accordingly, a fossil is significant but not communicative: the pattern *signifies* something other than itself but, in the strict sense, does not *communicate* to the person who can grasp the significance of this pattern. Strictly speaking, communication is that form of semiosis in which signification not only calls forth a response but also the response of one participant incorporates within itself the perspective of some other participant(s).

At the center of communication there is a give-and-take, a process of mutual influence. By virtue of this form of semiosis, we are always already thrown beyond ourselves, beyond the actual here-and-now of our immediate situation and unique perspective. Hence, communication is the process by which diverse perspectives fuse into more inclusive ones, but this fusion does not involve the obliteration of diversity. I respond as I to the other as other, but my response incorporates within itself the perspective of the other. To take a very simple example, when another shouts "Look out!" my *immediate* response to an immediate danger is one in which the here-and-now of my situated agency is transformed by the there-and-then of another. If the I-here-now were so hermetically sealed as to preclude the influence of other(s)-there-then, communication would be impossible.

Second, the word *transform* in my initial characterization of the communicative process is being used in a *very* broad sense, so broad perhaps as to be misleading. This term does not necessarily imply what would ordinarily be thought of as change. For example, if in a conversation I am strengthened in some conviction held prior to the exchange, this would count as a *transformation*; for my conviction has in a way been altered. It is something different—namely, stronger— than it was when I entered the conversation, even though it is, in another sense, the *same* conviction. This is what I take Peirce himself to have in mind when he identifies *habit-change* as the ultimate logical interpretant (see, e.g., CP 5.476.)

For Peirce no less than Plato, thought is best conceived as a form of communication: "thinking always proceeds in the form of a dialogue—a dialogue between different phases of the *ego*—so that, being dialogical, it is essentially composed of signs, as its matter, in the sense in which a game of chess has the chessmen for its matter" (CP 4.6). In other words, thinking which is other than mere reverie is a process in which the self of one moment struggles to communicate with its later incarnations. (Of course, even mere reveries can be taken by a subsequent self—the wakeful subject—to have a hidden yet decipherable significance.) The distinction of self and other is, accordingly, constitutive of not only sociality but also subjectivity: our *inner* lives are no less a dialectic of ego and alter than is our intersubjective experience.

Because the *process* of communication is one in which agents qua agents participate, it is appropriately called a *practice* (a distinction anticipated above). The communicative processes in which human beings take part are, overwhelmingly, historical practices (i.e., forms of conduct that have evolved over the course of history). The term *process* underscores the temporal character of communication. Practice highlights, in contrast, the fact that this process is initiated, sustained, and modified by the efforts and ingenuity of social actors; it also suggests that the form of conduct is either itself inherited (e.g., the enactment of an established ritual or the utterance of a traditional prayer) *or* dependent upon an inheritance (e.g., a code such as an alphabet or lexicon). Both terms might suggest that communication is encompassing: it is that in which beings are caught up or agents take part. If it is true (as Peirce suggests) that "we ought to say that we are in thought and not that thought is in us" (CP 5.289n1), then it is equally true (or perhaps the same truth stated in a different way) that communication envelopes us rather than the reverse.

The status of agents vis-à-vis processes of communication deserves comment here. This is especially the case since Peirce himself appears to grant greater autonomy to human language vis-à-vis human agents than does common sense. Recall that, in "Some Consequences of Four Incapacities" as well as elsewhere (e.g., CP 7.584ff), Peirce observes that: "Man makes the word, and the word means nothing which the man has not made it mean, and that only to some man" (CP 5.313). But this is only half of the story: "Since man can think only by means of words or other external symbols, these might turn round and say: 'You mean nothing which we have not taught you, and then only so far as you address some word [or other symbol] as the interpretant of your thought" (CP 5.313). This prompts Peirce to recognize the "fact" that humans and words "reciprocally educate each other" (CP 5.313).

What a pragmatically informed theory of communication attempts to illuminate is the way our communicative practices serve both as the matrix out of which distinctively personal agents emerge *and* also as the arenas in which such agents sustain and modify themselves and their forms of conduct. We are agents by virtue of semiosis, of our participation in processes leading to ever higher levels of autonomy. Processes of sign-use acquire their uniquely human form by virtue of agency, of the exercise of ever more refined measures of self-criticism (measures aiming at self-control). Peirce is quite explicit on this point. In a letter to F. C. S. Schiller, he states that the only pragmatically meaningful sense in which humans are *free* is that they are beings "with automatic controls, one over another, for five or six grades, at least" (CP 8.320; cf. CP 5.533) Immediately he goes on to confess that "I, for my part am very dubious as to man's having more freedom than that, nor do I see what pragmatic meaning there is in saying he has more. The power of self-control is certainly not a power over what one is doing at the very instant the operation of self-control is commenced."

What, then, is this power? For Peirce, it is essentially the capacity to engage in deliberation comprehensively conceived, taking this process to be one that truly, if only indirectly, bears upon the course of conduct. This capacity "consists (to mention only the leading constituents) first, in comparing one's past deeds with standards, second, in rational deliberation concerning how one will act in the future . . . third, in the formation of a resolve, fourth, in the creation of the resolve, of a strong determination, or modification of habit." This *whole* process, beginning with the recollection of what agents have done and concluding with the resolution of what they will do, might be called deliberation. Thus, what Peirce identifies here as *rational deliberation* is perhaps best conceived as a distinct phase in the deliberative process, a phase involving above all else (as Dewey makes clear) a dramatic rehearsal in the imagination of various courses of possible conduct.

Peirce also explicitly relates the distinctively human use of language to his own conception of autonomy. In a relatively late manuscript, he claims that the superiority of humans to other species of animals is due, above all else, to the "greater number of grades of self-control" that humans are able to exercise over their conduct (CP 5.533). He poses an objection to his own claim, asking "Is it not due to our faculty of language?" (CP 5.534). His response is worth quoting here: "To my thinking that faculty is itself a phenomenon of self-control. For thinking is a kind of conduct, and is itself controllable, as everyone knows [i.e., as common sense attests]. Now the intellectual control of thinking takes place by thinking about thought. All thinking is by [and in] signs; and the brutes use signs. But they perhaps rarely think of them as signs. To do so is manifestly a second step [or different level] in the use of language" (CP 5.534).

In any event, what a pragmatically informed theory of communication keeps in focus is our deep and pervasive dependency, precisely as agents, on various forms of semiosis. We are initially involuntary and unwitting participants in semiosis; eventually, we are, *by virtue of participating in semiosis,* reflexive and deliberative subjects. What such a theory refuses to countenance, however, is the effacement of agency.[50] On the question of agency, a Peircean approach to our communicative practices takes a doggedly commonsensical stand.

As we have already observed, Peirce was a pragmaticist in semeiotic. As we need to note now, he was a critical commonsensist in philosophical discussions. His commitment to a form of commonsensism is relevant to our sketch of a truly Peircean approach to communication. For this commitment is one firmly rooted in a recognition of the abiding condition of human beings: we are agents-in-the-world. (And the recognition of this condition should deeply and thoroughly inform a Peircean approach to human communication.) The root of this commitment becomes evident when we recall that, for him, common sense is principally a set of rough and ready maxims based on the actual experience of embodied agents, over countless generations. As a result of this experience, "there is not wanting a fund of propositions each of which is appreciably more certain than the most scientifically tested observations . . . inasmuch as they are shown to have the backing of the environment, not by superficial symptoms only but by the course of many generations of multitudes of men" (MS 326, p. 14). These propositions are "plain conditional maxims, not too rigidly [or precisely] defined" (e.g., if you want to relieve these pangs of hunger you ought to eat; if you want a family, then "you had better look for a nice girl, and having made a circumspect and not too passionate choice, and [had better] confide in her and govern your household in a measure yourself through her" [!]; if you are ambitious, then "you had better concentrate your desires upon one object and pursue that alone without turning aside from it"). For us, the world is first and foremost an arena of action. Peirce's opposition to epiphenomenalism is instructive in this context; for his rejection of this position is based primarily upon his refusal to reduce the role of human consciousness to that of an idle spectator. Against this reduction, he argues that the function of consciousness is to render self-control possible and efficient" (MS 318, p. 75).[51]

The effort to render all appeals to common sense problematic is characteristic of more than a few contemporary contributors to semiotics. But, in support of this effort, these contributors would be mistaken to try enlisting Peirce as an ally. It is true that, primarily because of the forbidding terminology and the incredibly complex classifications, Peirce's theory of signs does not *appear* to be vitally linked to common sense. Nor does it seem to be finely attuned to the actual character of our communicative practices. But this is largely the result of Peirce's principal interest in sign theory: his primary preoccupation was to investigate not the ways signs are actually used by humans but the manner signs might be ideally controlled in the interest of inquiry (that process by which beliefs might most reasonably and responsibly be fixed). Even so, he provides the resources to accomplish more than this principal objective. Stated positively, he fashions the means to offer a rich and nuanced account of our actual communicative practices.

For such an account, the role of speech cannot be exaggerated. As Peirce himself notes, "speech is man's instinctive vehicle of thought, even from himself to the self of a subsequent moment. . . . We know as yet little of how this faculty originated. But every mathematician and logician will tell the linguists [that] they [i.e., the mathematician and logician] are in possession of quite other systems of signs into which they are accustomed to translate words and forms of words and so to render them more intelligible" than is ordinarily possible by means of linguistic signs (MS 654, p. 5). As an actual medium of human communication, the importance of speech is paramount; as the most effective means for deliberate inquiry (put another way, for inquiry ideally designed to subject its inferences to criticism), speech is deficient in comparison with systems of signs based on the modality of sight (e.g., Peirce's own existential graphs, a system he designed to produce "a moving picture of thought" itself). Systems of aural signs *in actu* depend primarily upon *successive* differences: to speak not only takes time, but time is of the essence of speech. (For this reason, speaking may perhaps serve well as a model of time.) In contrast, systems of visual signs are ones very well adapted to present relationships *simultaneously*, even successive relationships and often ones (like those in mathematics) of staggering complexity (CP 3.418-19).

It is imperative to guard against drawing this contrast too sharply. For the use of aural signs depends upon a simultaneity made possible by memory, hearing later words while earlier ones still echo in our recollection. So too does the use of visual signs rely upon a successiveness made possible by the shifting of attention from this to that part (and back again) of what can to some extent be seen in a glance. It is arguable that our ability to hear music has been shaped by our use of visual signs (those signs most effective in attuning us to the grasp of relationships all-at-once) and, in turn, our ability to interpret diagrams has been influenced by our reliance on aural signs (those signs most influential in training us to grasp meaning over a stretch of time). This suggestion is, of course, highly speculative; but it seems warranted here since Peirce himself warned against our tendency to draw distinctions too sharply and absolutely.

No doubt, the place of speech in Peirce's semeiotic invites numerous comparisons (e.g., with Saussure's distinction between *langue* and *parole*, or language and speech; with various motifs in both Merleau-Ponty and Ricoeur). For our purposes, let me highlight but two of these. First, it would be helpful to see what role a Peircean should grant to the notion of code in an account of semiosis and, in particular, speech.

Second, it would be illuminating to link this discussion of speech with Derrida's vindication of arche-writing. (Below, I shall try to make clear why such a comparison merits attention.) In light of a focal concern of much contemporary semiotics,[52] it is also natural to inquire: Is there anything in Peirce's theory of signs that helps explain the role of codes in speech and other processes of communication? In light of Derrida's critique of a metaphysics of presence (a critique in which the priority of speech is challenged in the name of *writing*), we are prompted to ask: Is Peirce just another defender of presence, just another thinker nostalgic for a Being never at odds with itself and always accessible to us (provided, of course, we hit upon the right method or cultivate the appropriate virtues)? The question concerning the notion of code is best addressed at this juncture; the question of Peirce's understanding of speech vis-à-vis Derrida's critique of presence is best postponed until after the relevance of Peirce's categories to inquiries into communication have been discussed more fully.

The question of how fundamental a role codes play in our communicative processes and practices needs to be addressed here, if only briefly. In the semiological tradition deriving from Saussurean linguistics, the concept of code plays a prominent role. The work of Roland Barthes might be taken as emblematic of this tendency. In the semeiotic tradition deriving from Peirce's efforts to transform logic into a theory of signs in general, however, this concept appears to be all but absent. At least, the term itself is hardly used by Peirce and those followers who strive to remain rigorously faithful to his terminology. But this appearance is somewhat deceiving, for the Peircean notion of habit covers much of the ground encompassed by the semiological notion of code. At the very least, a code is a set of correlations providing the means for generating correlations at a different level (or of a different nature) than those making up the code. These correlations underlie the possibility of meaning; put alternatively, they are the means by which agents generate meanings, forge connections, and (on the basis of underlying connections) mark differentiations. For example, the correlations among sounds or phonemes, on the one hand, and words or concepts, on the other, make possible sentences— that is, correlations at a different level (or of a different nature). Such sentences, in turn, make possible yet other types of correlation (e.g., arguments or texts). One way to conceive the correlations comprising codes is in terms of how acculturated organisms are disposed to act in the presence of organisms having undergone similar acculturation.

In light of this, a code might be interpreted as a codification of the ways such organisms are disposed to act in the presence of one another or in that of artifacts dependent on these dispositions. Thus, while the notion of code is not a focal concern of Peircean semeiotic, it is (in my judgment) clearly explicable in terms of a fundamental pragmatic notion—habit or disposition. My suggestion is that, for the pragmatist, it is more fruitful to interpret codes as codifications of dispositions than habits as embodiments of codes, though the latter interpretation is legitimate and can undoubtedly be useful. It is also important to see that anthroposemiosis and some of the conditions for its possibility are embodied in human artifacts as well as in organic dispositions. As artifacts, the forms and conditions of semiosis can reach a degree of complexity and sophistication far beyond the ordinary reach of human sign-users. Think here of the immense difference between the linguistic competence of even the most knowledgeable person and the *Oxford English Dictionary*.

From the perspective of critical commonsensism, the phenomenon of human communication is, at once, a process and the interplay of a set of practices. It is the matrix out of which personal agents emerge and the theaters in which such actors perform their various roles. In situations requiring immediate action and thus swift deliberation, speech is more often than not the ideal medium, for it is (among other reasons) easily producible and producible in such a way as to leave the hands free for other tasks. In situations removed from immediate action and demanding the most carefully controlled processes of sign-use, visual signs are ordinarily superior to aural signs. In all situations involving communication, one or more codes can be supposed to underlie the possibility of our communicative processes and practices. These codes are explicable in terms of habits. This much we have already taken into consideration.

What remains to be discussed in this section is how human communication looks in light of *uncommon observation*—that is, the universal categories derived from phenomenological inquiry. The student of phenomenology needs, "first and foremost," that "rare faculty, the faculty of seeing what stares one in the face, just as it presents itself, unreplaced by interpretation. . . . This is the faculty of the artist who sees for example the apparent colors of nature as they appear" in all their subtle variations (CP 5.42). In addition, this student needs "the generalizing power of the mathematician who produces abstract formula that comprehends the very essence of the feature under examination purified from all admixture of extraneous and irrelevant accompaniments" (CP 5.42).

The most abstract of these formula are, of course, the three universal categories of firstness, secondness, and thirdness. Each of these categories designates a possible feature or facet of whatever we might encounter in experience or even simply conjure in imagination. In other words, they suggest what we should anticipate in the world of fancy no less than the world of fact. In the context of inquiry, they have nothing more than the status of hypotheses—that is, guesses: they dispose us to look in certain directions, to anticipate certain relationships. As descriptive terms conveying something of the phenomenological basis for the Peircean categories, I find the following most helpful: the firstness of *qualitative immediacy* (that aspect of a being such as it is, in itself, apart from anything else), the secondness of *brute opposition*, and the thirdness of *indeliminable mediation*. The ineffability implied by firstness, the perduring sense of struggle and the inevitable assaults on rationality implied by secondness, and finally the open-ended and self-propelled intelligibility implied by thirdness—all of this, and more, are suggested by Peirce's categories, especially when the descriptive phrases suggested above are used as clues to what the categories might concretely imply for an inquiry into signification and communication.

Communication is a process of mediation in which it is, in principle, impossible to identify any absolute *terminus a quo* or *terminus ad quem* (see, e.g., CP 5.311; also CP 5.259-263). This is part of what the thirdness of communication entails, recalling that thirdness itself entails a process of indeliminable mediation. We are always already involved in some form of dialogue; we are ever not yet at the point of closure, if this point be conceived as Absolute Knowledge or the full realization of an ideal consensus. In practice, however, more or less definite points of departure can be established ("for the purpose of this investigation or meeting or deliberation, we can start from ..."); so too can resolutions be reached ("For all practical purposes [as we so significantly say], we are done with our task"). There is, of course, no decisive or infallible way of determining either the *terminus a quo* or the *terminus ad quem* of communication; either can only be settled through the negotiations—and renegotiations—of the participants and possibly by interpretations put forth by "outsiders" (e.g., historians). Insofar as these participants genuinely form a community of inquirers, such negotiations stand a chance of being dialogically executed. But it is imperative to keep in mind that the community of inquirers is truly never anything more than a motley association of companionable antagonists. This is as good as it gets!

Moreover, communication is a process in which there is frequently, if not characteristically, the possibility of ever higher levels of self-consciousness, self-criticism, and self-control. The *self* here might designate the individual or some community—that is, any being who can, in principle, refer to itself ("I says to myself" or "We, the people . . ."). In this broadened conception of selfhood, the decisive criterion is self-referentiality, the capacity of an agent or quasi-agent to make itself the object of self-criticism and self-control.

Différance and Secondness:
A Difference that Makes a Difference?

Above, we noted that Peirce's views on speech invite comparison with various other thinkers, including Jacques Derrida. In very different ways and very different contexts, both Peirce and Derrida are trying to bring into focus the consequences of recognizing the ubiquitous role of indeliminable mediation. For Peirce, "there is no absolute third, for the third is of its own nature relative [or relational], and this is what we are always thinking, even when we aim at the first or second" (CP 1.362). For Derrida, there is no transcendental signified, no signified that is itself not also a signifer. Even so, it might appear that Peirce's claim regarding vocal signs being our instinctual medium of intra- as well as interpersonal, communication would align him, from Derrida's perspective, with the metaphysics of presence. Also, though somewhat paradoxically, it might seem that Peirce's privileging of visual signs because of their power to bring disparate features of a complex phenomenon together all-at-once would align him with this same tradition of metaphysics. But this appearance is misleading; for it prompts us to see presence as the point of difference, rather than different treatments of otherness (what Peirce calls secondness and Derrida *différance*). More accurately, the point of difference concerns *both* secondness and thirdness (otherness and mediation). In my judgment, Peirce has a more robust appreciation of otherness and a more plausible conception of mediation. But claiming this is jumping ahead of the story.

Derrida's desire to vindicate what he calls *writing* (also *arche-writing* as well as various other names) animates his critique of presence and, thus, his critique of metaphysics. For Derrida, Western metaphysics is nothing less than the epochal series of cultural struggles to conceive Being as what is or could be fully and finally present to human consciousness. In a sense, what Derrida intends by *presence* is, in effect, a double or doubled immediacy; for *presence* means, *on the one hand*, that which is what it is, in itself, apart from anything else (above all, that which is *not* defined in terms of either opposition or mediation—indeed, that which *cannot* be otherwise than itself or medi-

ated in any way by another); and, *on the other hand,* that which is immediately present to a conscious subject. In this twofold sense, *presence*
amounts to what Peirce would call firstness. The *metaphysics* of presence being attacked by Derrida is, at once, an ontology (a definition of
Being in terms of immediacy or in-itself-ness) and an epistemology (an
account of knowing in which immediacy or intuition is privileged).

   If we examine a notorious text ("there is nothing outside the text")
in its actual context,[53] we discover something remarkable. The distance
between Derrida and Peirce is not that great. For the section in which
Derrida makes this assertion ("The Exorbitant, Questions of Method")
begins by recalling Jean-Jacques Rousseau's claim that "For me there
has never been an intermediary between everything and nothing."[54] In
response to this, the author of *Of Grammatology* observes that "The
intermediary is the mid-point and the mediation, the middle term
between total absence and the absolute plenitude of presence."[55] It is in
the name of mediation or *mediacy* (what Peirce would call thirdness)
that Derrida undertakes his critique of Rousseau and other defenders
of presence. For "mediacy is the name of all that Rousseau wanted
opinionatedly to efface" and, in turn, the name of all that Derrida himself wants so puckishly to reinstate. For Derrida, the recognition of the
pervasive and ineradicable presence (!) of mediation has numerous and
profound implications. Some of these implications concern reading. In
particular, reading "cannot legitimately transgress the text toward
something other than it, toward a referent (a reality that is metaphysical, historical, psychobiographical, etc.) or toward a signified outside
the text *whose content could take place, could have taken place outside of language,* that is to say . . . outside of writing in general."[56] In an interview
with Richard Kearney, Derrida states that "It is totally false to suggest
that deconstruction is a suspension of reference. Deconstruction is
always deeply concerned with the 'other' of language. I never cease to
be surprised by the critics who see my work as a declaration that there
is nothing beyond language, that we are imprisoned in language; it is,
in fact, saying the opposite."[57] What deconstruction *does* try "to show is
that the question of reference is much more complex and problematic
than traditional theories suppose. It even asks whether our term 'reference' is entirely adequate for designating the 'other.' The other, which
is beyond language and which summons language, is perhaps not a
'referent' in the normal sense."[58]

   In light of these and other texts, the thrust of Derrida's insistence
that *il n'y a pas de hors-texte* seems to be that whatever counts as a referent does so only in and through the text itself and, more generally,
the possibilities of signification underlying the production of texts.

For Peirce, no less than for Derrida, it is a mistake to define Being in terms of presence or what might be called immediacy (that which is what it is, in itself, apart from all else). Even so, immediacy or firstness *is* an irreducible dimension of consciousness (see, e.g., CP 5.289) and, beyond this, of communication. But, then, so too are various forms of brute opposition and of indeliminable mediation. If we are to make sense out of either human consciousness or human communication, it is imperative to view our conscious life and our communicative practices in light of the irreducible and ubiquitous categories of firstness, secondness, and thirdness. But the recognition of one of these categories (in this context, thirdness or mediation) should not be purchased by neglecting the importance of the other two.

The firstness of secondness, the qualitative aspect of brute complusion (the *feeling* of being confronted by some actual, insistent other), is a prominent feature of our actual consciousness and our conversational exchanges. While there may be good or at least plausible reasons for trying to show that "reference is much more complex and problematic than traditional theories suppose," there are unquestionably weighty reasons to grant the obvious—within countless contexts, indexical signs perform their indispensable function in an entirely unproblematic fashion. These signs enable us to attend to what others have experienced or are now experiencing. Neither these others nor what they call to our attention should be construed as beings fully present to our consciousness. But their brute otherness, their irreducible alterity, should not evaporate into a play of differences. The rejection of meaning as absolute presence does not require defining meaning as endless deferral; indeed, the sense of such deferral is simply the shadow cast by the lingering presence of an enduring commitment to transcendent meaning in Derrida's own thinking.

For Peirce and (to be sure) for pragmatists of all stripes, meaning is in the making. It bears the weight of the past in ways Derrida and, to a far greater extent, many of his American disciples do not adequately recognize. It is open to the vicissitudes of time, the twists of history, in ways even the most imaginative of us could never anticipate. (This is, of course, the dimension of meaning highlighted by deconstructionism.) And meaning is more firmly established and reliably present than can be allowed by the characterization of meaning as a series of traces involving endless deferral.

Pragmatic idealism needs to be joined here to critical commonsensism. Peirce knew, all too well, that "there are writers who limit consciousness to what we know of the *past* which they mistake for the *present* and who thus think it to be a question whether we are to say the external world alone is *real* and the internal world *fiction* or whether we shall say that the internal world is the real and the external a fiction" (CP 8.284). For "the true idealism, the pragmatistic idealism . . . reality consists in the *future*." The real cannot be defined in terms of what can be grasped presently by any actual community, let alone any actual individual; it can only be defined in terms of what an infinite community, given an indefinite time, would discover. What this practically means for us, here and now, is that all of our utterances bearing on the character of the real are open to revision. It means, in short, a commitment to fallibilism; though a *contrite fallibilism* does not, for Peirce, rule out "a high faith in the reality of knowledge" (CP 1.14). And what *this* means is (as we noted above) that claims we make about our world and even ourselves are often practically warranted in the present but, simultaneously, indefinitely deferrable.

We must confess that we do not fully and finally know anything at all, but practically and provisionally know more than we can even imagine. Our belief in the reality of knowledge is based, above all, on our ability to meet intelligently, rather than blindly, a fair number of future events. The headlong rush of our lives toward the future is a process over which we exercise control. That the future is often *other than* my expectations is incontestable; but equally certain is that my habits of anticipation are more or less finely attuned to the habits of countless beings, encountered in the course of my practical engagements. There are no good pragmatic reasons to reduce this attunement to an ability to *cope*, a reduction intended to deny the title of knowledge to such attunement. We only truly distance ourselves from the epistemological obsessions of modern philosophy if we can reclaim for the expression *knowledge of reality* its proper (i.e., its humble and pragmatic) meaning, rather than jettisoning this expression altogether. Here, as elsewhere, Peirce's thought drives toward a tempered and tutored commonsensism.

Conclusion

Peirce's architectonic conception of philosophical inquiry should not be seen as an attempt to sketch a comprehensive and timeless framework "in which every other species of discourse could be assigned its proper place and rank."[59] Nor should it be viewed simply as an incredibly rich mine from which to extract conceptual riches. At the heart of this conception is, in effect, an integrated set of heuristic clues. They suggest not only directions in which inquirers might move but also sources upon which inquirers might draw (disciplines from which investigators might find illumination in the form of models and principles). In particular, Peirce's phenomenology and semeiotic are invaluable for an investigation of that array of processes and practices we ordinarily subsume under the heading of *communication*.

In these prolegomena to a distinctively Peircean approach to communication, I hope to have made this claim plausible or, at least, worthy of serious consideration. In other writings, I hope to make this case more fully and substantively, drawing explicitly upon the details of both Peirce's general theory of signs and his dialectical doctrine of the categories.

3

From Enthymeme to Abduction:
The Classical Law of Logic and the
Postmodern Rule of Rhetoric

⸙ ⸙

Richard L. Lanigan

The agonistic relation of logic and rhetoric is truly a historical contest of discourse and its human embodiment as practice. From Aristotle to the present day, philosophers are noted for their desire to refine thought *into discourse* as the inferential event that we retrospectively call modernity and its historical style that we know as modernism. And yet, rhetoricians from the Sophists onward are equally notable for their reverse desire to refine discourse *into thought* as the ahistorical event and inferential practice we now call postmodernity. In this pragmatic *agon* of discourse, modernity and postmodernity are respectively symptomatic (1) of *power* as the ability to exclude human beings from discourse (the human as *symbol*) and (2) of *desire* as the capacity to include persons in discourse (the human as *sign*).

Such a pragmatism in human communication, says Richard Rorty, "is the doctrine that there are no constraints on inquiry save conversational ones—no wholesale constraints derived from the nature of the objects, or of the mind, or of language, but only those retail constraints provided by the remarks of our fellow-inquirers."[1] Or as Charles S. Peirce might have rejoined the comment, "No communication of one person to another can be entirely definite, i.e., non-vague."[2] As such argues Peirce, the problematic of science and that of philosophy is the ground of a *pure rhetoric:* "its task is to ascertain the laws by which in every scientific intelligence one sign gives birth to another, and especially one thought brings forth another."[3]

On the one side we know as *power,* there is an exclusion by force of the ontology of thought enshrined as the *symbol* in the Aristotelian "law of identity," namely, that a thing is a thing (p = p). By such an operation of thought in which something is chosen, all other things are excluded from consideration. "The only sense in which we are constrained to truth is that, as Peirce suggested, we can make no sense of the notion that the view which can survive all objections might be false."[4] *Identity* as a discourse by *symbol (symbola)* becomes the *law of logic*, which should govern discourse, its existence and effect: the birth of modernity. "But objections—conversational constraints—cannot be anticipated. There is no method for knowing *when* one has reached the truth, or when one is closer to it than before."[5] Even Peirce's summary of the nature and function of logic has the tone of fallible human discourse: "Deduction proves that something *must* be; Induction shows that something is *actually* operative; Abduction merely suggests that something *may be*."[6] This is to say specifically, "abduction must cover all the operations by which theories and conceptions are engendered."[7]

But on the other side that we understand as *desire,* there is an inclusion by force of the ontology of discourse championed in the Peircian speculative rhetoric of abduction defined by the syllogism formula [rule + result = case][8]—namely, that a similarity [rule] between one thing and another [result] leads to the discovery [case] of both similarity as (1) a rule about things (consciousness) and (2) as a result to be anticipated in those things (object of consciousness). *Similarity* as a discourse by *sign (semeion)* becomes the *rule of rhetoric,* which should govern thought, its representation and influence: the birth of postmodernity.

In short, says, Peirce, "the universe must be well known and mutually known to be known and agreed to exist, in some sense between speaker and hearer, between the mind as appealing to its own further consideration and the mind as so appealed to, or there can be no communication, or 'common ground,' at all."[9] Rorty agrees by saying that we are led to similarity as a rhetorical rule about things, which is "to focus on a fundamental choice which confronts the reflective mind: that between accepting the contingent character of starting-points, and attempting to evade this contingency."[10] Yet we are also led to similarity as a result to be found in the very hypothesis (semiotic) of discourse—that is, "to accept the contingency of starting points is to accept our inheritance from, and our conversation with, our fellow-humans as our only source of guidance.[11]

In particular, we are alerted to the intuitive, human understanding that the *Real* (actual-ization as empirical signification) and the *Imaginary* (real-ization as eidetic signification) are both grounded in the *Symbolic,* which is a recognition that persons simultaneously makes judgments in *discourse* (actuality/reality as meaning) at several different levels of information (phenomenological awareness) at the same time and place illustrating distinction (symbol) by combination (sign)—that is, the both/and rule in communication theory.[12] The unsettling and insightful conclusion is that persons recognize that judgment in its postmodern conditions *begins* with the *failure* of Aristotle's law of non-contradiction. Human beings intuitively understand that the law of noncontradiction (and with it, the law of identity) fails at the symbolic level. The law asserts that a thing cannot both be and not be at the same time and place [-(p · -p)]. A symbol is a counter-example to the law, as exemplified in language, kinship, or exchange conduct. The symbol is *both* an eidetic *and* an empirical demonstration that the similarity of different levels of information can both be and not be at the same time and place.

As Apprey and Eckman have shown empirically, "it is a method that permits a heuristic dialectical generalization, *a dialectical generalization that includes what it denies*"—that is, the Jakobson *poetic* function of the symbol that includes (communication) at one level of judgment what is excluded (information) at the next level.[13] The proof of this thesis that "communication theory entails information theory" is enshrined in the famous Scholastic proposition defining the sign in discourse: *aliquid stat pro aliquo* [something stands for something else].[14] As Peirce argues, "a representation is that character of a thing by virtue of which, for the production of a certain mental effect, it may stand in place of another thing. The thing having this character I term a *representamen*, the mental effect, or thought, its *interpretant*, the thing for which it stands, its *object*."[15]

Enthymeme: The Classical Law of Logic
as a Discourse of Power

The more classical view of "our conversation" is embodied in the consciousness we know as dialectic and the relational experience that we understand as dialogue, both of which form a description. This new trivium of *description, dialogue,* and *dialectic* captures as meaning (capta) the structure of discourse that Aristotle calls the *enthymeme.* This enthymematic structure has synonymous names in the history of ideas—for example, the *telescoped inference*[16] or the conductive argument.[17] Since I have engaged previously an explicit technical and historical analysis of the enthymeme as the rhetorical species of Aristotle's syllogism as generic, in my present analysis I shall be summarizing and glossing that earlier essay in this part of my discussion.[18]

Using the new trivium as a guideline, we might posit that there are two approaches to a definition of the enthymeme, the *definition* being a logical counterpart to the rhetoric of *description*. In other words, the *dialectic of definition* offers one approach to the enthymeme, while the *description of dialogue* offers a second model. In a more cryptic view, we are to be confronted first with one model that offers us a logic of rhetoric and second with another, reverse, model suggesting to us a rhetoric of logic. In both models, the theory of *logic* dominates as a context for choosing a definition. In the tradition of our modern notion of *information theory*, we are confronted digitally with choosing *either* one model *or* the other, thereby confirming and legitimizing the theory (i.e., logic per se) already in place as a contextual hypostatization (an idea assumed to be an actuality) for the construction of a definition. Information, so discovered in awareness, is the discourse of modernity. And the continuing failure of this discourse to reach finality on its trip from originality is the rupture (Foucault's sense) that marks modernity as stillborn. The contextual alternative is, of course, the rhetoric of abduction grounded in *communication theory* that we shall take up in the next section of the analysis.

One traditional approach to Aristotle's enthymeme is a *logic of rhetoric*. This approach characterizes the enthymeme as a syllogism of formal validity, yet material deficiency in the use of signs and probabilities for evidence in argumentation. The alternative, second approach has Aristotle saying that the enthymeme is a *rhetoric of logic*. This is to say, the *enthymeme is a syllogism of material deficiency (certainty is only certain as persons can be—that is, awareness by signs and probabilities) that is also formally deficient with an unexpressed proposition operating in the rhetorical situation of the orator and audience.*

Aristotle's generic requirements for the construction of a *syllogism* specify what must be given (data) as evidence of judgment in argumentation. To be specific, the argument of a syllogism must be (1) a true inference, (2) a primitive inference, (3) an immediate judgment, (4) an inference more familiar than the conclusion, and (5) an inference more explanatory than the conclusion.[19] Aristotle sets out these *propriety* conditions in the *Posterior Analytics* as the required context of judgment for demonstration in science—that is, the construction of *definition*. On this ground for analysis, two approaches to the definition of the enthymeme are possible within the constitution of discourse as the power to judge.

The first modernist approach to enthymeme as a *logic of rhetoric* suggesting formal validity and material deficiency stresses the fact that Aristotle, and we, can differentiate among the species of the genus syllogism. The first species is a demonstration (science) by *description* where the three propositions of the syllogism are present as formally required and the distributed terms of the individual propositions are materially true, primitive, and so on. The second species of syllogism is known as *dialectic* (practical science), because it is formally complete with three propositions being present like demonstration, yet materially insufficient because the terms fail one or more of the criteria (true, primitive, and so on) for description. The third species (the first approach to the enthymeme) is the rhetorical syllogism where both formal completeness (just like science and dialectic) with a supplied "missing" proposition and material incompleteness (in positive comparison to dialectic; in negative comparison to science) constitute the *art* of judgment in *dialogue*. On this account, the audience *mentally, in the absence of discourse,* supplies *the* material terms that formally, and without any possibility of exception, would complete the syllogistic inference as unitary and original.

By contrast, the second postmodernist approach to the enthymeme as a *rhetoric of logic* suggests that it is a syllogism of (1) *material uncertainty,* defined by the signs and probabilities of human experience in which the asserted terms are fallible because they are present in discourse as oral comportment, and of (2) *formal deficiency* (nonstructural) with one of the three required propositions in the syllogism being left unexpressed or *suppressed* to use the traditional label. Any proposition supplied to replace the unexpressed proposition will exist in the speaker's and audience's mind as a silent, eidetic acknowledgment that is a *formal* (not material!) completion of the speaker's expression that is an encoded premise per se as "the expression of a train of thought,"[20] that is, a completion captured in Peirce's notion of *tone.*[21] Note in particular that the syllogism is *not* completed as a result of the audience's expression of material terms—that is, decoding as when a person reads a text or listens to a speech *as if* he or she were the originary speaker.

Ironically for modernist ears to hear, the second postmodernist approach to defining the enthymeme as a dialogue in discourse accords best with the Aristotelian corpus with its varied discussions of the rhetorical syllogism as the art of definition and the dialogic practice of discourse.[22] The postmodernist model is also the view that Peirce adopts in his various analyses of the Aristotelian enthymeme as an "incomplete argument."[23] And, it is this second view that accords with *Peirce's invention of the name* abduction as a neologism (1) to correct the traditional translation of Aristotle's usage from the Greek, and (2) to specify the enthymeme as the rhetorical species of syllogism in

Aristotle's logic,[24] most specifically in terms of Aristotle's four forms of causality (matter, form, efficient, and final) that ground both his and my own analysis of the enthymeme.[25]

Abduction: The Postmodern Rule of
Rhetoric as a Discourse of Desire

The notion of abduction [rule + result = case] will strike many as unfamiliar territory, especially those only accustomed to an either/or division of analysis into induction [case + result = rule] or deduction [rule + case = result]. These Peircian logics or *normative semiotics* are an expression of dialogue, dialectic, and description as we just encountered them in Aristotle's thinking.[26] Deduction is a demonstrative syllogism whose propositions are formally required [rule] and materially certain [case] so that the judgment [result] is true, primitive, and so on, in applied extension [the invention of power: results should not change; the law of identity]. In parallel fashion, the dialectical syllogism of induction is materially insufficient [case] and formally complete [result] so that there is a judgment [rule], but one of unknown consequence in applied extension [the invention of desire: rules should not be changed; the law of noncontradiction].

Recall that in the category of the rhetorical syllogism, there are two approaches to the enthymeme: (1) the syllogism is formally deficient [rule] and materially *certain* [result] as a judgment [case]; or (2), the syllogism is formally deficient [rule] and materially *uncertain* [result] as a judgment [case]. This second approach is the Aristotelian definition and the one that explicates a semiotic understanding in which the *symbolic capta* are the material under consideration. The second approach is also Peirce's understanding of *abduction* or the process of *hypothesis* formulation and selection.[27] By contrast in those situations which are nonsymbolic, hence nondiscursive (e.g., phenomena in nature such as chemistry, physics, etc.), the first approach to the enthymeme best accords with one modality of abduction that Peirce calls *retroduction* or the process of hypothesis testing. Post-Peircian scholars, such as Maurice Merleau-Ponty in the *Phenomenology of Perception,* use the modern label of *adduction* in place of *retroduction.*[28] In short, the same formula [rule + result = case] defines both abduction and adduction; yet, *abduction* is a *particular* and *a posteriori* claim, whereas *adduction* is a *universal* and *a priori* claim.

In the shift from a syllogism of scientific demonstration to the enthymeme of rhetorical dialogue, the symbolic constraint on discourse moves from the enthymeme as abduction to encompass the

enthymeme of adduction. In short, the symbolic as specific and experiential [abduction] envelopes the imaginary as general [retroduction]
and the real as prior to experience [adduction] much as a *cultural psychology* entails the *natural psychology* of discourse. Burks offers us an
illustration with the comparison between a person and a computer
wherein the human being can use abduction and the machine cannot.
"Thus according to Peirce's normative definition of inference a com-
puting machine fails to infer in two respects, conscious approval and
originality, both of which are essential to abductive reasoning."[29]
Richard Shweder elaborates this point clearly and concisely.

> If there is to be a cultural psychology it will have to synthesize ratio-
> nalism and empiricism into something else or provide an alternative to
> both. C. S. Peirce's notion of abductive reasoning as the indispensable
> assistant to the "unaided rationality" [rhetoric] of logic and sense data
> is a promising starting point. One version of Peirce's notion, if I under-
> stand it, is this: transcendent realities can be imagined but never seen
> or deduced, for they are constructions of our own making, which
> sometimes succeed in binding us to the underlying reality they imag-
> ine by giving us an intellectual tool—a metaphor, a premise, an analo-
> gy, a category—with which to live, to arrange our experience, and to
> interpret our experiences so arranged. In other words, the abductive
> faculty is the faculty of imagination, which comes to the rescue of sen-
> sation and logic by providing them with the intellectual means to see
> through experience and leap beyond empty syllogisms and tautologies
> to some creative representation of an underlying reality that might be
> grasped and reacted to, even if that imagined reality cannot be found,
> proved, or disproved by inductive or deductive rule-following.[30]

This very confrontation of power (natural psychology) and
desire (cultural psychology) in discourse forms the basis for Sabre's
problematical contention that "the difference between rhetoric and
inquiry can be explicated in terms of intent with regard to an audience," and his even more problematical conclusion that with regard to
the enthymeme, "Aristotle and his followers differentiate in terms of
subject matter, but do not make a clear case for that, nor the contention
that there is some fundamental difference in logical *form* between
demonstration and the other arts."[31]

Enthymeme versus Abduction: A Contest of
Desire against Power in Discourse

Sabre adopts a modernist literary (composition[32]) definition of
the rhetorical situation (the discourse of power) by asserting that "the
enthymeme is associated with a rhetorical context because a rhetorical

context involves an audience, a rhetor, and a subject about which the rhetor wants to convince the audience of some attribute." A parallel assertion is made for the conduct of science: "Inquiry is a triad of inquirer, audience and subject where once a hypothesis is formed, the inquirer is bound to persuade an audience expecting the use of established scientific procedures to determine whether a claim is acceptable."[33] In addition, the shadow of Stephen Toulmin[34] (who is never named by Sabre) emerges with the additional qualification that "the enthymeme is an argument which is established by a because-clause, the relevance and plausibility of which is established by a generalization or warrant it is assumed the audience would find plausible. The intention of the rhetor is to make a claim"[35] Of course, the because-clause is a theoretical construct in the discourse of desire belonging to Alfred Schutz (also never named by Sabre) as the *because-motive*.[36]

The first task in sorting out Sabre's position on the enthymeme and abduction is to recall that in Aristotle's *Rhetoric* that "rhetoric may be defined as the faculty of observing in any given case the available means of persuasion. This not a function of any other art. . . . It is not concerned with any special or definite class of subjects."[37] Of course, Aristotle had an *oral* art in mind so that a *rhetor* is a speaker *in situ* (phenomenologically here and now) among other speakers (an audience) who is speaking the sign of his or her mind *(semeion)*. The art is not a writer spatially and temporally displaced (there and then) from a possible reader by an intervening text *(symbola)* where writing formally records speaking and thus mediates its materiality. As Peirce would say existentially, the tone is lost in writing. The subject matter of Aristotle's persuasion is the *lived situation* of a shared *code* of meaning carried in the spoken discourse as materially, formally, efficiently, and finally *in praesentia*. Following Cicero, this *terminus a quo* becomes the *because-motive* in Schutz wherein discourse recalls in the pluperfect tense "what had been" as that *efficient form* in which we move to a *final material* judgment made here and now. A rhetor's speaking accomplishes this action with the use of an *enthymeme*. Yet persuasion as a result of an argument for the audience is the same situation, but with an unshared *message* of meaning carried in the perceived code of speech. This phenomenon is the *terminus ad quem* or what Schutz calls the *in-order-to-motive* in which discourse describes in the future perfect tense "what shall have been"as that *final form* toward which we move as an *efficient material* judgment about there and then. The audience's perception (sign) as an expression (probability) of thought accomplishes this action with the use of *abduction*.

It is this conjunction of enthymeme (here and now) and abduction (there and then) that makes a sign generate a symbol. This explication holds true, according to Peirce, even for a conception of the materially actual. As Turrisi suggests:

> Peirce's hypothesis is that the material universe, in its real uniformity, its regularity, its really operative laws of motion, is a "symbol" in the process of an argumentative elaboration of its successive "conclusions" in the mode of sensible "realities." The universe is an argument; an argument is a symbol.[38]

Or as Aristotle explicates the point at an eidetic level of formal actuality in discourse, speech is a sign of thought, while writing is a symbol of speech: *aliquid stat pro aliquo.*

The entire process of combinatory enthymeme and abduction is simply lost in a written text where the reader is confronted with a symbolic text (as an anonymous addresser) requiring a translation, which is both an absent code and a present message, and yet neither in the absence of the speaker's performance (tone) as the guiding inference (code selection; metaphor) of hypothesis (message selection; metonymy). As Jakobson continues to remind us, "we must consistently take into account the decisive difference between *communication* which implies a real or alleged addresser and *information* whose source cannot be viewed as an addresser by the interpreter of the indications obtained."[39]

In short, the Aristotelian requirement for *ethos* and *pathos* cannot be detached from the *logos.* Author intent (pseudo-ethos) frequently is manufactured to fill in this anonymous addresser void of contextual action (pseudo-pathos; actually it is known as *bathos* in speech). As we already know concerning the equivocation of sign and symbol (semeion; symbola),[40] Plato worried about writing as the loss of memory on this count among others in his dialogue *Phaedrus!*

Julian Jaynes makes the same point from the perspective of the oral rhetor whose persuasive discourse must always embody and heed this postmodernist maxim: "To be conscious of the elements of speech is to destroy the intention of the speech." This is to say you may adopt the modernist perspective and "try speaking with a full consciousness of your articulation as you do it. You will simply stop speaking."[41] In short, abduction is the embodied intentionality of speech as material uncertainty (discourse is only probable), while the enthymeme is abduction's articulation as formal deficiency (discourse is only a sign).

Next, a brief word needs to be said about Toulmin's theory of argumentation. It is a six-part model of discourse that grounds (1) a *claim* based on (2) *data* that are contextualized (3) by a *warrant* with (4) evidentiary *backing*, which may be influenced by (5) *reservations* about the evidence leading to a (6) *qualifier* on the claim.[42] The purpose of such a model is to explain the psychological connection of the rhetor and audience in the medium of the message and code—that is, the belief (a code that is a signifier of meaning) that contextualizes an interpretation (a message that is a signified of meaning) of an argument (a meaning as the sign or combined signifier/signified). Thus for Sabre, "a persuasive argument is the ability to appeal to beliefs held by the audience."[43] Here, the persuasive argument is asserted to be an abduction, while the appeal to belief is an enthymeme.

Sabre's view depends on the what he calls the *abductive cycle* in Peirce's description of the connection among deduction, induction, and abduction. Sabre's example is the syllogism in *first figure* BAR-BARA illustrated in Figure 3.1.

Sabre explains the argument cycle with this commentary:

> The abductive argument has the distinction of initiating the thought process by being a response of shock, question, puzzlement or assertion on the part of a person in viewing subject-S, indicated by the exclamation point. While the completed thought process is embodied in the explaining syllogism, the deduction, the thought process is initiated by (say) surprise and culminates in producing a hypothesis, all S are M [→], on the basis of a generalization or warrant, all M are P [←].

The hypothesis is that M explains the relationship between S and P.[44] On this modernist account, the rhetor or inquirer *invents similarity* between M and P because of the *statistical* similarity in the two inductive instances of S [All S are M; All S are P]. As Sabre notes, this induction is statistical by force of using Mill's method of *agreement*, that is, M and P have S in common.[45] But note, the statistic is used to *invent an identity* [S] as a definition [of M and P]. The definition is, of course, the syllogistic conclusion of the induction [All M are P] which supplies [←] the *major premise* in the deduction. But there is a logical alternative to inductive invention.

Abductive	Deductive	Inductive
		All S are M.
All M are P.		All S are P.
All S are P!	All M are P. ⟵	All M are P.
All S are M. ⟶	All S are M.	
	All S are P.	

Figure 3.1. C.S. Peirce's Abduction Cycle of Argument.

By shock, question, puzzlement, surprise, and the like, the rhetor or inquirer *discovers similarity* between M and S because of the *experience of consciousness* constituted in P,—that is, the abductive combination of [All M are P] and [All S are P]. This phenomenological starting point of intentionality (consciousness of P) as an essence S [All S are P!] constitutes the discovery of P as "bracketed" (Husserl's *epoché*) from other criteria for judging the phenomenon P (including, importantly, statistical generalization by induction!). As Peirce argues,"phenomenology has no right to appeal to logic, except to deductive logic. On the contrary, logic must be founded on phenomenology."[46]

By the procedure of *imaginative free variation*, the (1) phenomenological *description* [All S are P!] can be reflected upon and analyzed to also discover a second similarity to constitute a more precise description that *depicts* (not predicts as with statistical induction) a more precise description as definition. The rhetor or inquirer discovers, for example, that on reflection M is an essential characteristic of P because attribute M has a sign or symbol relation to P that destroys the essence of P if removed (a constitutive rule of discourse; metaphor). By comparison, the rhetor or inquirer may discover that, for example, attribute Z does not destroy the essence of P if removed during the free variation technique of conceiving the phenomenon P. Thereby, attribute Z is nonessential to understanding P (only a regulative rule of discourse; metonymy). The (2) phenomenological *reduction* produces the major premise of the abduction [All M are P]. Here is where the notion of enthymeme is so critically important! The major premise for the rhetor or inquirer is *unstated (not articulated)* and thus not the formal beginning of a deduction. The abduction is formally deficient, hence like (a *similarity to,* but not an identity with) a deduction, but *not* a deduction. Sabre misses this point in his account, which distinguishes abduction on the basis of logical *intent* rather that rhetorical discourse *form* (recall Aristotle's causality). The final step of analysis, (3) phenomenological *interpretation,* makes use of the syllogistic form to draw the conclusion [All S are M] which supplies [→] the minor premise of a deduction. The validity of the phenomenological method is thereby illustrated as the *rule of similarity* as described by the coincidence (Roman Jakobson's *rule of redundancy*[47]) of [All S are P] as the conclusion of the deductive syllogism (demonstration; science) and as "the abductive argument . . . *initiating* the thought process by being a response of shock, question, puzzlement or assertion on the part of the person viewing subject-S."[48] The shock, and so forth, is the realization (not actualization, which is yet to come in deduction) that M is yet another similarity discovered in the *appearances* of P in discourse (a similarity) as opposed to the invention of P as an ideal phenomenon (an identity).

The point is made clear and concise by Gregory Bateson in his definition of abduction (following that of Peirce): "**Abduction:** That form of reasoning in which a recognizable similarity between A and B proposes the possibility of further similarity. Often contrasted with two other, more familiar types of reasoning, deduction and induction."[49] In short, discourse as "a model becomes a tool for comparative study of different fields of phenomena. It is above all the tool of *abduction*, drawing from phenomena in different fields that which is shared among them."[50] The abductive symbol discovers the deductive sign. And, rhetoric (enthymeme) in science (abduction) comes to constitutes a *human science* appropriately called a *communicology*, or a *phenomenology* of conscious experience embodied in the model of *discourse*.[51] The phenomenology of Bateson's approach to doing science through a mediation of discourse follows the Peircian methodology for abduction—that is, *hypothesis* in Peirce's early writing:

> The truth is, that any two things resemble one another just as strongly as any two others, if recondite resemblances are admitted. But, in order that the process of making an hypothesis should lead to a probable result, the following rules must be followed:
>
> 1. The hypothesis should be distinctly put as a question, before making the observations which are to test its truth. In other words, we must try to see what the result of predictions from hypothesis will be.
>
> 2. The respect in regard to which the resemblances are noted must be taken at random. We must not take a particular kind of predictions for which the hypothesis is known to be good.
>
> 3. The failures as well as the success of the predictions must be honestly noted. The whole proceeding must be fair and unbiased.[52]

Given these methodological rules, an especially insightful version of Peirce's hypothesis argument occurs in Bachelard's blending of abduction, deduction, and induction as the enthymeme that is metaphor. Bachelard argues:

> To the extent that hypotheses have been linked to experiments, they must be considered just as real as the experiments themselves. They are "realized" [as in realization, not realism]. The time of the adaptable patchwork hypothesis is over, and so is the time of fixation on isolated experimental curiosities. Henceforth, hypothesis is synthesis[53]

Before illustrating the flaw in Sabre's analysis of enthymeme and abduction, it is helpful to follow our present discussion of discourse and see his analysis within the context of Toulmin's synthetic theory of argumentation. It is this approach that leads Sabre to ignore the

Aristotelian definitions of the genus syllogism and its scientific, dialectical, and rhetorical species and, thereby, conflate the phenomenon (sign) of orality and inscription in discourse (symbol) in the modality of enthymeme (the rhetor's art) and abduction (the inquirer's science). Recall, Toulmin's theory is illustrated by a six-part model of discourse that grounds (1) a *claim* based on (2) *data* that are contextualized (3) by a *warrant* with (4) evidentiary *backing,* which may be influenced by (5) *reservations* about the evidence leading to a (6) *qualifier* on the claim.

On Sabre's account (see Figure 3.1), the abduction creates as its conclusion (1: claim) a hypothesis [All S are M], which supplies [→] the *minor premise* (2: data) in a rhetor's deduction. This judgment is based upon the *major premise* (3: warrant) of the rhetor's deduction supplied [←] by the conclusion [All M are P] of an induction (4: backing). The deductive *conclusion* [All S are P] is susceptible to material error (5: reservation) since (a) it has already functioned as the all important minor premise in the abduction—a premise [All S are P!] intuitively (non-logically) generated in shock, question, puzzlement or assertion (6: qualifier), and (b) since the major premise of the deduction and the abduction are *identical* [All M are P]. Note that the deduction relies on the claim that M and P are *identical,* hence the hypothesis that P *either* explains the meaning of S *or* not. By contrast, the abduction relies on the claim that M and P are *similar,* hence the hypothesis that M explains the meaning of *both* S *and* P, as Sabre correctly notes for the wrong reasons. The right reasons involve a contemporary understanding of *tropic logic* as it emerges in rhetoric, not science. We shall come to this issue in due course, but for the moment we need to first recall the definitional characteristics of an enthymeme and then apply the differentia to Sabre's three logic example.

As I have previously demonstrated, the Aristotelian definition of the enthymeme derives from the following conclusions:

1. The conjunction of formal and material cause in expression is necessary to persuasion, but, probabilities and signs are the matter, while enthymeme is the form.

2. The enthymeme is a species of the genus "syllogism." This species is distinguished by probable or signified matter and an incomplete syllogistic form of three terms wherein one proposition (a premise or the conclusion) is unexpressed by the speaker.

3. Formal cause allows for the combination of an infinite number of probable ideas or propositions (material cause) that can be supplied psychologically in the mind of the speaker and each listener. Yet, the oral or mental process of supplying such material completion is a definiendum of persuasion for the listener, not a definiendum of the enthymeme as the speaker's method of persuasion.[54]

Given these criteria for understanding the Aristotelian enthymeme, especially as a logical form used by a speaker or by the scientific inquirer, we should reformulate Sabre's syllogistic example as given in Figure 3.2:

In this revised example, the selection of any one of the three logics for the speaker's or inquirer's expression in oral discourse constitutes a condition of persuasion (enthymeme criterion no. 1 above). The italicized propositions are *unexpressed* respectively as premises in abduction and deduction, and, as the conclusion in the induction (criterion no. 2). This formal deficiency defines the same rhetorical use of enthymeme *structure* in every one of the three *forms* of logic. At this point, we return to the suggestive Shweder distinction between a cultural psychology of the rhetor and the natural psychology of the scientific inquirer. This is to say, the discourse of the enthymeme is materially uncertain because the signs and probabilities of evidence are embodied in the rhetor (or scientific inquirer) in a formally deficient way: the rhetor or inquirer "cannot be viewed as an addresser by the interpreter" of the signs and probabilities following Jakobson's thesis. In a word, the audience addresses the unknown, which is to say, the symbolic. This cultural psychology accords with what John Searle calls the *background conditions* for discourse.[55] In particular, we need to take note of Searle's argument that "communicating is a matter of producing certain effects on one's hearers, but one can intend to represent something without caring at all about the effects on one's hearers."[56] By distinguishing communication and representation (information), we gain some insight about distinguishing rhetoric's enthymeme and science's abduction.

Communication is a cultural psychology of rhetoric manifest in tropes of speech, the empirical evidence of enthymemes. Yet representation is a natural psychology of science manifest in the logics of language, the eidetic evidence of abductions. In short, Searle is correct to

Abductive	Deductive	Inductive
		All S are M.
{All M are P.}		All S are P.
All S are P!	*{All M are P.}* ⟵――― *{All M are P.}*	
All S are M. ――⟶	All S are M.	
	All S are P.	

Figure 3.2. The Enthymeme Argument Cycle (with the suppressed propositions as a "blank" or "present absence" shown in brackets.)

argue that "one can intend to represent without intending to communicate, but one cannot intend to communicate without intending to represent. I cannot, for example, intend to inform you that it is raining without intending that my utterance represent, truly or falsely, the state of affairs of the weather."[57] So the formal cause of all enthymemes *communicates* orally a state of affairs by *representing* what is unexpressed (enthymeme criterion no. 3). Any listener who recognizes *anything* that fits the signified representation is, thereby, persuaded by the adduction resulting from the enthymeme used by the speaker or inquirer. As Peirce confirms:

> People commonly talk of *the* conclusion from a pair of premises [enthymeme], as if there were but one inference to be drawn. But relative logic shows that from any proposition whatever, without a second, an endless series of necessary consequences can be deduced; and it very frequently happens that a number of distinct lines of inference may be taken [capta], none of them leading into another.[58]

But note, the speaker using the enthymeme is using only that type of logic that is strictly an adduction, and not an abduction. The speaker's or inquirer's *abductive claim* is a *symbolic* relation by being particular and a posteriori (communication entails representation (information); "one cannot intend to communicate without intending to represent"). The abduction enthymeme, as I noted early on in my analysis, is a syllogism that is formally deficient [rule; in-order-to-motive] and materially uncertain [result; because-motive] as a judgment [case]. In short, the *abduction enthymeme* is Peirce's understanding of the process of hypothesis formulation and selection, a cultural psychology of the *rule of rhetoric as a postmodern discourse of realization by symbol*. Whereas, the listener's *adductive claim* is a *sign* relation by being universal and a priori (representation or information does not entail communication; "one can intend to represent without intending to communicate"). This adduction enthymeme is a syllogism that is formally deficient [rule; in-order-to-motive] and materially *certain* [result] as a judgment [case; because-motive]. The listener is forced into the process of hypothesis testing or what Peirce calls *retroduction* or "reasoning from consequent to antecedent" (= adduction).[59] The shift of the because-motive from the functive of *result* in abduction to *case* in adduction suggests the popular *falsification* view of science offered by Karl Popper where one counterexample (counter-case) points back (retroductively!) to a failed application of the rule. Hence, even Sabre is forced to conclude that "the enthymeme in a rhetorical context and the abductive argument in the abductive cycle [= adduction] are *identical* except for the inductive phase [= the selection of the case]."[60]

In the case of Sabre's syllogistic example, the listener is forced to choose whether to make the unexpressed (represented, but not communicated) proposition [All M are P] a major premise in the deduction or a conclusion for the induction. Either choice will merely confirm the syllogism as adduction because the same *maxim* results—namely, the combined propositions in the strict order [(1) All S are M; (2) All S are P]. For Aristotle the maxim is the enthymeme (the two expressed propositions) considered apart from the missing unexpressed proposition—that is, Searle's background knowledge or Shweder's cultural psychology.[61] Here, the rhetor and inquirer part company contrary to Sabre's analysis. The inquirer in the practice of science does choose deduction or induction as a confirmation of natural psychology by inventing (power) the proposition that [All M are P] as strictly *either* the beginning *claim* (step no. 1) of Toulmin's model and thus a major premise from which to invent a deduction, *or*, as the ending *reservation* (step no. 6) that is the conclusion of an invented induction.

The choice is demonstration or dialectic (representation; information), but not dialogue (communication), which would be the missing steps (nos. 2 through 5) in Toulmin's model of argument. The very process suggests the limits of the *scientific method* in actual human discourse, since the choice of deduction as an in-order-to-motive selects, at best, as its *case* [deduction: rule + case = result] a *probability* since there can be no material certainty as final cause. The *case* as a material *sign* for induction [case + result = rule] has exactly the same result as an in-order-to-motive (efficient cause), even though no argument for certainty is made by induction.

On the other hand, the rhetor does choose the abduction with its strict order [(1) All S are P!; (2) All S are M] because, as Sabre notes, "the hypothesis is that M explains the relationship between S and P."[62] This is to say, the intended communication of M is already represented as information in P! The communicated symbol already represents the sign, itself a signifier (expressed enthymeme: [All S are P!; All S are M]) and a signified (unexpressed premise: [All M are P]). All of Toulmin's steps, save the last (no. 6), are expressed in the enthymeme: the minor premise [All S are P!] is the (1) claim, (2) data, and (3) warrant validated by the conclusion [All S are M], which gives (4) the backing, (5) evidentiary reservation and (6) reservation awaiting argumentative fulfillment (persuasion!) by the appearance of any proposition that is (6) the qualifier to the argument. In Sabre's example, the M in the unexpressed proposition [All M are P] can be *anything* supplied by cultural psychology in the speaker/audience background.

The entire process whereby the desire of discourse (speech; orality; actualization) has priority over the power of discourse (language;

inscription; realization) can be illustrated now with a discussion of the *tropic logic model of rhetoric*, which informs the human sciences (cultural psychology) as opposed to the physical sciences (natural psychology). Following on the many analyses of discourse by Michel Foucault, I have called this model the quadrilateral discourse Model of *le même et l'autre*.[63] The model illustrates the definition of the abduction enthymeme, which I argue is the correct Aristotelian and Peircian view—namely, that it is a syllogism that is formally *deficient* [rule; in-order-to-motive] and materially *uncertain* [result; because-motive] as a judgment [case]. The model is constituted by the discursive rhetorical force of the French aphorism: *le même et l'autre*. This aphorism must be translated/transmuted simultaneously (material uncertainty of meaning) as both self and other, and as same and different, thereby creating Maurice Merleau-Ponty's notion of existential ambiguity or the *contingency* of the human experience (formal deficiency of meaning). The tropic relations and their definitions for the rhetorical formations (mutations in Hjelmslev's sense) that *derive from* the transformations can be illustrated in Figure 3.3.

If we can recall the Sabre syllogism example once again (Figure 3.2), we can then convert it to the tropic formulation that informs the discursive operation of enthymeme within each species of syllogistic

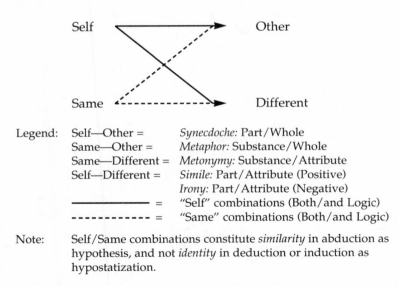

Legend: Self—Other = *Synecdoche:* Part/Whole
Same—Other = *Metaphor:* Substance/Whole
Same—Different = *Metonymy:* Substance/Attribute
Self—Different = *Simile:* Part/Attribute (Positive)
Irony: Part/Attribute (Negative)
————— = "Self" combinations (Both/and Logic)
- - - - - - - - = "Same" combinations (Both/and Logic)

Note: Self/Same combinations constitute *similarity* in abduction as hypothesis, and not *identity* in deduction or induction as hypostatization.

Figure 3.3 *Le Même et L'Autre:* A Tropic Logic Model of Rhetorical Argumentation.

reasoning that Peirce calls argument: "argument is of three kinds: *Deduction, Induction,* and *Abduction* (usually called adopting a hypothesis)."[64] Remember that the italicized propositions are the unexpressed propositions in the oral discourse of the speaker. With the appropriate tropic transformations of definitions for trope names, the syllogisms are now as presented in Figure 3.4.

It is important to realize on the analysis of this exemplar that science is rhetorical by force of the fact that the syllogism of demonstration (deduction) constitutes its inference by *metaphor* in which the defining semiotic relation of *same—other* (see Figure 3.3: metaphor = substance/whole) is the transformation/transmutation rule (see the terms *Same* and *Other* in the deductive syllogism in Figure 4.3). In this context of parallelism, the metaphor is a similarity and not an identity; it is Peirce's notion of the *hypoicon*. "But a sign may be *iconic,* that is, may represent its object mainly by its similarity [same], no matter what its mode of being [other]. If a substantive be wanted, an iconic representamen may be termed a *hypoicon*." Hypoicons consist of *images, diagrams,* and *metaphors*. "Those which represent the representative character of a representamen by representing a parallelism in something else are *metaphors*."[65] This rule of metaphor allows the deductive inferential conclusion [Self -> Different] because it is already grounded, as Sabre said, in the abductive "response of shock, question, puzzlement or assertion on the part of a person in viewing subject-S" that [All S are P!], which is to say with exclamation [Self -> Different!]:

> The abductive suggestion comes to us like a flash. It is an act of insight, although of extremely fallible insight. It is true that the different elements of the hypothesis were in our minds before; but it is the idea of putting together [metonymy] what we had never before dreamed of putting together which flashes the new suggestion [metaphor] before our contemplation.[66]

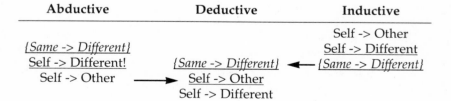

Abductive	Deductive	Inductive

		Self -> Other
{Same -> Different}		<u>Self -> Different</u>
<u>Self -> Different!</u>	*{Same -> Different}* ⟵	*{Same -> Different}*
Self -> Other ⟶	<u>Self -> Other</u>	
	Self -> Different	

**Figure 3.4. Term Specification of the Tropic Logic Model
(bracketed propositions are suppressed)**

It is precisely this insightful discovery of continuity in the *description, dialogue, and dialectic of the abductive enthymeme as metaphor* that drives the pragmatic argument that "the idea of a cultural psychology is the idea that individuals and traditions, psyches and cultures, make each other up." The tropic result, then, is to expose "one of the central myths [modernity] of the modern period in the West" which "is the idea that the opposition [different and same] between religion—superstition—revelation and logic—science—rationality divides the world into then and now [there and here], them and us [other and self]."[67]

In addition, the discovery of the Same— Other metaphor (see Figure 3.3) embedded in the abductive premise that "Self is [->] Different !" (see [1] in Figure 3.5) illustrates the Hegelian notion of a universal particular in discourse.[68] The Hegelian division of (1) subjective mind as the origin of consciousness, (2) objective mind as the signification of consciousness, and (3) absolute mind as the system of consciousness[69] grounds the Franz Brentano *rhetorical/symbolic* approach to a *nonpropositional* theory of categories. The categories are respectively (1) ideas where primary objects are representations (psychological objects) and secondary objects are physical objects, (2) judgments or universals, and (3) the unity of consciousness where emotion and volition constitute the basis of a nonpropositional theory of judgment.[70] The Peircian division of (1) type, (2) token, and (3) tone together with the respective *logical triplet* of (1) term, (2) proposition, and (3) argument follows in this phenomenological tradition.[71]

The nonpropositional categories of relation in discourse are, indeed, the ground of phenomenological (1) description, (2) reduction, and (3) interpretation as I am using them. Sabre notices a connection here as between Hegel and Peirce, but does not explore its consequence. He merely says, "This triadic formulation is similar to Hegel's."[72] Rather than a mere logical insight, the tropic infusion into abductive enthymeme is demonstrated both eidetically and empirically by both Maurice Merleau-Ponty and Michel Foucault.[73] In Merleau-Ponty's case, for example, the tropic logic can be used to prove the child's development of a cultural psychology noted rhetorically in learning the use of pronoun (language) reference (economic exchange) to oneself (kinship). This "system of four terms," as Merleau-Ponty calls it, depends on the Same—Other metaphor [You (personal) -> You (public)] being embedded in the abductive premise that Self is Different! [I -> Me!] as the child learns the embodied rules of existential discourse within interpersonal communication. The system of four terms is the child's learning experience of Searle's communication rule that "one can intend to represent without intending to communicate"

[You (personal) -> Same = You (public) -> Other], "but one cannot intend to communicate without intending to represent" [I -> Self = Me ->Different]. The system of four terms is the child's learning experience of Searle's two communication rules, namely (1) that "one can intend to represent without intending to communicate" [You (personal -> Same = You (public) -> Other], (2) "but one cannot intend to communicate without intending to represent" [I -> Self = Me -> Different]. The first rule states Jakobson's edidetic rule for *distinctive features*, while the second states his empirical rules for *redundancy features* in human communication.

It is also worth noting at this point that with the suppressed premise {Same -> Different; You (per) -> Me}, an addressee (listener) is confronted in discourse with decoding a digital (either/or) choice of logics: either an abduction (judgment follows from a suppressed major premise) or an induction (judgment results in a suppressed conclusion). The addressee literally does not know whether the judgment is coming (*terminus a quo*; because-motive) or going (*terminus ad quem*; in order-to-move motive). This very paradox of syllogistic form results in *both* (1) a functional reference that Gregory Bateson calls *play, and* (2) a disfunctional reference that he calls the *double bind*. The location of the suppressed premise is the key to this code priority problem. This is to say, which comes first in decoding as between abduction [Self -> Different!; (1) I -> Me!] and induction [Self -> Other; (3) I -> You (pub)]? Indeed, the addressee (listener) has a paradoxical choice (something will be lost) of codes from which to select one code, yet the selection of that code will be ambiguous (something else is gained) as a message. In Searle's frame of context, the addressee (listener) is driven to choose between either *play* (communication entails representation) or *double bind* (representation does not entail communication). Recall Jakobson's summary of this point that a person must constantly distinguish between *communication* with its "real or alleged [playful] addresser" and *information* (representation "whose source cannot be viewed as an addresser *by the interpreter of the indications obtained*" wherein the *source* and the *addresser* constitute a paradoxical *double*.

Returning now to Merleau-Ponty's example of communication in child development, the genus syllogism for the child come in three parts (bold numbering here matches that in Figure 5) with (1) abduction supplying the performance (desire) of speech (embodiment) in the *metaphor* of (2) deduction and then (3) induction as the competence (power) of language, exchange, and kinship (cultural memory).

By way of summarizing my analysis in this essay, let me offer Peirce's own phenomenological account of the *semiotic argument cycle*

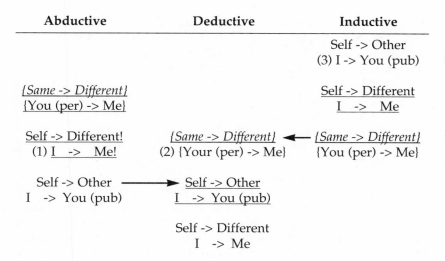

**Figure 3.5. Merleau-Ponty's "Child's Relation with Others"
Model Illustrated as a Tropic Logic of Existential Argumentation
(bracketed propositions are suppressed; per = Personal referent,
pub = Public referent).**

of rhetoric in which (1) abduction, (2) deduction, and (3) induction
account for Peirce's believe that "the truth of pragmaticism may be
proved in various ways":

> Abduction having suggested a theory, we employ deduction to
> deduce from that ideal theory a promiscuous variety of consequences
> to the effect that if we perform certain acts, we shall find ourselves
> confronted with certain experiences. We then proceed to try these
> experiments, and if the predictions of the theory are verified, we have
> a proportionate confidence that the experiments that remain to be
> tried will confirm the theory. I say that these three are the only ele-
> mentary modes of reasoning there are. I am convinced of it both a pri-
> ori and a posteriori. [74]

Merleau-Ponty's discussion of the child's relations with others
exemplifies this Peircian conclusion drawn from an *argument:*

> The argument is a representamen which does not leave the interpre-
> tant to be determined as it may by the person to whom the symbol is
> addressed, but separately represents what is the interpreting repre-
> sentation that it is intended to determine. This interpreting represen-
> tation is, of course, the conclusion. [75]

This is to say, like the child in Merleau-Ponty's analysis who is a rhetor (the Same) before being a scientific inquirer (the Other), we are treated to a wonderful postmodern enthymeme as *both* Peirce (the interpreting representation) *and* his words (the representamen) speak (the interpretant of *metaphor*):

I am convinced of it	All S is P!
both *a priori* and *a posteriori*.	All S are M.
I -> Me!	Self -> Different!
I -> You (public)	Self -> Other

This logical modern *discursive* enthymeme in its postmodern rhetorical function as an existential argument leads us to a material, efficient, formal, and final *motivation of the symbolic* where the Same—Other is a sign category of substance (a human self) that stands in place of a whole category (a human difference) as the very *pragmatic* definition of *metaphor* in the postmodern discovery of discourse as *capta*. The prior and posterior hypothesis define the *enthymeme* that is, indeed, the existential condition for Peirce and pragmaticism embodied in the argument that "A [hu]man has consciousness; a word has not."[76]

4

On Ethnocentric Truth
and Pragmatic Justice

<⊰⊱∘⊰⊱>

Andrew R. Smith and Leonard Shyles

Speaking one's truth can be treacherous. It can unnerve colleagues, alienate friends, encourage enemies, and threaten the sense of a community's integrity. As Socrates, Antigone (Sophocles), Copernicus, Rameau's nephew (Diderot), Thomas Paine, Black Hawk, Sojourner Truth, The Cherokee, Emma Goldman, Malcolm X, and other more obscure persons have discovered, speaking publicly about what one believes to be the truth of some matter can bring death, torture, confinement, restriction, exclusion, excommunication, and other forms of suffering that agents of a community so threatened may choose to inflict. There are, in fact, many historical and literary examples in which one person's perception and expression of truth was ridiculed or invalidated by his or her contemporary community of inquirers—or inquisitionists—only to be validated and praised in the future by persons who investigated the same, or similar, issues. Just as existential truth often contrasts sharply with communal interests in one's own time, so too do individual cultural truths often not fit coherently with transcultural, or multinational, concerns. Speaking one's truth in the former case may cause difficulties in, or perhaps loss of, a single life; speaking one's truth in the latter case may encourage embargo, war, or even genocide.

But what is this speaking one's truth anyway? Does not adherence to an idea, as Aristotle, Augustine, Peirce, Perelman, and others have argued, depend not only on existential insight, but also on *how* one's truth is perceived, spoken, and understood through signs that operate according to rhetorical arts and cultural norms? Why can we not just express the truth of a matter algorithmically without the contingencies of person, time, language, culture, or the exigencies of a

71

rhetorical situation? To think that any one person, or group of persons, can transcend these limiting factors through an *epoché* of conscious intent and arrive in full regalia at the *Truth* of a matter is, or course, the nub of one very significant issue in the modernist-postmodernist "conversation." We hope to elucidate in the following pages the degree to which the classical pragmatists, especially Peirce and Dewey, inform this conversation and link truth reciprocally to communal practice on one hand and temporarily on the other.

On the surface it seems that the possibility of justice would remain continually in the air in the communal and temporal play of truth. That is to say, justice would appear to be linked inextricably to the possibility of being proven wrong, being silenced, forgetting, remembering in politically expedient ways, or simply running out of time or up against a wall.[1] In this paper we raise the prospect, not of halting the juggling act of truth and justice by seeking transcultural truths that will hold over time in spite of others, but of generating intercultural truths that take hold on fragile and marginal ground and are sustained by the human forces—speech, time, emotion, cognition, conation, bodily bearing, spatial limits, relationships—that also threaten their existence.

An example might help to illustrate this point. Imagine that you are climbing cautiously over an outcropping above tree line on the upper slopes of a mountain. On the leeward side of the outcropping, in afternoon shade, you find to your astonishment a small patch of penstemon, paintbrush, and other wildflowers holding tenaciously to the soil they have created for themselves. The elements that brought this little community of diverse cultures into being—wind, rock, heat, cold, water, waste matter, and chance—also threaten to eliminate it. You think at that moment how remarkable it is that these flowers are flourishing in this desolate place. Justice may well be created and take hold in a similar, wholly remarkable, manner: through a temporary communion of diverse forms, in partial shade, against the wind, on previously barren ground, by a random mix of elements that include waste and chance, and by an evocative power to create the soil in which it takes root.

Given such metaphorical possibilities for justice—possibilities we hope the reader is able to imaginatively associate with his or her own experience—we wish to note that this paper was originally conceived out of an argument concerning the nature and function of truth. Shyles argued that if we, as educators, abandon the idea of truth—as the postmodernists apparently want us to do—then the profession of journalism would become illegitimate since the journalistic code states explicitly that the journalist's job is to ascertain and report the truth of a matter objectively and accurately. Educators should teach their students how to go about doing that job. Smith argued that journalists (and everybody else who witnesses and reports on an event) can only do the best they can depending on their perspective and the circumstances of the particular case. What journalists report is never the whole story, and readers need to piece together the puzzle of an event from a variety of sources if they wish to get close to the truth. Educators should teach their students how to think critically, to search out many sides of an issue, then do the best they can rhetorically to report or to judge.

In these very concrete, albeit simplistic, terms of journalistic and pedagogic practice, Shyles and Smith stand on two sides of the modernist-postmodernist debate; thus the "we" used throughout this paper is an ironic "we." It is not a unified voice, but an asymmetrical accommodation searching for harmony. The use of "we" in this paper is also an index of the problematic of truth that has so many people up in arms these days. How is truth formed? If it does not have transcultural or universal appeal, or cannot be known transparently by everyone, is it really not truth at all but something disguised as truth? Is the semblance of truth—verisimilitude—sufficient, as Aristotle noted, to warrant judgment or action? Is it culture specific or can it spread and hold across cultures like a propagated flower or a tenacious weed? To cull these questions we begin with a discussion of the limits and possible extensions of what modernists and postmodernists alike might term ethnocentric truth.

I

The idea of ethnocentric truth stems from two interrelated opinions about language and methodology, both of which have been discussed most cogently by Richard Rorty. A brief review should suffice for our purposes here.

The ethnocentric view on language follows the Nietzchean idea that truth is nothing more than a "mobile army of metaphors" through which we address selected problems at a particular time in a community that can assimilate and accentuate the metaphors we choose. According to this view, people create vocabularies in response to the problems they find most compelling, and their conceptions of truth become contingent on the language chosen and the uptake given by others. Truth loses its force as an ultimate or ideal end and becomes a provisional rather than strictly axiological concern. The second, methodological, view of those who advocate an ethnocentric orientation to truth is, quite simply, that a truth cannot be demonstrated in any other way than through procedures practiced by people living in a particular culture at a particular time. One society's procedures may differ from another's, but this does not mean that either society has a more or less privileged view of truth. Rather, different societies simply proceed toward the *truth* of a matter differently, and no one society should impose its procedure on another in an attempt to resolve that society's disputes or to demonstrate universal status.[2]

Any attempt at arguing against the idea that truth can only be known ethnocentrically runs up against a self-referential paradox that develops as follows: (1) Since every society determines the validity of arguments through language and procedures that are distinctly its own, and since (2) the authors of this essay are members of a particular society, then (3) any of our arguments that challenge the assumptions of ethnocentric truth operate ipso facto within particular cultural constraints. To demonstrate the truth of the proposition—truth is not merely ethnocentric—would mean that we simultaneously affirm its opposite. Such is the old sophistical trap laid out for those who think and argue dialectically according to strict deductive and inductive rules, or through what Lyotard might term the cognitive genre—that which can be shown to be the case through ostensive phrases.[3] We hope to show how classical pragmatism avoids this old trap without relinquishing creative ways of, and axiological stakes for, investigating the truth of a matter. We are especially concerned with situations in which different societies, cultures, individuals, or "a people" dispute the language and procedures by which truth is found and justice rendered.

We should be clear from the outset that we do not intend to argue against the idea that language and culture influence one's perception of truth and conception of justice; indeed, this is a reality to which we both adhere with confidence. Nor do we wish to argue that one culture or another has a better way of expressing truth and a smarter way of achieving justice in particular cases. Taking such a position would be naive and presumptuous, to say the least. Nor do we deny that the arguments we present here are conditioned by the social and cultural world in which we live. We wish to avoid self-referential paradox as much as possible. We do, however, intend to conduct an inquiry into the limitations, and possible extensions, of thinking of truth ethnocentrically—especially with regard to the possibility and desirability of reaching toward intercultural views of a phenomenon that are neither foundationalistic nor surreptitiously relativistic.

Some might ague that the procedures for adjudication in a liberal democracy come closest to achieving intercultural status, since, in such a society, the truth of a case is sought and justice ostensibly achieved according to rules meant to honor the legitimacy of diverse cultural orientations. It would appear that justice in a heterogeneous society would be impossible without some transcendence of specific cultural bias and social interest. An ethnocentrist would probably respond that a liberal democracy may, in fact, be as close as a society can come to the appearance of objectivity and equitability in deciding disputes that cross the lines of social class, gender, or culture, but the procedures used are still bound by a *Weltanschauung* that is, in fact, unique. Even a society made up of diverse social histories and cultural practices would be considered ethnocentric to the extent that all parties adhere to and participate in the same definitions of rights, and the same procedures for adjudication. But, we ask, how and for whom might these definitions and procedures be deemed insufficient?

Finding truth and rendering justice from an ethnocentric point of view would appear to be sufficient as long as the parties involved in a particular dispute feel that definitions of conduct and the available procedures for adjudication provide adequate and equal means for expressing their respective grievances. But what happens if a case arises in which different cultural agents—such as the American Indians and the United States government—are embroiled in a dispute (e.g., over mineral rights on reservation land) in which the definitions of property and the procedures used for adjudication favor one party (i.e., the U.S. government) over the other (i.e., the Indians)? Or what if one party to a dispute is powerful enough to ignore the decision of a court, as, again, the United States government did when it ignored the finding of the World Court over the mining of harbors in Nicaragua? What if the procedural forms used to adjudicate a dispute militate against an adequate expression of the wrong experienced by one party, as some people have felt when they have been silenced by formal procedures after filing or facing sexual harassment complaints in their work places? Or if, as Thomas Kochman discusses in one case of black and white styles in conflict,[4] the definition of an utterance in one culture (white) is considered conspiratorial, while in another (black) it is thought to be a typical way of expressing one's true feeling and not necessarily linked to an intent to act? In short, how might truth be found and justice served when the interests adjudicating the dispute, the definitions of acts, and the procedures used are themselves disputed by one of the parties involved, and these translative[5] wrongs are not—or by definition *cannot* be—acknowledged or remedied by the ruling tribunal?

We are interested in how the classical pragmatism of Charles Sanders Peirce and John Dewey addresses the force of the dilemma(s) just posed, and how the force of the dilemma(s) might help us to rethink the contributions of American pragmatism regarding issues of truth and justice in a democratic society. The following overview of neopragmatism helps orient our discussion of Peirce and Dewey since neopragmatism claims adherence to aspects of classical pragmatism while advocating forms of ethnocentrism and cultural relativism. The logic of cultural contingency appears to mark neopragmatism, and we examine how this contingency is actually configured classically as an abductive logic of sign relations. We then rearticulate the stakes involved in a fallibilistic mode of inquiry, and attempt to recover the progressive axiology offered by Peirce and Dewey that has been neglected or critiqued by many of the new voices of pragmatism.[6]

II

Both Richard Rorty in philosophy and Richard Shweder in cultural psychology adhere to different versions of an altogether *pragmatic* cultural relativism. In a well-known argument, Rorty states that we simply cannot get out of our cultural world and "there is nothing to be said about either truth or rationality apart from descriptions of the familiar procedures of justification which a given society—ours—uses in one or another area of inquiry."[7] A pragmatist should be ethnocentric, if we follow Rorty, and know that any translation from one cultural world to another is a fallible process that can rely on neither ideal formulations nor transcendental realities.[8] Rorty adheres to the Davidsonian view that, to be pragmatic, one should conceive truth simply as a "relation between a sentence, a person, and a time."[9] Judgment takes place as these relations are explicated and arranged according to the contingencies of the situation and the norms of a speech community. In response to the dilemmas we have posed, Rorty might argue that at least the disputants are recognized in a liberal democracy as having legitimate concerns; if they are not happy with the results of adjudication, they have recourse in the judicial system for appeal. What more can one do than play out the options available in the society in which one lives?

In a complementary vein, Shweder defends cultural relativism as the most viable tool for preserving diversity among and within societies, and for explicating the operative codes of meaning-constitution in a particular society's discourse.[10] In contrast to Rorty, Shweder takes a quasitranscendental[11] stance by admitting the existence of unseen or unarticulated realities at work in both cultural and intercultural discourse. These realities are, in effect, contextual references a person may sense or feel, but may not be able to express discursively at any one time or place. Just because a reality cannot be expressed—due to vagueness, prudence, propriety, or lack of language capability—does not mean that it is not a *felt* reality that impinges upon, or in some way constitutes the significance of, what *is* expressed in language. Shweder investigates how such felt realities are signs of larger cultural configurations, as well as psychological dispositions, that operate through communication practices. It is not uncommon when talking to another person, for example, that one feels something intensely, but the feeling remains in silence even as it struggles toward or against expression. Whether or not one attempts to express the feeling verbally depends largely on that person's willingness to, or capability of, playing with words and phrases; on his or her trust of the other, or on an interpretation of operative norms for trying to speak *that*. Moreover, if someone chooses to make contact with, or link onto, the feeling discursively, the actuality or truth of the feeling is generated through this very act of communication, and it is developed further through the response-ability of the other. A new social reality for both people is born, and it is possible that through their communication—however direct or indirect it may be—the function of previously taken-for-granted individual, social, or cultural norms are altered for them as well.[12]

Such alterity takes place among people in any particular social world all the time. When people from different cultures speak to one another and attempt to communicate in one another's languages as best they can, the felt realities recombine and reconfigure contextual references in unpredictable, tentative, and indeterminate ways. Shweder maintains that to the extent that understanding results, a person from one culture should recognize someone from another culture as a specialist who can "reveal hidden dimensions of ourselves," which in turn can help one understand the other in an even clearer light. This openness to something other than what one may already conceive as his or her own self-understanding promotes the attempt to enunciate realities that may have previously been hidden, or may have otherwise resisted expression in conventional cultural idioms. Shweder promotes cultural relativism as a way of encouraging an "open-ended self-reflective dialogic turn of mind" toward others who appear radically different.[13] Perhaps he would argue that those nondominant groups discussed previously should seek other communicative forums—both formal or informal—for adjudicating their disputes, and they should continue to struggle both inside and outside the institutional arenas until they feel justice has been served.

Both Shweder and Rorty draw upon the classical tradition of pragmatism as a backdrop for their highly palatable versions of rela-

tivism and ethnocentrism, respectively. They make relativism and ethnocentrism palatable because they agree that communication is not
merely an instrument for discovering or expressing preconceived
truths, but is a state of affairs where truths are created dialogically by
persons who are immersed in and continually coming to terms with
language. Interpersonal communication, and hence interpretation,
between people of different cultures is not contingent on each person's
ability to perceive isomorphic relations between their languages, histories, practices, conceptual schemes, and perceptions of things in the
world. Communication and interpretation are instead reflexive
processes through which people struggle to create meaningful and at
times asymmetrical fits with the way they perceive language, themselves, and one another. These are wholly pragmatic concerns—in the
classical sense—of clarifying and con-figuring meaning.

The crucial difference between Rorty and Schweder, from a classical point of view, pivots on their contrasting notions of reference and
transcendence. Rorty is more nominalistic than Schweder, even though
he would argue that he is certainly not an adherent of a metaphysics of
presence. He simply eschews any talk suggestive of essentialism. He
rejects any transcendental references that might lead to positing
abstract rational criteria for use in deciding the accuracy or legitimacy
of some communicated matter.[14] Weeding out vestiges of transcendence from classical pragmatism, and hence the notion of referential
thirds that situate judgment, is an attempt by Rorty to raise pragmatism
out of its Enlightenment moorings; to bring it into the postmodern era
of inquiry in which a sagacious ethnocentrism might reign. Rorty
argues that cultural dispositions rather than rationalistic models motivate our choices—what we think is rational is actually a cultural habit
of conduct—and the limits of our respective communities just cannot
be transgressed to achieve a transcultural view of things.[15]

In contrast, Schweder's ethnographic fieldwork has taught him
how transcendental realities (e.g., desires, unspoken feelings, social
obligations, presumptions about the nature and function of social relationships, and so on) do, in fact, operate continually in cultural and
interpersonal discourse. Especially in intercultural communication,
persons should be sensitive to, if not focus explicitly on, how they and
others conjure such realities reflexively in the act of speaking or in the
attempt at negotiating dilemmas that do not easily conform to criteria
set by their respective cultural, or personal, norms.[16] Drawing upon
Peirce's notion of abduction, Shweder suggests how this imaginative
and communicative conjuring generates conditions for an intercultural
moment that—though fallible and unpredictable—might negotiate dif-

ferences, produce tentative insight, and encourage understanding. He defines abduction in the following way:

> Transcendent realities can be imagined, but never seen or deduced, for they are constructions of our own making, which sometimes succeed in binding us to the underlying reality they imagine by giving us an intellectual tool—metaphor, a premise, an analogy, a category—with which to live, to arrange our experience, and to interpret our experiences so arranged. In other words, the abductive faculty is the faculty of imagination, which comes to the rescue of sensation and logic by providing them with the intellectual means to see through experience and leap beyond empty syllogisms and tautologies to some creative representation of an underlying reality that might be grasped and reacted to, even if that imagined reality cannot be found, proved, or disproved by inductive or deductive rule-following.[17]

Operating abductively in an intercultural context means that one does not only attempt to learn the other's linguistic rules and cultural codes, and then invoke these operations for practical purposes in a particular situation. One also conspires with another to transgress respective cultural modes of speaking, gesturing, and listening, and create new expressive—and hence poetic—idioms for acknowledging and knowing one another. We should take a closer look at this idea of new expressive idioms.

Any person who has experimented with another culture's language knows that communication with persons of that culture often produces an idiom of understanding that is native to neither oneself nor the other. Between Japanese and English speakers, for example, this very fluid idiom is affectionately called Japalish, and similar names exist for other hybrid languages. Such a language is created by each unique communication situation, which is, indeed, a very fluid, often delightful, and at times agonizing process in which axiological forms (personal habits, social customs, political dispositions, ethical constraints, and aesthetic codes) at work from each respective *Weltanschauung* are made critically self-conscious and often become the objects themselves for communication. Once in this metacommunicative mode, the sedimented language and meanings of each *cultural psychology* are made playfully problematical, and to the extent that the participants are willing to risk committing themselves to its development, a new speech is spoken. This new speaking could be considered the germ of a new culture that both manifests and transgresses forms of the previously taken-for-granted realities that had motivated habitual—or otherwise ethnocentric—conduct. However, it is crucial to keep in mind that any understanding of oneself, the other, or some *thing* (*pragmata*) produced in such a situation is accomplished to the extent that it moves poetically and practically against the grain of normal linguistic or cultural role-following, and is, hence, extremely fallible, contingent, and agonistic. That is, it is not easily replicable. But this does not mean that the truths revealed cannot form a web of hope for intersubjective understanding in the particular case, or in one space of time.

Just as two people in an intercultural situation develop new transgressive forms of language-use that do not strictly obey the cultural logic of their respective social worlds, so too can an inquirer develop the capability of grasping, reforming, creating, or managing through a provisional discourse those quasitranscendental forms that situate and mobilize understanding between himself or herself and the object or inquiry.

Furthermore, disputes between or among people from different cultures, classes, or genders can also be addressed abductively and potentially resolved to the extent that they are not drowned in the language and logic of a formal litigation.[18] But in taking the risks and commitments involved in such an informal mode of finding truth and developing terms for justice, persons confront axiological constraints emanating from each cultural world that continually threaten to impede or terminate the process.

There is more agony than delight in such a situation, and the parties can easily stop talking, go to war, or end up searching for a tribunal that can provide some semblance of impartial adjudication. In colloquial speech, we call such an agonizing situation "being at cross purposes." "Cross purposes" is a good metaphor because it suggests that the stakes involved in the dispute are linked to distinct and contrasting conceptions of "what happened," and, hence, of a future in which both people must live in the "same" or similar world. Abductive logic is a way of communicating in the present the operative axiologies that orient conceptions of "what happened" as a contingent and possible future. "What happened" is transformed into "what is happening" to use the Levinasian and Lyotardian suggestion. Abductive thinking makes such a transformation possible. It creates a communicative idiom in the here and now that enables disputants to challenge cooperatively the relative strength of any one image, meaning, or code brought to the dispute. They might then co-constitute a moment that produces new ways of thinking; ways that can take hold against the wind, on fragile ground, in partial shade . . . with some hope of peace and understanding.

For Peirce and Dewey, axiological questions are extremely important, and abductive experimentation in particular cases is fundamental

to being a pragmatist. Some might argue that focusing on value questions and experimental processes reveals pragmatism's modern foundations rather than postmodern potentialities. We beg to differ.
Discussing the relation between axiology and abduction is fundamental
to speaking and working with those who have been adversely affected
by a ruling consensus, with those who are excluded by the consequences—however justified or surreptitious—of political decisions and
economic circumstances, or with those who are involved in cases that
cannot be fairly decided according to the procedures of adjudication
available to them. Discussing axiology and abduction becomes even
more critical when dominant social, economic, political, institutional or
military-industrial interests routinely legitimize versions of reality
through hegemonic forms of communication that impinge upon particular questions of truth and justice. When the significance of a claim or
an event becomes interpreted according to a dominant group's interests,
and criteria for making judgments and taking action are constituted
according to the language and logic of those interests alone, then the
stakes involved for deciding the truth of a matter and defining the terms
for justice become very high indeed. Classical pragmatism offers ways
of thinking about truth and justice as consequences or ends conceived
through a complement of culturally contingent fallibility (ethnocentric
truth) and progressively sublime axiology (pragmatic justice). This com-
plementarity is a voice worth recovering.

III

The four principal terms in the title of this essay mark out a debate
in philosophy, rhetoric, and the human sciences that hinges on the
problem of communication and ethics. One of the primary vectors of
this debate concerns the difference between truth understood episte-
mologically—as contingent on a society's procedures for critical
inquiry—and truth as rational consensus that takes place among
inquirers in a community.[19] The latter conception limits the validity of
truth claims to neither scientific discipline nor cultural orientation, but
instead seeks a transcendental position through which new knowledge
can be developed and legitimized. Peirce and Dewey each share this
latter interest in what Hegel and critical theorists have termed immanent critique. But Peirce and Dewey's pragmatism also addresses the
contingent and fallible ways in which insight is generated and
expressed. Straddling these two seemingly opposing approaches to
conjuring truth, the classical pragmatists anticipated, and appear to

have offered a cogent response to, what has come to be known as the postmodern condition.[20]

One of the reasons why Peirce is perceived as an epistemologist is his love of logic, which is intimately tied to his notion of semiotics. This love is conditioned not by an infatuation with procedure, classification, or system-building, but by the imaginative process of gaining insight, generating new ideas about phenomena as a result of this insight, and testing these ideas with and through others dialogically. The notion of abduction is crucial, then, not simply for its methodological import, but for the way in which the outcomes it helps to produce engage others in the agnostic search for truth. In this sense, then, abduction is a communication concept that raises questions about the fallibility of accepted laws as well as the contingency of new knowledge; it also addresses the signification of consequences in inquiry, the relation of inquirer and object, and the axiological stakes of interpretation.

Peirce formalized abduction as [rule + result = case], in contrast to deduction [rule + case = result] and induction [case + result = rule]. Despite the numerous explications of these formulations by at least three generations of Peircean scholars, we wish to offer one that pertains explicitly to the process of communication in general, and to communication inquiry in particular.

The *rule* in abduction can be understood as those operative forms (laws, traditions, myths, precepts, beliefs) an inquirer takes as impinging upon or influencing his or her field of inquiry and which motivate the kinds of questions asked in that field, the language used for inquiry, how data are arranged and investigated, and so on. These are habits of conduct that in modern nomenclature are termed codes.[21] In a deductive scheme the rule is given as a first principle that is difficult, if not impossible, to usurp. In abduction the rule is made critically self-conscious; it is seen as requisite for asking questions, but not as an infallible principle. In a larger cultural sense, the rule is that *Weltanschauung* of sedimented forms and meanings that persons draw upon reflectively to speak and understand others, whether those others harken from the same or a different cultural world. The abductive rule is general and regulative to the extent, for example, that a bilingual/bicultural person chooses one language to speak instead of another depending on the perceived context for communication. In choosing that language, she or he chooses a cultural world that situates the constitutive rules of the language itself. For Peirce the abductive *rule* is a third par excellence that references and transcends immediate speech acts and the articulations of the constitutive rules for language use. Without it there is no sense, no bias, no culture, no difference. It is presumed sameness of selves in one cultural world that is recognized as different and other in intercultural contact.

The *result* is more difficult to pin down abductively, and for good reason. In the Hegelian schema it is that which is assimilated deductively into the overarching system of representation. But Peirce eschews his Hegelian enterprise to the extent that it militates against the capability of gaining insight into the particular case; of recognizing that case's singularity. For the classical pragmatist, normative languages, or genres, are necessary for the very recognition of that which cannot be assimilated by them, although in some cases a genre will work actively against the expression of difference. The dialectical forms of litigation, for example, influence the way a person working in that genre perceives, thinks, questions, and assimilates information. Those expressions that run counter to the dialectical rules, or for some reason cannot be assimilated by that genre, will be silenced or otherwise disregarded only after they are recognized as either threatening or irrelevant. In abductive thinking, however, the anomaly to normative expectations is that which the inquirer seeks, and if abandoning one genre, or switching genres, is the action required for a clearer vision or articulation of the phenomenon, then that is what should be done. Each distinct genre can serve as a *result*, but the proliferation of genres in a cultural world is also a *result* as is the capability of switching genres, and the building of new genres between or among existing ones. The upshot here is that the *result* is not *strongly* determined by the *rule* in an abductive scheme. The rule, in fact, creates the conditions for multiple results, or diverse ways of thinking, perceiving, questioning, and so on. Hence, critical inquiry for a pragmatist is a task of diversification and guesswork rather than assimilation and certain explanation in the Hegelian sense.

The modal + sign marking the relation between *rule* and *result* indicates a linkage that is both accumulative and progressive. There is virtually no limit, for example, to what people in a culture can absorb and produce; new, often hybrid, forms of dress, food, architecture, dance, theater, technology, and so on, are continually appearing. But any new production is impossible without first being in a particular cultural world (rule) with people who speak a language (result). When something new appears, it takes place and is judged according to a world of speech and language. This does not mean that existing rules and results determine the form and function of a so-called new phenomenon, but the new phenomenon cannot take form without in some way recombining the elements of existing cultural—or perhaps psychological—material. The elements were in our mind before, says Peirce, but it is the act of putting them together in ways that have never been done before "that flashes the new suggestion before our contempla-tion."[22] The new suggestion creates, or is equal to, the *case*. Superficially it would appear that abduction is an imposition of law and method on particular cases, but this is not so. Peirce was simply more willing than most to work through how existing habits of conduct and conventional methods of inquiry do influence what, how, and why we perceive what we do. And, in this sense, he acknowledged legitimacy of ethnocen-tric—or existential—truth, though his interest was in pushing beyond the limits of personal, cultural, or scientific determinism.

The *case* may be delusory or factual, but in either appearance it most certainly is a reality-posit, to use Shweder's designation. The *case* is not given in the positivistic sense of data being materially available prior to our appropriation of it. Rather it is real in the abductive sense of a singularity that takes on some form because we appropriate it as such. We may not yet know the validity of what we believe to be the case's most salient elements and functions, but we are capable of imaginative-ly varying these elements and functions, and generating ideas about their linkages and relations that can be tested in various ways. In short, the case is the as yet unverified phenomenon imagined, felt, perceived, guessed at, or otherwise experienced by the critical, ethnocentric, and perhaps crazy, inquirer. To the extent that the inquirer is ethnocentric, he or she first tries to frame the unknown in terms of a known genre, or genres, of disclosure. To the extent that one is critical, one takes the unverified manifestation as a way of challenging one's own habits of conduct, and perhaps those of a ruling authority. To the extent that one is crazy, one takes the incalculable risk of speaking the unspeakable in a language that nobody else understands. If nobody else is interested in understanding and speaking this apparently idiosyncratic language, the inquirer's community of inquirers are—we can only hope—obligated to rope one back into the folds of their scientific or rhetorical sanity.

Abductive thinking can, indeed, make one crazy since it involves a play of signs in the most radical sense of play.[23] True insight is possi-ble precisely because one is capable of stopping the process, however temporarily, at a moment that is often marked by redundancy. One keeps working through the semiotic differences (relations between and among terms, phrases, propositions, arguments, contexts, references, styles, methods, codes, contacts, and so on) and begins to recognize previously unrecognized associations, or possible linkages. In doing so, one realizes how the case is *different* from, or runs counter to, what was previously thought to be the case or what might have been the case. There is both a binding to a new possibility, and a rejection of taken-for-granted, or anticipated, possibilities. Because of this relation of negativity, one is able to suggest a *probability* that turns the corner on what others, or a community of inquirers, may already have accepted as the truth of some matter. The new actualization of truth, then, becomes not a matter of deduction [rule + case = result] but the *consequence* of inductive processes [case + result = rule] that play out, or test, the fallibilities of the abductive insight.[24] The situation may be, given dominant political interests, that the new insight is never tested. But if and when it is tested—through scientific, judicial, or other procedures—and achieves the consensus of a community of inquirers, it may radically alter previously taken-for-granted beliefs (rule) and normative modes of investigation (result). Inevitably something else—rule, result or case—becomes problematic; something other is excluded or skewed, and thus opens inquiry onto new terrain. We wish to emphasize that this negative movement of inquiry is made possible by the poetic play of semiosis, and the connotative differences this play engages are often overlooked by those who become stymied by the consensual, representational, or system formations in Peirce's architectonic.

One formulation that is particularly problematic for neopragmatists such as Rorty is Peirce's notion of ideal ends. How can a person advocate in one breath both the irreverent play of semiosis (think of abduction rather than system) and the piety of ideal ends (think of axiology rather than ultimate truth)? Peirce did so because of his appreciation for both ethics and aesthetics. The play of semiosis as we have defined it here would be pure chaos—or anarchy—without an appreciation for and accounting of potential ethical and aesthetic consequences. For Peirce, ascertaining the truth of a matter abductively is conditioned by one's capability of imagining possible ends—consequences of conceptions played out in conduct—as they are embedded in his or her communicative relation with that toward which inquiry is directed. The recognition and interpretation of truth is contingent, not merely on situational exigencies of time, place, person(s), and utterances, but on the potential consequences of the interpretation in the long run. Justice is conceived through this protention[25] of judgment.

Being able to signify the truth of a matter and generate the conditions for social justice through an invocation of possible ends suggests problems of reference on several levels of communication: (1) the intrapersonal (How are my prejudices influencing interpretation? How does my interpretation of the significant consequences of a case affect others as well as myself?); (2) the interpersonal (How will my conduct [statements, actions, beliefs] affect the other or reconstitute the case? How will my response-ability to the other orient the future of our relationship?); (3) the social (Does the state of affairs constituted by expert opinion, or other rules of evidence, create sufficient conditions for ascertaining truth and rendering justice in the particular case? Will judgments of the particular case alter the ways in which future cases are perceived and adjudicated?); and, (4) the cultural (Should adherence to customary procedures or traditional beliefs frame the contingencies of the case? Should habitual ways be altered as a result of findings in a case that render them problematic?).[26] The appearance of truth and the action taken with regard to this appearance become intimately bound with the problem of determining how significance is determined through these various levels of communication. How an expression is felt, valued, codified, temporalized, stylized, or spatialized—in short, *communicated*—in turn makes a significant difference with regard to specifying the terms for justice. But is it possible to address these concerns of communication without getting mired in representationalism; without succumbing to Cartesian doubt or elevating the referent to a self-evident position in the world?

Dewey believed so, and he discusses how in his treatment of the problem of reference and truth as they are linked to the perception and expression of social facts. According to Dewey, social facts change; they are processual, but not in the sense of physical events whose causes and conditions can be measured to a great degree of accuracy. Rather, social facts are inherently historical and thus a fact, in isolation from historical development, "loses the qualities that make it distinctively social." Moreover, "social phenomena involve judgments of evaluation, for they can be understood only in terms of eventuations to which they are capable of moving. Hence, there are as many possible interpretations in the abstract as there are possible kinds of consequences."[27] Simply providing information about a particular case is rarely, if ever, satisfactory. We want to know its significance in order to make informed judgments. Significance, to be satisfactory in the Peircean sense (CP 5.555–64), involves a reading of history in which the focus is upon "consequent phenomena; not upon precedents but upon the possibilities for action."[28] The historical consequents and situational conditions constitute the intricate web of truth about a case; *this is its significance.* Any attempt to isolate an inherently social fact as merely a piece of information, or an empirical fact of history, is an attempt to physicalize the event; and this, for Dewey, would be simply ridiculous.[29]

Invoking ends *ipso facto* places an inquirer—or disputants—in a position of interpreting the ethical and aesthetic, as well as logical or political, consequences of conduct. According to neopragmatists such as Rorty, assuming such a position is perilous because it may encourage the adoption of a dogmatic view on the one hand or an insufficiently ethnocentric one on the other. It would be dogmatic if one deductively applies an ethical or aesthetic system which would rule all conduct coming under its purview. Invoking ends would be insufficiently ethnocentric if the position—or result—taken situationally in one culture is *ipso facto* assumed to be operative in a similar situation in a different culture, or even at another time in the same culture. Peirce suggests a way out of choosing either dogmatism or ethnocentrism by linking the idea of correspondence with ideal end. He does so, not because he adheres to a correspondence theory of truth, but because the play of signs (one co–responding to another) is potentially unlimited. Without a consideration of ends, one person or another can easily become tied in knots, be overcome by chaos, or make judgments and take action based upon a purely fabricated reality. The end(s) imagined should encompass a possible state of affairs where communication is considered with reference to its full range of impact. The truth generated, however, "belongs exclusively to propositions" (CP 5.553); to a state of things rather than to the things themselves.[30] Hence, change of view is continually possible given new contingencies, insights, feelings, or events. Invoking ends for a particular dispute does not mean that the result of the dispute is necessarily going to hold for all time, or in any place.

Peirce suggests that pursuing a line of inquiry or settling a dispute on purely logical grounds is undesirable, and that to do so would amount to attempting to walk with one's legs tied together. The ethical and aesthetic orders or experience exceed, respectively, logical ways of knowing. Peirce implores inquirers to conduct inquiry according to ethical and aesthetic ends that they are prepared to adopt if their conceptions, descriptions, experiments, and actions are given their fullest play. He argues that since consequences are germane to voluntary action, inquiry should invoke the self-control necessary for such action in imagining consequences:

> An ultimate end of action deliberately adopted . . . must be a state of things that *reasonably recommends itself* in itself aside from any ulterior consideration. It must have an *admirable ideal*, having the only kind of goodness that such an ideal can have; namely, aesthetic goodness. From this point of view the morally good appears as a particular species of the aesthetically good. (C.P. 5.130; emphasis in original)

Living as we do after Auschwitz, it cannot be denied that aesthetic goodness can be used to justify ethnic cleansing, for example, or other forms of horror and terror. Those who cleanse argue that they are doing the world good by ridding it of selected others. This, of course, is not what Peirce had in mind. "A state of things that reasonably recommends itself in itself" should be conceived as a *sense* of—for example,

peace, justice, equitability, security, beauty, and so on—which motivates an enunciation of significance in the singular case. This sense and
the significance it breeds constitutes the ideal end.

Moreover, an ideal of goodness does not mean that inquiry could
or should come to a unified end, or that a paradigmatic metanarrative
needs to rule acritically over our thought and action. Such a concept of
end or consequence has nothing to do with Peirce's pragmaticism.[31]
Each person chooses his or her mode of being within a context of communication with others, and this community, however loosely organized, influences how thought and action associated with a particular
case would, or should, be interpreted. Choices of what to think, how to
interpret, who to speak with, how to speak with them, and so on, are
not merely personal arbitrary choices, but are motivated by wider
social, political, and historical concerns. Any interpretation of a case
that moves against the grain of accepted habits of belief and conduct in
a community should, through a concerted effort, reflect critically on the
ideal assumed in the act of the interpretation itself. Purposive—or
experimental—conduct thus entails a practical judgment whose stakes
are not defined according to one's own desires and idiosyncracies, or
for the interests of an exclusive institution, but according to a sense of
good for a larger, perhaps extraordinary, community.

Peirce's theory of abduction pivots on transgressions from ruling
routes of thought and action as a way to improve life, advance knowledge, and test new ideas for the common good. If consensus or convergence is the necessary condition for improving life, then divergence or
dissensus should be understood as the sufficient condition. This does
not appear paradoxical if we consider that criticism presupposes the
existence of accepted customs or truths, and truths make no sense
unless some apparent falsehood, wrong, injustice, or disparity appears
to be operative.

As already suggested, Dewey agrees with Peirce's claim that logical, ethical, and aesthetic dimensions of truth are part and parcel of
projected consequences of inquiry.[32] And even though his notion of
experience is linked to, if not synonymous with, his definition of culture, [33] he warns against accepting acritically the moral prescriptions
and proscriptions of social custom, or the aesthetic, and hence cultural,
construction of lies. These distinctions are discussed perhaps most
cogently in a series of three lectures entitled "The Problem of Truth."[34]
Here Dewey presents the idealist-realist debate and critiques both sides
from a basis in the pragmatic perspective of truth, for which the present
realization of a case, and the purposive hypothesis developed there-

from, is imbued with communicative consequences rather than normative antecedents. However, this is not to say that antecedents have no
significance in the definition of a case. In fact:

> The ordinary misconception of pragmatism . . . is that it neglects
> entirely the *other* or antecedent factor of existent conditions. On the
> contrary, pragmatism holds that the idea or proposition is framed
> with reference to them; but with reference to *using* them in a certain
> way, not with reference to reduplicating them in a knowledge order
> separate and ultimate.[35]

Antecedents include already existing beliefs, moral orders, aesthetic preferences, cultural logics of common sense, and habits of conduct in every conceivable design and magnitude. These influences
organize communication among people, and a proposition is often
believed to be true to the extent that it coheres with these influences in
common understanding. In this sense, then, social custom, and the procedures for justification that emanate from social custom, dictate what
is believed in a circle of meanings that tend toward dogmatism. If we
think of the ethnocentric as being defined by such a circle, then
Dewey's definition of culture as experience, and inquiry as progress, is
decidedly not ethnocentric. The point of pragmatism as a philosophy
and as a methodology for human progress is to link the social with the
scientific so that the authority of custom can be disbanded without succumbing to the temptations of either absolutism or skepticism. Truth,
then, is free to roam among the discourses of possible beliefs, which
multiply by virtue of the very course that they set for inquiry.
Consequences have a moral dimension to the extent that a community
agrees with the desirability of ends or aims as possible states of affairs,
and this desirability is contingent on how ends fit with social prosperi-
ty and goodness. For Dewey, such social evolution toward freedom,
happiness, and justice is possible only through a human scientific practice that is free from the shackles of modern dualisms:

> My hypothesis is that the standpoint and method of science do not
> mean the abandonment of social purpose and welfare as rightfully
> governing criteria in the formation of beliefs, but that they signalize a
> profound transformation in the nature of social purpose and social
> welfare. The role of scientific truth in the social medium is an emanci-
> pation of goods, purposes, and activities, producing the transition
> from a stationary society to a progressive society.[36]

The ethically good for Dewey becomes defined by an art of emancipatory progress. But how does the aesthetic fit with such progress?

Dewey uses the example of a ship that relies for its journey on a compass that directs its movement toward a desired port. The needle of the compass does not present antecedents, where the ship has been, but "the port that is to be attained. And it presents this in terms of the existing movement of the ship, thereby making the end a present factor in facilitating the gaining of the desired haven."[37] The movement of the ship points true to the extent that someone (the steersman) reads the compass correctly and has a sense for the end to which it points. Dewey shows how such reading is analogous to the interpretation of propositions or judgments. There exists some convergence, some end, toward which discourse aims, and the movement of inquiry is determined by the projection of this convergence. Orientation to such consequence requires imbuing the present with its future possibilities and contingencies so that a course can remain true. Imbuing is a practice of arrangement, of *disposition*, of fitness and adaptability, of pleasing quality and coherence. A sense of where one is aiming defines such a disposition. Convergence, then, becomes understood as a dis-position that requires a conceptualization of future orientation if one wishes to achieve an understanding of the present course set.[38]

The course set is a search for legitimacy of a truth perceived, a search for where one might end if inquiry into a singular case—or course—is played out to its fullest. Hypothesizing pragmatically about these aims presupposes a way of orientating ethically, as value or worth, and aesthetically, as fitness or disposition. But despite the harmonizing of inquiry and ends, of convergence of aim and the course set, the search itself, from Dewey's point of view, requires a proliferation of beliefs and assumes that we are not necessarily familiar with the ends we seek. Progress is defined by not always knowing where we will end, despite the fact that we have set our course according to the coordinates that we know. The only way to keep guessing right is through discourse with others who have embarked on a similar course—or perhaps on a different but intersecting course—and have likewise shed, or are willing to shed, the prejudices of custom and shackles of dogmatisms. So-called objective truth, for Dewey, becomes:

> [equivalent to a] primitive . . . human sense of truth: truthfulness—
> generous, frank efficiency of communication. Truth, in final analysis,
> is the statement of things . . . as they are in a shared and progressive
> experience. Friends, said the Greek proverb, have all things in com-
> mon. Truth, truthfulness, transparent, and brave publicity of inter-
> course, are the source and the reward of friendship. Truth *is* having
> things in common.[39]

IV

How can the pragmatic notion of consequences as ends that surpass the customary limits of ethnocentrism be linked to critical communication practice and pragmatic justice in social inquiry? We believe
the following linkages are plausible: (1) by not taking as self-evident the
significance attributed reflexively to cases, the inquirer becomes critically self-reflective (fallibilistic) about criteria formation—both with
regard to ruling references and to his or her own tendency to invoke
prejudicial ends; (2) by being willing to try out (or try on) other beliefs,
habits, desires, perceptions, roles, and possibilities—thereby at least
attempting to embody the strangeness of the other; (3) in the recognition that some features of cases are selected as essential while others are
ignored or left out, the inquirer, if a pragmatist, would imaginatively
vary the consequences of some selections over others and argue for the
relations of co-respond-ence one believes to be true, good, and fine in
the context of ever-wider and diverse communities of interest (group,
region, nation, world); (4) in writing or speaking, one should become
cognizant of what type of emphasis is given stylistically to cases, especially in the use of images and symbols that legitimize particular social
or political interests.

Truth in the most pragmatic sense is contingent at least upon
these referential choices. Any sense of objective truth, in turn, depends
ironically upon heterogeneous communities whose members continually argue and question in the spirit of friendship and common interest
in a progressively "secure, more varied and more free" environment
for communication.[40] Different views exist, and the means for justifying
these views do vary ethnocentrically across communities. The fact of
this relativity does not mean that we should completely abandon our
own sense of truth and justice in the particular case, nor should we dis-
parge others' sense of truthfulness. Rather, it means that we converse
about intercultural issues by rendering fallible—at least for the time
being of the issue under consideration—our own customary language
and procedures.

As Davidson argues, reference is not truth;[41] it is the context
through which conditions for truth are realized. Truth, then, becomes
coherent—or harmonious—with communicative agreement on these
conditions. If, for example, we are operating from distinct contexts
(social, political, cultural, and so on), then we have great difficulty finding a common language of truth—although we hope we have shown in
this essay that such coherence is, in principle, possible without going to
war or to court. The point is to keep talking even if this means that we

agree to disagree in order to keep talking. If we are operating from contexts that overlap one another, then we have a better chance for coherence or at least agreeing to disagree on certain conditions temporarily in order to accomplish a task. The greater the contextual coherence, the greater the possibility for a collaborative enunciation of the truth of some matter. When such an enunciation becomes manifest, we take for granted that certain logical, ethical, and aesthetic norms are at work. When such an enunciation is problematic, reconciliation of views is possible only when the presumed normative conditions for communication are made critically self-conscious through metacommunication. This agonizing but sometimes playful process is a way to recognize assumptions—or operative intentionalities, if you will—so that disputes have a chance of being reconfigured idiomatically. Playful agony, which requires a recurrent questioning on various levels of communication, constitutes the purposeful dimension of fallibility—a dimension that pragmatism by definition should not live without.

Seeking the truth of a matter and rendering justice is problematic to say the least. Understanding and acting upon the significance of a case can be accomplished objectively, as Rorty continually points out, only to the extent that we agree on certain conventions for justification within a speech community. But since world events cross many communities, and since frames of reference shift disparately within one community as well as across many communities, rendering significance objectively appears virtually impossible. Despite potential dispersions of meaning, we can still make an offering about events in the world, enjoin that offering with other offerings, and play out the possible convergences and divergences through conversation and argument. Even though we may fool ourselves into thinking that one proper significance of an event exists, and indeed such foolishness is endemic to some forms of critical communication practice, we should not despair at being fools. Adhering to a belief with one's head above ground means that one is willing to entertain the possible fallibility of that belief in the context of the potential viability of other beliefs. Recognizing the strangeness of the other in ourselves means, in turn, that communication among us might still yield some common coherence. At least it will keep us questioning and disputing ruling references, which is at heart an honest attempt at actualizing social and political justice.

In closing, we should address the analytic preference for locating truth in the content of sentences, and we would like to suggest that even Davidson moves beyond such a nominalistic bias. It appears that Davidson actually aligns himself with Peirce and Dewey with respect to finding a way of taking into account the purposeful, interpretive, and fallible dimensions of belief and reference. When read in a communication context, we believe Davidson's statements corroborate most, if not all, of what we have been arguing concerning the relation classical pragmatism nurtures between abduction and fallibility on one hand, and axiology and ends on the other:

> What matters is this: if all we know is what sentences a speaker holds true, and we cannot assume that his language is our own, then we cannot take even a first step towards interpretation without knowing or assuming a great deal about the speaker's beliefs. Since knowledge of beliefs comes only with the ability to interpret words, the only possibility at the start is to assume general agreement on beliefs. We get a first approximation to a finished theory by assigning to sentences of a speaker conditions of truth that actually obtain (in our own opinion) just when the speaker holds those sentences true. The guiding policy is to do this as far as possible, subject to considerations of simplicity, hunches about the effects of social conditioning, and of course our common sense, or scientific, knowledge of explicable error.
>
> The method is not designed to eliminate disagreement, nor can it; its purpose is to make meaningful disagreement possible, and this depends entirely on a foundation—*some* foundation—in agreement. The agreement may take the form of widespread sharing of sentences held true by speakers of "the same language," or agreement in the large mediated by a theory of truth contrived by an interpreter for speakers of another language.[42]

Again, despite Davidson's nominalistic and metatheoretical overtones, we must admit that, given potentially different views of the significance of a phrase, for example, abstracting beliefs or agreed-upon meanings about that phrase is, indeed, the first pragmatic move toward an enunciation of its truth. And particular consequences are embedded in the very act of that enunciation. How far do we go in conceiving of these consequences? "As far as possible," says Davidson. In order to achieve what? "To make meaningful disagreement possible," he says. How do we get there? Through "hunches . . . common sense . . . explicable error."

In the same vein we ask: When a legal, political, or institutional judgment is made by a person or people from one community (class, culture, party, gender, discipline, rank, etc.), but felt by one or many others in a different community to be unjust, what recourse does one, or do they, have other than challenging the ethnocentric or idiosyncratic interpretation of phrases, exposing operative beliefs inherent in that interpretation, and demanding a more intercultural view so that justice might be served? In such a situation, communication becomes not simply an exchange of messages redolent with preconceived meanings (i.e., beliefs) that might be independently verified by a judge or other third party, but a production of feeling and sensibility in language that promotes and is itself conditioned by struggle, insight, clarity, fallibility, obfuscation, frustration, vulnerability, desperation, and, at times, laughter. Keeping the conversation going in this context is avoiding silences that allow an authoritative judgment the time it needs to sediment and take further hold of a person's or a people's lives. It is in such a situation that the classical pragmatism of Peirce and Dewey helps an inquirer (conceived in the broadest sense) to actualize the response-ability of truth and the remark-ability of justice.

III

The Ends of Communication

5

The "Cash-Value" of Communication:
An Interpretation of William James[1]

<ato ato>

Isaac E. Catt

Although pragmatism was the invention of C.S. Peirce, William James is generally considered the "father of pragmatism."[2] James probably had more influence on our way of thinking than any other American philosopher, and this is perhaps attributable to the fact that he intentionally spoke the language of common sense. As always, however, the attempt to find common denominators in the media of exchange is not without its problems. James referred, in his essay "What Pragmatism Means," to the need to bring out from words their *practical cash-value*.[3] This rhetorical gesture was reiterated more than once in his works and was intended to convey, in words easily understood, that to be useful, ideas must have consequences. The *cash-value* metaphor was perfect, though unfortunate. Its meaning was clear, but it spoke to the individualistic frontier American spirit in a way that reified and sanctioned practice over theory. This was not James's intent, but it was a consequence of his linguistic choice.

Today, research and pedagogy in communication are carried out with an eye toward the cash-value of communication competence. It is difficult to argue with Canary and Spitzberg's assertion that "few concepts present more potential for integrating the diverse landscape of human interaction than that of competence."[4] The history of communication study and the voluminous research on competence combine to create a habitualized way of thinking about communication.[5] At least on the surface, this does not seem problematic; after all, what could be more obvious than that communication is a means by which those most knowledgeable in its processes and skilled in its practices best achieve their distinctly human purposes?

Spitzberg and Cupach justify in theory this *natural attitude* of common sense wisdom. Communication is the instrument of *control, collaboration*, and *adaptability*. It is essential to an individual's ability to effect *mastery* over the social and physical environment, to relate with others in the accomplishment of shared objectives, and to sustain a flexible behavioral repertoire with which to impress the public.[6] The lack of competence is associated with personal and social maladies inclusive of mental disorders, anxiety disorders, relational disorders, academic disorders, developmental disorders, and occupational stress.[7] We might think of communication as the practical philosophy for, lacking its effective use, not only have ideas no consequences but illness ensues.

This paper calls into question the emphasis on communication competence as the concept we should invoke in order to integrate the human sciences. The thesis argued here never suggests that competence is unimportant, nor does it even argue against the view that competence is an essential aspect of the field. Rather, the intent is to impose some limits on the research exuberance associated with the concept of competence, to argue against an unnecessarily narrow definition of communication, and to expose the ideological bias of the competence metaphor.

The competency issue is a pragmatic concern in communication pedagogy and is likely to remain so. However, the empiricists' naive *pragmatics* of communication education that would seek to integrate knowledge of communication is ironic. It is problematized by the *fluency* of communicative experience as conceived in philosophic pragmatism[8] as well as by the *fluidity* of postmodern academic life, which is essentially antidisciplinary.[9] This is to say in one breath that the lived-experience of communicating is not limited to deliberate speech, and that the study of communication entails much more than the transmission of ideas that are formulated elsewhere in the exclusive provinces of the traditional liberal arts curriculum. Furthermore, what we have here is not merely the usual case of pedagogy that tardily translates contemporary research into the curriculum, but, rather, entrenched resistance to a dramatic paradigmatic shift[10] in the very conception of communication.

As the metaphysics of presence[11] slides into distant memory, so too should the idea that competence in communication consists merely in proper training in presentational skills. This essay is intended as a contribution toward the rethinking of competence that is necessitated by postmodern theories of communication. The concern here is unabashedly pedagogical, a perspective that would certainly not be lost on the originators of the philosophy of pragmatism, each of whom was considered a great educator. *My purpose is to establish in pedagogical practice what we already know in theory. Namely, the identification of competence in communication with proper training in self-presentational skills, in whatever pedagogical context and regardless of ideological purpose, is now defunct, a necessary consequence of the critique of the metaphysics of presence.*

My task entails three steps. First, the social condition that constrains research and pedagogy to an emphasis on communication practices is adumbrated. Second, it is argued that the father of American pragmatism was a phenomenologist who had a much richer idea of the pragmatic than is evidenced by the current focus on competence. Third, the benefit of conceiving the competency issue from a pragmatic critical-phenomenological perspective is demonstrated.[12]

Respectively, communication competency is shown to be consistent with and in service of a *consumerist* or *careerist* interpretation of higher education. Competency as a predictor of efficacy is argued to be inherently dependent on a pretense to value-free research and pedagogy. James's existential phenomenology rejects such an approach as impractical because it is not truly empirical. James's pragmatism is explicated as a focus on the lived-experience of the whole person, which includes but is not limited to behavioral skills. Contemporary phenomenology, on which James is a strong historic influence, offers both eidetic and empirically based insights into the communication of persons and their lifeworlds. As such, it is a critical and ethically based practical philosophy.

The first step of the inquiry is to show how far the discipline is from a truly pragmatic approach.

Communication Inquiry as a Social Institution

Social institutions normally conceived as bureaucratic structures are also repositories of cultural myths, harbingers of social habits, and environments conducive to ideological practices. The communication disciplines of higher education are not exceptional in this regard. They exist to serve society, a society whose expectations are not always critically assessed. Seen from within the careerist/consumerist perspective on education, institutions of higher learning have a strong vocationally oriented responsibility. From within this frame, communication study could be viewed as but one *business-like* disciplinary-specific activity that occurs in the academy. The academy, in turn, often subscribes to a *corporate* model of operations, consisting as it does of various so-called *shops* with dean-managers and chair-foremen. Students are frequently discussed as *clients* and are, upon graduation, the institution's products.[13] These products are *sold* into a labor market. The *success* of the academy and its multifarious academic shops is measured by *outcomes assessment,* which, whatever else it includes, emphasizes jobs. The academy's future share of the market is contingent on its ability to maintain a satisfactory public relations image as a respectable route by which students may become employed.

Education is assumed to be the panacea for a perceived lack of worker productivity caused by a so-called crisis in human capital.[14] The deterioration of the nation's *competitive edge* in the new global economy is a responsibility laid squarely and unhesitatingly in the laps of American workers and those who educate them.[15] To cure the problem, Rosenberg calls for a "science of human performance technology"[16] dedicated to *human resources development,* which would improve the performance of individuals; *organizational development* to improve the performance of groups; *human resources management,* which is "dedicated to managing the performance of individuals and groups"; and *environmental engineering* which would "provide the tools and facilities that support improved performance."[17] The core problem addressed in this body of literature is a lack of competence of employees, a lack that Rosenberg indicates is being addressed by "human performance technology."[18]

Central to the competence issue in the *crisis of human capital* is the problem of communication. Briefly stated, workers are not regarded as having sufficient communication skills. Inman argues that "the number one problem facing American managers is communication" and that this is costly to those wishing to successfully compete.[19] Reece [20] and Inman agree that "the best communicators are those who possess *interpersonal competence.*"[21]

The link between pragmatism and competence is very old in the study of communication.[22] However, the focus on information handling, on rudimentary skills, and on responding to a narrowly defined conception of life after college graduation is a relatively recent arrival. Scholars in communication have not always addressed this point with a critical eye. Though Rogers and Chaffee, for example, hint at the ideological constraints placed on the academic field, they seem most concerned with how well the academy will respond to society's invoice; that is, their concern is with whether societal demands for trained communicators will be satisfied.[23] Still others have accepted the discipline's role in the academy and have set about devising behavioral assessment instruments by which social expectations can be engineered.[24] Thus, research on competence in communication has taken a decided turn in favor of *method* and away from critical reflection on the concept itself. This has occurred despite the fact that "in educational systems the concept [of competence] is a relatively new way of describing old concepts—basic skills."[25]

Particularly given a basic skills emphasis, it may come as a surprise that the implied model of communication pedagogy in competency research is that of "the lay person as scientist." White describes the model:

> In the lay scientist model the judgments and procedures of the professional scientist and statistician are regarded as optimal or normatively correct, and the layperson is viewed as aiming to conform to the standards of inferential competence established by the professional.[26]

Behind or above the research and pedagogical assumption that there is a lack of communication competence lurks an implicit standard by which to diagnose this lack and to effect an adequate prognosis. The appropriateness of the medical metaphor used here is clearly established by the literature which alludes to *in*competency, which is *dis*ordered and results in a variety of illnesses. A rationalist's sense of order is at work here, and it suggests that individuals must conform to scientifically derived standards of action. The rationalist thesis could not have been more aptly expressed than in an essay that equates being with knowledge *about* being. In an "An Exploration of Ontological Knowledge," Hazleton and Cupach describe knowledge of being from a functionalist standpoint as the ability to act.

> They assert: "Ontological knowledge," entails beliefs about the essential nature, properties, and relations of being. Operationally, ontological knowledge is reflected in communicators' ability to describe, predict, and explain human behavior.[27]

That the lay scientist model inheres in competency research results from the fact that it is based on the paradigm of empiricism. Here, however, is a very strange case in which empiricism, as practiced in communication, has explicitly co-opted the philosophy of pragmatism. Wiemann describes the battle for *communication literacy,* which is "the ability to enact all possible behaviors a person needs in order to respond appropriately to communication tasks at hand."[28] Hewes and others similarly argue:

> The value of interpersonal communication research, and much of its popularity in the classroom, stems from its applications to everyday life. The study of interpersonal communication must be, first and foremost, practical[emphasis added][29]

Rubin admits that the communication discipline is susceptible to being drawn "away from eloquence and toward minimal competence."[30] Nevertheless, it is most certainly as communication skills instructors that professionals in the discipline are prominently conceived both inside and outside the academy. This is the social condition that constrains research as well as pedagogy. Hewes and others, in a review of the state-of-the-art, are explicit. They state that "we focused on *skills* and the abilities that support them because they constitute the most *pragmatic* way to view interpersonal communication."[31] [emphasis added].

White's argument with the model of the lay scientist is that it does not square with the lived-experience of the person. Though he writes as a social scientist, his position is phenomenological. His theme is the development of a contrast between the former model and that of the *lay pragmatist*. The concerns of the latter are those of everyday life and are neither to be equated with nor dominated by the epiphenomenal (abstracted) world of scientific rationalism. White's conclusion echoes, but does not quote, the early James of "The Sentiment of Rationality."[32] White's practical advice is:

> The optimal strategy for the pragmatist is not one that produces scientifically accurate judgment, but one that achieves the most successful compromise between conflicting practical concerns. It is this, and not informational uncertainty or judgmental inaccuracy, that constitutes the major problems and sources of error and failure in the real world.[33]

And, most particular to the concerns of this paper, White further advises :

> Rather than a view of laypeople as imperfect or informal versions of professional scientists, which is, in any case, based on an idealized view of science, the view of the pragmatist model is of professional scientists as potential victims of concrete and practical considerations.[34]

White challenges the claim of pragmatism in normative communication research and introduces a philosophically informed view of pragmatism consistent with its American founders. Step two of the paper contrasts the claim of pragmatism in the communication competency literature with the original pragmatist, William James.

The Pragmatics of Everyday Life

The difference between communication conceived abstractly as a social institution and the pragmatics of communication in everyday life could not be more stark. The empiricist's precision in method is sacrificed by the lay pragmatist in favor of the ordinary conscious experiences of mundane existence. What the lay pragmatist lacks in precision, however, is duly compensated by a fertile imagination necessitated by the factual texture of life as it is really lived. It is this latter world of which the empiricist can say nothing, for it precedes all rationalist science and cannot be subsumed as objectified data.

The lay scientist conception is, to put it precisely, distinctly *non*-empirical. It is reductionist science that does not account for conscious experience but, instead, relies on abstract taxonomies pertaining to *competence*.[35] Phenomenologically speaking, competence has to do with necessary and sufficient conditions, not of knowledge *about* life but *of* life. That is to say, phenomenological competence consists in an awareness of ontological evocation, the cultural and social contexts that condition the call-to-be, and in which we establish the very style of our existences by making the mundane choices of everyday seeing-saying-acting. This is an important distinction between the *empiricistic* and the *empirical*. It is a distinction well understood by the father of pragmatism. "Knowledge about a thing," he declared, "is not the thing itself."[36] Likewise, it should be understood that the idea of pragmatism is not pragmatism.

James formulated a *radical empiricism* that contrasted sharply with the British empiricists. Although his explication of human consciousness is generally considered in terms of his famous work, *The Principles of Psychology*, his phenomenological orientation is most clearly seen in his essay "The Sentiment of Rationality," and in his masterpiece, *The Varieties of Religious Experience*. A number of philosophers have convincingly demonstrated that America's leading pragmatist was, in fact, a phenomenologist.[37] Interpreters tend to cast James as either an existential phenomenologist (Wild) or a transcendental phenomenologist (Edie). However, James would have little to do with such labels. He saw himself as a pragmatist and an American, and he had little sympathy with the vocabulary or the general theoretical proclivities of the continental philosophers. Of course, Sartre rejected the label of existentialism and Foucault refused to see himself as a poststructuralist. Each is nonetheless so classified. What, then, are the features of James's phenomenological pragmatism relevant to this essay? A complete picture cannot be drawn here, but salient and interrelated features follow.

In rejecting empiricism of a rationalist type, James interested himself in what Dallmayr calls the "interpretive and concrete existential underpinnings of cognitive pursuits."[38] This is probably best indicated in James' argument that there exists, beneath rationality, a *feeling* for it which is its phenomenal ground. The whole reason for scientific or philosophic endeavor in the first place, from this point of view, is to re-create the sufficiency of the moment, a moment that had been interrupted by a need to justify it. He referred to this as the *sentiment of rationality*.[39] The scientist is called upon to be distant from this sentiment and to endlessly classify objects of perception, but James reminded us that "custom *per se* is a mental sedative."[40]

On the development of taxonomies, James made the point that concepts must always be rooted in experience as it is lived:

> Every way of classifying a thing is but a way of handling it for some particular purpose. Conceptions, "kinds," are teleological instruments. No abstract concept can be a valid substitute for a concrete reality except with reference to a particular interest in the conceiver.[41]

The interests of the conceiver are founded on the primacy of perception, a common thread in the fabric of phenomenological literature. James said:

> A concept can only be designative; and . . . the concept 'reality,' which we restore to immediate perception, is no new creation, but only a kind of practical relation to our Will, perceptively experienced .[42]

A careful reading of James indicates that "traditional theories of knowledge are too speculative because they ignore the origins of knowledge in the life world."[43] The primacy of perception provides human behavior with an experiential base. However, the expressed world of human action is not privileged over the perceptual, nor vice versa. The concrete world is experienced *because* it is a correlate of consciousness.[44] Of course, this perspective is at odds with the received view of meaning in a neo-Kantian epistemology.[45] James himself said, "concreteness as radical as ours is not so obvious. The whole originality of pragmatism, the whole point of it, is its use of the concrete way of seeing."[46] Thus, consciousness is never a mere matter of the mind knowing another entity.

Additionally, human consciousness can never completely realize itself. There is an essential incompleteness to reflection, leaving room for mystery and, therefore, openness to the world. This openness is not unlike that expressed by Heidegger.[47] It is ethical and democratic to its core. The ethical aspect is apparent throughout James, but particularly in his essay "The Will to Believe"[48] and especially as interpreted by Barrett.[49] Relevant to the point of this paper, Wild noted:

> The intimate fusion of consciousness with action has often been interpreted by American commentators in a pragmatic, or voluntaristic, sense, as though ideas, according to James, were only instruments for action. This is a misunderstanding. The two factors are fused, it is true. But it is the conscious vision which guides, not the action. As James puts it [Psychology II, 531], "in action as in reasoning, then, the great thing is the quest of the right conception."[50]

The *right conception* is determined through the interpretive act of understanding, but such understanding is not to be subjectivized. Because James's understanding is based on intentionality (the conscious field of experience), it is akin to the position taken up by Bernstein. Bernstein, as interpreted by Dallmayr, considers understanding to be an *event* that can occur only to the extent that the individual loses a sense of self in the process.[51] This position is made specific to the question of interpersonal competence by Deetz and is addressed below.[52]

If ethical, James's pragmatism is also democratic. As such, it stands against the integration of knowledge as a totalizing function of empiricistic method. He was ready to accept any and all ways of knowing, so long as they were grounded in human praxis. Specifically, in regard to the issue of communication competence, Seigfried is helpful:

> The whole world of rational explanation epitomized by philosophy, which privileges the articulate, nonetheless has its own roots in the preconceptual world of experience. The limited world of coherent discourse can avoid sterility only by acknowledging its dependence on "the aboriginal flow of feelings."[53]

Finally, it is important to note that James was acutely aware that subsequent interpreters of his work might narrowly cast his pragmatic philosophy as mere competent practice. Seigfried explains:

> The determination of "concrete fact" and of "conduct consequent upon the fact" should not be narrowly construed as an empiricist appeal to sense data or to behaviorist analyses, but requires an understanding of "the living facts of human nature," or of what is later called by Heidegger a phenomenological analysis of Dasein.[54]

In contrast with the empiricistic conception that equates communication competence with the pragmatic, as Seigfried goes on to say, James "deplores the fact that practical workings as a criterion of truth has been taken in a narrowly useful sense."[55] Throughout the philosophy of William James, she concludes, "the practical is being used in its broadest, most inclusive sense as a synonym for his phenomenology and therefore refers to his basic methodological procedure."[56]

Step three of this paper looks more closely at the issue of pragmatism in relation to interpersonal communication competence.

Communication Praxis

Bochner,[57] Lanigan,[58] and Deetz,[59] have made concerted efforts to show the limitations of contemporary research and pedagogy in interpersonal communication. All have taken pragmatic orientations in the Jamesian democratic sense. That is, each author, in his own way, speaks out against the tyranny of method, each urges a broadening of perspectives, and each is concerned with ethics.

Since Bochner wrote his comprehensive review of research approaches to interpersonal communication in 1985, the discipline has not fundamentally changed. For example, *Human Communication Research*, perhaps the journal most highly regarded by interpersonal communication scholars, remains dedicated to empiricism. Of course, Bochner did not call for the termination of such research; he merely pointed to its limits. In Jamesian style, he offered pragmatism as a way of avoiding the pitfalls of either/or thinking. He primarily relied, however, upon Rorty and not upon the original philosophers of pragmatism.

Bochner subscribes to Rorty's view that differences in perspective are principally differences in the vocabulary used to talk about phenomena. Bochner divides approaches to interpersonal communication into three paradigms: empiricism, hermeneutics, and critical theory. He is aware that there are more poststructuralist approaches than are encompassed in his categories, but his scheme serves his purpose. Namely, he summarizes the three aims of science accordingly as "prediction and control," "interpretation and understanding," and "criticism and social change."[60] He is also aware that these are, in the latter two cases, interrelated and overlapping. His summary discusses the objects of discourse ("view of phenomena"), functions of discourse ("functions"), the activity of discourse ("how "knowledge" is produced"), and discourse criticism ("how truth claims are judged").[61]

The Bochner piece is an exemplar of interdisciplinary thinking. Not only does it provide a comprehensive review of the discipline, but it draws upon the philosophy of science to situate interpersonal discourse within the context of contemporary intellectual thought beyond artificial disciplinary boundaries. Nevertheless, two problems in the analysis are worth mentioning.

First, the allegiance to Rorty's egalitarian notion of research territory, while difficult to deny as a gesture of good will, assumes that distinctions between theoretic approaches are noncompetitive or, better, that they should be. Quite another way to think about this is to regard the linguistic choices as deliberate. Words, after all, have consequences. Metaphors that are grounded in the language of economics, for example, bespeak a mind-set that carries with it a certain set of cash-values that excludes the non-economic. Pertinent to the study of communication, I have elsewhere depicted the distinctive paths of research in communication to which we are preconsciously led by ostensibly innocuous choices of metaphors by which to organize a description of communication. For example, describing communication as a process *naturalizes* the research task limiting it to observation of behavior and a focus on interferences in or barriers to communicative effectiveness. Eventually, and almost imperceptibly, the premise that all behavior communicates (i.e., has message value) leads researchers to equate communication with behavior. On the other hand, the text metaphor employed in some deconstructionist accounts leads critics to *read* communication as though it were fixed in time and space. In the latter perspective, logocentrism replaces homocentrism, but the problem of foundationalism remains. The incommensurablility of research metaphors is not an issue easily dismissed.[62]

In fact, the *crisis of confidence* in empiricism so well summarized by Bochner belies his attempted fairness. He provides no good reason to continue adherence to a paradigmatic choice that has been cast out of serious philosophical consideration for the past twenty years. To the contrary, his critique of empiricism is so telling that its goals, view of phenomena, functions, and the like, seem to pale in probable insight to alternative modes of theorizing. The conclusion can only be that empiricism is old-fashioned communication theory, the paradigm assumptions of which are dubious.

Second, Bochner addresses but glosses over ethical distinctions between the paradigms. His interrogation of the *aims of science* brings the issue of research motives into full view. The critical reader of Bochner is forced to contemplate the respective ethics of empiricism's desire to control other beings, the hermeneutic desire to interpret and understand others, and critical theory's desire to effect social change by appeals to reasoned discourse.

Explicit in this analysis is the assumption that the communication field has more to offer than training in minimal competencies. From this point of view, a choice of paradigms is *necessitated;* the exigencies of life praxis do not allow continued allegiance to nonpragmatic premises. It is not pragmatic to suggest the possibility of agreeing on a variety of scientific vocabularies, as do Bochner and Rorty, while avoiding the possible pitfalls of paradigm competition. The ethics of speech inheres in speaking, and this applies to all languages, scientific or not. Furthermore, no theoretical language is particularly imaginable that is truly exterior to a worldview. Pertinent to this inquiry, Hook and Kahn pose the practical question:

> By recognizing the job as the prime target of college education, by inviting the student to enjoy the college community with that idea in mind—when he or she already has this notion in dire excess—is not the college offering an implied contract for a job it has no moral right to offer?[63]

Scholars of communication might well wish to interrogate their own academic curricula along these lines. Central to the interrogation should be the issue of the extent to which the discipline has unwittingly served the dominant culture. Certainly, it is clear that the choice of the competency metaphor by the empiricists is an *ethical choice* preconsciously made. Recognizing that the definition of competence makes a significant difference to research methods, Rubin offers a "consensually shared" view:

> Communication competence is knowledge about appropriate and effective communication behaviors, development of a repertoire of skills that encompass both appropriate and effective means of communicating, and motivation to behave in ways that are viewed as both appropriate and effective by interactants.[64]

Rubin thematizes research in communication competence into "three main types based on common theoretical bonds—cognitive, social/interpersonal, and communication skills."[65] Research so conceived leads to behavioral approaches and a focus on the problematics of method. Methods include the gathering of data in the form of self-reports, behavioral observations by experts, and reports of interactants' perceptions of one another. Measurement and behavioral change are the general research objectives. The research model borrows heavily from traditional behavioral sciences and is implicitly justified by *the* scientific method of the natural sciences.

In a lengthy but telling passage, Murchland forewarned of the current situation:

> The principal trait of cognitive rationality, and what most sets it off from the liberal arts tradition, is its stance of value neutrality. It is nourished by an ideology and supported by a methodology that

shields it from the domain of values with a veritable arsenal of carefully worked out distinctions: subjective-objective, rational-emotive, ought-is, and so forth. These distinctions are guaranteed to keep what counts as truly knowable on one side of the hyphenations, with what is merely felt on the other. Facts are one thing; values another. Never shall an ought be derived from an is. Rationality thus defined and circumscribed is a hallmark of modernity and a source of our recurring dilemmas.[66]

Murchland argues that "the unexamined society is not worth living in," and that "our political alienation and social malaise are directly related to the eclipse of the liberal arts."[67] Given the foregoing analysis of the ideological context of contemporary higher education and the paradigm that supports the status quo arrangement, the need for alternative theorizing appears axiomatic.

Such an approach is offered by Lanigan's semiotic phenomenology. It produces the kind of pragmatic knowledge for which James called, relying as it does on a synthesis of the parallel triads of *data, capta, acta;* syntactics, semantics, pragmatics; and, ultimately, philosophy, linguistics, and communication. To appreciate this approach, it is necessary to briefly consider Lanigan's assessment of the state-of-the-art of competence research in communication.

As a theory of human communication praxis, semiotic phenomenology does not exclusively rely on methods borrowed from other disciplines and modeled after the natural sciences.[68] Rather, it justifies itself based on its long history, dating back to Aristotle and Plato. Its methods are eidetic and empirical, and its aims are descriptive and critical. The research focus is on human conscious experience, which is always synthesized as the reversible relationship of perception and expression, person and world. How, then, might Lanigan's synthetic theory differ from normative investigations of interpersonal communication competence?

Semiotic phenomenology is concerned with the experience of signs and the process of semiosis. It is not the purpose of this paper to address this theoretical approach in detail. However, as one outgrowth of James's radical empiricism, it brings a significant potential contribution to the competency issue. Namely, it may be used to show how normative research has unnecessarily fragmented *the experience of communicating.* By dividing the fundamental person-world correlate of the field of consciousness into discrete linguistic realms, an unfortunate dualism results between cognition and behavior. By contrast, the phenomenological perspective studies the person-sign-world relationship holistically. Thus, the competence research themes of the cognitive, the social/interpersonal, and communication skills become, respectively, *langage, langue,* and *la parole.* These correlate to the familiar syntactics, semantics, and pragmatics of linguistics. Syntactics *(data)* is concerned with the experiential boundaries imposed by language. Semantics *(capta)* is the realization of social conventions. Pragmatics *(acta)* is the act of speaking. Communication is more complex, yet more practical regarded this way. The richness of the field is enhanced by a synthesizing perspective, rather than limiting research to a narrow focus on disembodied behavior. The latter empiricistic approach is more simplistic and this allows it the false impression of being more practical. However, James realized the point of diminishing returns in such thinking. He maintained that "a simple conception is an equivalent for the world only so far as the world is simple—the world meanwhile, whatever simplicity it may harbor, being a mightily complex affair."[69]

Critical-interpretive approaches, including semiotic phenomenology, are not limited to the expressive (behavioral) aspect of being. They appreciate the preconscious ground of all behavior. This is consistent with James:

> To explain a thing is to pass easily back to its antecedents; to know it is easily to foresee its consequents. Custom, which lets us do both, is thus the source of whatever rationality the thing may gain in our thought.[70]

While we may be accustomed to a behavioral focus in communication inquiry, our habitualized way of thinking is forgetful of the temporal aspect of speaking activity. Experience, as Lanigan has taken great pains to point out, is the reflective condition of human consciousness, not consciousness itself. Being cannot be made the object of inquiry for the human sciences. Being is, after all, no-thing; that is to say, it resists objectification as behavior or as mere messages. Being is realized in and as its relations to the world. In this sense, consciousness may be said to be persistently valid, and experience more or less fidelitous. That is, experience, as I have elsewhere argued, is a matter of fidelity, of interpretation and, ultimately, of ethics.[71] If consciousness is being awake, experience is its correlate, which directs us to our morning coffee, but it may also appear that this situation is reversible and that the directedness of experience (the scent of coffee) affirms our being. Just so.

For this reason, the central concerns of postmodern theories of communication must be human experience and its social conditions. This inevitably leads to axiology, but not to ethics considered in its usual sense:

As Ralph Barton Perry has pointed out, with great penetration, the philosophy of James is neither a philosophy of objects and actions nor a philosophy of ideas; it is a philosophy of the *experience* of objects and actions *in which the subject itself is a participant.*[72]

The quality of the subject's experience is simply not reducible to the issue of behavioral effectiveness. Even if it were, however, a question of ethics would remain. In the philosophically defunct empiricist paradigm, education in communication competence is reduced to mere training in self-assertion. (Perhaps this accounts for the implicit admiration in this type of research for the *clinical* psychology of behavioral science.) Effectiveness is determined by assessment of results, but is *appropriateness* of behavior not a matter of social conscience as well as individual consequences? Perhaps alternative ways of thinking about communication should be more fully considered. One such alternative is to think in terms of developing interpersonal *understanding*, as opposed to training in self-assertion. Understanding itself, however, must be reconceived so as not to limit it to the behavioral domain.

It is misleading to characterize understanding as an "activity of a subject." It is true, of course, that understanding requires effort and care, imagination and perceptiveness, but this is directed to the pathos of opening ourselves to what we seek to understand.[73]

As Dallmayr expresses it, "interpretation from this perspective means participation in a 'play' that 'fulfills its purpose only if the player loses himself.'"[74] Whereas in the behavioral model, research and pedagogy always presume a completed self who then may be groomed to act appropriately—that is, effectively—upon the social and physical world, an approach from the refined conception of human understanding is radically different. In this scenario, it is necessary to rethink the customary conception of the person. Behind the presumed person is a network of social and linguistic relations in need of investigation. As Deetz indicates:

In light of modern communication theories, contemporary conceptions of individual autonomy, democracy, and ethics (if they can be reclaimed at all) must consider the social production of knowledge, experience, and identity rather than attending primarily to their expression. The conditions of the construction of experience through communication are of more concern here than the '"free" expression and "reasoned" collective decision.[75]

Deetz suggests that the system that produces the self in the first place can no longer be ignored. This is important because:

> Individual behaviors take on meaning from their system function rather than from the speaker's intent or external social conventions. In this sense the system produces meaning and individual identities which individuals take on as their own as they participate in the system.[76]

Systemic ethics becomes the focal point of inquiry as individual actions are no longer assessed as if in a social and linguistic vacuum. "Systems and structures have important ethical implications that cannot be assessed from looking at individual behaviors and attitudes."[77] The objective of communication study then shifts to "the development of relational systems where responsible action is possible," and where mutual understanding is the goal.[78] Scholarly attention to effectiveness continues but is regarded differently. For example, "from the ethical standpoint of mutual formation of understanding, the least effective thing a person might do in interaction is to convince others."[79] Such a display of competence in interaction might be the death nell of the further goal of keeping the conversation going and the experience open to possibilities.

This is not at all meant to suggest a closed systems approach in which adherence to pregiven standards of conduct is the objective. Instead, the point is to learn that the *strategy* of communication,[80] already structured by historically sedimented cultural and social conditions, provides the parameters in which the *tactics* of communication may be creatively discerned and functionally appropriated. To paraphrase an old saying, genius that does not know the rules has no possibility of transcending them.

When contextualized by human understanding, the explanations provided by social systems become the discharge of psychological obligations. Both understanding and explanation, as Schrag has taken great care to indicate, are necessary moments of interpretation.[81] Or, in Lanigan's vocabulary, human gestures are choices of context, not the other way around.[82]

Conclusion

The point of this essay has been to indicate that research and pedagogy in the human sciences unduly emphasize an empiricist notion of communication competence. Analysis of the social constraints placed on communication as an academic discipline leads to the conclusion that the competency focus serves ideology. The unwitting partner in service of this ideology is empiricism, which has co-opted the communication discipline as its pragmatic influence. This influence is based on the cash-value of training in communication competence.

In sharp contrast, the phenomenology of William James posits a much richer and more complex view of human conscious experience. The interpretation of James discards the normative paradigm as impractical because it is nonempirical. Postmodern theories of communicology owe much to James who developed a protophenomenology based on the primacy of perception. These postmodern approaches are not only a means by which the limits of the normative paradigm may be indicated, but they are also major constructive contributors to a fuller understanding of communication. They are not necessarily intended as substitutions for traditional theory, but they do offer deeper insights into the experience of communicating.

Conscious experience is itself a communicative project; it is the reflective possibility of a hermeneutics of signs. Communicology, the new name for this turn in the human sciences, is a pragmatic philosophy. It draws our attention to the complex interrelationship between the background of constraints on our speech (ideological discourse) and our expressive/actional possibilities. Consistent with James, we must contend that it would not be advisable (practical) to consider behavior (pragmatics) as the sum of experience and in isolation from its historical syntax and semantic context. As a practical consideration, communication exceeds its behavioral manifestation and is always embedded in, as well as structured and systematized by, the parameters of culture and the social circumstances that call it out. The empiricist's narrow focus on the competent deliberations of the intending self, even if we could suppose to know them, could never give a sufficient account of the conscious experience of communicating.

Normative research may speak *about* competent communication as the behavior that measures up to preconceived standards of ethical conduct. However, it may not speak *of* communication competence. Communication is as indeterminant as experience; it is not subject to a single, unified, and integrated way of being in the world, whether it be conceived as competent or incompetent. From the standpoint of communicology, being human is a project subject to hermeneutic disclosure.

James might have agreed, for he posited the idea that there are many worlds of consciousness, not merely one. It is thus to James that this essay again returns:

There is no ringing conclusion possible when we compare these types of thinking, with a view to telling which is the more absolutely true . . . . Common sense is better for one sphere of life, science for another, philosophic criticism for a third; but whether either be truer absolutely, Heaven only knows. . . . Profusion, not economy, may after all be reality's key-note.[83]

6

Devising Ends Worth Striving For:
William James and the
Reconstruction of Philosophy

◁ᴣ▷ ◁ᴣ▷

Charlene Haddock Seigfried

Pragmatists characteristically appeal to experience as justifying their claims. But, as Richard Rorty so strongly reminds us, their very demonstrations of the irreducibly finite, human dimension of experience destabilizes any naive appeal to an experiential given. Experience, as lived, is both more and less than nature; more, because it includes subjectivity; less, because we occupy and are aware of only a part of the cosmos. Pragmatists plainly want it both ways: the objectivity of the facts of nature and the subjectivity of humanly diverse appropriations. According to John Dewey, for instance, "experience is *of* as well as *in* nature."[1] It is the bar before which interpretation pleads its case. Even though it is historical, organic process, it is still objective and accessible. But it is also inseparable from our subjective apprehension: "Only analysis shows that the *ways* in which we believe and expect have a tremendous affect upon *what* we believe and expect."[2]

Dewey explains experience as a dynamic reciprocity between organism and environment, between undergoing and doing.[3] Rape, for example, is first undergone and interpreted as a violation of one's autonomy, which begins with bodily integrity, before it is named as such and the event contested in law courts. It produces its own evidence on the bodies and clothes and in the minds and memories of those involved. Such undergoings, however, are not merely passive. As participants we also anticipate, welcome or reject, are spontaneously reactive. The assailant's or lover's and the victim's or partner's versions of the event, or that of bystanders or forensic experts, are required to turn inert clothes and observable bodily marks into evidence. But the

background of desire and revulsion, of beliefs of permissible and for-
bidden sexual activities, of culturally traditional and feminist contesta-
tions of the meaning of rape—which exhibit both stability and change
over time—are constituent features of both the *original* event and the
interpreted event.

The nature of the event, both as event and as reconstructed in
moral or legal judgment, can only be determined within a horizon of
enacted meanings. This horizon is inextricably both cultural and personal—that is, bounded by socially constructed and individually
appropriated ends-in-view or purposes. But actual results accrue as
these are acted upon. Pragmatic determinations of objectivity, therefore, focus on beliefs as rules of action. They inquire into what distinguishes satisfactory from unsatisfactory beliefs or assertions about
reality. Justificatory appeals to reality, as Dewey's theory of inquiry
consistently argues, can only refer to the outcome of certain ways of
behaving, of acting on one's beliefs.

For William James, too, experience is inherently ambiguous or
vague because it always includes interpretation.[4] He says in some
unpublished notes that even if reality is "fixed in itself," it "permits of
an indefinite variety in our ways of knowing it truly. We make our contribution to the truth product and the same reality may be the object for
many formulas, none false, and none irrelevant."[5] Interpretations can be
more or less satisfactory as clarifications of events or happenings or factual occurrences, but they cannot simply disclose being as it is. Events
are always events-for-us and therefore can only be understood in relation to our intentions or ends-in-view. For James both realism and idealism "must admit the minimal fact to be the full phenomenon—i.e.:
the-object-given-to-the-subject."[6] The positivist program of ignoring
intentions in order to insure a neutrally objective standpoint, therefore,
cannot succeed, since its findings will be accurate only within operative
parameters that remain unexamined because unrecognized.

The Concrete Perspective: A Pragmatic Phenomenology

James pioneers a shift away from speculative theories of knowledge to a consideration of the cognitive process as it emerges in an
investigation of our conscious being in the world. He does so by taking
states of consciousness holistically, recognizing that earlier states influence later ones. In this ongoing process we are always moving on from
one topic to another by introducing new ends-in-view. He thus substitutes his concrete analysis for the foundational role that epistemology
had usurped in modern philosophy.

The distinctiveness of James's view of knowledge is best expressed as arising from its attempt to describe knowing as it exists concretely in contrast to the popular or usual epistemological view, which only describes the results taken abstractly.[7] Reflections on the storm of controversy raised over the pragmatic theory of truth led him to realize that "concreteness as radical as ours is not so obvious. The whole originality of pragmatism, the whole point in it, is its use of the concrete way of seeing."[8] The concrete level of analysis is also called the "practical and psychological point of view."[9] Dewey recognized the revolutionary change such an emphasis on the concrete situation would bring about and argues in "Context and Thought" that "neglect of context is the greatest single disaster which philosophic thinking can incur."[10] He concurs with James that "context includes at least those matters which for brevity I shall call background and selective interest."

To the very end of his life James sought to distinguish his own position from the humanism of John Dewey and F.C.S. Schiller, but without much success. He characterizes them in a letter to Schiller, April 27, 1910, as being deeper and more radical, in contrast to his own *more superficial* handling of problems.[11] But it turns out that the superficial plane he works from is the phenomenal or common sense level. A week later he points out that he, like Schiller, had always held that percepts are as much artifacts as are concepts—that is, they are both human constructs, but that he chose not to emphasize this in *Some Problems of Philosophy* because it was written as a textbook for students.[12] He reiterates that for didactic reasons he begins on the common sense level whereas Schiller characteristically begins from a more fundamental ground and describes the process of knowledge "from an initial zero," presumably meaning as a pure construct, without any presuppositions. James says that he has never placed himself on such a fundamental ground and that the practical function of concepts should not obscure the fact that by this time some of them should have been established *in pragmatic solidity.*

James's philosophical project is characterized by his rejection of a presuppositionless starting point.[13] His supposed "superficiality" consists in his adoption of the natural history point of view in his writings, which means for James a careful description of phenomena, abstraction, hypothesis formation and validation.[14] He consistently limits himself to the level of concrete or phenomenological description, often to break an impasse generated by the formulations of particular problems by idealist and empiricist philosophers, and in view of establishing the fundamental facts of human experience. His radically empiricist analysis of concrete experience "describes" or sets up the world in which our activities take place. Explanations are justified insofar as they take account of these findings and rejected by showing exactly how they do not. Metaphysics is not rejected outright, but only those versions of metaphysics that de-realize the only world we know. But this includes all metaphysics except the humanist, of which his own is a variant. James rejects metaphysics as the disclosure of being but not as a human effort to unify experience.

At Home in the World

James approvingly quotes Hegel on the aim of knowledge, which is "to divest the objective world of its strangeness, and to make us more at home in it." But he adds that different persons "find their minds more at home in very different fragments of the world."[15] While for Hegel, the attainment of a universal, rational appropriation of the world will divest it of its alien character by stripping away the limitations inherent in a merely human understanding, for James we can never know the world except partially, nor do we ever lose the particularity of our appropriation. The goal of knowledge is not merely passive assimilation to what is, whether this means the particularity of the empirically given or the ideal rational explanation of everything, but the active transformation of the world into a better place to live.

The world is *unheimlich*—that is, we do not feel at home in it, insofar as we feel that it is not susceptible to our efforts to transform it according to our moral vision. If our efforts are doomed to failure from the start, inasmuch as the human animal is just an evolutionary aberration that will have its day and then fade out of the universe leaving no more traces than if it had never been, then there is no escape from pessimistic nihilism. But where can the hope that our efforts will prove both adequate to the transformation and definitive of the future find any guarantee outside blind faith? How can it become rational—that is, defensible intellectually?

James argues both that it is a necessary condition of the human appropriation of the world that we postulate the genuine efficacy of our efforts, and it is the philosopher's task to demonstrate the legitimacy of this postulate. James had no difficulty with the proof on practical grounds—that is, in establishing that it is a genuine condition of human action. We would not act, not constantly incorporate the world into our activities and impose ourselves on it, if we believed that there were no point to any activity at all. We need a motive for our will and will supply one if it is lacking. Purposeless action, random groping, is not a characteristically human form of life, and insofar as it manifests itself in a human being we take it for a sign of something amiss, such as a loss of conscious control, brain damage, or some such breakdown. Dewey also opposes "the humdrum; slackness of loose ends, submission to convention in practice and intellectual procedure" to the unity of experience paradigmatic of being human.[16] But is there anything objective that confirms this subjective necessity?

To see in what such objectivity would consist, it should be understood that James assumed that the link of particular, limited means to ends was conditioned by their link to more encompassing ends. Persons would not get out of bed in the morning, for instance, if they did not believe that the change of state was more desirable, not only in the short, but also in the long run. Thus getting up contributes, if only incrementally, to the total good of the universe. Insofar as humans differ from other animals, they do so precisely in the fact that human activity is not limited to proximate means to ends, but these narrower ends are themselves conditioned by wider ends-in-view. Meaning in the narrow, linguistic sense, is parasitic on meaningfulness, in the sense of overbeliefs. We do not eat just because food is placed in front of us, but because we must eat to live and living is perceived as good. If it is not, we do not eat. In the absence of wider ends, the proximate ends no longer function.

But although it is easy to demonstrate that certain means must be undertaken to attain particular ends, and that some particular ends are more valuable than others, James was ultimately stymied in his attempts to demonstrate that the more encompassing guiding ends are not only subjectively necessary for action but are also objectively true. Is the universe better off because we participate in it? Are we adding to the total increment of good in the universe? Will our efforts be sustained throughout all coming time or are we just a passing phenomenon? Are we to approach life with the high seriousness that the task of working for a better world demands or are we just the brunt of a colossal joke? Philosophy cannot proceed in a post-Newtonian world, unhinged from a guiding, rational providence, unless it has the resources for overcoming the nihilism of a meaningless universe.

Since James thought philosophy differed from the particular sciences precisely by taking as its task the demonstration of the ultimate grounds for all things and the justification of ultimate purposes, he both continued to identify himself as a philosopher and tried to fulfil its traditional task until his last crisis, when he gave up rationalism.[17] But he succeeded only in contributing to a strong subjective foundation for ultimate ends, without ever developing any objective ones. Worse, he developed more and more arguments against the very possibility of an objective grounding. His last crisis was overcome in the same way as his first one, which determined the course of his intellectual career. At that time he overcame suicidal tendencies brought on by a nihilistic loss of meaning in a ready-made, rational universe by deciding that since one must believe to act, then this practical necessity was adopted as sufficient grounds for belief.[18] Where earlier James simply put off the demand for an ultimate grounding to give himself time to develop one, at the end of his life he denied the legitimacy of the objective demand. The fulfillment of its conditions is in principle impossible, since ultimate goals differ from particular ones precisely because we can never prove beyond the shadow of a doubt that what we subjectively believe about the ultimate nature of the universe is objectively true. Since we can never satisfy the rational demand for an irrefutable proof that each person's limited contribution to the betterment of the world will finally bring about a final transfiguration, then that demand is not to be taken seriously. Because the conditions set are impossible to obtain, the demand must be mistaken. We cannot have a rational obligation to fulfill the impossible.

In denying rationalism's veto, James also denies the philosophic project. He is beyond rationalism, beyond philosophy. But we can wonder whether he is only prephilosophical and not postphilosophical. Perhaps he is only clinging to beliefs without seeking to justify them, just as were those Athenians whom Socrates scoffed at because they had many beliefs but no justified, true beliefs. What price has James paid to keep his "overbeliefs" intact? He finally gives up trying to prove that there is an objective basis for the subjective conditions for human action and being in the world. But he does not give up the belief that they are objectively true. In this he does not seem to differ from the religious believer.

There is some evidence for this interpretation of James's final position as yet another example of his tendency to justify by subjective need what cannot be demonstrated on objective grounds. But the texts also lend themselves to another, equally plausible, interpretation that I think is both more promising and confirms James's sense that his final position represented an advance and a resolution of his earlier dilemmas.

We can grant, for instance, for all the reasons James has given, that rationalism is bankrupt and ultimately indefensible as traditionally understood, and therefore the practical grounds he has advanced are not lacking anything from not fulfilling the rational demand for absolute certainty. But there still remains the question of whether the overbeliefs he therefore accepts have been shown to be practically necessary. It could be the case that James, for all his astuteness, misunderstood the basis of his own escape from nihilism or mistakenly took an aspect of it that was true enough of his own experience as being a characteristic of any overcoming of nihilism.

James willed to believe that life was ultimately meaningful, in the absence of any proof that it was so, in order to literally give himself time to work out its meaningfulness.[19] He located this meaning in the ultimate meaning of the universe. His own creative imposition of order, arising out of the values in which he believed, took place for him within a wider, harmonious moral order that he could glimpse only mystically in literary or religious garb. In order to show that James is not just reverting to a naive belief in the ultimate intelligibility and purposefulness of the universe, I will draw on a similar explanation in Friedrich Nietzsche.

Like Nietzsche, James recognized that many traditional religious beliefs could not withstand the corrosive effects of modern science. He likewise recognized that these religious beliefs had also provided a foundation for rationalism, despite the fact that their Greek origins had not depended on the Christian religious synthesis. Also, like Nietzsche, he located the invention of rational principles and beliefs in the necessity of carving an ordered world out of the chaos of passing sensations. For both, the particular world we experience is the result of our needs and of the success of our past inventions as much as of the world encountered. But where Nietzsche emphasizes the destructive force of both rationalism and Christianity, James only deconstructs rationalism and the particular Christian belief in an omnipotent, omniscient Being. Nietzsche shows that the belief in a better world, which is beyond this world, can ultimately destroy everything of value in this world. James equally exposes the danger of substituting a parallel rational world of being to this one, because to do so can only undermine our limited, but genuine mode of being in the world.

But James does not apply this same rationale to the belief in a utopia of the final harmony of all things, which is the goal of both rationalism and religion. This is not because Nietzsche and James adopt different criteria. They do not. Even their genealogies are parallel: all human organizations of experience, from the organization of knowledge into sense data and concepts to scientific and religious institutions, are expressions of the drive to order our surroundings. They are expressions of those values that we have developed over time as most efficacious to what we have taken to be our well being.[20] Particular explanations are accepted or rejected insofar as they further or hinder the will to power. Nietzsche expresses this as the exuberant oneness with the ever-changing forces of life, while James says that interpretations are acceptable insofar as they allow us to reform experience congruent with the powers we possess, in a "kind of living understanding of the movement of reality."[21]

Using these same criteria, Nietzsche concludes that all beliefs in ultimate harmony, whether of a Christian heaven or of total rationality, are destructive of our taking full control of and responsibility for our lives and our appropriation of the world. This view contrasts with James, who distinguishes between beliefs in an existent, perfect Christian heaven or in an already achieved, complete rational reconstruction of the world and beliefs, whether religiously based or not, in a utopia yet to be achieved in which our deepest values are perfectly translated into a harmonious world. James finds the former destructive but the latter, not only not destructive, but a necessary precondition for the full engagement of our powers.

A condition *sine qua non* is that the ultimate harmony does not now exist and, in fact, will never exist unless we bring it about. But such a hoped-for consummation also means that if we do cooperate, we will finally succeed. Ultimately, James's utopia is only another way of expressing belief in our own powers and our continuity with life. Its correlate in Nietzschean terminology is the justification of the will to believe in its conformity to the life process. James recognized this in his understanding of the Nietzschean *amor fati.*[22]

Knowing as it Exists Concretely

James's analysis of reasoning is meant to be a phenomenology, or in his words, a description, of "living acts of reasoning," or "concrete acts of reasoning" and not an analysis of logical forms, although it superficially resembles the logic of syllogisms.[23] He is not interested in systems that are true in virtue of stipulative definitions and rules of transformation because such self-enclosed systems do not illuminate reasoning as we actually engage in it, nor how we appropriate the world, nor how we distinguish between true and false appropriations. Both the sterility and fundamental skepticism of much of modern philosophy derive from increasingly favoring free-floating formal systems in the largely successful effort to place epistemological analysis at the heart of philosophic discourse. As a result, most of current philosophical writing still resembles late medieval Scholastic exercises of refining formal systems, as if the mere perfection of the system would somehow put us in closer touch with reality, in a contemporary version of idealism or misplaced assumption that an absolute lawgiver both thinks logically and creates a natural world according to this predelineated model.

We are thus distracted from the more difficult task of discerning how we can reason correctly about the world, which entails subordinating epistemological analysis to an ontology of our being in the world and requires a "concrete" or phenomenological, descriptive methodology. Closed systems are inherently more attractive to philosophers because any problems that arise are resolvable without going outside the reasoning process itself, while a description of the living act of reasoning requires empirical information. It is one more sign of the increasing preference for casuistry and extreme spcecialization in philosophy that James's early writings would now be categorized as either "psychology," "philosophy of psychology," or "philosophy of mind." If his thought is to be recovered as an alternative to sterile philosophizing for its own sake, however, it has to be understood as a thoroughgoing attempt to reconstruct the philosophic enterprise itself, and not just as a series of brilliant contributions to one or other of its branches. But such phenomenological analysis is naive to the extent that it isn't also hermeneutical, that is, if it doesn't recognize that any such description of the facts of experience is contingent on the selective interests that constitute human spontaneity.[24]

Consistent with this hermeneutic insight of the partiality and distortion involved in all conceptualization, James argues that "emphasis and selection seem to be the essence of the human mind".[25] But in the very same sentence where he seemingly falls back into a realistic essentialism, he reminds us that he is offering an explanatory hypothesis that seems called for by those characteristics of *finite and practical nature* that are disclosed from the point of view of his guiding interest in determining how we choose rightly out of a phenomenal totality. The temporal finiteness is stressed in the first part of the sentence, where he says: "To me now, writing these words, emphasis and selection seem to be the essence of the human mind." The word "seem" calls attention to the hypothetical character of the proposal. And in the following sentence he stresses the "practical" as also a condition of the determination of essentiality: "In other chapters other qualities have seemed, and will again seem, more important parts of psychology."

In his early writings James still held that there is a total truth that can be contrasted with the partial truth he has been explicating, and he wavers between locating this total truth in the idealists' absolute totality of being and "the world's concrete fullness"—that is, in an ideal totality or in an empirical totality.[26] But this truth of the experienced fullness of reality is not the modern philosopher's truth of propositions or the traditional correspondence to the truth of being. It is rather the ground for the possibility of the necessarily partial truths that can be articulated within the human dimension of experience and reflection, and is finally explicable as a phenomenological "totality,"—that is, the "horizon" within which particular organizations of experience can emerge. As a necessary postulate of the rationalist worldview, its ideal and empirical dimensions are only finally dropped by James in his last period, although he expressed doubts about them much earlier.

Interpretive Strategies: Aesthetic and Practical Rationality

James understands rationalism as the cognitive dimension of the drive to order our experiences satisfactorily—that is, to bring about a world in which we can be at home. The self is an organizing center, an "activity-situation" characterized by personality.[27] Dewey also characterizes organic selves as "individual centres of action" and as a "centered organization of energies."[28] We organize experience rationally both aesthetically and practically, according to James.[29] Aesthetic ordering consists of two opposite but complementary moves. One is to evermore comprehensive simplification—that is, reducing the maximum number and kinds of phenomena to the least number of explanatory rules. The other is the gathering and identification of as much of the variety of experience as possible. The first is called by James "simplifying" or "unifying," and the second is "clarity." But this effort to organize the many into one is characteristic of all fields of endeavor, not just the philosophical and scientific. In the fine arts, for instance, acrylic can be shaped into a construct determined by the artist's intent.

We can ignore the practical dimension of rationality and simply order the variety of experiences aesthetically. Aesthetic relationships are analogous to the unity of purpose by which we impose a teleological order on the world. Parts of the world experienced seem to tell a story. This expressive ordering can be understood dramatically. "Retrospectively, we can see that altho [sic] no definite purpose presided over a chain of events, yet the events fell into a dramatic form, with a start, a middle, and a finish."[30] But these dramas tell only partial stories and gather in only limited numbers of actors. The beginnings, middles, and ends of various dramas run parallel, overlap in various ways and separate again, but do not seem to be a part of one world play. Aesthetic unification is therefore dramatically pluralistic.

This is not to say that these separate dramas may not be imagined into a single, overarching drama. Dante's *Divine Comedy*, for instance, reconstructs the world into such a coherent dramatic unity. But we believe in such "monistic dogmas" at our own risk. To this dramatic rendering of many worlds into a single world, James opposes a contrasting pluralistic vision expressed in the simile of a rope composed of many fibers. Each single strand is continuous in extent and "each fibre tells a separate tale; but to conceive of each cross-section of the rope as an absolutely single fact, and to sum up the whole longitudinal series into one being living an undivided life, is harder."[31] We can cut through a cross section and expose an ordered array of fibers, but this "nextness" is less cohesive than that of a single strand in its full extension. Each strand, even when bound together, retains its individuality, to which it will return when unbound. According to this angle of vision the rope is "really" made up of many units, which get their unity as individuals. A single strand, for instance, can become part of different ropes successively.

Although James argues for this pluralistic interpretation, he does not privilege it as revealing the inner nature of reality. He acknowledges that according to another angle of vision, the unity is that of the cross section, since every strand can be identified in relation to every other strand in the rope bundle. Neither way of perceiving the unity more accurately represents the world of the rope. The advantage of his interpretive angle of vision is that it recognizes its own limitations. He can conclude that "*absolute* aesthetic union is thus another barely abstract ideal," but those who believe in such absolutes cannot acknowledge the finite context of their claims.[32] Such absolute, non-negotiable claims are terroristic, even if well meant. When we instead recognize and acknowledge the perspectivism of concrete experience—that is, when we refuse to let the pleasure to be gained from aesthetic union blind us to the multiplicity of experienced relations—then "the world appears as something more epic than dramatic." There is indeed more unity to our experiences than appears on the surface, but not enough to turn what may be a legitimate hypothesis into a dogmatic affirmation that there is "one sovereign purpose, system, kind, and story."

He adamantly opposes any plan of unification that does not preserve and enhance the proliferating richness of burgeoning ways of life. "In a life at first hand there is something sacred."[33] This is because we are finite, temporal beings. Each person is a unique and irreplaceable angle of vision. We will be confirmed in our precarious sense of being only to the extent that we sympathetically try to apprehend those ordering values that center other persons' lives.[34] Concomitantly, no one's angle of vision can encompass the whole without distortion and loss. Our lives are fragmented; we are part of many partial stories, and the pain of isolation can be relieved by cooperative ventures. The drive toward inclusivity can be pursued cooperatively or oppressively.

The world appears epic because of the episodic nature of our lived experience. One thing happens after another, with local battles, triumphs and failures. Our experiences are not bounded as in the drama with a defining beginning and an end; there is no identifiable grand denouement or purpose, the achievement of which brings the drama to a resolution. Although our birth can be precisely dated, there is no such neat beginning to our conscious experiences. Our end is likewise final, but is not written into the script. "If we were *readers* only of the cosmic novel, things would be different: we should then share the author's point of view and recognize villains to be as essential as heroes in the plot. But we are not the readers but the very personages of the world-drama."[35] We imagine ourselves taking up the various parts. If I cast myself as the hero, then I determine who my enemies are. The absolutely right reading, even if it be understood as being that of the author, is spoiled by the different ways each of us can identify ourselves with the different characters.

Aesthetic rationality is but one stage in concrete rationality. It can resolve the dilemmas it raises only through serving practical rationality.[36] But neither are self-sufficient. James's explanation of rationality in its fullest sense is based on his revision of the reflex-action theory of mind.[37] He says that "if the human mind be constructed after the triadic-reflex pattern we have discussed at such length,"[38] then every universal formula and system of philosophy must satisfy "all three departments of the mind." These are (1) our impressions of sense or facts of nature, (2) the theoretic or defining department and (3) our fundamental active or emotional powers (which require "an object outside of themselves to react-on or to live for").[39]

The third department is called "practical rationality" in the narrow sense, but in the broad sense, the other two (aesthetic) stages also "subserve and pass into" this third stage of action.[40] We delude ourselves about the second or middle department of definitions and general essences, of totalizing worldhood, when we take it as final rather than as a transitional stage. Its function is to transform the first department—that is, "the world of our impressions[,] into a totally different world—the world of our conception; and the transformation is effected in the interests of our volitional nature, and for no other purpose whatsoever."[41]

Pragmatic rationality is rationality taken in its lived or fullest sense. Favoring only aesthetic or only practical rationality cannot be finally satisfactory, although it may be sufficient for organizing any particular person's life. As Dewey puts it, we are live creatures constantly interacting with the world in which we live. We act on the world and the world acts on us. Such experiences are cumulative and therefore we can reflectively revise the way we find ourselves in the world. The world becomes part of us, just as we leave our mark upon the world. "Through habits formed in intercourse with the world, we also in-habit the world. It becomes a home and the home is part of our every experience."[42]

But we have learned through ecological investigations just how fragile our home is. We can enhance or destroy it. Even with the best intentions—and we often act on lesser motives—what we consider the conditions for making ourselves at home in the world may turn out to be ultimately destructive. Pragmatism constantly reminds us that we have no privileged perspective and that we proceed at our own risk. Politicians, religious leaders, even poets like Emerson, who exhort us to adopt the viewpoint of the absolute, are not only asking for what is impossible, they are advocating a perspective of infallibility that has borne bitter fruit. Against such self-serving claims James retorts: "I am finite once for all, and all the categories of my sympathy are knit up with the finite world *as such,* and with things that have a history."[43] Pragmatic optimism is a guarded optimism. We find ourselves in "an uncertain, incomplete and precarious universe," according to Dewey.[44] And James says of pragmatists that "neither in the theoretic nor in the practical sphere do we care for, or go for help to, those who have no head for risks, or sense for living on the perilous edge."[45]

A Hermeneutics of Cooperation

Sympathetic apprehension of the point of view of the other is central to James's philosophy. Feminists have shown us concretely how different our interpretations of humanity and rationality are when they incorporate the varied viewpoints of women and other disadvantaged groups. In the absence of any absolute point of view, truths are matters of finite experiences that support one another. If they clash, then pragmatic truth has not yet been obtained. James argues that rationality is better understood as intimacy rather than transparency. We are united in a common destiny since "the common *socius* of us all is the great universe whose children we are."[46] We must learn to share, accommodate, or negotiate each other's point of view at the peril of failing to survive at all. And the ultimate good that pragmatic truth serves is value for life.[47]

James's more moralistic epistemological view is complemented by Dewey's more socially oriented epistemology. They agree on cooperative communication as indispensable to the process of coming to know in the concrete world of experience. For Dewey, "a democracy is more than a form of government; it is primarily a mode of associated living, of conjoint communicated experience . . . so that each has to refer his own action to that of others, and to consider the action of others to give point and direction to his own."[48]

It is well known that, with the exception of *Principles*, most of James's writings were first lectures. What is not as well recognized is that he took oral speech to be linguistically privileged over written speech because it better incorporated his model of a hermeneutics of cooperation. Unlike the privacy of composing the written word, oral speech requires an audience or listeners, appeals to their interests, and must illuminate their experience if it is to be successful. The communicative context is explicit, and success or failure to communicate genuine insights is often immediately apparent.

Oral speech itself is a concrete expression of that communicative praxis that founds knowledge claims. For James communication is fully, dynamically embodied: "Before I can think you to mean my world, you must affect my world; before I can think you to mean much of it, you must affect much of it; and before I can be sure you mean it *as I do*, you must affect it just *as I should* if I were in your place."[49]

Without interactive confirmation there is no way to know that our beliefs are justified. But such interactive confirmations themselves can take place only within a horizon of shared meanings and values. Once we have given up any claim to having a privileged insight into being, then our task as thinkers is simply to "offer mediation between different believers, and help to bring about consensus of opinion."[50] Such consensus, of course, is predicated on a willingness to enter into the inner life and values of each other.

The goal of philosophy for pragmatists is not to develop the best epistemology or philosophy of mind, but to cooperatively formulate hypotheses and develop such methods as can improve human lives. As Dewey puts it: "It will not stop with analyzing and classifying as science does, but must devise ends worth striving for, and must find what resources we have for accomplishing these ends."[51]

IV

The Process of Communication

7

John Dewey and the Roots of Democratic Imagination

❦❦

Thomas M. Alexander

The Renewal of the Question of Democracy

The question of democracy urgently and insistently presented itself at the beginning of the century, and the major trials of its first half—the Great Depression and two world wars—can be understood as trials of democratic hope. But the aftermath of World War II ushered in an era shadowed by the threat of nuclear annihilation and that political Pleistocene known as the "Cold War." Philosophical thinking about democracy, even during the civil rights era, was put in cold storage: professional philosophy in the Anglo-American tradition concentrated on the logic of moral language which Continental political philosophy worked mainly within the framework of Marxism.[1] The two foremost exceptions, John Rawls and Jürgen Habermas, turned back far beyond recent phases of democratic theory to the Enlightenment for their models of personhood, rationality, and choice, each delineating in his own way the ideal, objective, logically-purified space of decision-making and communicative praxis.[2]

These cases for democracy seem to stand with a resurrection of the Enlightenment as the only counter to the excesses of the later Sartre's politics, the anarchism of Marcuse, the individualism of Lyotard, the dirge of Adorno's "negative dialectics," and the Nietzschean reconfigurations of history as power exhibited by Foucault. Radical defenders of democracy, like C.B. Macpherson, toyed with classifying the regimes of Third World Marxist-nationalists as "non-Western" modes of democracy merely on the basis of their professed if rather general and long-range aims of improving the welfare of their citizens. Others, like Richard

Rorty, have nothing better to offer in defense of liberal democracy than a groundless "ironic" hope tinged by sensitivity to the petty humiliations as well as the grosser sufferings of others.[3]

I begin by recruiting these well-known facts because I believe that, with the great thaw of the post-Cold War era, the question of democracy must be asked anew. In Eastern Europe, especially in the former Yugoslavic and in the new Commonwealth of Independent States (the confederacy of former Soviet republics), democracy once more struggles with dangerous and confusing consorts such as chauvinistic nationalism and ethnic racism.

Over against the Enlightenment's nationality and ethnically indifferent concept of the *person* stands a dangerous exclusionary image of democracy as the direct, uninhibited expression of the *will of a people* of definite contextual and historical character. Which shall it be: liberal democracy, which uses the empty, formal token of abstract individualistic personhood endowed with rights, or nationalist democracy, with its immediate, concrete palpitating desires for freedom mixed with equally powerful ideals of racism and ethnic collectivisms? Shall ethnic Russians be allowed to be citizens of Baltic republics? Shall there be a national Polish religion? What political principles will be used to oppose the resurgence of anti-Semitism? Is nationalism the first step to ethnic cleansing? Are Rawls and Habermas correct: that the only stem to the confusion of democratic theory with specific historical contexts and localized voices are the transcendental ideals of the Enlightenment?

This dilemma poses a serious practical as well as theoretical problem for the post-Cold War era. I believe that by examining the idea of democratic communication, we may be able to explore an alternative non-Enlightenment model, largely based upon the work of John Dewey and George Herbert Mead. I want to propose here what might be called a concept of democracy based on a view of *pluralistic rationality* in which diversity of outlooks, the cultivation of a social imagination, and a pervasive context of mutual care are intrinsic features. My claim, in brief, will be that this model of democratic rationality (or "intelligence," as Dewey preferred to say, a term I will hereafter adopt) requires, first, a number of *different communicating points of view* in order to work.

The way these differing viewpoints come to understand each other requires, second, the use of a *social imagination*—that is, an ability to understand in a concrete and emotional way, as well as in a cognitive manner, the lives and values of others. Indeed, we only come to have a distinct organized self at all insofar as it emerges from a long cultural process of engaging in communication with others. This capac-

ity to understand the viewpoint of another from his or her own historical or embodied context is radically different from trying to think in
the neutral, contextless abstractions of universal personhood.

Third, at the root of our ability to communicate, indeed at the
very root of our existence, is a context of mutual care and support. This
ability to be related by an *underlying disposition to care for and be cared
for by others* is, so to speak, the *transcendental erotic structure* of human
understanding presupposed in all mature, explicit, self-reflective, and
cognitive endeavors. The democratic context will be one that exhibits
not just mere toleration, which is the art of *indifference*, the social per-
mission for the development of a wide range of individual preferences
and beliefs, but rather one that fosters active and responsive *dialogue*
between different perspectives for the sake of a shared life, which realizes in as integrated a manner as possible the diversity of values that
give meaning to human life. Thus, by exploring the idea of communication in the democratic process, one comes to see the *need* for pluralism, for a style of intelligence that relies upon imagination as well as
reason, and for an erotic context of care above and beyond mere self-
centered toleration of differences.[4]

The life of democracy, Dewey repeatedly insisted, was the life of
the community, and the life of the community was one that sustained
the process of communication. Democracy, ideally, involved the use of
social intelligence to realize each member's potentialities as much as
possible to live a life imbued with a deep, underlying sense of intrinsic
meaning and value. Far broader and richer than the mere transferal of
information, communication involves the realization of shared experiences through cooperative action that dyes our verbal and practical
encounters with each other in the hues of tacit, aesthetic understanding
and emotional comprehension.

One of the primary facets of a community is its creative ability to
care for the young and educate them so that they come to be participants in the culture, sharers of the world or universe of meanings and
values that sustain the drive of human existence itself. In short, democracy is based on fostering an educated imagination and the social dispositions to engage others through a mutual contextual understanding
of each other's beliefs, needs, desires, feelings, traditions, and identities.
Together, these features might be termed the *aesthetics of democracy*.
Over against the Enlightenment model of the state as founded on the
rationally self-evident rights of autonomous individuals—a model that
was never endorsed by any anthropological inquiry—stands the possibility of communitarian models of democracy, such as that recently
explored by Robert Bellah and others in *The Good Society*, that take an

ecological or transactional view of the way individuals exist in relation to each other.[5]

The topic of communication is critical for such approaches because it is in the processes of communication that the community arises, exists, and develops. Communication is thus not only a basic issue for political theory, but for any theory of meaning and value. From the Deweyan point of view, the labor expended on the theories of meaning in this century would have done well to take the expressive process as primary rather than to search for the absolute grounds, phenomenological or logical, of meaning in itself.

Communication is a creatively developing, historically contextualized, mutually organized process with aspects of ambiguity as well as clarity, with unconscious but pervasive depths as well as its conscious, cognitive surface. This is not to say that a theory of democratic communication is necessarily uncritical or must blandly endorse *any* point of view or agenda. Pluralism is not subjectivism. To be constructively critical, we must speak from within the framework of shared but different contexts, which can *listen* to each other and search creatively for integrative, mutually sustaining frameworks. Speaking for "our" position will not be assumed to be speaking from some ahistorical, acontextual, impersonal, universal rationality, which speaks through us as its mouthpiece. But that does not mean "our" position is groundless any more than it means it is absolute. It denotes the context from which we speak and whereby we also listen in order to establish a shared horizon with the other who speaks to us. It is this effort to incorporate the viewpoint of the other that gives rise to the possibility to self-criticism. As Donna Haraway says, "the only way to find a larger vision is to be somewhere in particular.[6]

The Enlightenment Model of Democratic Communication

It must be evident that the model of rationality—of *intelligence*—offered here is seriously at variance with the standard Enlightenment model bequeathed by Locke, Hume, Kant, and the rest. It would be worthwhile to discuss this point briefly, insofar as classical liberal democracy stems from these thinkers and their inheritors: politicians, philosophers, and citizens. It is clumsy, perhaps, to speak of "the Enlightenment concept of rationality" as if that complex historical movement presented a single, rather simple facade. It was the century of such pre-Romantics as Shaftesbury, Hutcheson, Rousseau, Vico, and Herder, as well as Leibniz, Newton, Locke, Condillac, Diderot, Reid, and Kant. Nevertheless, such a consummate scholar of the epoch as Peter Gay has dared to aim at such generalities.[7] If I now speak of the Enlightenment's view of reason, I intend to denote primarily the cluster of ideas that stemmed from the conjoint picture of the universe and human nature bequeathed by Isaac Newton and John Locke to the French *philosophers*, the American Founding Fathers, and Kant.

Rationality, according to this view, is an autonomous but rule-governed power, a universal faculty residing in particular individuals, able to manipulate ideas and recognize truth, which can be put into action by the auxiliary faculty of the will. The mind (the collectivity of these powers) recognizes discrete unitary objects (or complex objects which can be analyzed in principle into their simple components) called *ideas* and their relations, which, in turn, stand for or *represent* their *causes*, either in the external world or in the internal world.[8] Language comes about, as Locke says in the third part of his *Essay*, when humans, who desire to form a society, agree upon common signs to stand for common ideas. And so the project of communication becomes clear: Communication presents a common set of shared conventional symbols in a certain pattern that represents the pattern of ideas in the communicator's mind. If I am making truth claims, then I believe that the pattern of my ideas (or the *logical form of propositions* as later positivists would say) corresponds to the pattern of *states of affairs* in the world or descriptions of my internal constitution (such as when I say "I love you" or "I am sorry").[9]

The aim of improving communication will be the derivative one of mechanics. If presented with confused ideas, I can analyze them to see what their components really amount to, what they *mean*. It was on just such a basis that the Enlightenment could pronounce the host of technical terms inherited from Greek and Scholastic philosophy as meaningless, a project extending into this century with positivism and ordinary language philosophy. To learn the meanings of new terms, one needed to have corresponding experiences with which to match them. Having learned whatever arbitrary signs are used for those objects, the only problem remaining is to form, as exactly as possible, verbal models of ideas and their relations, which then can be understood by anyone who also has had those basic experiences and knows the reference of the signs. Communication is thus *a mechanism for establishing an isomorphic structure of representative ideas in two or more minds*.

The primary concern is simply with the correct *analysis of ideas* into their components and discerning the *laws* (or conceptual and categorical structures) that govern their connections. Just as Newton had resolved nature into its elements and laws, and given them a universal mathematical expression, so could the mind, these thinkers hoped, be brought into the domain of science.[10]

Obviously this model still compels us, however far we have gone from Locke's *simple ideas and relations* or Kant's twelve categories. Yet I think this model is wrong for a number of reasons—for so many reasons, in fact, that I cannot offer a critique here, for they reside upon extensive metaphysical and epistemological assumptions. I can simply indicate, first, that studies in the psychology of learning and language acquisition strengthen the belief that our modes of categorization, thinking, and representation emerge as developmental processes resulting from the primary act of communication.[11] Learning a first language is not an irrelevant process that may be ignored when we deal with the issue of justification, category clarification, object identification, concept structures, and so on. A case is being mounted that the Enlightenment view of concepts is, to put it bluntly, empirically false.[12] Not only is our world organized by family resemblances rather than algorithmic essences, but these structures are dynamic patterns that provide ways in which new experiences and meanings come about. This comes far closer to Dewey's view of meaning, which emphasizes the transformational, creative nature of the process. For Dewey, we can find a paradigm of meaning in the way a work of art *transforms* our experience in emotional, tacit, noncognitive ways as well as directly. [13]

Furthermore, one should reflect on the primary language situation described by Locke, one in which the essential problem is for two already rational beings merely having to *agree* on an arbitrary terminology. This is possible only for people who *already have a language*—which is to say, already have a culture. Human beings do not begin as solitary wanderers who then somehow manage to agree to invent a language. If they agree they must *already* be communicating; if they want to invent a common symbol system, they must already know what it is to *have* a symbol system; if they consciously want to learn each other's language, they must know what it is to have *learned* a language.

Presupposed at every stage of Locke's example is the fact that without having been raised in a language-using culture, there would be no possibility of communication. The model of communication as a case of transferring one pattern of ideas from a speaker's mind to another person's mind by the artificial medium of neutral signs arbitrarily and conventionally agreed upon is based upon a thoroughly derivative, limited, and fairly late instance of communication in the experience of every human being. This is not how we grow up and not how we learn. Even in his later work, Wittgenstein was fairly indifferent as to how people agreed to change the rules of language games or moved from one "form of life" to another. Rorty, too, sees shifts in the patterns governing language as irrational, arbitrary intrusions into the process of meaning.[14] The result is a paradigm of meaning as something that is rigidly rule-bound and whose translatability lies in finding exact equivalences—in other words, the paradigm of meaning is still the Enlightenment's ideal of mathematics.

This model has had political consequences. It must be granted that Locke's critique of meaning, which forced every idea to be connected at some point to direct experience if it were to have any content, thoroughly threw into question the notion that meaning could be established by authority, especially merely textual authority, but also the authority of those who claimed to have arrived at truths not easily grasped by the senses or by the ordinary yeoman. If the Middle Ages begins with Augustine's "I believe that I may understand," it ends with Locke's discussion of language in the *Essay*. A concept of liberal democracy follows from this change. Whatever the inconsistencies between the empiricism of Locke's *Essay* and certain rationalistic appeals to "the light of nature" in his *Second Treatise*, this is their common, underlying unity. The problem of society will be to ensure that each invididual is as free as possible to judge, to test experience, to communicate with fellow citizens as effectively and openly as possible.

It will be necessary to have as many facts available as possible, and as clear a language as possible for representing them. Criticism will be required to check the fancies generated by passion and enthusiasm. Of beliefs concerning those things that admit of no empirical support, as long as they do not harm, they can be tolerated. Toleration itself will be understood as *indifference* to private beliefs, which have no common, empirical bearing. It will be Voltaire's right to be wrong: the freedom from persecution because of difference in belief. Education can be secular and oriented toward the acquisition of facts and skills of analysis and inference.

I do not mean to trivialize the important values that classical liberalism generated. A brief review of humankind's effort to enforce some dogmatism or other, such as is provided by the Reformation, Counter Reformation or the Thirty Years War (events vivid to the Enlightenment theorists), shows the ideal of toleration as a genuine watershed in the history of civilization. When placed against the highly questionable values passed on by romantic nationalism—think of Rosseau or Hegel (or of Marx's romantic internationalism or Nietzsche's romantic anarchism—they become even more attractive. But insofar as they may be grounded upon a problematic model and have certain limitations resulting from that model, it becomes desirable to explore the alternatives, especially in the presence of those very romantic and emotional appeals that nationalism can use against the colorless values of testable empirical claims, toleration of difference, passionless objectivity, and rational analysis and criticism.

Liberal society seems susceptible, especially lately, to criticisms that it has ultimately failed in the social project of establishing culture. Alasdair MacIntyre, among others, has offered powerful criticisms that rationality cannot be ahistorical, but must grow out of establishing a continuous, critical tradition. Likewise, he argues, mortality that tries to rise above the mere relativism of conflicting desires must appeal to such a tradition. Liberalism, in his view, unfortunately cannot even *have* a tradition (or recognize one—which amounts to the same thing) because of its ahistoricist ethical and epistemological presuppositions.

Educational writers like E.D. Hirsch worry about whether communication will be possible if there is not even a minimal cultural historical context shared in common. Allan Bloom's jeremiad on the dangers of the "open" American mind ("open" because it is "empty" and "indifferent" to the Great Truths and Absolute Values of "The Tradition") as rushing down the dark road to nihilism because of the sinister influences of Heidegger and rock 'n' roll are well known.[15]

Dewey's Reconstruction of Reason as Intelligence

The question to be faced now is whether there is an alternative model for democratic intelligence that can secure the genuine benefits of the Enlightenment's political ideals without relying on its concept of reason, knowledge, and communication. It will be the argument of the rest of this essay that there is, and that its parameters were largely discerned in the work of John Dewey and George Herbert Mead. In his psychological research of the 1890s at the University of Chicago, Dewey, working with Mead, developed an alternative to the classic *reflex arc* model of behavior, a *circuit* of action and readjustment. The old reflex arc model saw the organism as a passive mechanism, waiting for the environment to act on it, and then reacting to it. The circuit proposed by Dewey saw the organism as actively motivated from the start to organize and develop an intelligent continuity of experience. The implications of this new model were of utmost importance for Dewey: it signaled his abandonment of idealism for a naturalistic philosophy, as well as his rejection of the notion that knowledge must aim at certainty and rigorous justification. Instead, the ideals of learning and discovery became the central themes of intelligent inquiry. In short, Dewey's circuit of learning came to provide the model for his view of the interactive nature of experience that would characterize his mature philosophy. It provides, I will argue, the basis for his theory of communication.

The article in which Dewey expressed this idea most thoroughly, "The Reflex Arc Concept in Psychology," appeared in 1896. This became the basis for the theory of learning and communication worked out in *Democracy and Education* (1916). But the theory itself was only adequately developed only thirty years later in the fifth chapter of his magnum opus, *Experience and Nature* (1925). Its political implications can be seen as the underlying theme of Dewey's major work on democratic theory, *The Public and Its Problems* (1927). I hope to indicate that the model that Dewey worked out in his earlier piece, which focused simply on individual organic activity, came to be applied to the social process of communication itself in these books. After briefly summarizing the major claims of these discussions here and in the next section, I will go on to indicate how they provide for a theory of democratic communication in which pluralism, imagination, and creativity function as central components of public intelligence.

In "The Reflex Arc Concept in Psychology," Dewey complains that certain tacit assumptions, inherited from the two thousand years of philosophy separating *mind* or soul from body, are still present in scientific psychology of the day, and that the description of the *reflex arc* is a case in point. There is first of all a *passive* organism (or nervous system) waiting to be acted upon by the environment (or external stimulus), a biological or neurological version of Locke's famous *tabula rasa*. Secondly, there is a dualism in the notion of the relation of nervous stimulation and the formation of a conscious idea, which then somehow motivates the *response*, reversing the line of causalty from the *internal* back to the *external* world. Cognition here will be essentially a matter of identification of the external fact, letting the reaction follow as a logically disconnected response expressing the emotive value preferences of the individual. In brief, Dewey says, "the reflex arc is not a comprehensive or organic unity, but a patchwork of disjointed parts, a mechanical conjunction of unallied processes."[16]

Dewey rejects the mechanical model in favor of a genuinely organic one that (1) stresses the primary *activity* of the organism as a whole that exists in dynamic relation with an environment, and which (2) seeks for *coordination* or *integration* of action in a continuous way resulting in a dynamic process of *growth* or *learning*, in which identification of *facts* and formation of *values* are functionally related phases of organizing the *meaning of the situation*. It should be emphasized, perhaps, that Dewey's concept of the activity of the organism is not like

that of the windowless Leibnizean monad, a pure center of action dis-
engaged from any direct response to its world. The organism is a
process that *intends* an environment; its activity is outwardly directed
and seeks to become determinate and focused.

Let us take a closer look at this claim. Organisms, especially
human infants, from birth on are not passive. Though Dewey makes
this point rather laboriously in this article, the essential idea is more
succinctly expressed years later in his *Ethics* of 1932:

> Observation of a child, even of a young baby, will convince the
> observer that a normal human being when awake is engaged in activ-
> ity; he is a reservoir of energy that is continually overflowing. The
> organism moves, reaches, handles, pulls, pounds, tears, molds, crum-
> ples, looks, listens, etc. It is continually, while awake, exploring its
> surroundings and establishing new contacts and relations. Periods of
> quiescence and rest are of course needed for recuperation. But noth-
> ing is more intolerable to a healthy human being than enforced pas-
> sivity over a long period. It is not the action that needs to be accounted
> for, but rather the cessation of activity.[17]

In the "Reflex Arc" article, Dewey reinterprets the classic example
of the child seeing a candle, reaching for it, getting burned, and with-
drawing its hand. There is not initial passive reception of light followed
by a response of reaching. In the beginning is the activity of *seeing*—that
is, of *looking for objects to see*. The whole sensorimotor movement is the
condition for the possibility of the act of seeing the candle: "the real
beginning is with the act of seeing; it is looking, and not a sensation of
light."[18] The response itself of grasping along with the act of seeing are
but phases of one comprehensive coordinated action. Nor is the act of
reaching isolated from seeing—there is a constant interplay between
the eyes and the hand, one guiding and modifying the other and vice
versa. In short, the act of reaching depends upon *communication*
between the visual and motor centers of the nervous system, which
aims at a single integrated result. Sensation has not been replaced by an
act of motor response; but the circuit of activity has expanded and
developed, not just been restored.

Dewey's next point is extremely significant: The fact that there is
an expanding process of activity in which the various sensorimotor
phases communicate with each other is what makes it possible for
learning to occur. In the example, the child gets burned. But organisms
can be burned without any further modification of behavior: Merely
suffering an experience does not guarantee learning. So how does the
child learn that "the candle burns?" It will only be because the burning
experience is directly seen as the *result* or the *outcome* of the *developing*

act of seeing-reaching. It is seen as "the completion, or fulfillment, of the previous eye-arm-hand co-ordination and not an entirely new occurrence."[19] The experience of the pain is not simply a new experience, but a transformation of the initial experience, with the result that it radically reinterprets the *meaning* of the whole experience as such.

The ongoing process of experience is just such a search for stimuli that significantly determine the meaning of the activity. In other words, a stimulus cannot be taken as prior to the response or *action*. One only responds to stimuli insofar as one bears upon directing action. We do not respond, for example, to any and all excitations of the sensory nerves. If we did, we would have what James called a "blooming, buzzing confusion." Rather, what we do is *focus* on those stimuli that have import—that is, meaning and value, with respect to organizing and directing activity in a coherent way. This holds as much for our highly developed conscious cognitive activity. What is a scientific experiment but such an experience, intentionally set up, which will produce the meaningful *stimulus*—the observed event—which will organize and determine the meaning of the whole situation? By flying in an airplane during a total solar eclipse, light from a star near the sun was observed to be closer than it should have been, thereby proving that the sun's gravity bent the light, an experience that did much toward establishing Einstein's theory of relativity.

Thus, in this crucial article, Dewey established an important alternative model that substituted the continuous organic process of active coordination for the passive-reactive, mechanistic model inherited from Locke and others. In the former, learning is not only comprehensible, but essential; in the latter, learning is left a mystery. The focus instead is on how mental "states" could correspond to external "states of affairs." The mechanistic model continues in various theories, from Skinnerian behaviorism to those that analogize the mind to a computer where *output* depends on *input*.

An important advocate and developer of the Deweyan point of view can be found in the work of James J. Gibson's "ecological realism." "If behavior does not consist of responses what does it consist of?" asks Gibson. "The failure of the stimulus-response formula in psychology is being recognized more and more widely, but what do we have to take its place?" This formula, he argues, "should be abandoned. A substitute formula might be that behavior consists of *postures* and *movements*." These are controlled by a *flow* of information (which is not composed of signals). More specifically, "a posture is an *orientation to the environment*. . . . The postures and movements are felt and seen *relative to the environment*." The perception of environment and self reveals the "behavioral geometry," or, to use Gibson's term, "affordances," of possible actions that organize and orient the whole organism and its activity to its environment.[20]

This model led Dewey to formulate a radically different model of rationality. Instead of regarding rationality as a fixed universal consensus *grounded* upon self-evident principles of justification, rationality is the *process itself* of transforming an ambiguous, tensive, unresolved, or *problematic* situation into one which has a settled resolution contingently open to revision by future experience. In short, *rationality* is better revealed in the methods of intelligent inquiry, in insight into the meaning and scope of the problem at hand, in creative responses to ambiguity, and continuous evaluation of the situation in light of past histories and anticipated outcomes. *Rationality* will be all one with the issue of *learning*. Finally, one of the central features of rationality will *not* be its a priori universality, but its capacity to use *social imagination*, which can take into account not only the variety of different interpretations and responses possible in one's own experience, but in the experience of others as well, and use these diverse possibilities as a means for communication in hopes of articulating commonly fulfilling, regulatory ideals. Rationality will be most evident in the social process of exploring possibilities. We can now see how this new conception led to Dewey's theory of communication and his democratic ideal of social intelligence and imagination.

Communication and the Social Imagination

"The Reflex Arc Concept in Psychology" offered a view of how a single organism could be capable of continuously coordinated activity. Sensory and motor activity work together, linked in intimate communication through the nervous system. But what of organized activity located in a group of distinct organisms, not simply in one single organism? How would it be possible for just such coordination to occur without any one physical medium, like the brain, to control the activity? Though Dewey obliquely addressed this topic in his work from the 1890s on, it was only explicitly handled in *Experience and Nature*. Here Dewey was drawing on ideas worked out much earlier with Mead, while Dewey was at Chicago, and subsequently after Dewey's move to Columbia in 1905. Mead himself gave perhaps the most sophisticated version of the theory in his lectures on social psychology, assembled posthumously under the title *Mind, Self and Society* (1935). It is appropriate that the theory of *the social self* and *symbolic gesture*, which underlies Dewey's analysis of social intelligence, should be the product of a relationship of mutual dialogue and deliberation.

Clearly, if organisms are going to achieve a kind of integrated behavior that is genuinely the result of intelligent coordination and not chance or mechanistic compatibility (which could be accounted for on evolutionary principles alone, such as the symbiosis reached by certain organisms with each still acting for its own sake), then there must be some way for each member to understand both oneself and the other members *as* members working for a common end, and have some way of interpreting and adjusting to the actions of others in light of that end. In short, there must be a basis for communication. There must be a way of explaining how an individual organism can come to see itself from the *social standpoint* and to communicate with others.

Certainly an important initial condition is a shared bodily framework, a common physical way of interpreting and acting. This does not merely require similar organs, such as eyes with retinas that can respond to a limited band of the radiation spectrum in the same way. It includes a whole range of ways of schematizing our preverbal experience.

It has been forcefully argued by Mark Johnson that our cognitive, conscious understanding is not only pervaded by a variety of such flexible, dynamic, organizational "image schemata," but that they actually establish the *conditions* for our rationality. Against those views that have sought to describe rationality or mentality as some sort of autonomous realm perhaps at best abutting the body, Johnson claims that our living bodies provide the resource for further conscious, cognitive structures. The mind, in other words, *grows* from the vital configurations the human body endows in organizing its experience. Thus among beings who have similar ways of encountering the world, similar ranges of image schemata, there is at least a primary condition for mutual comprehension and shared experience, and so of communication. But a problem still remains: How can such communication be achieved?[21]

The central theme here must be concerned with the development of symbols in lieu of anything like a physically shared nervous system to achieve the end of organized conduct. The result of such an *invention* clearly marks one of the most crucial transformations in human history: The use of symbols not only let us communicate consciously, but let us develop self-consciousness and the self-reflective arts of intelligent inquiry. Through social communication, we could come to demarcate and experience our *selves* meaningfully. Mind and civilization were the result. The brute events of nature thereafter could be significant of past histories or future consequences. Human existence could interpret itself likewise so that having a coherent narrative of one's past and one's anticipated future controlled the meaning of the present, making it possible to experience the *self* as a process of meaning.

The problem to be dealt with is how genuine participation can emerge from natural association or interaction. Mere noises or movements are not inherently *expressive*. One may scream in pain, but that is not intentionally conveying the thought "I am in pain" either to oneself or to another. Meaning arises from the *use* of such cries or gestures so that "a context of mutual assistance and direction" is achieved.[22] A whimper may be *used* to call attention to another that I am in pain. An infant may *learn* to cry to tell its parent of its discomfort. The physical event, whether sound or gesture, is treated as a means to a desired end in which the activity of another is crucial and necessary. The other is not treated as an indifferent object, but as someone who can *participate* in bringing the desired end about. The other can participate because he or she can *understand the end to be realized*. Moreover, the other will understand the end as an end not for himself or herself, but for the one in need.

From this comes the possibility of interpreting one's own behavior in light of how one imagines it will be understood by *another*; one can then respond to *that* point of view, controlling one's action from this anticipation of the other, from the social standpoint. In other words, by projecting oneself into another's position, one is able to interpret and guide one's own behavior, trying to see it as the other would, in order to achieve mutual coordinated action for realizing a desired end. When this happens *in the other as well*, then there is the possibility for communication. Communication relies upon the capacity of the members to project themselves imaginatively into the standpoint of the others in order to comprehend the dimensions of the situation as a *whole*, in terms of its *possibilities* as well as actualities.

An example may help clarify this important thesis. A father and an infant daughter may be playing with a ball. The infant has a natural desire to hold the ball or manipulate it. If the ball rolls away, she may cry until it is retrieved. From this, the child may learn to cry whenever the ball rolls beyond her grasp in order to attract the parent's notice. This would be the first step toward communication. But let us imagine a further stage of development. The father rolls the ball to the girl, and she gleefully grabs it. Wishing to repeat the joy of capture, the successful use of hand and eye to secure a prized object, she rolls the ball back to the parent so he can roll it back to the child. The child has now taken a step toward seeing herself from the parent's point of view, the one *to whom* the ball is *going to be thrown*.

Note the objective case and the future tense: in light of anticipated future activity, the child can interpret herself as the object of the action. She sees the ball functioning in the other's experience as well as in terms of her own. Indeed, this move to seeing the ball from the other's role allows, for the first time, her to become aware of her own role, her own point of view (here, the catcher).

We obviously have here the elements of a game. In throwing the ball, the thrower just does not "throw," but throws *to* the catcher. To do so, he must see his throwing from the catcher's point of view. This is what guides his own act of throwing. The better one controls one's coordination, the more likely it is that one throws the ball directly to the catcher's hands. Furthermore, the thrower knows that the catcher is not simply a passive receiver, but one who is trying to interpret her own activity, catching, by taking *the standpoint of the thrower*. She is trying to read the gestures of the thrower as indications of the thrower's action. Both players are taking the standpoint of the other, using that standpoint to guide and control their own actions, in order to bring about a common end: the playing of catch. By virtue of this, a pattern of communication (and miscommunication) can be established. By throwing back one's arm, the thrower can say, "I will throw this one far." If after doing so, he rolls it on the ground, the catcher can understand either that she misunderstood or was "faked out" in a joke:[23]

> The heart of language is not "expression" of antecedent thought. It is communication; the establishment of cooperation in an activity in which there are partners, and in which the activity of each is modified and regulated by the partnership. To fail to understand is to set up action at cross purposes.[24]

This "fusion of horizons," to use Gadamer's expression, allows objects to be perceived in terms of their meanings. Objects are comprehended in light of shared and sharable projects of action in which goods can be realized or fail to be realized. A ball bouncing wildly over a field can become, instead of mere visual object, a "foul ball" or a "home run." "To *perceive*," says Dewey, "is to acknowledge unattained possibilities; it is to refer the present to consequences, apparition to issue, and thereby to behave in deference to the *connections* of events."[25] This is what allows one to treat the present as full of meaningful portent: One takes the immediate as a symbol of a process full of potentialities, and one can then respond to those potentialities in light of the values they portend—good, evil, or indifferent. From the social point of view, then, we are able to symbolize the meanings of events in light of mutual projects of activity.

Symbolization, in other words, is constituted from the *shared, social capacity to imagine participatory activity*. Through the *social imagination*, we are able to have a world of meaning. We not only imagine the other as participating in our action, but we imagine ourselves in the other's action and both actions together as determined by a shared, communicated objective or end to be realized in time. The present moment is continuously interpreted in light of its possibilities for this end—and the end itself may be changed or modified in light of what the present reveals about it.

Finally, the *horizon of time*, which allows objects to be interpreted as *symbols*, is a horizon only revealed through this mutual act of *social imagination*. By communication the experience of action itself as a developmental, temporal, end-oriented structure embracing past, present, and future, emerges and is symbolically expressed. This *shared* discovery of symbols through temporality discloses the possibility of having a *self*, a *life* that develops in time and has meaning—not the *meaning* discerned in propositional attitudes about states of affairs, but *narrative* meaning. We understand ourselves in terms of being able to tell stories of our family and parents, our childhood, the decision we made or the trials that befell us, and such stories are *mutually comprehensible*. In fact, one of the best ways to become familiar with an alien culture is to be told the life story of one of its members, as many of the classics of anthropology do, showing us what it means to be an individual in that context. To have a self is to have a history and a future, a culture, a language, a mythology—in short, a *world* that is not the purely objective world viewed by impersonal, acultural, atemporal rationality.[26]

The self thus discovered in time is discovered along with other selves. To put it as succinctly as possible: Without the social imagination, there would be no sense of temporality, no symbolization, no sense of individual selfhood. One discovers the self not as lost in the anonymous herdlike character or "the They" (or, in German, Das Man) but as a distinct, individual participant in a mutual project. The self, in other words, does not emerge as a self-sustaining atomic unit which then *happens* to be externally related to similar units by universal, rationally apprehended *laws*—the old Lockean model.

Human beings *may* be thus related, as when they unintentionally bump into each other in a crowded hall. There may even be situations where *at first* they may be so related, as when strangers are thrown together in some disaster or as inmates may be initially thrown together in a prison. But such situations usually get readily transformed into social situations in which mutual coordination and organization are established and communication occurs. After bumping, people may apologize and change directions; survivors will work together; a prison evolves into an extremely hierarchical social order in which minor social gestures, like lending a cigarette, may come to indicate weakness or dominance. From mere physical proximity, from merely being *along-side* others, because of developed social skills, individuals can come to form a community.

The self, then, which becomes the reflective, responsive, and interpretive core of identity, is a self that arises from its capacity for imaginative embodiment of others as a basis of communication. It does not merely exist alongside others, but participates with them as a fulfillment of the meaning of its existence. As the anthropologist Clifford Geertz notes, there is a cultural *style* to having a self, whereby one may speak of having a self *Balinese style* or *Moroccan style*.[27]

The self has such a deep impulse for its social realization that it experiences a crisis when its social identity is put under stress or conflict, or is altogether shattered. The symbolic life of a culture articulates in a vivid and dramatically concrete manner the shared life of the community. From such projects comes the *idea* of civilization. An individual life takes on its significance because it inhabits a world as well as an environment. Worlds are those symbolic systems that are shared by members of a culture. They include mutually comprehensible ways of designating the ways of meaning within that culture as well as the modes of valuation. When the idea itself of securing a meaningful, value-rich existence becomes consciously articulated, it is the idea of civilization itself functioning as a guiding ideal of social action. The aim of civilization is to secure those conditions whereby genuine human communities can flourish. This is to say, civilization is the effort to establish those physical and cultural conditions whereby people can meaningfully live together, and this requires above all the possibility for communication in the deepest and richest sense that term can have.

Pluralistic Intelligence

Beginning with his novel account of organic behavior, Dewey was led to a model of communication in which different points of view within a shared activity were required in the very idea of symbolic interaction. If intelligence lies in the exploration and evaluation of the various possibilities of a shared situation so that meaningful and fulfilling conduct may result, then it seems highly desirable to have a number of *alternative* perspectives that nevertheless are in contact with each other and can work together toward a common end.

Just as eye and hand establish a mutually coordinated path for coherent action, and just as the slightly different perspectives of each of the two eyes result in a form of stereoscopic vision in which objects have depth, so a community requires a plurality of *adjacent*, communicating foci for its own cultural world to have direction and depth. Imagination may be defined as the ability to project possibilities from actualities. It is because we see the possibilities of something that it appears as an *object* in the first place. Here again, the views of classical pragmatism and the work of James Gibson agree. The object has meaning because we anticipate modes of possible conduct. As we shift possible horizons, the object acquires its defining *profile*, its definiteness.

Vision allows us to see a world not merely because we have two angles of perception, giving us double profiles of the same objects. Each eye is in constant motion, shifting its own view of the world back and forth. This process also makes the world of objects have definition and proportions. Experiments show that with one eye closed and the other rendered immobile, the visual field loses its clarity and intelligibility. In the same way, it is because we are constantly in the *process* of shifting possibilities around the objects in the world that they gain their *edge* and focus. The Cartesian mind is like the fixed eye: it aims at one changeless point of view. Deweyan intelligence is like the mobile plural centers of vision, multifaceted and engaged in imaginative play. It is this latter process that sees a world in its complexity and depth. The plurality of communicative centers, their different perspectives on the world, and the dynamic process of communication itself whereby these imaginative horizons are not only put in play, but shared, is what gives us a meaningful world.

The kind of culture that fosters and utilizes this kind of pluralism enhances the very possibility for the development and maintenance of communities in which human beings can live meaningful lives. Communities arise from the act of communication, and communication is an art in which the social imagination allows one to take a number of different perspectives of the same situation. Organizing these different perspectives depends upon working out coordinating frameworks, general ends of action, which can be used to interpret, regulate, and evaluate the specific actions of the participants. To attain this end, it is necessary for the members of a community not only to develop reliable critical methodologies, but they must also be able to frame *integrative ideals* that have *aesthetic power* to organize and attract the desires of the members of the community. Resolutions of conflicts must seek new avenues of action that maintain otherwise conflicting values and perhaps even transform old, cherished values in light of new values that grow out of past activities. For a community to maintain itself, it must have ways of symbolizing itself *as* a community *to* itself; this has been one of the primary functions of mythology in culture.

More importantly, perhaps the primary type of communication that occurs in communities is the transmission of culture—that is, the process of teaching and learning. The imaginative and aesthetic context in such a situation is one of care and support. At the root of the social imagination, in the very process of learning, there is a presupposed context of love that is vital for communication to succeed. Dewey's term for such a community secured by the cultivation of intelligence was *democracy*.

One of Dewey's most significant discussions of communicative practice is found at the beginning of *Democracy and Education*. This is not accident: The entire question of education itself for Dewey is a primary instance of the need for an imaginative, intelligent manner of communication by means of which the values and meanings of a culture are transmitted and transformed.

Rawls sees the primary instance of democratic rationality in the enlightened self-interest of isolated rational beings placed behind the "veil of ignorance." Habermas looks toward establishing the ideal conditions for communicative praxis aimed at rigorous justification for truth claims—any contextual claim is ultimately critiqued from an ahistorical, *transcendental* point of view. Not only do both views ignore the role of imagination, both ignore the need for an erotic horizon of care as fundamental for a community. Human rationality cannot be separated from the fact that it has been developed in each person by a social process in which the welfare of the learner was the primary good aimed at.

Dewey, on the contrary, sees the type of communication that occurs in the ideal learning and teaching situation as providing the paradigm mode of democratic intelligence. The teacher must be able to understand the concrete characteristics and capacities of the students, and to work with them in such a way that they come to acquire new methods for cooperation and communication, as well as new information and expanded experience.

Educational communication, says Dewey, is a prime necessity of any society because we are all going to die. Without the transmission of culture through definite means, each generation will have to acquire all its arts for itself. Indeed, for any community to operate and survive, those arts must be in place at least to some extent. In a strong sense, then, the need for culture, and thus for education, is an intrinsic feature of human *biology*: We need it in order to survive. The helplessness of the human infant indicates the need for an organized, communicating group for its nurture to succeed. This is what it means to say that we are cultural beings and, in a fundamental way, learners rather than knowers:

> Society not only continues to exist *by* transmission, *by* communication, but it may fairly be said to exist *in* transmission, *in* communication. There is more than a verbal tie between the words common, community, and communication. Men live in a community in virtue of the things which they have in common; and communication is the way in which they come to possess things in common. What they must have in common in order to form a community or society are aims, beliefs, aspirations, knowledge—a common understanding—like-mindedness as the sociologists say. . . . The communication which insures participation in a common understanding is one which secures similar emotional and intellectual dispositions—ways of responding to expectations and requirements.[28]

Individuals come to form a community not by merely coexisting in physical proximity, nor even by working for a common end, for this may be accomplished automatically, as with the parts of machines working together without necessarily involving any conscious, guiding awareness of a shared end. A community, for Dewey, lies in the fact of *participation*; they all imaginatively share each other's world. If the various individuals involved are

> all cognizant of the common end and all interested in it so that they regulated their specific activity in view of it, then they would form a community. But this would involve communication. Each would have to know what the other was about and would have to have some way of keeping the other informed as to his own purpose and progress.[29]

There must be "a sharing of purposes, a communication of interests."[30] What constitutes a community, then, is not a Rawlsian sense of *fairness* arrived at by self-interested rational individuals, nor some transcendentally grounded context of absolute truth, but a contextualized, ongoing activity in which members come to participate in or share the ends or ideals that guide and control the meaning of those actions. There is a set of values, usually aesthetically envisioned rather than merely cognized, which coordinate the various activities of the members into a continuous, progressively directed experience.

It is important to stress that the primary relation of individuals to each other presupposes a context of care and love. This, too, is a fact of human biology. A community survives by nurturing its young, raising them, and gradually imparting to them the skills for being fully participating members of the society, ready, in turn, to become caregivers. This context of care is presupposed in the very process of educational communication. It is deeply linked with our ability to learn. If the teacher is *careless* with respect to the subject matter and the students, or even worse, filled with hatred and disdain, it will be nearly impossible for learning to occur. This erotic horizon of care if probably one of the most neglected preconditions for understanding. The openness that learning requires for self-transformation assumes an environment of love.

From the natural capacity of the organism to respond and form habits to features in its environment, social methods can be used so that the younger members of a group gradually come to anticipate the distinctive ways of the group. From this they gradually come to apprehend the ends in light of which they become active participants rather than mere accessories. The sense that they are being cared for by those who teach allows them to become open to the possibilities of conduct that are taught. The bridge between mere behavioral training and genuine responsive, affective understanding must be crossed:

> Setting up conditions which stimulate certain visible and tangible ways of acting is the first step. Making the individual a sharer or partner in associated activity so that he feels its success at his success, its failure as his failure, is the completing step. As soon as he is possessed by the emotional attitude of the group, he will be alert to recognize the special ends at which it aims and the means employed to secure success.[31]

Thus, by a mutual effort between those educated in the culture of the group, those who inhabit the communicative world, and those struggling to become members, there must be an imaginative—and erotic—effort on the part of both to grasp the experience and world of the other in a mutual project of care, if education is to occur. Intelligence (which includes the emotional and affective dimensions as well as the cognitive) is called forth for two such diverse worlds to come together.

The process in which this happens is a genuinely *transformative* one for the experience of all members, for the world of the communicator as well as that of the recipient:

> Not only is social life identical with communication, but all communication (and hence all genuine social life) is educative. To be a recipient of the communication is to have an enlarged and changed experience. One shares in what another has thought and felt and in so far, meagerly or amply, has his own attitude modified. Nor is the one who communicates left unaffected. Try the experiment of communi-

cating, with fullness and accuracy, some experience to another, especially if somewhat complicated, and you will find your own attitude
toward your experience changing; otherwise you resort to explica-
tives and ejaculations. The experience has to be formulated in order to
be communicated. To formulate it requires getting outside it, seeing it
as another would see it, considering what points of contact it has with
the life of another so that it may be got into such form that he can
appreciate its meaning. Except in dealing with commonplaces and
catch phrases one has to assimilate, imaginatively, something of
another's experience in order to tell him intelligently of one's own
experience. All communication is like art. It may fairly be said, therefore, that any social arrangement that remains vitally social, or virtually shared, is educative to those who participate in it.[32]

In any communicative act whereby social participation is realized
and a community comes to be, Dewey is saying, there must be an imaginative, artistic transformation of the experiences of those involved.
This imaginative act is not merely creating new ideas or modes of
expression. From the beginning, each tries to embody the role of the
other as concretely as possible, not merely in terms of who the other is
right now, but in terms of *how the other can develop and grow*. Such an
imagination is intrinsically *social* and *erotic*. It is in the process of developing and using our social imagination that we discover our own
unique, distinctive ways of exploring possibilities, and transforming
our experiences so that they become meaningfully expressive. The personal imagination grows out of the experience of the social imagination. Just as the young are transformed through the educative process,
we should see communication (and meaning) as a transformative
process itself. This is far from the Enlightenment ideal of discovering a
bare identify so that an isomorphism of cognition and object is realized.
The process has a continuity that has meaning, but its identity is the
identity of the growth of a story rather than a fixed, bare self-sameness
underlying the phenomena.

Democracy as the Culture of Communication

I think we can now see that Dewey holds that communication carried to its fullest development becomes art. One merely has to turn to
Dewey's *Art as Experience* to see that this is so. There is no space here to
carry out this analysis further, especially since I have done so elsewhere.[33] It is important to grasp that communication is the basis of society for Dewey, and at the heart of communication we find the themes

of the social imagination, education, care, and artistic expression, themes that stand in opposition to the Enlightenment models of Rawls and Habermas.

Human beings are cultural animals born to die. For this reason the young must be born into a world of love and care. Culture exists because of the process of education, and the young come to have their identities shaped as learners of a civilization. This is done through communication, whereby they learn to embody imaginatively new and diverse standpoints, which allows the meaningful use of symbols to occur. The exploration of imaginative possibilities transcends any finite algorithmic concept of rationality. Most fundamentally, the communication involved especially in education presupposes a tacit context of care. The young are raised not only to be communicants in the world of the symbols of the culture, but caregivers and teachers in their turn. The nature of intelligence is to share in the capacities for the meaningful transformation of experience.

The implications of these conclusions for a theory of democratic culture are too vast an undertaking here. "Regarded as an idea," says Dewey in *The Public and Its Problems*, "democracy is not an alternative to other principles of associated life. It is the idea of the community itself."[34] A democracy is a community that sees its primary task as the realization of communication in the profoundest sense possible. It is because the members of the community can project the possibilities of action and see the consequences of lines of conduct that they can come to make intelligent decisions. Whatever natural enjoyments result from human association, "they demand *communication* as a prerequisite."[35] This is why Dewey saw education as the most significant process in any society, for it is the means whereby a society can become a community. "To learn to be human is to develop through the give-and-take of communication an effective sense of being an individually distinctive member of a community."[36] The life of a democracy in particular is bound up with the art of its communicative abilities.

We can discern that a theory of democracy is primarily a theory a *civilization*, not just a political theory. Without a democratic culture in which the social imagination is developed and used, no formal set of political procedures will be effective. Political structures exist to help develop the ability of the members of a community to live lives that are imbued with a rich aesthetic sense of significance and worth.[37] Such communities must be efforts to organize stable horizons of care in which the young can grow to maturity with a sense of progressive participation and worth. Without this most fundamental security, the freedom from violence and hatred, care for one's deepest physical and

emotional needs, there is little possibility for communication or, consequently, for community.

A democratic culture needs to be trained in the arts of imaginatively embracing a diversity of perspectives; this is the primary condition for communication. The unifocal, atemporal "God's-eye view' of
Enlightenment rationality cannot do this. The democratic imagination
understands others in order to talk with them; it talks with them in
order to work out conflicts so that values can be successfully integrated cooperatively.

This does not eliminate the need for criticism. Criticism emerges
from this mutual exploration of possibilities and is most effective
when presented in a context of care rather than one of hostility and
self-certainty.

New ideals may also be discovered through this exercise of critically disciplined intelligence as well as imaginative idealization. For the
democratic imagination to flourish, it must have a strong grasp of the
historical traditions by means of which people come to identify themselves as members of groups. It requires a discipline of the aesthetics of
human existence—those compelling worlds of symbols within which
the human project of trying to live with a pervasive sense of meaning
and value may be realized. This is why the humanities and the arts as
well as the sciences are vital components of a democratic education, for
they do not only provide the contextual means for understanding others, but call upon our own imaginations to become, even if only for a
moment, the other.[38] When this process becomes reciprocal, then there
is the chance for communication and the possibilities for respect and
understanding, and, perhaps for love.

8

Pragmatism Reconsidered:
John Dewey and Michel Foucault
on the Consequences of Inquiry

⊰≈⊱ ⊰≈⊱

Frank J. Macke

Conceptions of Deweyan Pragmatism as Problematic

Richard Rorty has, within the last decade, gained a very strong following among theorists and researchers in the social and human sciences.[1] Especially for those who are disenchanted by the staid, uncritical, and linear approach of *empirical* research (within the normal science paradigm) and who are, at the same time, mystified by the difficult—and often conflicting—positions and polemics of postmodernist discourse, Rorty has seemed to emerge as a clear-thinking, straight-talking voice of reason. One important consequence of his popularity is that he has played a key role in bringing the concept of pragmatism back into vogue. Rorty seeks to extend the late modern and poststructuralist inquiry into humane, emancipatory practices by recovering the spirit of practical liberalism found in the work of John Dewey.[2] Yet, as helpful as Rorty has been in restructuring and redirecting some important epistemological concerns of philosophy and the social sciences, his invocation of Deweyan pragmatism as a watchword for the future of critical inquiry and *social hope* requires closer investigation.

Rorty's interest in reinvigorating the important work of John Dewey—or the interest in Rorty among social and human scientists, for that matter—is certainly not what is at issue. Instead, and as I will argue throughout this chapter, my primary complaint resides in what I take to be an absence of intellectual depth and consistency that accompanies the current use of pragmatism in a number of social science works and, most surprisingly, in the work of Rorty himself.[3] The idea of the pragmatic in these works is frequently taken to mean practicality, utility, "matter-of factness"—connoting, at least to me, a species of situational ethics rather than a concern for the human consequences of theory and reflection. Who is to say, after all, what is *practical*, what is *of use*, and what the relevant facts, in fact, *are*?

Further, the term is used on occasion without a clean grasp of the complex philosophical interests and doctrines of Peirce, James, and Dewey—or (as with Rorty) an appeal is made to the sensibility of Dewey or James, but without properly situating them in the discursive context to which their respective works are addressed. In other words, if the doctrine of Deweyan pragmatism is to be plucked out of its historical, epistemic context—*id est*, turn of the century American bourgeois liberalism—and placed in the middle of late modern, poststructuralist, or postmodernist debate, the doctrine may well appear trivial and fossillike. Or worse, the doctrine might be used to trivialize or repress certain aspects of postmodernist thinking in order to advance a particular aspect of ostensibly necessary (i.e., practical and useful) bourgeois liberal culture.[4]

Of even greater importance, however, is the following implied concern: For what purposes has the work of Dewey now become relevant? More than just a few twentieth-century doctrines, pseudodoctrines, and discursive practices operate under (or at least are commonly associated with) the name of Dewey. And, as Alexander reminds us, decoding Dewey's work—despite the numerous stereotypes and applications of his doctrine of instrumentalism that have found their way into the fields of education and social philosophy—is not a simple matter.[5]

It is well known that Dewey began his philosophical training as a Hegelian. But this matter of historical fact serves less to clarify than it does to confuse. And this is because Hegel, as a name for philosophic inquiry, is without a fixed referent. Quite simply, there are at least two versions of Hegelianism. First, there is the Hegel whose name denotes a mode of dialectic inquiry whose work has served to frame a conservative, if not reactionary, critique of the development of modern thought. Hegel's *synthesis* here can be said to *positively exist*. For example, if we are to make the claim that bourgeois liberalism is the finest form of government we could ever achieve—a point that Rorty himself has made in *Consequences of Pragmatism* and *Contingency, Irony and Solidarity*—we then see it as the *end of history*, and we vow to preserve it on that basis. Second, there is the Hegel whose dialectical system and whose concept of the history of experience has inspired a century of radical thought. It is this latter sense of Hegel that bears the closest resemblence to Dewey's thinking, and it is from within this latter sense that we can gain the clearest picture of the value of a sensitive reading of Dewey's work.

This chapter seeks to develop a concept of Deweyan pragmatism as a contemporary doctrine for the human sciences. I will focus on three important aspects of pragmatism and the human sciences relevant to Dewey's work. First, I will examine the question "What is pragmatism?" in the context of contemporary discourse, paying particular attention to pragmatism's function as an analysis of sign production and social meaning. Second, I will examine the function of art and the concept of aesthetic experience—which is "the very heart and center of Dewey's thought." Dewey's concern for creativity and art in experience, as well as his notion of intentionality (the reflex arc), habit, and the role of the body, is highly compatible with the phenomenology of Maurice Merleau-Ponty, and thus can be read as thematically consistent with the post-Hegelian interests of what was later to become postmodernist discourse.[6]

My argument is that Dewey's emancipatory interests were, for their time, very much in keeping with those of Foucault—particularly with respect to the role of art and experimentalism in the human sciences. Thus it would be a mistake to read Dewey as strictly tied to the tenets of late nineteenth-century liberalism. In a final section, the chapter will offer some observations on the status of communication inquiry as *writing*, as well as the desire to address some of the discipline's fundamental theoretical problems by way of conservative, *reformist* rhetorical devices—such as solidarity and conversation.

In short, Dewey's instrumentalism, viewed as a relevant, consequence-oriented species of pragmatism (of the type that Rorty and his many followers seem to desire), cannot, properly, be taken as a philosophical doctrine to be appended, uncritically and carelessly, to the modernist conception of "man," knowledge, institutions (i.e., power), and the subject. Rorty's concept of emergent critical discourse as *solidarity* (or Bochner's *pragmatist* conception of inquiry[7]) succeeds only in circumventing, in postponing the challenges that postmodern critical theory poses for the status of knowledge and discourse in the human sciences.

Precisely because it is concerned with the consequences of critical and reflective activity, pragmatism cannot assume a neutral philosophical stance. Thus, the dialectical tension that obtains between the *normalizing* discourse of modernist social science and the emancipatory interests of Foucault's human sciences can only be sustained as a form of theoretical equivocation. If the interests of a thinker like John

Dewey are to be invoked as a response to knotted matters of inquiry, they ought not be used as a shortcut.

The Meaning of Pragmatism

Any reflection on the meaning of pragmatism will inevitably remind us that pragmatism is in essence a discourse on the consequences of thinking. It is the self-consciousness of discourse: thinking aware of its own presence and its own history—discourse manifest to consciousness through the moments of its effect. Interestingly, this mode of thinking itself has its own consequences. One possibility is to consider the effect as the ground of thinking, in the sense that we are all borne as effects of discourse into a world already in motion. As such, effects and their traces form the context and the direction for discourse, which in turn frame the range of meaningful performative possibilities and effective practices for persons, institutions, and human organizations. Another possibility, one that is less a matter of discourse's self-fascination—in effect, valuing, measuring, and counting both its attributes and its admirers—is to consider the effect in the moment of its birth. Here, we ask: What does it mean for an effect to become known as such? Or more precisely, What forces combine to yield the effect that now anchors the time of our discourse?

In an important sense, the answer lies in the odd transformation that occurs when one shifts from examining the idea of *work* as a verb to the idea of *work* as a noun. The latter, it can be said, appears to us as the effect of the former. Input generates output. But it can also be said with equal facility that the latter guides the former. Our work, after all, is not "for nothing." Work, as noun, would then describe the empirical representation denoting the achievement of an objective: an ideologically driven labor. We can imagine the painter, the woodcarver, the factory worker, the writer, fixed upon the object of his or her work, willing it to its proper completion. Yet at the same time we are well aware of the limits of this portrait. The mature noun eventually detaches itself from its parent verb and assumes an existence of its own. At the moment the labor is given a name it is already complete; as such, it no longer belongs to the imagination—that is, the will—of the laborer.

Moreover, we are also quite aware that the laborer (even *as* willing creator) does more than dream about the completion of the object. He or she will grow hungry, sleepy, bored, lonely, and the object, the effect of work, will become a surrogate for many longings and aspirations—perhaps to the point of signifying its own disappearance. It is almost as though we could assert that for the worker there is no work, there is no object precisely because the object in itself, the intended effect, is no longer important. It disappears in the moment of creation, only to reappear in the name of the mature work in the moment we can observe its deployment as a tool in yet another creative act.

The work, then, becomes a stranger to the labor of creation. Or, in Foucault's thinking,[8] the working becomes not the cause or even the motive, but the threshold for the work: the verb is only a threshold for the noun. The working doubtless entails a completed notion of the work. On this basis we can also say that once visualized, the creative act, the working, is already complete. But even more fundamental to the creative act are the instruments implicated in the moments of production, of which antecedent work is certainly one.

But this is not to make pragmatism speak the language of an exhausted Marxism. Pragmatism is certainly not a discourse on the alienation, victimization, and enslavement of labor. To the contrary, it might well be argued that pragmatism as a modern framework for philosophic inquiry is very much intended to *displace* the romantic, nostalgic inclination to somehow reconnect the life and motif of the worker—and the event of creation—with the work produced.

Pragmatism, after all, is situated in the legacy of modern thought as a thematic of work and production (or, as Thayer phrases it, of *meaning* and *action*[9]). From the theoretical stance assumed in this essay, I will assert that its primary original contribution concerns the experience of creative work (both verb and noun), not its political structure (or its disavowal). In this sense, pragmatism is about the genealogy of performance. It addresses the cultural and historic conditions (i.e., discourse) of authentic production as an inspired act. And on this basis, it has little to do with the psychology and economy of production as matters of material cause. But it can also be said that if pragmatism succeeds in this displacement of an earlier romantic impulse, it does so as a kind of inverted positivism, reasoning from *effect* to *cause*, and reconceptualizing the meaning of both.

It acknowledges, fundamentally, the consequences of human action: the effects given birth by both the activity and the sleep of reason, which in turn define the presence of human existence, effects that outline the basis of all human action in their signification of the time of our thought, configuring the *momentous* as both the premise and the course for reason. It is from this perspective we can perhaps begin to gain a sense of how Peirce, James, and Dewey adopted a view of pragmatism that can only be labeled as a species of both empiricism and existentialism.[10] It is well known that during the period marking the birth of the modern era, the focus of philosophic inquiry turned from idealism toward materialism and existentialism, from what *ought* to what *is*, from eidetic form to empirical content. Pragmatism, in this sense, stands as a logical extension of the Enlightenment's passage. As a philosophical system, its invention and application signify rationality's continual insistence on the development of a positive empirical foundation for the material things that are, ostensibly, of consequence.

The consequence of human action, the effect, becomes a sign, a manifestation—or as Foucault has termed it, a *positivity*.[11] These positivities, finite in number and therefore saturated with significance, define our presence. They constitute all that is within our grasp. Ultimately, the discourse of these positivities (a discourse that is spun into networks, revealing itself only in fits and in tangled codes) becomes that which beckons us to reflect and understand. Through, over, and under these positivities (sign-effects) an interminable number of possibilities cross. Simply, in the life of the human being who generates a work and in the field of creator-creation (or what Deleuze and Guattari designate as *desiring-production*[12]), there is a multiplicity of elements defined by the presence of a sign. Pragmatism's work, thus, is to bring to the surface all the elements within a given, momentous positivity—a consequence that for the elements is *of consequence*— and let them speak.

I am fully aware that for many this will appear a strange view of pragmatism. It may well be argued that this interpretation of pragmatism is more a sketch of postmodern rhetoric of the sort one might find in the work of Foucault, Derrida, or Lyotard than it is an explication of pragmatism as an American (U.S.A.) school of thought. Perhaps so. Yet—and especially in the context of what has happened in the last half-century of modern thought—one can only ask: But what else would pragmatism be? What else remains for pragmatism, considered as an intellectual doctrine to be taken seriously, to do?

Pragmatism, viewed from the standpoint of the current intellectual milieu, is certainly not reducible to the set of assumptions that frames, say, policy analysis in a liberal democracy or rational argumentation in the social sciences. It is simply not the mastery of thought directed toward a particular, albeit desirable, outcome. Or, perhaps it may have been just that at one time, at a time when Enlightenment concerns dominated the historical framework of both science and pedagogy. But it can no longer function as an intellectually satisfying mode of discourse if this remains its sole capacity. It is not simply a matter of observing that the intellectual winds have shifted away from the revolution in consciousness implied by the Enlightenment—away from the end of history, dialectical materialism, psychology, structuralism, hermeneutics—and toward so-called avant-garde modes of criticism. Instead, it is a matter of how we are to approach the creative process; it is a matter of how we frame the process of production. So, the issue is, no doubt, one of sign production, but the question that will emerge time and again concerns not how a sign-effect is engineered by the activities of reason (which Foucault, in *The Order of Things*, discusses at length in terms of *general grammar*[13]), but how the activities of reason are linked, through a normalizing process, to the valuation of certain sign-effects.

To focus on the creative *process* as a logic of invention—that is, to insist that a particular manner of creation plus a formal mode of inquiry (and scientific communication) is inextricably linked both to the production and existence of a given effect as a matter of causal correlation—is, ultimately, to dwell along the contours of the absurd. It is as if we were to think that the American Revolution led to the invention of constitutional democracy, or that the so-called Dark Ages gave birth to the Renaissance. It is to insist that the consequence of mind, the effect, is enveloped by the creative process—and that we have a clear idea of what this process is and how it works—when in fact it is the other way around. The creative process, the activity of mind, is enveloped by the effect. The effect is always immanent—and imminent: a clear and present body both in outline and in substance. In essence there are so few valued and expressive materials—materials given birth as effects of a truly nameless process (perhaps an impression, a dream, a delirium, an accident)—and so many thoughts that flow among them.

Dewey, the Creative Process, and Pragmatism's Connection with Continental Thought

It can well be said that art, creativity, and imagination figure prominently—if not centrally—in Dewey's philosophy of instrumentalism (especially in his later works). As Alexander has concluded:

> Nothing in Dewey's philosophy makes sense without understanding his philosophy of experience, and it is impossible to comprehend this without coming to full terms with the aesthetic dimension of experience. This is no external or superfluous part, but rather the innermost living heart of everything Dewey had to say. . . . We may have a legitimate basis for regarding Dewey, along with Wittgenstein and Heidegger, as one of the truly monumental thinkers of the century, not because of his negative "deconstruction" of "the tradition," but

because of his courageous promise of a creative and yet critical vision of human life.[14]

But having identified creativity as a central component of Dewey's work, we will nevertheless be sorely disappointed if we are to insist upon reading his philosophy of creative experience as some sort of logic or method of discovery.

For Dewey, the work of creativity is signified by its effect (in the name of *art*); the creative process is understood by way of his metaphysics of experience. Here, a meaningful experience is one that both arises from activity and possesses a unity of sense. Dewey describes it as "defined by those situations and episodes that we spontaneously refer to as being 'real experiences'; those things of which we say in recalling them, 'that was an experience.'. . . In an experience, flow is from something to something. As one part leads into another and as one part carries on what went before, each gains distinctness in itself. The enduring whole is diversified by successive phases that are emphases of its varied colors."[15]

Dewey's Hegelianism might suggest that he, like Hegel, views experience as an eidetic progression, as a chain of semiapprehensible *shapes* of consciousness. But Dewey's Hegelianism only marks a jumping off point for his thinking. He abandons the idealist conception of *Spirit* and *reflective consciousness*, and speaks instead of embodied response, of activity, of experience not as a progression or series, but as a course—or, rather, a *mosaic*—of creative exploration. Alexander, on this very basis, interprets Dewey's concept of experience as creative, holistic, and aesthetic, and his work makes a novel and compelling case that Dewey's inquiry into the domain of experience is, simply put, a journey along the contours of feeling.[16]

Alexander succeeds in underscoring Dewey's emphasis on organic elements in his particular doctrine of instrumentalism. The term organic is important. Dewey thought it quite important to identify not the cause or origin in creative or artistic production; instead he was concerned with the *nature* of creative experience and artistic work. And in his conception of the nature of primary experience, Dewey pays particular attention to the feelings and life world of the subject as designating the primary *form* of experience. The feeling and sensation of a subject inhabiting and thus fully immersed within the living environment—his or her vital experiential grounding—constitutes the instrumental value of all experience.

Smith has summarized Dewey's concept of experience as a journey along the contours of *lived sensation*: "Primary experience consists of all the encounters, the doings and sufferings of experiencing subjects in the surrounding world. It is this experience which sets the problems and provides the data for the construction of secondary objects of reflection."[17]

What becomes particularly clear at this point is the manner in which Dewey's *instrument* merges, so to speak, with Merleau-Ponty's (and Foucault's) *body*.[18] *Instrument* describes the lived conditions of experience and the existential basis for all artisitic expression. Similarly, the *body* constitutes the domain, or *inhabited* realm, of all expression and perception. Moreover, the syncretic operation of sensation in the body is such that the functions of perception and expression cannot truly be separated. This particular conjunction of Dewey with Merleau-Ponty and the French tradition succeeds in shedding new light on the existential and semiotic phenomenology of human perception, and it permits us to assert the following: perception, in other words the speaking of the world into and through our domain of sensation, is meaningful, instructive, and, importantly, *sensuous,* and erotic precisely at the point where it is expressive.

Moreover, the body's expression (i.e., its rhetorical being) to a caring other, is meaningful, instructive, sensuous, and erotic when it is perceptive. Perceptive expression and expressive perception, then, combine to denote a significant thematic of the creative person—for both pragmatism and phenomenology—as a performed-performing instrument of consubstantial and coextensive artistic experience.

On this basis it may well be argued that Dewey's concept of experience is *best understood as a phenomenology.* And, in this important respect, it is most apparent that Dewey's concept of lived experience is not qualitatively or perceptibly different from that of Merleau-Ponty (although, it should be noted, each derives from somewhat different Hegelian traditions). The discovery of the *habitual body* is as much a Deweyism as it is a hallmark of modern French phenomenology. Alexander has noted that, for Dewey, "the habitual body is the primary means and material of expression; it is the primary medium of meaning."[19] As such, habits are

> capacities for treating different situations similarly in terms of relevant similar features. They constitute a complexly structured reservoir. Therefore, Dewey oberves, "Repetition is in no sense the essence of habit." Repetition is not what makes habit possible; habit is what makes repetition possible. . . . Habits are the constitutive structures of organized responses. Any particular adjustment in one part of the field may mean a transformation of the whole system. Dewey is insistent on this point that "The whole organism is concerned in every act to some extent and in some fashion."[20]

The sensation and vitality of the body within the space and movement of a gesture finds its energy in artistic form. This, in a number of ways, is a statement that not only succeeds in capturing a key element of the concept of experience upon which Dewey's instrumentalism is based, it also serves as a thematic reflection of Merleau-Ponty's phenomenology, Heidegger's ontology of the work of art, and Foucault's genealogy. In this formulation, feeling (or, more specifically, passion or *eros*) is not reducible to the mere performance of a *necessary function*. Instead, as primary experience, it energizes the perceptive/expressive moments of dwelling among and within the known—and soon to be discovered—effects of discourse. As Dewey concludes:

> Tangled scenes of life are made more intelligible in esthetic experience: not, however, as reflection and science render things more intelligible by reduction to conceptual form, but by presenting their meanings as the matter of a clarified, coherent, and intensified or "impassioned" experience.[21]

And on this very basis, we can take note of an even more important point of merger between Dewey's instrumentalism and the lived body experience of French phenomenology and postmodernism: it is only in passion that we can find the birth of meaningful art, reason, and instructive experience, as it is only in passion that we can find the birth of ourselves. As Foucault has claimed, it is in the instances of rupture, in the intense, erotic, and frenzied moments of transgression that we are exposed, and given over to the possibility of primary experience: in the space of such a moment, we are both shaken from the fragile foundations of the infinite (language's false promise, its tragic heaven) and riveted to the astonishing, enveloping, and exorbitant encounter with the speechlessness that reminds us of our ultimate limit.[22] It is in this moment of possession—an infinite moment within our finitude—that we are lead to say what cannot be spoken. It is in this moment of artistic stammer where the idea or form of the work (or *statement*, as Foucault elaborates in his *Archæology*[23] is not so much revealed as given birth. It was in this moment where, according to Foucault "death *communicated with communication.*"[24]

So, it seems fair to conclude that Dewey's instrumentalism, as with Foucault's postmodernism, is an inquiry into the limits of communication. Dewey's work is an inquiry into the formation of habit as it relates to the vitality of speechless primary experience. On this basis, it serves as a critique of limiting and imprisoning institutions (education and pedagogy in particular), institutions that have failed to address the modern emancipatory imperative—and, more importantly, institutions that have failed the culture they were designed to serve, the culture of critique: science, art, and inquiry. Dewey's work, looked at from the inside out, identifies the experience of artistic expression and perception in terms of its function in discursive praxis.

The most prominent stereotype of Dewey that has emerged, however, places Dewey in the role of advocating modern practical discourse. This, it seems, is the result of looking at his work from the outside in—that is, taking note of his political commitments prior to examining the metaphysical premise of his philosophy of creativity. Instances of Dewey's writing, it is true, give off the clear impression of Dewey being a modern yankee patriot, a social reformer, and a bourgeois liberal philosopher. And on the level at which he produced such statements, perhaps such an impression does offer a fair characterization of his relationship to his time. But it is also true that writers cannot fully choose the social milieu into which they were born to speak. More to the point, for the very same reasons that nostalgia makes for poor critical reflection, we are in error when we study too closely the visible and overdetermined markings of the time and place situating a writer's thought. While it can be said that these monuments tell a part of the story, we cannot let the ephemeral drown that which is eternal in the work; we cannot lose sight of the topology when we find ourselves entranced by the topography.

So, Dewey's relevance to the emancipatory interests of semiotic phenomenology, poststructuralism, and postmodernism—particularly as they have been articulated in the French tradition—has been rarely appreciated. Aside from his development of a theory of learning (and education) related to experience, Dewey is rarely credited for having articulated much of anything important to the work of contemporary thought.[25] This is largely a matter of historical development and emphasis, and, as historical events go, seems rather unfortunate. Unlike James and Peirce, Dewey's work has been read mostly in America. And aside from the recent work of Alexander, Kestenbaum, and Rorty,[26] Dewey has been, according to Gunn, "misapprehended for the most part either as an educational philosopher with a penchant for democracy, or as a moral philosopher almost naively committed to the application of scientific methods to the solution of social problems."[27] Since he was not basing his work on Husserl, Heidegger, and Freud, but on American Hegelianism, Emerson, James, and Peirce, he simply was neither read nor given due credit by the influential writers of the first half of the twentieth century who addressed similar intellectual problematics and thematics.[28]

But, like Foucault, his work is about art, passion, experience, and life. The moment of rupture possessing the artist who steps beyond the limits of communication is not for nothing and it is not for its own sake; it can equally be said that it is, as well, a moment (and crucible) of rapture. Perhaps this idea finds its clearest expression in Foucault's brief reflection (1977, p. 51) on the work of Michel Leiris: "Perhaps this 'difficulty with words' also defines the space given over to an experience in which the speaking subject . . . is brought back to the reality of his own death: that zone, in short, which transforms every work into the sort of 'tauromachy' suggested by Leiris, who was thinking of his own action as a writer."[29]

Tauromachy, literally a bullfight—a contest of wills between the capability of the trained reactive performer and the energy of the enraged beast—represents the difference between artistic creation as discursive practice and artistic performance as practical discourse. In the former, sensation gives birth to thinking (in other words, lived experience produces discourse); in the latter, thinking merely gives birth to itself—or, rather, discourse reproduces, so to speak, asexually, mechanically, without the benefit of experience, without the vitality of human energy. "The bull's keen horn . . . gives the torero's art a human reality, prevents it from becoming no more than the vain grace of a ballerina."[30]

Pragmatism as Experimentalism: Dewey and Foucault

The encounter with the existential *limits* (as opposed to *uses*) of language does not on first glance appear to belong to the agenda of pragmatism, even when viewed in the context of postmodern discourse. Yet when one examines Peirce's elaborate theory of signs, sign production, and meaning, and the broad problematic to which it is addressed, as well as Dewey's theory of art (as both effect and event) and experience, one begins to notice that semiotic production and translation are helplessly tied to one another: we simply cannot speak a thought if we are not first aware of a manner of expressing it in another way.[31] Again, pragmatism begins with the self-consciousness of discourse. It attempts to match discourse with the presence of its effect and the rules for its generation. Another way of putting it is to say that although there is *a process* (for lack of a better term) for arriving at or expressing an original idea, we have been tragically deluded about what this process is or how it is to be carried out. We have through the development of Western consciousness been led to think that the limit of language and its meaning is located in its articulation rather than in the presence, finitude, and capacity of its forms.

In his early and much ignored work on the intriguing turn-of-the-century writer Raymond Roussel, Foucault observes:

> The prisons, the human machines, the tortuous ciphers, the whole network of words, secrets, and signs issue marvelously from a single fact of language, a series of identical words with two different meanings, the tenuousness of our language which sent in two different directions, is suddenly brought up short, face to face with itself and forced to meet again. . . . The identity of words—the simple, fundamental fact of language, that there are fewer terms of designation than there are things to designate—is itself a two-sided experience: it reveals words as the unexpected meeting place of the most distant figures of reality.[32]

It is well known that Roussel's work, elusive and cryptic—and particularly difficult to appreciate in its English translation—was inspirational to André Breton and a generation of surrealists.[33] The surrealist project was in large part a matter of Marxist rebellion toward the Enlightenment canon of artistic and scientific representation combined with an attitude of playfulness. Their work was an artistic negation of historical form, and they saw Roussel as making a compatible political statement. Despite the fact that their group constituted the one continuous source of praise for his work, Roussel nevertheless had little use for the surrealist project, dismissing it at one point as *"un peu obscur."*[34]

Foucault's study of Roussel reveals, in Rousselian fashion, that Roussel as an experimental artist was in fact much more concerned with the *density* of an artistic sign than its *destiny*. His concern was not to waken the public to the presence of truth whose revelation would alter the progress of human events, but to problematize the meaning of art by disrupting the coherence of its most recognizable signs. For Roussel and for Foucault, any sign can be read as a heterotopia, a common locus of chance encounter "like the umbrella and the sewing-machine on the operating table."[35] Through clever machines designed to produce odd, circumstantial, schizoid, and strangely logical effects of language, Roussel assembles on the surface of the recognizable literary and material sign incomparable and incredible things, "splendid particles"—monstrous plants, crucified jellyfish, adolescents with sea-green blood.[36]

Roussel's talent was to show that the *unpresentable* not only was *not excluded* from the realm of discourse, but was embedded in its most mundane and indifferent expressions. A community's hospital has both a maternity ward and a morgue, and this very same maternity ward will yield murderers, geniuses, lawyers, farmers, rapists—so, how will we regard this hospital, this indispensable sign of a community's well-being? The sign that names the space of a hospital, or any sign, is at once the site of at least two interpretations. As Foucault writes:

> Language is a thin blade that slits the identity of things, showing them as hopelessly double and self-divided even as they are repeated, up to the moment when words return to their identity with a regal indifference to everything that differs."[37]

The distance that separates the presentable from the unpresentable, music from noise, an original work of art from a repetition of form, vanishes when one examines them in a light that collapses all rules of proportion, interior qualities, and boundaries of distinction. These rules, qualities, and boundaries are only historical fixations; confronted with an inquisitive science, with an attitude of experimentation, with techné in its pure sense, history momentarily vanishes.

In a sense, the argument that flows from Foucault's critical discussion of Roussel establishes a foothold for the position he later takes in the *Order of Things*, a position that problematizes the concept of discourse—in all its manifestations—as representation. While it is quite true that Foucault's conceptualization of the problematic of representation cuts in directions generally unheard of in the American pragmatist tradition (as it has evolved to this point), his concern for what a creative artist must endure (as both sign-producer and person) in the theater of rule-giving institutions is very much in agreement with the position taken by Dewey in his *Art of Experience.*

There is actually more than just a compatibility that obtains between the experimentalist thinking of Dewey and Foucault. The emancipatory interests of Foucault are clearly relevant to Dewey's concern for the relationship of history and human experience, particularly in terms of the culture that has come to contextualize the processes of inquiry and the institutions that contain the activity of learning. It can well be said that the nucleus of Dewey's work (that is, the creative dimension in experience) must either be read alongside the interests of contemporary philosophical discourse, or we will only succeed in doing violence to the originality of his thought. Or, as Giles Gunn has emphasized, "it would scarcely be an exaggeration to say that John Dewey is presently the most misunderstood major thinker in America today."[38]

There is a very important sense in which Dewey's concept of æsthetic experience offers significant depth to the role of the philosopher implied by Foucault. This is not to suggest that Dewey's work entails a program of activity that could serve to pin Foucault's postmodernism down to some sort of liberal, progressive, reformist agenda.

Although Rorty as a recent champion of Dewey's work has time and again argued such a position in defense of his preference for bourgeois liberalism as an end of history,[39] there is a rather strong case to be made against this interpretation of Dewey.[40]

For example, Rorty, after reflecting on the connections between Foucault and Dewey with respect to their mutual dissatisfaction with the social sciences, makes the following argument:

> Man as Hegel thought of him, as the Incarnation of the Idea, doubtless does have to go. The proletariat as the Redeemed Form of Man has to go, too. But there seems no particular reason why, after dumping Marx, we have to keep on repeating all the nasty things about bourgeois liberalism which he taught us to say. There is no inferential connection between the disappearance of the transcendental subject—of "man" as something having a nature which society can repress or understand—and the disappearance of human solidarity. Bourgeois liberalism seems to me the best example of this solidarity we have yet achieved, and Deweyan pragmatism the best articulation of it.[41]

Rorty's reading of Dewey is indeed faithful to Dewey's text—that is, as far as he is capable of situating it. The problem here is that Dewey's articulation of pragmatism as a political doctrine for his times is clearly no longer relevant, particularly if the only problems of art, experience, and understanding (and, as well, of ethics) are the *practical* ones on which Rorty has tended to concentrate.

Perhaps this argument is best expressed by way of a simple formula. If it is the case that Dewey's so-called practical—or bourgeois liberal—focus on art and creativity is in fact a broad inquiry into the received view of history and ethics, it should follow that Dewey's thinking on creative praxis *as doctrine* can only be understood if it is read alongside other such doctrines. It makes considerably less sense to examine Dewey's doctrine of creative praxis in terms of his liberal optimism.

My argument all along has been that Foucault is probably the most relevant contemporary exponent of this sort of thinking. Rorty's attitude toward Foucault is dismissive, to say the least. Rorty chooses to problematize Foucault by reducing the substance of his work to a matter of utility. Rorty writes: "I disagree with Foucault about whether in fact it is necessary to form a new 'we.' My principal disagreement with him is precisely over whether 'we liberals' is or is not good enough. Foucault would not appreciate my suggestion that his books can be assimilated into a liberal, reformist political culture."[42] This is a tired reason to invoke Dewey's political agenda. In essence, it typifies a kind of reactionary response to postmodernism that has become prevalent in the social sciences: the lament that *hope* must necessarily be yoked to a patriotic sentiment, or nostalgia, for traditional, liberal practices. The silent assumption embedded in such nostalgia is that hope can and should legitimately exist in the political implications of the current intellectual climate because it seemed to exist at one time; or, possibly, that hope ought to endure in liberal praxis (as well as the theory that feeds it) given that a philosopher of Dewey's stature appeared to believe in it so strongly.

What is most fascinating is that Rorty's interpretation of what Dewey has in mind for pragmatism *and* what Dewey valued as a philosopher is surprisingly off the mark. It is not at all clear in reading Dewey, especially in tracing the development of his metaphysics of experience and in his unique perspective on science and art, that his political writings (on liberal culture) and his theory of progressive education best describe the nucleus of his philosophy. Dewey is indeed concerned with praxis as a function of a pragmatic view of experience and culture. However, if one follows Dewey's model of the philosopher as artist, particularly in the reading given by Alexander, one begins to see that the idea of philosophy that begins to take shape is not significantly different than that offered by Foucault.

For both Foucault and Dewey, the philosopher must experiment. Foucault writes:

> The role of an intellectual is not to tell others what they have to do. By what right would he do so? . . . it is, through the analyses that he carries out in his own field, to question over and over again what is postulated as self-evident, to disturb people's mental habits, the way they do and think things, to dissipate what is familiar and accepted, to reexamine rules and institutions.[43]

From this perspective, we gain a clear sense that Foucault does not view philosophy—that is, the work of intellectuals and the sign-effects (i.e., the texts) that they produce, as fundamentally different from the approach taken by Roussel toward writing. To test ideas in her or his own field, to question, to disturb, to dissipate the familiar—these are the tasks of any artist whose objective it is to both live and express oneself in an original way. And if, as Foucault argues in the *Order of Things*, the intellectual is by nature of his or her task a human scientist (as opposed to a social scientist),[44] then we see that for Foucault the scientist and artist are one and the same.

This is the same argument that Dewey makes in *Art as Experience.*[45] Although Dewey does not approach the problematic of art and the museum in quite the same fashion that Foucault discusses the life of the sign and its doubles, they both appear to have arrived at much the same argument. This point is made by Alexander: "Dewey finds in the work of art the distinctive ability to bridge the dualism of modern culture which seeks to separate the æsthetic from the world of ordinary experience."[46]

So, if at this level one is to insist that we must name the difference between the positions taken by Foucault and Dewey, the difference would clearly reside in a matter of focus. Dewey examines the duality of art as a manifestation of experience and as a meaningful sign-effect from a broad, social perspective. His work is a critique of historical and cultural practices that separate the existence of the art object from the life of the community, and that mystify the process of creativity, establishing a logic of cultural valuation based on principles of exclusion and separation.[47] Foucault's position zeros in on the instrument of the artist *as writer*. What Dewey might say about a painting or a musical composition, Foucault could say about words and language. Each and every word and grammatical sign is a union of history and culture, of experience and resemblance. Language possesses an undeniable material and monumental quality. We speak with it, and it addresses us. But we experience it as well. It affects us. As we concentrate on the markings of what was once said, we journey through their forms and rhythms, and get lost in the fold.

Toward a Radicalized Conception of Science/Art

To pursue life and experience as art, thus, necessitates an active commitment to imagination and experimentation. And it entails a commitment to respond to the logic of exclusion and isolation, a logic that can be traced back to a desire inherent in the manner in which history is practiced—namely, the desire to perpetuate itself. In this sense, all history is about the same thing: it is about extending the narrative. This narrative, that narrative, any narrative, is grounded in the fear of one's nonexistence, of one's own extinction. Put simply, we shape the future to incorporate ourselves.

The purpose for the production of a narrative form and content, as Bataille reminds us, is grounded in a "a desire to modify the relations that exist between a man and his fellow-creatures."[48] And in this modification, the unacceptability of the present and the markings of its terminal direction emerge as the *motif* of desire to modify human relations—in other words, to classify, construct, reconstruct, limit, or otherwise modify human communication. So in addition to saying that we shape the future to incorporate ourselves, we seek to protect our imagined presence from those elements that threaten to contaminate or defeat the corpus of our works (in other words, the traces that document our identity across time). It is the narrative that places us, our works, and our name in proper perspective.

It has become an established point that, irrespective of who is telling the story, a primary narrative function is to treasure—in what might be described in Freudian terms as a neurotic cathexis—a certain continuity for experience.[49] (The story's audience will always encounter its primary narrative forms as forms of the familiar.) In this narrative event, this decisive, ego-centering moment of condensation, a moment of ecstasy—an encounter with power—is sustained by the subject privileged to speak and be taken seriously. If this telling is done in the context of the authority of inscribed history, the historical subject is then formed (as, for example, the community's responsible individual) and his or her experience becomes subject to what Deleuze and Guattari have termed *territorialization*.[50] Communication ethics is reduced to a kind of social grammar.

To respond to the rules demanding a closure of experience's space is to live both inside *and* outside them. Which is to say that they must be viewed as a threshold of possibility (and thus fully tested and transgressed) and not taken as ends in themselves. The ethic that emerges is certainly not to be taken as a kind of *postmodern imperative*. Rebellion for its own sake, or rebellion practiced as a new morality or late-modern virtue bespeaks a devolution of discourse into noise. Rather, the ethic that lies at the edges of this discussion, understood as a kind of expressive ecology, describes the space of artistic experience. It is the embodiment of the creative act. It is a discursive encounter with discourse wherein discourse comes face to face with its limits; it is discourse's encounter with itself.

In *Tombeau de l'Intellectuel*, Lyotard asserts that "an artist, a writer, a philosopher . . . experiments. He does not need to identify himself with a universal subject and to take in charge the responsibility of the human community in order to assume those of creation."[51] What Lyotard suggests is that we find the creative dimension of experience not in the denotative or performative constitution of rules (i.e., in their economy), but in the general notion of "making of one's life an experiment." In a sense, this entails an active deconstruction of such deceptive notions as the *ethical self*, the *judicious individual*, the *reasonable man*—or even more perplexing, the life that teaches by example. What, after all, does a life teach? What is given in the lesson, and what is made unthinkable? What is kept secret, and what is disavowed? The artistic instinct, thus, is given birth by a peculiar indifference to the history of what constitutes *great persons*. It is fueled by a bemused understanding that the consciousness generated by the artistic sign may well be taken as the thinking and laboring of a *madman*, or what Foucault has termed a *dangerous individual*.[52]

As such, experimenting artists live with, and perhaps thrive from, suspicion. They must know that they can take temporary refuge only behind their work, and that their public will always attempt to sniff them out, to make them speak, and to give narrative form to their secret experimental urges. Artists must know that in speaking, they are being asked to redefine the limits of expression—almost, perhaps, to remove such barriers for others (i.e., the less courageous)—and to affirm this limit for themselves.

Artists are then faced with the inescapable knowledge (*savoir*) that their experience, life, and name are inseparable from their work. Or, as Dewey contends, it must be understood that they *are* their work.[53] They constitute the surface over the underground force from which artistic expression is sprung. Although Dewey's metaphysics of experience can be traced closely along the contours of the phenomenology of Merleau-Ponty, Dewey charts his course for a somewhat different purpose. His interest in locating the perceptual process undergirding lived experience outside the pattern and flow of narrative history, of course, is to highlight the principal source of dualism in the life and language of the human actor. But it is also to set a path for the philosopher.

By way of an experimental method—in which the philosopher quite literally sacrifices herself or himself to the machines and traps of language in order to master them from the inside out—the philosopher offers a key to unlock the secret tucked deeply inside the folds of discourse. The machines of language are the philosopher's science. The philosopher then *becomes* art. His or her life and work, inseparable, occupy the form of a gesture; his or her life and work become the instrument that is played.

Postscript: Writing about Communication

This essay began as commentary, as a missive issued in response to a certain tendency of writing. In effect, it began as communication about writing. I would like to end by giving consideration to the idea of writing *about communication*.

Writing, and its speech, is the art of the philosopher. It is an intellectual work, yet in its constitution it resurfaces and refigures what being *intellectual* or being *an* intellectual might mean. Writing names the presence, the space, of the writer. In its mirth or desperation it corresponds to the tonality of music or the texture of the plastic arts. In its effect and in its form it is curved. In the spontaneity of its construction—all semantic and syntactic decisions, after all, are carried by a flow of feeling, regardless how labored they may seem!—it only hits its mark (so to speak) with a glancing blow, knocking it to one side, bumping it, nudging it, perhaps caressing it, but never penetrating it at its core. When its object anticipates its touch, it will prepare itself for its arrival and exchange. The intellectual who merely reiterates the work of her or his history, who merely attempts mastery of the rules of the game as played out by the grand masters, is always fully anticipated. A bed will be made for her or his arrival.

To be art, writing must, therefore, generate the pleasure, the ecstasy, of surprise. It must say something new and we must be able to locate something new in reading it. What is most important is that it is never a formal exercise. If it is true that in its ecstatic element it produces a moment and thus refigures the time of our thought, it is because the experience of the writer—her or his doubts and urges—has brought us to a different threshold; a new plateau and a new field of inquiry.

Writing, as both an artistic and philosophic mission constituting the legacy of our intellectual work, must then become self-conscious in its creation—as pragmatism first taught us that we must (because we *can*) view discourse and its double, its effect, simultaneously, as one. Pragmatism's essential ethical doctrine is that a thinker does not think just anything, and that the thinking that emerges over time can be examined in terms of the history of its effect, its praxis, instead of the authority of its history. Pragmatism, viewed as the self-consciousness of discourse, guides the work of the creative intellectual by way of a sensitive responsibility to the consciousness and history of practices and their sign-effects. Pragmatism as an intellectual movement in the United States, thus, has been an attempt to free the intellectual from a dogma embedded in the narrative of Western thought.

As the example of Roussel demonstrates, writing is the praxis of artistic vision. It is an example of what Lyotard refers to as "the increase of being and the jubilation which results from the invention of new rules of the game."[54] The act of writing thus entails an experiment with familiar forms, with the connection and unity of objects that inhabit our space. And because these familiar forms are "already there" in our silence, they occupy a fixed position in our speech. Because of their fixedness, they develop a certain gravitational pull, they crowd our movements, and they distract our imagination.

In what has long been labeled *natural science*, the horizon of knowledge has been continuously redefined by the scientist's creative vision enacted through experimentation. The philosopher is similarly committed to such experimental praxis. As a science, this praxis is fundamentally about communication. It dwells in a world to which only the scientist is privy, and in its movement out of this world and into another it is heard to speak in a language never before articulated—comprehensible, at first, only *as language*, but later through its forces of attraction, the hypnotic powers of its mystery and elusiveness, it begins to register new forms of perception and thought, coupling and decoupling images from their concepts. This science ultimately becomes poetry, but it never abandons its experimental vision for the romance of its lyric, and its urges can never quite escape its environment of doubt.

Dewey captures the essence of this work in his reflection on Keats—which could just as easily apply to the work of Roussel: "Ultimately there are but two philosophies. One of them accepts life and experience in all its uncertainty, mystery, doubt, and half-knowledge and turns that experience upon itself to deepen and intensify its own qualities—to imagination and art."[55]

Lyotard offers a similar comment0 concerning two forms of knowledge:

> It is therefore impossible to judge the existence or validity of narrative knowledge on the basis of scientific knowledge and vice versa: the relevant criteria are different. All we can do is gaze in wonderment at the diversity of discursive species, just as we do at the diversity of plant or animal species. Lamenting the "loss of meaning" in postmodernity boils down to mourning the fact that knowledge is no longer principally narrative. Such a reaction does not necessarily follow. Neither does an attempt to derive or engender (using operators like development) scientific knowledge from narrative knowledge, as if the former contained the latter in an embryonic state.[56]

Lyotard reminds us here that experimental method is not something that is already laid out, like the shiny instruments on an operating table, ready to be performed. There is nothing particularly recognizable, particularly conversant, or particularly communicative in the work of writing. It is directed toward the horizon of narrative knowledge, but it cannot be accounted for in the logic of the narrative.

Richard Rorty claims that he is following Dewey in his argument for a *cultural conversation* of philosophic and scientific inquiry.[57] In this model we seek to find, among all the confusion and disparate vocabularies and purposes, some common ground—and thus a basis for positive understanding. Despite its appeal, or perhaps because of it, Rorty's conversation ultimately fails Dewey, as it ultimately fails the authenticity of knowledge borne by transgressive experimentation in the human sciences. In the end, Rorty and his many adherents would like to drag all the pieces in the mosaic of contemporary intellectual work onto familiar ground. As Lyotard warns, this in effect is history, the familiar narrative, swallowing up the curiosity of scientific labor. Although curiosity may eventually kill the cat, its absence transforms it into a four-legged zombie.

So, the communication that I have been writing about in a section playfully labeled "postscript" is that which has come to be equated with conversational, recognizable, familiar exchange. As such, it is no accident that Rorty's attempt to recover Dewey's liberal, reformist politics—and then deploy it as a grounding for the private romance of intellectual adventure—has been taken as a matter of long-awaited common sense in the field of study that now calls itself *communication*. For communication not only studies discourse in terms of its familiarity, it judges its effect in terms of its relation to narrative knowledge. In the end, one can only see that the logic of our contemporary communication ethic is circular. That which is worthy is that which communicates, and given that our fundamental epistemic truth is "you cannot not communicate," one finds little space for unfamiliar discourse—that is, discourse whose very design is to endanger the rules of the game. Narrativity has fully emerged as the *altar*[58] of communication studies wherein matters of structural/performative coherence and consistency are not simply matters of taste, they are matters of function and sense.

Moreover, as long as communication remains faithfully bonded to a pursuit of narrative knowledge in its ethnography, group and organizational theory, and performance studies, as well as in its post-Enlightenment humanist and futurist ethics, it will have only occasional *use* for the human science of philosophic inquiry, particularly in terms of its praxis of writing about communication. In short, writing will always seek to excite, refigure, and expand communication, but communication will invariably choose to disarm writing.

V

The Effects of Communication

9

George Herbert Mead and the Many Voices of Universality

❖ ∘ ❖

Mitchell Aboulafia

There are many ways to frame the so-called debate between modern and postmodern thinkers, even as we struggle with the attendant difficulties of deciding what we mean by these camps and who precisely are their members. One of the ways to approach the divide is through the concept of progress. While there are clearly modernists who would not wish to be associated with this notion, numerous figures in this camp have defended some version of it. Postmodernists, on the other hand, have been quite articulate in specifying their varying degrees of hostility to the idea, in part because it is viewed as inevitably leading to metanarratives that obscure the idiosyncratic and deny difference.

The sheer multiplicity of approaches to the idea of progress serves to recommend caution. There are those, for example, who might declare that they are for progress in the same breath that they disparage theodicies that promote teleological end runs around history. Others would argue that we had best cast aside this troubled and mystifying term, while certain pragmatists would defend it as an essential feature of emancipatory discourse. For thinkers in this last school, progress can in large measure be evaluated by looking at the degree to which parochial views and prejudicial behaviors—those that subvert respect for persons based on accidents of birth and circumstance—no longer dominate our interactions.

George Herbert Mead would have supported this form of enlightened cosmopolitanism. Yet his universalism was tempered by a commitment to local and individual experience. This showed itself in his interest in the novel and unique, and in his account of the multiplicity of *generalized others*. His theory of linguistically grounded intersubjec-

179

tivity can be viewed as an attempt to negotiate a path between the twin dangers of abstract universalism and romantic particularism. In the pages that follow I will address Mead's standpoint with an eye toward understanding why he thought increased understanding between diverse groups valuable and likely. I hope to show that his concept of the generalized other can serve as a key to Mead's qualified universalism, as well as to his nonpositivistic understanding of science.

I should note in advance that I will not be concerned with evaluating the accuracy of Mead's portrayal of the science(s), but with how his views of science reflect political and ethical sensibilities that are still worthy of our attention. The first part of the paper provides an overview of Mead's position on these matters. The second takes up some of the key concepts of his model of intersubjectivity. The final section examines Mead's notion of universality by addressing the relationship between authorial voice and the generalized other.

I

George Herbert Mead was committed to the notion that science, properly understood, and social progress are intimately linked. (The call of progress had for Mead, as it had for Dewey, an Aristotelian ring: human flourishing through the actualization of socially redeemable potentialities.)[1] Why this faith in science? Because Mead saw it as a method that enhanced natural human capacities to solve problems and because of its ultimately democratic character. In Mead's view science should be approached as a conversation, guided by a general method, among those dedicated to fostering verification of hypotheses in a manner that does not bow to political and economic power. He would more than agree with his good friend John Dewey when the latter declares in *Individualism Old and New:*

> No scientific inquirer can keep what he finds to himself or turn it to merely private account without losing his scientific standing. Everything discovered belongs to the community of workers. . . . the scientific attitude is experimental as well as intrinsically communicative. If it were generally applied, it would liberate us from the heavy burden imposed by dogmas and external standards.[2]

This view of science will appear as simply naive to many contemporary readers, mistrusting as they do discourses claiming any form of general validity, especially when they happen to be promulgated by technocratic *elites* who make proclamations regarding objectivity as they serve those who finance their research. But this obviously would not be the *ideal* of science for figures like Mead and Dewey. As a matter of fact, only by turning to ethical and political concerns, as opposed to purely epistemological ones, can we appreciate the importance of science for thinkers in their camp. Science held out the promise of a sphere of influence in which each would be entitled to his or her say without class, economic, or racial biases subverting claims. Further, science in Mead's (and Dewey's) view is a methodical extension of a rather commonplace competence—that is, problem-solving reflective thought—and not an abstruse methodology that only experts can understand or avail themselves of.

> Scientific method . . . is nothing but a highly developed form of impartial intelligence. . . . It is not teleological in the sense of setting up a final cause that should determine our action, but it is as categorical in insisting upon our considering all factors in problems of conduct, as it is in demanding the recognition of all of the data that constitute the research problem.[3]

This activity, and the knowledge gained from it, could assist in breaking down, for instance, damaging barriers between men and women, and between various ethnic groups. It had the potential to accomplish this by establishing unbiased investigation as a valued norm and through enhancing our understanding of the sources and character of these divides. In its method and results, science had much to offer a democratically oriented society, not least of which was its potential to create a language that could transcend local and national boundaries. Mead, after all, was a dedicated internationalist who could declare, "We are struggling now to get a certain amount of international-mindedness. We are realizing ourselves as members of a larger community. The vivid nationalism of the present period should, in the end, call out an international attitude of the larger community."[4] And he thought that he had discovered just the type of scientific social psychology that could support such enlightened goals.

Mead developed a desire to extend the range and quality of interaction between individuals and groups rather early in life, and it remained a lifelong end. As a young man he seriously considered a life in Christian social work because it would allow him to serve others. But this option posed a problem, which he noted to a friend in 1884. "I shall have to let persons understand that I have some belief in Christianity and my praying be interpreted as a belief in God, whereas I have no doubt that now the most reasonable system of the universe can be formed to myself without a God. But notwithstanding all this I cannot go out with the world and not work for men. The spirit of a minister is strong with me and I come fairly by it."[5] And he could still write in 1923 in the context of a discussion of democracy as an ideal:

> The most grandiose of these community ideals is that which lies behind the structure of what was called Christendom, and found its historic expression in the Sermon on the Mount, in the parable of the Good Samaritan, and in the Golden Rule. These affirm that the interests of all men are so identical, that the man who acts in the interest of his neighbors will act in his own interest.[6]

It is worth noting that Mead's father, Hiram Mead, was a minister in the Congregational Church and a teacher of homiletics at Oberlin Theological Seminary. His mother, Elizabeth Storrs Billings, whose career included serving as president of Mt. Holyoke College and teaching at Oberlin College, was a deeply religious woman.[7] Oberlin was an institution with a culture that had long viewed improving the lot of humankind as a religious duty, and it became a center for liberal theology and progressive thought in the 1880s and 1890s.[8] Mead attended Oberlin, beginning his studies in 1879. His lifelong penchant for universalism can be traced in part to his Christian roots, and it no doubt would have placed him in the camp of secularized Christian apologists for someone like Nietzsche. Mead was not a believer, but neither was he a pagan, at least not in Lyotard's sense.[9]

I raise this aspect of Mead's background to suggest that the almost missionary zeal with which he spoke about enhanced possibilities of human communication was not an accident of his conversion to pragmatism or social behaviorism. Quite the contrary. I also raise it to suggest just how far removed Mead is from certain Nietzschean and Heideggerian sensibilities that permeate postmodernism, in spite of his affinities with specific aspects of it—for example, its antifoundationalism. Internationalism was no less than a moral calling.

Yet focusing solely on the importance of universality at the expense of the individual, local, and particular can be seriously misleading. Mead was not Condorcet. He had read his Hegel and nineteenth-century romantic thought. His goal was not to eliminate difference but to somehow maintain it in a larger whole, a whole that for Mead develops in part through enhanced opportunities for communication. The postmodern response, if one can speak of one response, would be to suggest that this is often the claim of totalizing thinkers, Hegel being the most infamous example. The given becomes subsumed or drawn into a metanarrative that only pays lip service to difference.[10] Mead no doubt would rebuff such charges, citing his concepts of the "I" and the generalized other, which I will discuss below, as paths for addressing the issue.

There was indeed a lifelong tension in Mead's thought between romantic impulses and enlightenment ones, between the longing to give the unique its due and the drive to see commonality.[11] The unique for Mead is neither an unfathomable idol nor an illusory surd. In the context of historical "development," unique and novel events should be viewed as transformative moments insofar as they become integrated with other (past) events and conditions to shape new presents. The continuity that results is defined from the perspective of the present, for it is in the domain of the present that past events live.[12]

In short, in Mead we have a secularized (left) Hegelian alternative to postmodernism. It tells us that difference and novelty can be respected while some form of historical continuity is maintained. And this continuity occurs not simply because it is the winners who write history, but because the dynamics of historical interactions allow for concrete developments that may alter who we are in a coherent (and at times progressive) fashion. As a matter of fact, this version of events would have it that it is only after certain attitudes are developed—for example, seeing others as part of a common humanity, and an ensuing denunciation of prejudice—that particularity can be given its full due; that is, it is only in light of discourses on universality and universalistic attitudes that hostility to, or grudging tolerance of, difference evolve into sanctified norms that speak to acceptance and affirmation of the other. That we have often failed to realize this ideal would not diminish its importance for Mead. In the modern world, due to specific historical conditions, we have unrivaled opportunities for realizing it.[13]

Mead's stress on (possible) historical continuity in the face of the novel, as well as his emphasis on the defining character of the present, will strike some as proof that he lacks an understanding for peoples and persons of the past, especially those that have been left by the wayside as the juggernaut of the Western (or any) world rolls by.[14] No doubt this is a serious issue and would require an extended discussion, one that would have to include an evaluation of Mead's concept of sociality and his claims regarding the objective validity of perspectives. Instead I will turn, momentarily, to Mead's contentions regarding the importance of localized communities in the emergence and sustenance of mind and self in order to address his sensitivity to particularity.

But what specifically do Mead's musings on democracy, science, and progress have to do with Mead as a communication theorist? We might begin to answer this question by pointing out that a necessary condition for progressive political achievements—for example, the extension of the franchise to those who do not have it—is being able to see the excluded other as part of the same (or part of an interlocking) communication network(s). This appears to be trivially true in the sense that one must share common frames of reference in order to be defined as a citizen (or even a human being for that matter), and that the task of including the excluded entails bringing them into the fold, or revealing that they already are in it.

In Mead's case, however, there is an interesting twist to the process. The possibility for expanding such frames of reference is not seen solely in political terms (in a narrow sense of power politics), but in social psychological and linguistic terms; that is, it is to be found in the manner in which mind and the self originate in symbolic interaction and develop through enhanced opportunities for communication. Habermas has a natural ally in Mead, and it is no accident that he drew so heavily on him in his *Theory of Communicative Action*. Mead tells us:

> The advance in the practice and theory of democracy depends upon the successful translation of questions of public policy into the immediate problems of the citizens. It is the intensive growth of social interrelations and intercommunications that alone renders possible the recognition by the individual of the import for his social life of the corporate activity of the whole community. The task of intelligence is to use this growing consciousness of interdependence to formulate the problems of all, in terms of the problem of everyone.[15]

For Mead, modern historical conditions and human psychology conspire to lay the groundwork for the (possible) realization of his prescriptive aspirations. What then are the basic elements of his social psychology?

II

As a young man Mead brought back from his studies in Germany—which included studies with Dilthey—certain ideas that would later become mainstays of his position. Among them were ideas on the *gesture* that Wundt had developed. The gesture proved to be the perfect concept for linking animal and human communication, while at the same time allowing Mead to articulate crucial differences. (No doubt for Mead the dedicated naturalist, committed to the idea of emergence, our continuity with other organisms is as important as are our differences.) A gesture is a movement or sound produced by an animal that influences the behavior of another animal. The example

Mead liked to use was of two dogs, where the first dog's snarl would set in motion the second dog's snarling back or perhaps its running away. Meaning in these situations is defined by what the second animal does in response to the first—that is, snarls or runs. Gestures, then, have objective meaning in these situations, although the participants obviously cannot articulate what they are.

Gestures are transformed in human interaction into something quite unique, for human beings not only gesture, they use significant symbols that allow them to be aware of the meanings of their gestures. Unlike mere gestures, significant symbols are gestures whose meanings human beings are reflexively aware of as they employ them. If I shout "Fire!" at you in a crowded theater, I have a tendency to respond as you do, and I am aware of this tendency. I can anticipate your response because I "feel" it in myself. "Gestures become significant symbols when they implicitly arouse in an individual making them the same responses which they explicitly arouse, or are supposed to arouse, in other individuals, the individuals to whom they are addressed."[16] By taking the position of the other with regard to my own gesture, I become aware of its meaning; I learn to respond to the symbol even in the absence of the other. I might very well "shout" *Fire!* to myself in a crowded theater, and then respond accordingly. The question is, of course, how did human beings move from using gestures to significant symbols?

Mead's answer is that it was the development of *vocal* gestures, which were made possible by the evolution of a sufficiently sophisticated central nervous system, that enabled human beings to become reflexively aware of meanings. "The critical importance of language in the development of human experience lies in this fact that the stimulus is one that can react upon the speaking individual as it reacts upon the other."[17] I can hear myself as you hear me when I speak. This allows me to respond to my own stimulus. To your overt (explicit) response, I respond covertly (implicitly).[18] I could do the same using a hand sign language, for I can see my hands' movements as you do. But while hand sign languages are clearly possible for Mead, he emphasizes the unique importance of the vocal gesture in the genesis of human language.

Habermas argues that Mead's model must be augmented if we are to understand how our ancestors moved from dealing in gestures that merely provided similar (functional) responses to stimuli, to situations in which identities of meaning are found. (I want to know that you understand a gesture in a way that is identical to my understanding, as opposed to merely responding in a similar manner to the gesture.)

To fully understand how this is possible, Habermas tells us that we are going to have to appeal to a notion of linguistic rules that define and confirm meaning, and address the ways in which rules are generated. He believes that Wittgenstein's understanding of rules can be used to complement Mead's model, while Mead's approach can be of assistance in explaining their development.[19]

In order to generate identities of meaning, according to Habermas, individuals must at minimum have developed a facility for anticipating the responses of others, and must also have learned to take yes/no positions with regard to the actual responses of others. I must be able to say that you have or have not violated my expectation of a certain behavior, a certain response. And you must be able to do the same. In intersubjective give and take, in the testing entailed in the taking of yes/no positions regarding expectations of behavior, identities of meaning arise in the context of evolving linguistic rules. Oral discourse is privileged over written discourse here, at least with regard to the evolution and maintenance of identities of meaning, for it would seem that one can never question a text in quite the same way that one can question and be questioned by another. (The necessary qualification is, of course, that sophisticated grammatical structures allow certain presumptions of meaning with regard to written texts.) Habermas notes that Mead fails to address the evolution of language from the (merely) symbolically mediated to the grammatically nuanced, but instead "goes abruptly from symbolically mediated to normatively regulated action,"[20] action in which the existence of language with sophisticated rules is presumed. And I am afraid that for the present paper I will be doing the same as I now turn to address the self.

Mead defines the generation of *mind*, which must be addressed before turning to the self, in terms of the development of significant symbols.

> Mentality on our approach simply comes in when the organism is able to point out meanings to others and to himself. This is the point at which mind appears, or if you like, emerges. . . . It is absurd to look at the mind simply from the standpoint of the individual human organism; for, although it has its focus there, it is essentially a social phenomenon; even its biological functions are primarily social.[21]

For Mead, the use of language entails a reflexive awareness of meaning or a self-consciousness of meaning. I am in a sense self-conscious when I use the term "Fire," because I have an awareness of its meaning—that is, an awareness of possible responses to it. But there is another use of the term *self-conscious* in Mead; that is, when he refers to the explicit awareness of having a self, an identity. The self is, for Mead, a set of unique meanings that depends on language development. And as we shall see, Mead's notion of the generalized other proves crucial here.

We can approach Mead's notion of the self through his theory of roles. For Mead we are role-taking creatures. In learning to use a significant symbol I must become aware of the response of the other to my vocal gesture. Meaning is attached to the word in the context of its use. As I grow more sophisticated in learning the responses of others, I gradually develop repertoires of responses. I learn not only to take over specific responses but whole sets of responses, which may include nonverbal behaviors. These sets of responses can be spoken of as roles. "The child says something in one character and responds in another character, and then his responding in another character is a stimulus to himself in the first character, and so the conversation goes on."[22] One learns to play doctor by playing the role of patient and vice versa. One must become aware of one's own responses from the perspective of the other in order to take roles.

Learning numerous roles, and being aware of them, is not enough to constitute a self for Mead. There is a wholeness to a self that incorporates specific roles that we take. Mead attempts to approach this wholeness by introducing his concept of the generalized other, in which specific roles are incorporated into a larger whole.

> The organized community or social group which gives to the individual his unity of self may be called the "generalized other." The attitude of the generalized other is the attitude of the whole community. Thus, for example, in the case of such a social group as a ball team, the team is the generalized other in so far as it enters—as an organized process or social activity—into the experience of any one of the individual members of it.[23]

The key phrase here is *organized process*. To be a pitcher I must know not only the roles of pitcher and catcher, I must have an understanding of the game as a whole, and the rules that make it possible. Mead is seeking to illustrate the idea that we often take perspectives on our behaviors that require us to frame our responses in something more than role-to-role terms. In other words, systemic interactions—for example, those that we might find in a family as well as on a ball team—have the potential to provide the perspective of generalized others. And when we view our (possible) actions from such a perspective what we "see" are not isolated responses, but a self. This complex set of responses or "object" that we view from the perspective of the generalized other Mead calls the *me*. That which does the "view-ing" he designates as the *I*. But the *I* is more than a position for "view-ing" the *me*. It is also the locus of spontaneity for Mead, and as such supplies an avenue for bypassing the pitfalls of an overly socialized conception of the self. This said it is important to note that the *I* is a *functional*, not substantive, subject for Mead. It is also worth noting that at times the term *me* is used synonymously with the term *self* by Mead, while at other times *self* is used to suggest the combination of the *I* and the *me*, that is, a complete personality.[24]

For Mead, there are numerous possible generalized others corre-sponding to various social groups:.

> Some of them are concrete social classes or subgroups, such as politi-cal parties, clubs, corporations, which are all actually functional social units, in terms of which their individual members are directly related to one another. The others are abstract social classes or subgroups, such as the class of debtors and the class of creditors, in terms of which their individual members are related to one another only more or less indirectly.[25]

Each of us has more than one self, and these selves correspond to various generalized others. This is not to claim the absence of a "meta-self" (or selves) for Mead—that is, a self that can unify numerous gen-eralized others. Such a self would have to be capable of "incorporating" less generalized voices in some manner. For Mead, we clearly have the capacity to identify with and be shaped by such unifying perspec-tives—for example, the perspective of an "abstract" group that defines itself in terms of mutual rights.

> There are what I have termed "generalized social attitudes" which make an organized self possible. In the community there are certain ways of acting under situations which are essentially identical, and these ways of acting on the part of anyone are those which we excite in others when we take certain steps. If we assert our rights, we are calling for a definite response just because they are rights that are uni-versal—a response which everyone should, and perhaps will, give.[26]

Mead's approach to these more inclusive, universalistic, selves (or self) is intimately bound up with his vision of ethical progress. This is not to say that all institutionalized generalized others are progressive simply by virtue of being general. Mead, after all, was quite critical of ossified religious perspectives and the selves that they gave rise to.[27] For Mead, the generalized others of "properly" universalistic (ethical) com-munities appear to share certain characteristics: they permit the functional integration of various roles and selves, allow for the preservation of that which they integrate, and remain open to creative modifications.

That individuals are capable of defining themselves in the more universalistic terms of (ethical) communities that transcend localized generalized others, should not be read as militating against the unique experiences of individuals.[28] Quite the contrary. Mead thought that by ridding the world of narrowly defined communities, such as castes, we would be making room for greater differentiation. Since we are social beings, our differences from others need to be recognized by others if they are to inform the self in any permanent sense. But our (potential) differences cannot be recognized unless we live in communities that both allow us to actualize a multitude of roles and behaviors, and provide opportunities for being confirmed in these roles by others. And such communities, tied together by various "abstract" generalized others, are becoming more prevalent in the modern world.

> It is often assumed that democracy is an order of society in which those personalities which are sharply differentiated will be eliminated, that everything will be ironed down to a situation where everyone will be, as far as possible, like everyone else. But of course this is not the implication of democracy: the implication of democracy is rather that the individual can be as highly developed as lies within the possibilities of his own inheritance, and still can enter into the attitudes of the others whom he affects.[29]

No two persons are ever exactly alike for Mead, for even in terms of specific generalized others, each will reflect social wholes from (slightly) different vantage points.[30] But we must be able to *enter into the attitudes of others*, and they must be able to enter into ours, if we are to be confirmed in our own attitudes.[31] This point can be approached from a more concrete, if somewhat simplistic, angle. We all have idiosyncratic memories, which differ because of our different individual histories and biological endowments. These memories become meaningful and vital parts of ourselves when we are able to share them with others (even if the others are absent/imaginary audiences). You may never have taken the trip to India that I just have, but you have traveled, and as a traveler I can share my experiences with you in a way that I cannot with friends from the "backwoods." And after I do so, my memories are in a sense more fully *me* than they would have been without you. The breadth of your experience, informed by certain generalized others that we have in common, does not suspend my differences from you, but actually assists in their flourishing. So it goes for a myriad of distinct but related activities.[32] This is not to say that "backwoods" cultures are obligated to become cosmopolitan ones, and I will return to this troubling issue below.

Individuality is maintained in spite of the fact that with greater degrees of intercommunication, more "abstract" selves come into being. Although the more general does challenge the exclusivity of one's prior *selves*, it offers in return an enhanced number and range of communities that one can participate in, including former ones. "A member of the community is not necessarily like other individuals because he is able to identify himself with them. He may be different. There can be a common content, common experience, without there being an identity of function."[33] To follow the thread of Mead's vision requires that so-called abstract inclusive communities be viewed in terms of their potential for assisting in the differentiation of individuals, and not merely as threats to concrete life practices.

Earlier in this paper I quoted Mead on international-mindedness. Here is the quote again, this time with the lines that preceded it now incorporated:

> We all belong to small cliques, and we may remain simply inside of them. The "organized other" present in ourselves is then a community of a narrow diameter. We are struggling now to get a certain amount of international-mindedness. We are realizing ourselves as members of a larger community. The vivid nationalism of the present period should, in the end, call out an international attitude of the larger community.[34]

In the days ahead there will be new opportunities for the ideal "that the interests of all men are so identical, that the man who acts in the interest of his neighbors will act in his own interest."[35] For as interdependence and intercommunication grows, so too will new possibilities for common bonds amid diversity.

III

There is another important and perhaps crucial dimension of the generalized other that links it to Mead's claims regarding science, social groups, and the question of universality. To address this aspect of Mead's thought I wish to appeal to the work of a group of thinkers known as systematic pluralists. According to the work of Walter Watson and David Dilworth, there are four basic levels at which authors and texts need examining if we are going to make clear-headed comparisons between them.[36] We should investigate: authorial voice, method, ontological focus, and governing purpose or principle.

To focus on texts in this manner seemingly inverts the deconstruction-ist paradigm. Texts are seen to function in terms of principles that guide or work through signifiers, as opposed to being at their mercy. For heuristic purposes only I wish to appeal to Watson's and Dilworth's notion of authorial voice.

Texts can be written in four basic voices according to this model.[37] Dilworth summarizes the four voices as follows:

> *Personal.* This is the self-referent, idiocentric presence of an author or authors—in the first person singular or plural—that shapes his world view. . . . *Objective.* This authorial perspective dispassionately observes the world's objects and their practical effects. . . . *Diaphanic.* This is the standard voice of religious texts. It bears witness to a high-er wisdom or the revelation of an absolute knowledge . . . . *Disciplinary.* The disciplinary perspective presupposes an ideal com-munity of like-minded readers; it typically takes the form of the first person plural. [38]

Much ink has been spent in recent years debating whether Mead was actually a hard-headed scientist, using an objective perspective as did Peirce, or whether he was more of a Jamesian, biased to the per-sonal and idiosyncratic.[39] (In the latter case he would be seen as emphasizing the importance of the I over the *me*.) I would like to sug-gest the following. There are indeed elements of both present in his thought depending on which Mead you are reading: the more *scientif-ically* attuned pieces emphasizing social behaviorism, or those stress-ing the dynamics and importance of spontaneity in the life of an individual and culture.

But in fact both of these readings miss the mark. Mead's real bias, if we are talking of authorial voice, is in the direction of a disciplinary perspective: expert knowledge, communities of knowers and inter-preters.[40] Hence, while you will find him singing the praises of the sci-entific method, which appears to suggest an objective perspective, a closer reading reveals that he is only talking about a general method of problem-solving. When we actually look to different subject matters we find that there will have to be different approaches. Consider the following:

> The difference between the physicist and the biologist evidently lies in the goals which their sciences contemplate, in the realities they are seeking. And their procedure answers to their goals.[41]

> Outside this field of appreciation and criticism, the method of study in the field of the humanities is just as scientific *as the subject-matter with which it deals allows.* . . . .The ideal of modern education is the solu-

tion of problems, the research method. And this research method is no
less dominant in the humanities than it is in the natural sciences *so far
as the subject matter permits."*[42] [emphasis added]

The phrase, *so far as the subject matter permits*, is just the sort of
qualification one would expect from someone attuned to a disciplinary perspective, as was Aristotle, the preeminent disciplinary voice
of his day. But the major piece of evidence for Mead's attraction to
this voice comes from his analysis of the generalized other. The generalized other orders our experience in terms of groups, and we
become cognizant of ourselves in terms of groups. We speak (or eventually must speak) with the voice of a group whenever we communicate, and this holds true for scientific matters. Of course, generalized
others may undergo transformation, but this need not lead to the
purely personal or idiosyncratic, for they are then reconstituted as
new disciplinary voices. In Mead's terms, an *I* transforms a *me*, but we
only become aware of the work of the transforming *I* through the new
(social) *me* that arises.

The fact that we are dealing with groups and perspectives does
not eliminate the notion of universality for Mead. Recall that for Mead
significant symbols arise in the interactions of agents:

> "But signification is not confined to the particular situation within
> which an indication is given. It acquires universal meaning. Even if
> the two are the only ones involved, the form in which it is given is uni-
> versal—it would have the same meaning to any other who might find
> himself in the same position." [43]

We can call universals of this type functional universals. And
Mead understands them and employs them in a fashion that clearly
suggests his disciplinary orientation, which views the world in terms
of *we* who define the terms—not subjectively—but in a manner that
would be true for anyone who can stand in our place. It is the perspective of groups, groups skilled at interacting with the world in particular ways, and which are organized in terms of generalized others.

Communities, whether they be seen in political or scientific terms,
define themselves by a common *voice*, a generalized other, a universal.
Scientific communities define themselves in terms of the common perspectives of the different sciences—for example, biology, sociology,
and physics—and knowledge is understood in terms of the perspectives of the investigators. Because it is so understood, there is more
knowledge, not less. The reason for this is that limits are seen here as
allowing for richer experience by revealing what would not have been
seen without them.[44] This by no means denies the possibility of inter-

disciplinary cross-fertilization, or keeps new disciplines from arising. Mead in this sense was a preeminent interdisciplinary thinker. Further, the notion that limits provide fuller insight into the world, as opposed to somehow violating it through essentialist structures (as many postmodernists might argue), is one that extends far outside the scientific domain. Communities live through their generalized others, their defining limits for Mead. The issue, then, is whether or not this manner of seeing the world enriches or violates (or perhaps sometimes enriches and sometimes violates) the other according to fixed and arbitrary categories.

Mead, no doubt, would not have seen himself as a defender of totality and a despoiler of the other. He clearly would have wanted to make the following claim: it is wrong for social groups to violate the reality of others simply because they possess enough power to do so. The question is, of course, on what grounds is it wrong. One obvious objection Mead would make, though by no means the only one, is that such a course would eliminate possible perspectives for understanding and appreciating the world; in short, it would reduce the realizable potentialities of humanity. More "abstract" groupings should not seek to eliminate the more "restricted" voices, but maintain them as the means through which persons can "hear" aspects of themselves, and hence continue to be themselves. Mead would have defended this right on both ethical and conceptual grounds. Serious difficulties, of course, are raised by the existence of groups that believe that their survival depends on excluding others, or who believe that the very existence of other groups, or universally minded folk, constitute a nonnegotiable threat to their way of life that must be overcome. I cannot hope to do justice to these concerns in the context of this article. But I hope that I have at least shown how Mead's international-mindedness was not a call to do away with difference per se, but to find commonalties that would allow diversity to flourish in a nonthreatening fashion.

In one respect communication for Mead is limited by the generalized others that help constitute the self. We must speak through group voices if we are to be heard and if we are to remain intelligible. But groups are increasingly less isolated. The assumption of growing collective interdependence that allows truly international sorts of communities to arise is basic to Mead's vision. There will be increased interaction in the years to come, and new skills and forms of communication will have to develop to meet new needs. We will have to learn to take of the *perspective of the other* more frequently.[45] International-mindedness will go hand in hand with new and often wider ranging (disciplinary) perspectives. Again we see that Mead looked forward to concrete conditions conspiring to fulfil his prescriptive aspirations.

Mead was not unaware of the importance and power of nationalism.[46] He lived through World War I and he knew that nations would not disappear in the foreseeable future, if ever. As a matter of fact, the problem of nationalism was in part a problem of insecure national identities for him. "For at this period of the world's history there is no point of national honor and peculiar interest which is not open to reasonable negotiation in a community of self-respecting nations as any of the so-called justiciable and negotiable issues, if we were sure of ourselves. But we are not sure of our national selves. . . . . We cannot attain international-mindedness until we have attained a higher degree of national-mindedness than we possess at present."[47]

Until nations and other social groups are allowed to determine and define their own voices, we will continue to live in a world of parochialism that breeds hostility, not international-mindedness. The growth of universality in international terms depends on the flourishing of particular social groups, whose particularity is itself defined in terms of functional universals, generalized others. For Mead, particularists need not fear his sort of universalism, but they had best keep a wary eye on their parochial neighbors.

10

Philosophy of Language and Philosophy of Communication: Poiesis and Praxis in Classical Pragmatism

❦ ❦

Lenore Langsdorf

Of all things, communication is the most wonderful. That things should be able to pass from the plane of pushing and pulling to that of revealing themselves . . . and that the fruit of communication should be   participation, sharing, is a wonder by the side of   which transubstantiation pales. When communication occurs, all natural events . . . are re-adapted to meet the needs of conversation, whether it be public discourse or that preliminary discourse termed thinking. Events turn into objects, things with a meaning. . . their meanings may be infinitely combined and rearranged in imagination, and the outcome of this inner experimentation—which is thought—may issue forth in interaction with crude or raw events.

—John Dewey, *Experience and Nature*

All linguistic philosophers talk about the world. This is the linguistic turn, the fundamental gambit as to method, on which ordinary and ideal language philosophers (OLP, ILP) agree.

—Gustav Bergmann, *Logic and Reality*, cited by Richard Rorty in *The Linguistic Turn*

Mind arises through communication by a conversation of gestures in a social process or context of experience—not communication through mind.

—George Herbert Mead, *Mind, Self, and Society*

> The abductive suggestion . . . is an act of insight, although of extremely fallible insight . . . the different elements of the hypothesis were in our minds before; but it is the idea of putting together what we had never before dreamed of putting together which flashes the new suggestion before our contemplation.
>
> —Charles Sanders Peirce, *Collected Papers, 5*

It would be unfair, as well as contrary to the theme of this essay, to compare these remarks directly. Many years and substantially different intellectual and political contexts separate the Dewey, Mead, and Peirce quotations from the Bergmann quotation and Rorty's use of Bergmann's phrase as the title of his first book.[1] I set them together here not to argue their comparative value, but as emblematic of a crucial difference between classical pragmatism and neopragmatism. I would summarize that difference as one of conceptualizing human communication as based in poiesis (Dewey, Mead, and Peirce) in contrast to a basis in praxis (Rorty).[2]

Substantiating that claim begins by noting an evident difference: Dewey, Mead, and Peirce speak of communication, conversation, and connection; Bergmann, and thus Rorty, of language, method, and world.[3] The more we read of the work surrounding these quotations, the more we come to recognize that this difference is neither a chance occurrence in these particular remarks, nor reflective of a mere difference in terminological preference. It is, rather, symptomatic and symbolic of pervasive differences between classical pragmatism and neopragmatism. Rorty borrows Bergmann's phrase to characterize what became the dominant mode of academic philosophy in mid-century. The Peirce, Mead, and Dewey remarks bring together two strands of philosophy—process metaphysics and philosophy of mind—to form a thesis basic to pragmatism: the human self and its objects of inquiry are formed through a particular sort of experience.

In what follows I propose that communicative poiesis (originary creative doing that extends beyond existent symbolic structures), intrinsically linked to communicative praxis (production that has a linguistic product as its goal), is at the core of this formation. This proposal is basic to my more encompassing project of articulating a philosophy of communication, based in classical pragmatism, that is quite distinct from the philosophy of language at the core of Rorty's neopragmatism.

A conception of communication that relies upon poiesis may be found in more or less explicit form throughout the classical pragmatists' work. But it is most explicit in Dewey and Mead. Perhaps this is because their thinking was rooted in the real political context of their lives: democracy as lived in the United States during the first half of this century was the ever-present context of their work, and how to create the conditions for living in and expanding that democracy was at the center of Dewey's work, in particular. Dewey's "plane of pushing and pulling" is a public domain, and especially, an educational one. The educational theory he developed combines participation in "inner experimentation" or thinking with embodied experimentation with "crude or raw events," and both ends of that spectrum are present in his sense of "the needs of conversation."

This focus on the public domain—and especially, on political and pedagogical issues—is the primary reason for my relying most on Dewey's work in delineating a philosophy of communication dependent upon the creative thrust of poiesis rather than the productive force of praxis. Mead is also important to this delineation, by virtue of his focus on the emergence of mind, self, and society within acts of cultivated or mediated response to an organism's environment. Peirce's work—with its explicit focus on the logical structure of language use and relative neglect of actual communication processes—is less crucial, although his concept of abduction tells us much about the character of poiesis. All three classical pragmatists share an innovative, rather than reproductive or representational, understanding of communication.

The claim that communicative poiesis is basic to the investigations of the classical pragmatists requires reflection on several orientations—the good, being, knowing, doing, and making—that philosophy may take toward investigating any subject matter, including communication. Although these need not be exclusive interests, philosophers typically have chosen to explore these orientations as separate research specializations. One of classical pragmatism's distinctive features, however, is an insistence on holding these orientations together. Most importantly, a pervasive interest in *doing* the *good*—a meliorative rather than purely theoretical interest—may well be the crucial factor that differentiates classical pragmatism from Rortyean neopragmatism. The more usual separation of interests means that an interest in the good typically inclines philosophers toward formulating ethical or political theories, which may imply policies that promote particular conceptions of value, as exemplified in certain modes of behavior. But those implications fall outside the philosopher's self-concept. Classical pragmatism avoids theorizing the good in abstraction from inventing ways to practice the good, and does so out of convictions concerning the meliorative possibilities of theory that is generated from, and returns to, practice.

A dominant interest in being or knowing in isolation from doing does have the virtue of avoiding the high level of contingency involved in ascertaining and promoting the good. Metaphysics can proceed as an abstract study of what is, and even, what must be, the case. This is a relatively object-oriented, in contrast to subject-inclusive, interest, and tends toward static descriptions of being. (Process metaphysics rejects that tendency, however—and not coincidentally, is a strand of pragmatism.) Correlatively, epistemology can be done in isolation from the contingencies of actual searching for knowledge about a particular subject-matter. If values are the objects of an orientation toward the good, and things (or their representations) are the objects of an orientation toward being, the correlative object for this epistemological orientation is thoughts. Although the epistemologists' concern for how we can know inspires a search for methods that will enable thought to know things, an abstracted interest in knowing can lead away from doing, to theorizing: in this case, it may lead to theories that explain correspondence between mental and physical entities (thoughts and things).

All three of these historically predominant orientations are inscribed in the institutional structure of academic philosophy. Research and teaching typically are categorized as axiology, epistemology, or metaphysics. Attention to the other two possible orientations for philosophy—doing and making—has most often come from outside academic philosophy, and has either bypassed philosophy or been critical (in the negative sense) of its ways.

For example, critical theories that are rooted more or less directly in Marx's identification of material production as the basis of what is, what is good, and how we know, are an example of negative critique that is centrally concerned with praxis. Contemporary deconstructive theories that are rooted in textual production (another form of praxis) declare a determination to terminate, or at least bypass, philosophy. Classical pragmatism, however, is pervasively concerned with doing, rather than making, and with the particular sort of innovative doing that occurs by virtue of communicative poiesis, rather than by virtue of the praxial function of communication. Not coincidentally, Dewey and Mead are far more interested in communication (the process) than in language (the product we make in that process). The quotations with which we began provide examples of that diverse focus. Looking in some detail at this difference in focus as embedded in the historical division between philosophy and rhetoric will help in specifying both the link between poiesis and praxis and what distinguishes them.

Bergmann's identification of the linguistic turn as a methodical gambit on which both (ordinary language philosphers) and (ideal language philosophers) agree suggests that there is much about which these philosophies of language disagree. That disagreement, I would suggest, derives from the divergence of rhetoric from philosophy in Western intellectual life. Rhetoric, in Aristotle's well-known definition, is the study of all available means of persuasion. That orientation toward what is *available* indicates a need for study of how language actually is used, at particular times and places and for particular ends.[4] Perhaps only because of the institutional structure of scholarship in ancient Greece, that need set rhetoric's origins within the public life of the polis. This was precisely the territory Plato shunned in specifying the life of the philosopher, although it is the territory investigated by contemporary ordinary language philosophy.

Through one vivid metaphor after another, Plato tells us quite clearly that the philosopher must climb a ladder of abstraction away from the polis, the many, the particular, and the situated. Philosophy is to concern itself instead with dwelling among the Forms; with discerning the one fixed Idea or concept rather than searching out the many changing things or instances; with specifying the universal, atemporal, or ideal stasis rather than describing the ways of particularity (which he disdains as inundated with temporality and immersed in real flux); with following the stipulations of the philosopher-king who represents a concept of reason that rules over will and affect, rather than with participation in the deliberations of citizens who embody a concept of reason that chooses among the often conflicting needs of volition and emotion. That dichotomy was deepened in subsequent historical epochs as philosophy's otherworldly leanings were joined to comparable ones within Christian tradition and logic was rooted out from rhetoric.

The very length of time it took to totally divorce rhetoric and philosophy (roughly, two thousand years; from Plato to Peter Ramus) and the very brief period of thorough separation (roughly again, three hundred years; from Descartes and Francis Bacon to Austin and Perelman) suggests that the division between (formal) philosophy and "ideal" language, on the one hand, and (empirical) rhetoric and "ordinary" language, on the other, is more a dialectic than a dichotomy. Bergmann's identification of an area of linguistic agreement between "ordinary" (empirically-oriented) and "ideal" (formally oriented) language philosophers confirms that at least some area of discussion exists. Yet (as Bergmann recognizes) ordinary-language philosophers can simply join ideal-language philosophers in some limited agreement about the value of the linguistic turn as an alternative to stalled epistemological disputes. They can then turn their backs not only on those disputes, but on any practical quandaries—difficulties arising within human endeavors of valuing, being, knowing, doing or making—that may have instigated those theoretical disputes.

In other words, the linguistic turn circumvents certain traditional problems of philosophy, but it cannot in itself offer any convincing practical argument (as Rorty is very aware) for why one should take it, other than to avoid problems intrinsic to certain metaphysical and epistemological discussions. Thus the linguistic turn shifts philosophical discussion from things to words without making any substantive headway—formally or empirically—toward knowing what is, or what is good, or what ways of knowing may lead us to know how things are or how to do what is good.

Rorty's advocacy of the linguistic turn at the very beginnings of his neopragmatism retains both the virtues and limitations Bergmann saw, and leads directly to his well-known prescription for postrepresentationalist philosophy: philosophers are to join extant intellectual conversations with no more substantive goal than to keep them going. This advice is consistent with the linguistic turn in philosophy in both its empirical (ordinary language) or formal (ideal language) modes, for that orientation was toward "a suitable language" (the phrase is Bergmann's) for talking about the world, rather than toward doing or making, in themselves or in relation to being, knowing, and the good. Their concern was rather to reform or resolve—and even, as far as some practitioners were concerned, dissolve—such traditional problems of philosophy.

Rorty's own linguistic turn accords with that concern, and may be a wise prescription for institutionalized philosophy's future, as well as a politically astute means for diminishing certain historically cherished assumptions about academic philosophy's superiority to other intellectual endeavors. Those are both commendable aims, and I would go no further toward arguing against Rorty's counsel as to how to bring them about than to mention that his prescriptions may not be the only or the most effective ways to bring about those commendable ends. I do want to propose, however, that classical pragmatism has some particular and especially valuable, because relatively neglected, content to add to the conversation. Appreciating that content, however, depends upon appreciating basic differences between the philosophy of language and the philosophy of communication. Dewey's portrayal of a shift in the history of science from an empirical to an experimental attitude provides a model for discerning those differences.

From Aristotle to Galileo, Dewey tells us, inquiry into experience was empirical, in the sense of delineating a realm of inquiry and describing what is the case for entities identified within that realm. [5]

Not surprisingly, this endeavor placed a high value on stasis: it is far more difficult, after all, to describe a body in flux than to describe one that is settled. Thus practical considerations joined ingrained philosophical considerations, rooted in Plato's valorization of stability over change, to produce some persistent assumptions about the subject matter of any theoretical inquiry. Most basically, that subject matter was to be abstracted from time, place, and human circumstance so that it could be described as independent of context and immutable—although no investigator ever encountered such items. The result of that conception of subject matter was a decided isolation of practice from theory: practice remains in the flux of mundane experience, a matter of perception and sensory evidence, which enable, at best, belief about the particulars comprising an environment.

Dewey was concerned with just that flux of mundane experience that is neglected by this tradition of theoretical knowledge. He identifies inquiry that remains concerned with actual, mundane experience as "commonsense knowing . . . concerned with *facienda*, with things to be done and/or made."[6] This is a knowing that remains "enmeshed in the individual situation" (343). "Scientific knowing," in contrast, "liberates itself from the individual situation and its pressing practicality"—a liberation that is "facilitated by . . . the creation of a scientific language" that is "completely neutral"; a "code by means of which that which happens at any specified place and time is capable of translation into what happens at other places and times" (342–43). Inquiry, in this conception of science, is constructed in reference to conceptual items formulated in that special language and available only in that linguistic form. It is purified (which is also to say, bereft) of the particularity and mutability intrinsic to spatio-temporal existence and sensory engagement.

What Dewey notices is that this conception of theory embodies the assumptions of pre-Galilean science, prior to the shift from an empirical to an experimental attitude. Experimental science, far from continuing a Platonically informed distanciation from changing things in order to produce certain knowledge of immutable conceptual entities, mandates increased involvement with, and even deliberate changing of, the objects of inquiry. Dewey substantiates his claim that this is a radical change by itemizing the many details that constitute the shift from descriptive empiricism to active experimentalism:

> In classic Greek-medieval theory science is of that. . .which so transcends space and time as to be unaffected by differences of place and date. In modern practice natural science has to do inclusively and exclusively with events . . . particulars are scientifically known when they are specifically located and dated in a system of interconnected

events. Again science in the classic scheme was of fixed natures . . . all
classic scientific knowledge was taxonomic . . . scientific knowing
today substitutes for the isolation between species or kinds demand-
ed in the classic scheme a continuity. (338)

Within this integrated subject matter, as he goes on to say, "reflection or inference can travel freely." This freedom enables us to use
Peirce's conception of "abductive suggestion . . . putting together what
we had never before dreamed of putting together."[7] This is an imaginative, insightful, and innovative form of reasoning that, I propose, is
the very essence of poiesis.

The subject matter of experimental science is sensory as well as
imaginative: "Greek scientific knowing was of the universal; sensation
or sense-perception was of the particular . . . In the present . . . sense-
perception is doubly involved . . . in the occurrence of a problem. . .[and
also] in the testing of the proposed solution" (338–39). The need for sensory evidence requires nothing less than a shift in the conduct of
inquiry from distanciation and deduction to involvement and induction. Dewey emphasizes the inquirer's active participation in the "revolutionary change-over from the Greek to the modern method of
scientific knowing [that] was effected by the use of experiment," which
he defines as "the art of conducting a sequence of observations in
which natural conditions are intentionally altered and controlled in
ways which will disclose, discover, natural subject-matters which
would not otherwise have been noted" (339).

This active intervention in knowing also resulted in changing the
character of theory: Theory thereby lost, once and forever as far as concerns the conduct of scientific knowing, the Greek status of finality and
acquired the modern status and office of a working hypothesis" (339).
The entire process of knowing is no longer a matter of distanciation
from flux and positing a static subject matter, but one of participation
in situated events: "the experimental method of scientific inquiry
broke down the wall that had been erected between theory and practice. . . . Knowing involved some kind of doing and making. It turned
away from immutability toward process, change . . . from the past
toward the future, from precedents to consequences; from isolation to
continuity" (339).

Without explicit announcement, then, science after Galileo (which
is to say, experimental in contrast to empirical science) became "concerned with *facienda*, with things to be done and/or made." But that
lack of explicit announcement enables both popular and institutionalized conceptions of science (in the broad sense of systematic inquiry) to
retain certain comforts of the earlier model. The philosophy of lan-

guage provides an example, by virtue of the enduring presence of pre-Galilean assumptions about knowing and theory in its self-conception and method.

Even browsing through the essays in Rorty's *The Linguistic Turn* reveals that language philosophers (especially those of formal/ideal orientation, but also empirical/ordinary language philosophers) assume that the practicing subject (the inquiring philosopher) observes and reports on the theoretical object (the nature or use of language). It does not engage in reflection on the language philosopher's own practice: "language" is posited as a theoretical entity for analysis apart from the doing and making of the philosopher. When we look at this research attitude through the lens of Dewey's analysis, the doing and making accomplished by the philosopher in order to say anything about language is evident. Failing to acknowledge and reflectively examine that active role raises questions as to the value of a philosophy of language that restricts its attention to a product, in isolation from its productive process and in particular, from the creativity that evokes the nonlinguistic environment in and by means of that process.

In other words, philosophers of language study the result of a production process without attention to the process itself, or to their involvement in the process—either as users of the language or as formulators of their research questions. Nor are they concerned to relate their reified subject matter to actual practice. This separation of theory and practice, I would argue, reiterates a Cartesian separation of mind and body—often in the guise of separation of the private and public, and despite the pervasive anti-Cartesianism that marks contemporary scholarship, including philosophy of language. It reinscribes the search for certainty within inquiry by taking as its object a circumscribed reification, purified of the contingencies endemic to any process embedded in human affairs.

In its more rarified forms, the philosophy of language more resembles the formal sciences (mathematics and logic) than it does the human sciences (sociology, economics, etc.). The radical change in the way science actually happens remains unannounced—and even ideologically denied—outside certain relatively esoteric and often denigrated orientations in the philosophy of science. Thus the philosophy of language benefits from its association with a culturally valued, although factually inaccurate, set of assumptions.

Against this background, we can turn to considering the impetus that classical pragmatism gives for developing a philosophy of communication that incorporates Dewey's "experimental" orientation "concerned with *facienda*, with things to be done and/or made" rather than the "empirical" orientation concerned with things (such as language) that are residuals of processes already done, and are investigated in reified form—which is to say, as products already made. Once we begin to think of the process and the product as a continuum, all aspects of which are equally although not uniformly amenable to inquiry, we are liberated in quite a few ways. Perhaps most importantly, for academic research interests, we are able to see that methods that may be appropriate for the study of relatively fixed "things," such as the syntactic and semantic features that comprise the structure of any language, need not be forced on intrinsically processual "things," such as communication events. More specifically, we are liberated—and even required—to study communication events in which we ourselves are intrinsically and thoroughly involved. The very writing of this chapter, for example, can be investigated in an "experimental" manner. Perhaps that would be an appropriate way to illustrate what Peirce, Mead, and Dewey have noticed about communication.

In order to investigate the writing of this chapter in an "experimental" way, as an instance of verbal doing that exercises communicative poiesis, I begin by reflecting on the still ongoing event of generating a coherent account of processes that I have not previously identified as a unified (processual) "thing." This would be a highly problematic, if not simply unacceptable, undertaking to philosophers of language with "empirical" convictions—for I am inventing, in the rhetorical sense, rather than discovering or simply using, as a given, the object that I investigate, as I conduct the investigation. Yet this is a clear instance of experimental science in Dewey's sense. "Experiment," he writes (as quoted earlier), "is the art of conducting a sequence of observations in which natural conditions are intentionally altered and controlled in ways which will disclose, discover, natural subject-matters which would not otherwise have been noted" (339). This is why I noted that involvement in the events under analysis is "required" in Dewey's analysis of actual contemporary science. I cannot intentionally alter and control anything with which I am not involved.

Along with continued involvement with my subject-matter, I distanciate myself conceptually—although not spatiotemporally—from this object under study (and still in process), by the very act of "conducting a sequence of observations" rather than simply continuing to write the chapter. My attitude toward the ongoing process now has two distinct foci. On the one hand, I am attending to a praxial activity of using language to make a linguistic product. On the other hand, I am attending to a creative doing—communicative poiesis—that only partially and uncertainly anticipates the linguistic product that will result from it. In other words: my inquiry is directed at generating the account (doing), while also treating that account as a distinct thing (an object made in the course of my doing). In the midst of this rather dense multivalence, I "disclose, discover" what "would not otherwise have been noted": all of my communicative activity, since it involves what Dewey calls "transactions" between communicating parties, displays both those modalities. Somebody—perhaps, only I myself; perhaps, an other—hears or reads the product that is made in my doing. (Mead's analysis of the person as both an "I" and a "me" helps here conceptually, but may complicate initial understanding: "I" am doing what is also made by "me.") This is very difficult research on which to report, at least in part because it requires us to reject the "empirical" mindset, which we have been taught to value, and we are not quite sure of the value or even the legitimacy of that rejection.

What has unquestioned value, we can now recognize, is the "product" rather than "process" aspects of a communication event: empirical science begins and terminates in "things," such as language, which are already made. Although there is a good deal more that I could add to this start toward disclosing what "would not otherwise have been noted" in a communication event in which both doing and making can be discovered, a shift to analyzing particular elements of the "doing" aspect more closely may disclose some alternate value. Dewey's definition of experiment provides a starting point here: he notices that what we do, when we engage in experimentation, is intervene in the "natural conditions" for the subject matters under investigation—and that there is an "art" in doing so. The notion of "conditions" may well be as vague as the notion of "art" is disputed. As it turns out, they are very closely aligned in what Mead and Peirce, as well as Dewey, notice about "doing."

"Art" has three general senses within Western thinking. Two of them, mimesis and expression, were distrusted (at best) by Plato. His condemnation of mimesis is explicit: he finds no value in uncritically copying nature, which in turn (in his metaphysics) copies the immutable Forms: art is merely third-rate reality, and the philosopher is directed to live as best he can in the second-rate (mundane experience; a world of mere belief, without stability or certainty) while nurturing the soul's efforts to escape that sensory environment and dwell among the Forms (within an immutable conceptual reality admitting of knowledge). Along with Plato's clear disdain for mimetic art, there is an implicit condemnation of art as expression (a view that came to dominance much later, during romanticism) in his work. Human beings, in his view, live an uneasy truce among warring factions in the soul: intellect, spirit, and desire struggle for domination. Intellect should rule; thus insofar as art expresses the "lower" elements within us, it must be brought under the rule of mind. There is a long history of contention concerning both of these views. Without meaning to declare Plato (or platonism) the victor in that dispute, we need to recognize that the value of "art," in either the expressive or mimetic sense, typically is problematic in our culture.[8]

The third sense of "art" is less clear and closer to Dewey's thinking. It is documented in everyday discourse when we speak of the "art of medicine" or of someone who exemplifies "the art of living well." What is involved here is a creative (rather than mechanical) know-how that enables the practitioner to transform conditions, whether that be by sifting through available possibilities so as to gather up elements into a good life or by diagnosing the probable cause of distress from observation of symptoms and prescribing meliorative remedies.[9] This is the sort of creative, innovative, doing that I have aligned, throughout this discussion, with poiesis. Poiesis is the transformation of conditions by using know-how or skill; the Greek term is *techné*. Correlatively, praxis produces results or products—things in the everyday sense of independent tangible items and in the intellectual sense of concepts or ideas. Praxis is instructed, at its best, by the practical wisdom summarized in the Greek term *phronesis*. Philosophy typically has been more concerned with knowing of a more abstract sort, often referred to as epistemic and informed by theory; the correlative Greek term is *theoria*. Both poiesis (creative doing) and praxis (productive making) are encompassed in practice, in the sense of everyday practical matters that is usually associated with pragmatism.

Dewey's work and life is a record of pervasive concern with art in the sense of developing skill in transforming the conditions for human experience. That this goal was easily misunderstood is evident in even a cursory examination of his biography. The diffusion of that misunderstanding in commonplace beliefs about pragmatism is documented by the frequent association of the term with expedience, self-interest, and an over-optimistic confidence in progress. Those beliefs, I would argue, are largely a product of confusing transformed conditions with revolutionized consequences. Reflecting on just what "conditions" are, and how they stand in relation to consequences, provides the last element we need to appreciate the function of communicative poiesis in a philosophy of communication informed by classical pragmatism.[10]

"When communication occurs," Dewey tells us in the quotation that opens this chapter, "all natural events . . . are re-adapted to meet the needs of conversation, whether it be public discourse or that preliminary discourse termed thinking." This process of readaption is a curious one, for it is neither creation from nothing (there are "natural events"), nor mere reproduction. Most crucially, it is not a making—a production of any real (spatiotemporal) entity, that can be considered in isolation from its productive process—at all. Rather, it is a *doing* that remains within the realm of *possibilities; of conditions* for the making of things. As the later part of the passage (quoted at the start of this chapter) tells us, this is an experimental, imaginative process of recognizing what is and knowing what is good, in a particular context of needs. It is on the basis of this re-adaption of elements that we are able to make something new—"objects"—from pre-communicative "events" that were the *conditions* for those objects.

What occurs in the very core of the communicative process, then, is hypothetical rearrangement, recombination, and re-connection of conditions, not things; of events that are adaptable into objects which may, or may not, suit anticipated needs. Most immediately, these are the "needs of conversation." Ultimately, however, Dewey reminds us that this process "may" surpass conversation: we can develop competencies that allow us to turn again to "interaction with crude or raw events." Analysis of this readapting process enables us to "disclose, discover natural subject-matters which would not otherwise have been noted." But our usual conceptions of how things are produced are inadequate to appreciating what we have noted, because those conceptions are modeled on making, not doing; on producing things, rather than on creating that surpasses conditions. The difference in analytic strategies is substantial, for the result of a process of making—a product resulting from praxis—is subject matter that allows analysis into its components (both material and processual) which are directly discernable in that product. Once we identify the core of this process as poiesis rather than praxis, however, and thus recognize that we are concerned with adapting conditions rather than producing things, we are free to use methods other than analysis by composition and division. Peirce's term for the sort of method appropriate to this endeavor is abduction: "an act of insight" which he summarizes (in the quotation at the start of this chapter) as hypothetically gathering up elements for innovative rearrangement, recombination, and reconnection.[11]

From a reflective vantage point informed by classical pragmatism, then, conversation appears not as the sole or necessary end of thinking, and so philosophers ought not take the production of conversation as their goal. Rather, conversation—and communication of all sorts—is a brief linguistic hiatus in an ongoing process of action and reflection, doing and making. The goal of this process is not talking about things; nor is it simply "things . . . revealing themselves." For Dewey, the highest goal of this process is expanding innovative capacities so as to increase our ability to do the good. For Mead, the goal of analyzing communication's blend of poetic and praxial functions is understanding the formation of those cognitive patterns we associate with selfhood: "Mind arises through communication . . . not communication through mind." Dewey discerns the same order of formation: "through speech," he writes, "a person dramatically identifies himself with potential acts and deeds; he plays many roles . . . in a contemporaneously enacted drama. Thus mind emerges."[12] Mind encompasses a multitude of ways of knowing and being in relation to things. A philosophy of communication that appreciates the functioning of both poiesis and praxis in mind's emergence understands those responses as rooted in innovative and insightful, and also inherently fallible, processes of generating possibilities for adapting conditions, within the goal of responding to the changing needs of human being.

VI

Neopragmatism and Communication

11

Talking-With as a Model for Writing-About: Implications of Rortyean Pragmatism

❧ ❧

Arthur P. Bochner and Joanne B. Waugh

Of the many consequences that Rortyean pragmatism may have for communication theory, there are two that strike us as especially important. The first follows from pragmatism's criticism of essentialism—a position that Rorty shares with other pragmatists. It requires a reconsideration of orthodox accounts of *theory* in general, and traditional conceptions of communication in particular. This consequence is largely critical and, in that sense, negative. Rortyean pragmatism, however, may also provide direction for introducing optional metaphors for conceiving of and studying communication. This consequence is more positive and, at the same time, more tentative.

In what follows we ask why communication theory should conform to a model of theory that takes its task to be the *description* of objects when communication is not an object, nor a discipline studying objects, but rather sequences of interactions, and the activity of studying them. We think it is peculiar for orthodox communication theorists to continue to conform to this model of theory when it is by no means clear that the conception of science that inspired this view of communication as a discipline, and the model of theory that this conception of science employed, can be sustained.

In place of what has become the orthodox view of communication theory, we propose that communication theorists take as the model for their activity not *writing-about* or *describing* but *talking-with* or negotiating meaning. On our view, the study of communication is not a matter of discovering how we think and feel and act, but coming to think, feel, and act in certain ways by using language—that is, having conversations with others and ourselves. We expect, of course, that some readers may find this type of *theory* not to their liking, since our proposals for communication theory are at odds with some of its tradition's more deeply entrenched ideas about language, knowledge, and certainty. We hope to show, however, that these ideas about language, knowledge, and certainty are in conflict with some of the other commitments made by contemporary theorists in the philosophy of communication.

I

The assumptions and terms by which the study of communication as a social science has operated are due not so much, if at all, to the "essential" nature of the phenomena of communication as to a certain view of theory that has been dominant in Western thought since the Enlightenment. On this view, for a theory to meet the standards of science it must conform to certain criteria, the purpose of which is to yield descriptive statements—that is, statements that correspond to an independent, physical reality by employing "neutral" or "value-free" terms that denote *publicly observable* features of this reality.[1] The "neutrality" of this language is thought to result, at least in part, from the fact that the observer is an observer of, and not a participant in, what is being described.

Accordingly, both *external reality* and the language that represents it are seen as distinct from the mind, consciousness, or *interior reality* of the observer, and from the language used to express this internal reality to *outsiders*. Unless the *interior reality* of observers has some external, publicly observable consequences, it cannot be studied scientifically: it does not exist so far as science is concerned. Indeed, on more stringent views, *science* deals only with physical reality. The study of human behavior, if such behavior is seen as an instance or a sign of something nonphysical, is not *science*, though it may employ some methods or procedures used in the physical sciences. On this view, needless to say, any nonphysical external reality could not be studied scientifically. Even for those who are content to call a study *scientific* if it employs the scientific method by applying the criterion of validation of scientific explanation, or by employing quantitative analyses of publicly observable events, the study of nonphysical reality cannot be scientific unless it has observable consequences.[2]

On this view of what makes a study scientific, language is of interest only insofar as it can achieve its denotative and referential function of describing things in a world *out there*, apart from and independent of language users. There seems to be implicit in this account an emphasis on words representing *the* world, rather than language-users specifying *a* world. In conforming to this view of scientific study, orthodox communication theory sees messages and meanings as merely *transferred* from one person to another, and reduces the problematics of communication to metaphors of *information processing, social exchange, transmission* or *attributional errors*. Communication thus becomes itself a kind of *external object*, which can be seen as a commodity to be packaged and exchanged.

Qualifying as a scientific study would not be so important were it not for the fact that not just knowledge but rationality itself has been equated with being scientific. The result, Rorty notes:

> Any academic discipline which wants a place at the trough, but is unable to offer the predictions and the technology provided by the natural sciences, must either pretend to imitate science or find some way of obtaining "cognitive status" without the necessity of discovering facts. Practitioners of these disciplines must either affiliate themselves with this quasi-priestly order by using terms like "behavioral sciences" or else find something other than "fact" to be concerned with. People in the humanities typically choose the latter strategy. They either describe themselves as concerned with "values" as opposed to facts, or as developing and inculcating habits of "critical reflection" . . . [but] society tends to ignore this kind of rhetoric. It treats the humanities on a par with the arts, and thinks of both as providing pleasure rather than truth. Both are, to be sure, thought of as providing "high" rather than "low" pleasures. But an elevated and spiritual sort of pleasure is still a long way from the grasp of a truth.[3]

Rorty suggests that "worries about 'cognitive status' and 'objectivity' are characteristic of a secularized culture in which the scientist replaces the priest" (p. 35). In such a culture, the only power other than themselves with which humans could be in contact is nature:

> The scientist is now seen as the person who keeps humanity in touch with something beyond itself. As the universe was de-personalized, beauty (and in time, even moral goodness) came to be thought of as "subjective." So truth is now thought of as the only point at which human beings are responsible to something non-human. A commitment to "rationality" and to "method" is thought to be a recognition of this responsibility. (p. 35)

Thus, concludes Rorty, the scientist becomes something of a *moral exemplar* because of his constant exposure to the *hardness of fact*.

A genealogy of the vocabulary of *objectivity, rationality, truth,* and *scientific method* shows the increasing hegemony of science as Western culture became secularized and the scientist replaced the priest. A genealogy of this sort also reveals that the notions *objectivity, rationality, truth,* and *scientific method* have been formulated so as to suggest that they have always implied each other, and are not the product of developments within intellectual history. Inasmuch as science's view of itself, or at least the view of itself that science prefers to promulgate, denies that a genealogy of such conceptual linkages is necessary for understanding rationality, scientific method, truth, or objectivity, challenges to science's preferred view of itself continue to be largely ignored in English-language scholarship. Also ignored is the genealogical spade work challenging this view of science done by such philosophers as Hegel, Marx, Nietzsche, Peirce, and James in the nineteenth century, and Dewey, Wittgenstein, Heidegger, Foucault, Derrida, Quine, Sellars, and Davidson in the twentieth.

Rorty's work in the last dozen or so years, viewed as a whole, has advanced this genealogy, showing that whereas certain traditional concepts associated with a nonhuman reality—for example, God—have been explicitly put aside as unscientific, irrational, or outside the boundaries of scientific method, *rational, objective,* and *scientific explanations* continue to make use of ideas that such orthodox concepts had allowed or required.[4] Accordingly, *scientific rationality* continues to promote the orthodox view that the world is split up "into sentence-shaped chunks called 'facts'"; that *out there* lies nature's vocabulary, "waiting for us to discover it;" and that certain languages or vocabularies correspond to a language the world proposes for us to speak.[5] These assumptions were part of an earlier worldview that held that the nonhuman reality that exists besides us—the world—was the creation of a Thinking, Speaking Being—God—or identical with such a Being. To understand why, in the absence of this belief, anyone would claim or even imagine that what exists besides us conveniently takes the shape of *sentence- shaped chunks* to which the sentences of our *current* scientific theories correspond, requires going back, albeit rather breathlessly, to earlier episodes in the history of philosophy. However, even a quick survey of modern thought should be sufficient to show how problematic this assumption is.

The quest for certainty in modern philosophy begins with Descartes' search for the indubitable. His certainty of his existence as a thinking thing, which counted among its inner representations clear and distinct ideas, followed from, if not constituted, the primary instance of the incorrigibility of those inner states about which a subject cannot be mistaken. But the insistence that the clarity and distinctness of some representations compelled certain beliefs about them was simply Descartes' application of an idea that goes back at least as far as

Plato—the idea that parts of the mind or parts of the body might be compelled to believe a certain proposition or representation true because of some characteristics or powers of the object represented, described, or referred to by the proposition.[6] Rorty, after Heidegger and Dewey, believes that the analogy prompting this idea is one between knowing and visual perception, an analogy they see as Plato's gift to epistemology.[7] This analogy lies behind traditional theories about *theory*: once *knowing* a proposition to be true is identified with being caused to do something by an object,[8] the relation and position of humans to the external world (whether natural or transcendent, and to our *inner* world, for that matter) becomes one of *describing or writing-about* rather than of *interacting or talking-with*.

Plato's preference for ocular rather than auricular metaphors is central to the development of philosophy as a genre of writing, notwithstanding either his use of the dialogue-form or the reservations Socrates expresses about writing in the *Phaedrus*. If, as Derrida suggests, philosophy as a genre of writing *disguises* that it is a genre of writing and that philosophical *speech* is parasitic on philosophical *writing*—if philosophy only *appears* to privilege speech over writing— discussions of the sort found in the *Phaedrus* are just what we should expect.[9] If language gives voice to thoughts or representations that mirror some *transcendent* or *external* reality that causes these thoughts or representations, *our* giving voice to them or writing them down is nonessential or accidental. The truth or necessity of these thoughts or representations has nothing to do with their utterance or inscription by us.[10] To quote Rorty:

> The idea of "necessary truth" is just the idea of a proposition which is believed because the "grip" of the object upon us is ineluctable. Such a truth is necessary in the sense in which it is sometimes necessary to believe that what is before our eyes looks red—there is a power, not ourselves, which compels us. The objects of mathematical truth will not *let* themselves be misjudged or misreported. Such paradigmatically necessary truths as the axioms of geometry are supposed to have no need of justification, of argument, of discussion—they are as undiscussable as the command of Zeus shaking the lightning, or of Helen beckoning to her bed. (Putatively rational *ananke* is, so to speak, just a sublimated form of brute *bia*.)[11]

Yet, as both Derrida and Rorty have noticed, while truths, or the *facts* to which thoughts or representations correspond, do not depend on our uttering or inscribing them, they must be inscribed somewhere, at least metaphorically. It is this inscription in nature, or in Platonic

Forms, or in the soul's innate ideas or recollection of these Forms, that supposedly guarantees the necessity of these truths.

Writing "fixes" language; an inscription preserves a statement or utterance for others to "find." Writing thus enables special kinds of utterances or statements: statements about what is fixed, as things are fixed when Zeus nods; statements about what is universal, intelligible, and necessary; statements about things that are not the result of our doing, but that come from a power other than human; statements of truths that are found rather than made. Thus *philosophical* writing as a genre pretends (or *pretenses*) that the writing of philosophy has no effect on how one *does* philosophy—that *philosophical* writing merely records or inscribes philosophical speech, because *philosophical* speech simply states what has been *written in Nature's Own Vocabulary*, or in the mind of God, or in innate ideas in the human mind, or wherever the One True Vocabulary is allegedly found.

Philosophical *speech* does not *appear* to be parasitic on writing, because *our* inscriptions are merely tokens of some original inscription *of which we are not the authors*, but *see* or *discover* or *read* in Nature or Reality or the Mind. Since this original inscription has *fixed* these truths, the philosophical statement of these truths can appear to be grammatically tensed but logically tenseless. Philosophical *speech* can appear to have a certain independence from its historical and cultural context and from the occasion of its utterance or inscription. As such it can serve as a foundation for the rest of what we know or believe.

In short, philosophical *speech* can appear to consist of propositions about abstract concepts or classes. Philosophical speech is not, of course, ordinary language—the language of everyday speech in which we talk to others or to ourselves. Indeed, it is not clear in what sense a kind of reading off or deciphering of truths inscribed in nature or mind by some power other than ourselves should be considered *speech* at all. What is read off or deciphered is the *message* or *proposition* the world causes us to believe, and the medium in which it is communicated— speech or writing—and the style in which it is communicated are *ex hypothesi* irrelevant as long as the message is not *obscured* by the medium or style.[12] Because "writing entrusts communication to a set of signifiers that remain or can remain constant through an unlimited number of transmissions" (p. 44) it is suited to the communication of propositions, but not to single speech acts. To quote Thomas Cole:

> if a written message is much less subject to distortion when a series of
> transmissions is involved, any single transmission by means of writ-
> ing involves certain ambiguities from which oral communications are
> largely free. It usually occurs apart from any situational context, with-

out the clarification that intonation, phrasing, gestures and other aspects of delivery bring, and without the presence of the transmitter to explain, rephrase, and repeat in an effort to minimize or correct misunderstanding. (p. 44).

The inscription of propositions enhances their timelessness, which, for Plato, is a cause of our being certain of them. For Descartes, certainty results from introspection; from attending to the clarity and distinctness of our representations. In both cases the justification for believing something was identified with the cause of the belief. For Locke and the empiricist tradition associated with him, the justification for believing something was again identified with the cause(s) of the belief. A representation was *privileged* if a *mechanistic* account could be given of how one came to have it, where *mechanistic* referred to the processes by which physical objects caused sense impressions in the mind, just as a seal can leave impressions or an imprint on a wax tablet.

The problem with Lockean empiricism is that it confuses, indeed, *must* confuse, as Rorty points out, a representation as some quasi-object in inner space, and a representation as a true judgment about an object.[13] The representation as a quasiobject in inner space is, at least for Locke, in some respects an image of the object in outer space that caused the sense impression. It is through sense impressions, then, that the *mind* can know something extramental, which Locke identifies as material or physical reality; thus is the mind the *mirror* of nature. The representation as a true judgment about an object is a proposition, a conceptual or linguistic entity that does not resemble something extramental or nonlinguistic, as Berkeley was to point out in insisting that an idea can only be like another idea. Knowledge qua propositions or judgments, then, is not justified by knowledge qua acquaintance with images of objects, for, as Hume made painfully clear, propositions are not given in sense experience, nor are the *important* ones simply relations of ideas—that is, analytic truths.

Kant's response to Hume was to *save* the preferred *representations* of the new science by identifying the foundations of empirical knowledge with conditions for intelligible experience imposed by the knowing subject—that is, by arguing for synthetic a priori truths. This meant that the mind did not *mirror* Nature, but instead provided the conceptual framework that allowed nature to be known. Knowledge was no longer conceived as simple acquaintance with what was *given*, which in turn justified propositions about this *given*. The way things are independent of our sense experience could not be known, since the sensory input that came from outside the mind *could not be known by the mind without being synthesized*—that is, reproduced and organized in *inner space* in conformity with certain rules (the a priori forms of sensory intuition and the a priori categories of judgment) that were *inscribed* in the subject, albeit the *transcendental subject.* Neither the things-in-themselves outside the mind—that is, the *noumena*—nor the mind's processes in turning the sensory manifold generated by the things-in-themselves into things-as-they-appear—that is, the phenomena, could be known through Cartesian introspection or Lockean experience. An a priori synthesis cannot be known *incorrigibly* through introspection or experience, but only as the conclusion of an argument or *deduction* about the possibility or conditions of knowledge.

Thus the certainty that attaches to knowledge as a consequence of Kant's *epistemological* turn comes not from the relationship of the mind to extramental objects of knowledge, but from the relations of propositions to judgments, or to forms of judgments that are universal and necessary. The specific intuitions and categories of the knowing subject that were allegedly a priori and, as such, supposed to guarantee the universality and necessity of Newtonian physics and Euclidean geometry, ended up looking very much like remnants from a web of beliefs that constituted Western philosophy and science at a particular point in its history. The notion that the self has a priori concepts, like the idea that the self has innate ideas, or a rational essence, or some other sort of vocabulary that transcends the vocabularies and practices of particular societies at particular times and arrives at what is universal, seemed to be a remnant of a worldview that saw humans as the creation of a Thinking, Speaking Being, or as identical with such a Being. Indeed, the notion of the self as something over and above a web of beliefs, desires, and performances seems to be a vestige of this earlier web of beliefs.[14]

It is not surprising that the response to Kantian a priorism was first an Idealist turn that emphasized that phenomena are appearances, albeit historical ones, of noumenal reality, and then a linguistic turn that looked for universality and necessity, and for the logical grounds of empiricist and phenomenalist doctrines, by analyzing language's contribution to what is given.[15] Certainly English-language epistemology proceeded on the hope that language might supply *the universal scheme for all possible content.*[16] Logical positivism attempted to distinguish between statements that were true by virtue of their meaning and thus necessary, and those that were true by virtue of experience. The latter, though not incorrigible, at least had the status of *privileged* representations because of their origins.

The notion that we could distinguish between responses made because of the compulsion of language and those made because of the compulsion of experience was challenged, however, by philosophers influenced by Wittgenstein's *Philosophical Investigations*. Wilfrid Sellars, for example, argued that awareness of facts, particulars qua particulars, resemblances between particulars, and particulars qua instances of *classes* or *kinds* is a linguistic affair."[17] This type of awareness Sellars describes as "being in the logical space of reasons, of justifying and being able to justify what one says." It is thus different from the prelinguistic awareness of babies or the discriminative behavior of other entities in responding to stimuli.[18] This means, as Rorty notes, that while behavior of the latter sort may be a causal condition for knowledge, it does not provide a *ground*—that is, a justification—for beliefs.

Moreover, whatever *knowledge* we may have of particulars or classes is abstracted from propositions. As Rorty remarks, "there is no such thing as a justified belief that is nonpropositional and no such thing as justification which is not a relation between propositions."[19] Quine's inscrutability of reference thesis—the claim that we cannot determine how words *hook on* to the world simply by observing a speaker's responses to sensory stimuli—also undermined the notion that we can separate responses compelled by *experience* from those compelled by language, as did his claim that there is no noncircular way of explaining an analytic truth—that is, a statement that is true by virtue of its meaning.[20]

Thomas Kuhn's study of episodes of major theory change in the history of science also undermined the logical empiricist's hopes of formulating a "neutral observation language" into which at least the empirical consequences of conflicting theories could be translated in order to choose between them.[21] Noting that any set of data admits of more than one interpretation, Kuhn argued that the "facts" used to decide between competing theories during *revolutionary* episodes in science are not independent of some *paradigm* or global theory that identifies them as "facts." Because of the "inscrutability of reference," as Quine put it, a certain indeterminacy attaches to any translations between languages or theories. This indeterminacy underscores the difficulty of both identifying a *neutral observation language* into which the empirical consequences of conflicting theories could be translated and of translating the *facts* of one theory into any language, neutral or otherwise. While Kuhn continued to argue that *paradigm* changes in science were different from those in the arts and humanities, in his later writings he acknowledged that even if global theories were to *share* certain methodological and axiological criteria, these would not be sufficient to *determine* theory choice.[22]

By establishing that the criteria we call the *scientific method* may not be sufficient to explain how theory change in science is *rational*,

Kuhnian and post-Kuhnian philosophy of science undermined the attempt to shift objectivity from objects to the *method* used to establish truths about objects, and the notion of truth from what causes beliefs to what justifies them. Roughly, this attempt consisted in holding that knowledge claims may be justified if they were the result of applying explicit criteria or principles formulated in advance of the specific knowledge claim, because these criteria define an *ideal situation* in which "all residual disagreements will be seen as 'noncognitive' or merely verbal, or else merely temporary, or at least capable of being resolved by doing something further," where what matters is "that there should be agreement about what would have to be done if a resolution *were* to be achieved."[23] As Rorty notes, however, this notion of objectivity presupposes that there are "rules which constrain inquiry, [and] are common to all discourse," or at least to every discourse on a given topic. Thus epistemology proceeds on the assumption that "all contributions to a given discourse are commensurable."[24] Accordingly, *commensurable* means "able to be brought under a set of rules which will tell us how rational agreement can be reached on what would settle the issue on every point where statements seem to conflict," and not by "assigning the same meaning to terms."[25]

But it is by no means evident that there is a set of rules that will clearly demarcate between *rational* disagreements and those that are *noncognitive, verbal, or temporary*. Traditionally the distinction between cognitive and noncognitive disagreements has presupposed the Platonic distinction between reason and desire. Reason, on this view, is simply and wholly cognitive—that is, independent and distinct from any feelings. Thus reason can be exercised without being accompanied by emotion, and edification plays no part in rationality. Barring belief in Platonic *nous* or the Christian soul, it is not clear on what basis we can divorce rationality from edification, or, if the two are not divorced, why rationality should be limited to the type of edification one gets from transforming simple forms into complex sequences by the application of mechanical rules—that is, staying in the *logical space of science*—or to the type of edification one gets from overdetermining meaning and thus bringing the world and ourselves under a simple vocabulary and a fixed description by which one may attempt to *predict* future events and *control* others. Trying to tie the notion of criteria to that on which all subjects must agree, is not very helpful, for that not only begs the question, but also invokes a subject-object distinction that is not unproblematic, just as the notion of a *merely verbal dispute* invokes an equally problematic distinction between words and the world.[26] This is not, of course, to deny that a nonlinguistic reality exists; rather, it is to emphasize *how problematic the claim is that in our experience of this reality we can separate which of its features are due to linguistic factors and which are due to nonlinguistic factors.*

Indeed, that we cannot separate nonlinguistic from linguistic factors in our experience means, as Donald Davidson points out, that we can assume neither that "communication is possible between people who have different schemes . . . for we have found no intelligible basis on which it can be said that schemes are different," nor that we have found that "all speakers of language . . . share a common scheme and ontology. For if we cannot intelligibly say that schemes are different, neither can we intelligibly say that they are one."[27] The notion of a language or conceptual scheme that exists somehow in separation from the content of the world invokes, once again, the notion of linguistic or conceptual forms inscribed somewhere *prior* to their performance by speakers.

Davidson proposes an alternative view of language in which language does not give form or structure to the world, nor is it a medium linking nature to the mind. Rather, it is part of the actions and events in the world, a part of our actions and behavior, a matter of getting around in the world. Getting around in the world entails, among other things, being able to communicate by speech with others, and this requires that one be able to engage in off-the-cuff interpretation, that one has the ability to construct what Davidson calls a *passing theory* of interpretation. A passing theory, according to Davidson, is a theory that the interpreter actually uses in understanding the speaker, and a theory that the speaker intends the hearer to use. It is what is constructed during the course of the performance—while the speaker is talking and the hearer is interpreting what he or she is saying.[28] *A passing theory, then, is constructed by the speaker and the interpreter while communication is taking place; they "negotiate" meaning as they communicate.*

Although a passing theory is what enables an interpreter to understand a particular utterance on a particular occasion as the speaker intends that utterance to be understood on that particular occasion, it would be a mistake to confuse the ability to construct a passing theory with knowing a language. To the degree that the speaker and hearer communicate, what they share "is learned and so not a language governed by rules or conventions known to the speaker and interpreter in advance; . . . what the speaker and interpreter know in advance is not (necessarily) shared, and so is not a language governed by shared rules or conventions" (p. 445). If we were to label a passing theory a language, there would have to be a different language not only for each occasion, but for each turn in the conversation, each malaprop, intentional or unintentional, each joke.

> A passing theory is not a theory of what anyone (except perhaps a philosopher) would call an actual natural language. "Mastery" of such a language would be useless, since knowing a passing theory is only knowing how to interpret a particular utterance on a particular occasion. Nor could such a language, if we want to call it that, be said to have been learned, or to be governed by conventions. Of course things previously learned were essential to arrive at the passing theory, but what was learned could not have been the passing theory. (p. 443)

The things that a speaker and interpreter must have learned in order to construct a passing theory need not include mastery of a language in the traditional sense. Not even the prior theory with which a hearer is prepared to interpret an utterance of a speaker, and the prior theory of the speaker, which is what he or she believes the interpreter's prior theory to be, conforms to the standard conception of a language. Thus the ability to communicate by speech, on Davidson's view, is not a matter of mastering what we usually mean by a *language*:

> It is only when we look at the structure of this ability that we realize how far we have drifted from standard ideas of language mastery. For we have discovered no learnable common core of consistent behaviour, no shared grammar or rules, no portable interpreting machine set to grind out the meaning of an arbitrary sentence. We may say that linguistic ability is the ability to converge on a passing theory from time to time. . . . But if we do say this, then we should realize that we have abandoned not only the ordinary notion of a language, but we have erased the boundary between knowing a language and knowing our way around in the world generally. For there are no rules for arriving at passing theories, no rules in any strict sense, as opposed to rough maxims, and methodological generalities. A passing theory really is like a theory at least in this, that it is derived by wit, luck, and wisdom from a private vocabulary and grammar, knowledge of the ways people get their point across, and rules of thumb for figuring out what deviations from the dictionary are most likely. There is no more chance of regularizing or teaching the process of creating new theories to cope with new data in any field—for that is what this process involves (pp. 445–46).

The construction of a passing theory entails just those aspects of the communication situation—situational context, intonation, phrasing, gestures, the presence of the speaker who by explaining, rephrasing, and repeating the performance minimizes or corrects misunderstanding—that are lost or ignored when it is assumed that writing can preserve the communicative act by transmitting *meanings* or propositional core in an unmediated manner. As Bateson showed, the multiple levels of abstraction involved even in the simplest acts of classification indicate that there is no such thing as a simple message.[29] To interpret one message we must rely on other messages that qualify, modify, or frame its meanings—"without context, there is no communication." Yet it is just these metacommmunicative aspects of the communication situation that orthodox conceptions of *theory* have traditionally considered unimportant or irrelevant. Thus, most conventional theories of communication have been based on conceptions of messages that do not take into account interactive practices by which humans communicate by speech. If communication theory is to be responsive to the interactive practices of communication, it will have to abandon the traditional idea of theory, where theory describes what is already inscribed in mind or nature, and focus instead on *how meaning is performed and negotiated by speakers and interpreters.*

II

The purpose of this brisk excursion through the history of epistemology has been destructive. We wanted to show that the epistemic assumptions on which the orthodox theory of theory is based cannot be sustained. The world empiricists seek to describe does not exist in the shape of the sentences they write when theorizing about it. Seeing, reading, or writing the world are problems that cannot be resolved simply by anticipating a day when our science will mature. What we come to say about the world involves the indistinguishable provocations of the world *and* the mediations of language by which we make claims about it.

Like other academic disciplines emerging in the twentieth century, communication wanted a place at the trough of academic respectability, and that meant it was more important to be true to the practices of science than to the practices of interactive communication. The result has been the development of a research tradition that is built on the decaying foundation of the orthodox theory of theory. Attempts to defend these orthodox research practices now sound hollow, as in the case for empiricism developed by Bostrom and Donohew, which rests on appeals for more data, an optimism about the impending maturity of communication studies as a science, and a few cheap shots at the character of those who would question communication *science.*[30]

Our goal is modest. We want to clear a path that legitimates optional forms of representation, forms that take into account narrative dimensions of knowing and telling. What is needed, we think, is a transformation from description to *communication*. In contrast to the orthodox *theory* of theory that takes what the world causes us to believe as a model for writing about or describing it, we want to make the practices of communication in ordinary human interaction—that is, how meaning is performed and negotiated, the model for telling about the empirical world. Talking-with, then, would become a model or *theory* for writing-about or knowing-about. An epistemology of interactive communication that *privileges* the ways we are part of the world that we investigate, and the ways that we make the world and change it, would dislodge the epistemology of depiction that *privileges* modes for inscribing a preexisting and stable state of affairs.

This change from a causal to a conversational model would mean that participating-with-the-other in the active and interactive world of communication praxis would replace what Dewey once called the *spectator theory of knowledge*,[31] an epistemology that, as noted above, historically has separated subject from object, observation from participation, and reflection from direct experience. The ways in which we *make meaning* in a world of others, by hearing and talking in addition to seeing and writing, would become a focal point of our work. An interactive conception of communication—how the practices of speaking, writing, and reading enable us to make our way through the world—would displace the transmission or depiction notion of communication in which language is viewed as nothing more than a vehicle or tool for describing or inscribing a preexisting ontological world. The vocabulary of facts, objectivity, neutrality, detachment, and correspondence to reality would give way to a terminology that focuses on meanings, subjectivity, emotional involvement, and coping with reality. Indeed, when all these terms are seen as metaphors we choose, the discontinuities between scientific and humanistic inquiry may disappear. As Rorty says, "on this view, great scientists invent descriptions of the world which are useful for purposes of predicting and controlling what happens, just as poets and political thinkers invent other descriptions of it for other purposes."[32]

To see fictional accounts of events as *made-up stories* and scientific descriptions as *discovered facts* is to ignore or trivialize the burdens of authorship and contingencies of language shared by all writers (and speakers). The crisis of representation provoked by postmodernism has made it nearly impossible for scientists to cling to the presumption that the world decides which descriptions of it are true or false.[33] The world

cannot speak for itself. Attempts to represent reality involve transforming a speechless social world into a discursive form that makes
sense (has meaning for or to someone). As historian Hayden White
observes, to the extent that descriptions of the social world involve
translating knowing" into telling they may be viewed as narratives.[34]
Thus social scientists' descriptions of social life, such as the world of
communication, are stories that interpret, construct, and assign meaning to the patterns of lived experience that have been observed. All
such accounts of human beings and their actions convey evaluations;
they are stories that make a point.

The contrast between a causal model and a conversational model
draws attention to the distinction between a science of description (corresponding to the way the world *is*) and a science of communication (a
way of getting around in the world). The former conforms to the practices and methods of doing science; the latter, to the practices of interaction, the application of passing theories by which we make sense of
the world and our places in it, and share our meanings with others. The
causal story is a restless search for enduring truths and universal generalizations; the conversational story fits willingly with plurality,
embracing the power of language and metaphor to make new and different things possible. The causal model emphasizes how we know
about the world and tries to explain it, whereas the conversational
model focuses on how we talk about the world and tries to deal with it.
The causal story talks about order, stability, routine, and control; the
conversational story recounts improvisations, changes, contingencies,
and ambiguities. The differences between causal and conversational
models are real enough, but that is all they are—*differences*; as Rorty
says, not issues to be resolved, only differences to be lived with.[35]

When Thomas Kuhn showed that the match between the ontology of a theory and its correspondence to a reality in nature was illu-
sive in principle, he was saying that the history of science could offer
no warrant for thinking it is possible to distinguish unequivocally
between what is in our minds and what is *out there* in the world.[36] One
of the lessons we should have learned from Kuhn was not to expect so
much from science and to guard against being smug about pushing the
rhetoric of objectivity and value-neutrality. The problem is not with science but with a reverent and idealized view of science that positions
science above the contingencies of language and outside the circle of
historical and cultural interests. Scientific method per se does not make
it possible for the mind to transcend the skin.[37] In the final analysis,
what we are left with is ourselves, the institutions *we* have constructed
and developed, one of which is science. Science *as an institution* may not

have lived up to—indeed, cannot live up to—its ideal of objectivity, but as an institution science has and can exhibit the solidarity that, as Rorty notes, is what makes science useful (pp. 21–45).

The model of talking-with requires a radical shift in the way we construe the connection between ontological and experiential reality— that is, the world *out there* and the world we know. On the whole, social scientists still tend to think of reality as something to get in touch with *as it is*, independent of our participation in it. Most empirical research proceeds on the premise that scientific method provides a means for *receiving knowledge*—that is, procedures for objectively describing the "real world" in a fashion that removes the influence of the knower or experiencer. This goal is presumably accomplished by mandating that the investigator be positioned as morally neutral, detached, and disinterested, a spectator in the game of knowledge. What our brief journey through the history of philosophy shows, however, is that the very foundations of "the mirror of nature" from which persons and groups have securely represented each other and made their claims to knowledge have been dislodged.

Science, it turns out, is positioned within, not above, historical and linguistic processes.[38] This point is made forcefully by biologist Humberto Maturana in his ontology of scientific explanation:

> Since the observer cannot make any cognitive statement about anything independent of his or her operation as a living system, the notion of nature constitutively can refer only to what the observer does (in language) as a human being explaining his or her experiences as such, and, hence, it cannot refer to anything deemed independent of what the observer does. (p. 44)

In a human science of communication that embraces talking-with as a model for writing about or speaking-about, the ideal of a detached observer using neutral language to produce an unmediated mirroring of reality is replaced by the premise that attempts to speak for, write about, or represent other people's lives necessarily are partial, situated and mediated ways of creating value and inscribing meanings. The texts that we craft to represent Other(s) become, as Laurel Richardson says, "a site of moral responsibility."[39]

One of the reasons social scientists have resisted the transformation from description to communication is a desire to cling to traditional distinctions between science and literature and between the "objectivity of methods" and the "utility of narratives."[40] If social sciences were seen as continuous with literature, it would become necessary to concede the legitimacy of anecdotal and narrative modes of scholarship that do (sometimes better) what many of the best exemplars of social science traditionally have done—offer intelligible interpretations of people and actions that have been ignored, forgotten, neglected, or misunderstood.[41] What we hope for from social scientists," Rorty argues, "is that they will act as interpreters for those with whom we are not sure how to talk. This is the same thing we hope for from our poets and dramatists and novelists."[42]

Another reason *talking-with* has not been given legitimacy as a model for writing-about is that *telling* and *narrativizing* as modes of scholarly activity have remained secondary to *knowing*. Thus the questions "How do you know?" or "What methods do you use?" have been regarded, in principle, as the first questions to ask about inquiry. When "objective" descriptions of the social world are viewed necessarily as a translation of knowing about something into telling about it, however, then a question that needs to be asked is not so much "How do you know?" but rather "Why do you talk that way?"[43] Inquiry aimed at prediction and control thus becomes only one among several optional ways of talking about *knowledge* and helping people get on in the world—that is, cope with the contingencies of lived experience. As Rorty and his fellow pragmatists want to say, we have talked that way for a time, now let us see what would happen if we talk this way. Instead of conversing about the objectivity of methods and the validity of results, we could talk about the utility of narratives and the call of stories.[44] Our research practices, whether they are aimed at predicting, interpreting, criticizing, changing, or creating, could then be seen, with humility, simply as discursive strategies that are potentially useful ways of talking (modes of describing) for certain purposes.

Talking-with redefines how we see ourselves positioned in our research; that is, who we are in relation to the others we study and who they are in relation to us. Michael Jackson contends that "our understanding of others can *only* proceed from within our own experience, and this experience involves our personalities and histories as much as our field research" (p.17). Once we are liberated from the ideal of a detached observer who uses neutral language to explain raw data,[45] we will be released from the obligation to hide or deny the experiences of our own lives and the connections between these experiences and those of Others we choose to study and represent. Henry Glassie says, "we study others to bring our own humanity into awareness."[46] The converse fits as well; that is, the awareness we have of ourselves is what arouses our curiosity and interest in the lives and experiences of other humans. Talking-with means acknowledging the ways in which we may be a part of *our data* and thus the ways in which we proceed from our own experiences and our own life stories. It also means, as Heinz von Foerster suggests, that "we see ourselves through the eyes of the other,"[47] examining how we as researchers (and as human beings) are constructed by the others whose experiences we are trying to represent, as well as by the cultural texts that construct us as Others (one of which is social science research). Henry Glassie eloquently articulates the premises of a human science that takes *talking-with* as a model for knowing about:

> Our study must push beyond things to meanings, and grope through meanings to values. . . . Our need is for a sustained investigation of alternatives, a human science in service to morality. . . . Studying people involves refining understanding, not achieving final proof. Ethnography is interaction, collaboration. What it demands is not hypotheses, which may unnaturally close study down, obscuring the integrity of the other, but the ability to converse intimately. (pp. 12–14)

The model of talking-with dissolves the rigid distinctions that have divided self from others, objectivity from subjectivity, and rationality from emotion. As Barbara Myerhoff says, the others, then, are seen as "part of me, not *they*."[48] As the boundaries between self and others dissolve, it becomes unclear whether writings about others are about them or about ourselves. For in looking at them we are inevitably looking at ourselves; our research is a form of reflexive self-examination.[49] "When I judge these people," writes Myerhoff, "I judge myself" (p. 28). Neutrality thus gives way to what Victor Turner once called "compassionate objectivity,"[50] a commitment to enter the space where feelings merge with facts and self engages others in the quest to understand the forms through which we make our lives meaningful. And, as Rorty reminds us, the moral imperative of identifying with the details of others' lives in this way is "to keep trying to expand our sense of *us* as far as we can."[51] The result is a radicalized empiricism that "accommodates our shifting sense of ourselves as subjects and as objects, as acting upon and being acted upon by the world, of living with and without certainty, of belonging and being estranged."[52]

III.

In this final section of our chapter, we want to formulate some goals for a human science of communication that takes talking-with as the model for writing-about or speaking-about, and provide a few exemplars that blur the narrative genres dividing literature and social science. Our concerns here are practical, not ontological. There is nothing about the *nature* of social life that makes it necessary to confine research on communication to the goals of prediction and control. It is up to us as practitioners of communication research to decide whether we want to talk more about the validity of methods or about the usefulness of narratives, about the representativeness of samples or the meanings of lived experiences, about how to improve our predictions in order to reduce uncertainty or how to facilitate dialogue between investigators and subjects (or writers and readers) in order to keep a conversation going, about staying in touch with reality or coping with contingencies of relationships, about letting our data speak for themselves or assuming responsibility for how we speak about them.

Lessons we have learned from the history of philosophy and of science is that we are not going to discover the way the world *is*, because as Nelson Goodman once observed, the world "is as many ways as it can be truly described."[53] Our model of talking-with draws attention to the question of how we position ourselves in the processes of inquiry, the constraints imposed by conventions of writing and modes of description, and the intrusive forms of mediation that fall between reality and data, data and text, text and reader.

An interpretive human science of communication would encourage attempts to reproduce and underscore experientially the practices of communication and joint action (passing theories) that are played out in the moment-to-moment contingencies of living *in*, *through*, and *out of* the open-ended processes of social life. One of the goals would be to construct a multivocal text in which alternative voices and perspectives would be invited to participate in the construction of meanings attached to the experiences being represented. Research would be targeted at simulating the processes and procedures by which partners co-construct the meanings of their experiences for themselves, as well as for others, and to show how these meanings may change as partners confront the constraints and demands of negotiating *what things mean* with each other and conveying those meanings to relevant third parties.

The products of such research would highlight the force and relativity of different modes of description, conventions of writing, and styles of expression. Instead of bracketing reflexivity *in the name of science*, research would be premised on the reflexive goals of exploring how communication is used practically to reveal ourselves (and our meanings) to ourselves, and the ways in which the texts we produce subsequently produce us.

Our model of talking-with would also advance forms of scholarship that radically reframe the conventional sense we have of *self as observer* and *other as subject*. By entering into an interactive relationship with the people we are studying, we create an opportunity to focus on the ways in which our experience of ourselves is changed by them, as well as the ways in which we may be altering their experience. Research on others thus becomes a fervent exploration of a broadened self. As Rose explains, "it is another way to make ourselves more available to ourselves" (p. 6). Accordingly, research may be premised on the assumption that the researcher and the subjects are co-participants and, as a result, the ways in which *they* (the subjects) construct *us* (the observers) are as important as the ways in which we represent them (and a part of the process).

This approach to research fractures the boundaries between subject and object, and detachment and involvement, that have traditionally privileged what we have to say about them and what they can learn about themselves from us, over what they have to say about us and what we can learn about ourselves from them. The research products in this case would be multivocal and dialogic; we would be getting to know (and thereby acquiring knowledge of or learning to talk with) the others by being with them in a way that would inspire conversations in which we exchanged views and experiences with them, challenged each other's points of view, and placed their ideas on a par with ours. Our research texts would include their voices and intelligibilities as well as our own.

Bochner has discussed three overlapping categories of social research that embody the goals of talking-with as a model for writing about.[54] These include: (1) first-person accounts, including autobiographical *true stories*, memoirs, and personal tales; (2) co-constructed multivocal personal narratives, twice-told tales, and performed ethnographies; and (3) interactive fieldwork and self- reflexive ethnography. Space limitations preclude a thorough consideration of exemplars here. We will conclude, however, with a brief description of three exemplars that blur traditional distinctions between literature and social science description, and fall within the boundaries of the goals we have in mind for a human science of communication.

Patrimony is the *true story* of novelist Philip Roth's intimate bond with his elderly father during the last few months of his father's life.[55] Forced to reassess his appraisal of his father in the light of old age and chronic illness, Roth achieves an empathic understanding that reframes his father's most offensive characteristics simply as what it took to survive for eighty-six years. Told in the first-person, this unmistakably autobiographical account plunges the reader into the emotional trauma many people experience when they become parents to their parents. Recognizing that "if not in my books or in my life, at least in my dream I would live perennially as his little son, with the conscience of a little son, just as he would remain alive there not only as my father but as *the* father sitting in judgement of what I do" (pp. 237–38), Roth neverthe-less musters the courage to take charge of the man who had terrorized him as a boy, ushering in "the end of one era, the dawn of another" (p. 83). Often sad, sometimes funny, Roth's narrative paints a rare portrait of an ambivalent son trying to "do it right" for his father, coming to grips with "the overpowering force of bloodbonds," the workings of a mind seeking to detach itself from "the agonizing isolation of a man at the edge of oblivion" in order to find comfort as a member of a clan, and the dissonance arising from the necessity of uniting into a single father, the fierce and vigorous father of his childhood with the fragile and stricken father of the present moment.

In Cancer in Two Voices, Sandra Butler and Barbara Rosenblum use essays, journal entries, and personal letters to tell their story of what it was like to live with terminal cancer and to be the partner who survives.[56] Beginning to write within only a few days of Barbara's diag-nosis of advanced breast cancer, Butler and Rosenblum define their narrative as "a story about loss and the gifts it brings" (p. 1). In Barbara's voice, we hear a candid assessment of what she did to mobi-lize the help and love of her friends to help her cope with the fear of this scary disease, of her feelings about the war being waged inside her body, of her growing recognition that the cancer spreading inside her was *hers* not theirs and that she would ultimately have to fight it alone, of how she and Sandra "closed ranks" to face their crisis together, of how her friend of so many words became mute as they became trapped in their own terror and were unable to reach each other, of what it was like to face the "if only" days" after mastectomy and to want desperately to squeeze life out of every minute of the day, of the changing images of her concepts of a future and the meanings of money, sexuality, and love, of the ironies of being kept alive with poi-sons that cause fatigue and depression, of her hope for miracles and the aloneness of one who faces death squarely within a finite body that is changing radically every day, and finally of being too weak to speak, or interact, or care.

In Sandy's voice, we hear her fears of losing herself in her part-ner's needs, of trying to stay calm in the face of her partner's terror, of sometimes being angry at Barbara for getting cancer and ruining their lives together, then wanting to protect her to keep the cancer away, of her growing feelings of disengagement and loneliness, of what it was like to begin to imagine life without the person she had wanted to grow old with, of their fight for meaning and for maintaining connection, and of her remembrances throughout of the way things used to be, of how Barbara's body became *the* body in their lives and how she became only an extension of Barbara's physical capacities and, then, of the guilt of survival and comparison.

"Living on Tortoise Time" is Mark Neumann's narrative account of an oppositional form of travel in which "tourists" attempt to "get off the beaten track" and recover a sense of identity and meaning by escaping the traditional structures and conventions of tourism.[57] Drawing on his own experience as a participant on the nine-day Green Tortoise Bus Tour, a trip that "self-consciously pits itself against the organizing structures typically associated with mass American tourism," Neumann used fieldnotes, interviews, and correspondence with participants after the tour was completed to recreate a story of what it meant and what it felt like to be on the trip. Reframing the bus trip as a "form of pilgrimage" in which travel "becomes a journey toward the experience of belonging and community bonding" (p. 2), Neumann's first-person account vividly juxtaposes the adventure and intrigue of spontaneous and intense relating on "tortoise time" against the secure and stable routines of ordinary life. Ironically, Neumann's story shows that the Green Tortoise's resistance to conventional orders of tourism cannot overcome the dialectical necessities of individual spontaneity and organizational control that, in this case, offer an "opportunity to run away from the demands and routines of one form of social organization only to find themselves making another" (p. 38).

As it turns out, the cohesion and feelings of unity that formed among these "oppositional tourists" was not based on their escape from the beaten track. As Neumann tells it, "we ultimately kept finding ourselves amidst others—in buses, campers and automobiles—who were traveling the main stem of tourism" (p. 34). Rather, it was the sense in which those on "tortoise time" were able to set themselves apart as a community, however temporary, from the community of "mere tourists" whose lifestyles and conventions they opposed, even if they could not literally escape "the beaten track," that made Green Tortoise travel meaningful. In the final analysis, Neumann concludes, "the pleasure of travel for these persons "is not in the destination, but in experiencing the world with a group of like-minded cohorts, people who symbolically reveal their opposition to others" (p. 38).

These brief exemplars of first-person accounts, twice-told tales, and interactive ethnographies blur the boundaries separating humanities from social science. They exploit what Henry Glassie calls "the synthetic power . . . of a unified program for the study of human beings . . . (where there is) one enterprise, the wholeness of life . . . where old categories slip and shift and then melt away as we find the place where social science joins the humanities, where art and culture and history, time and space, connect, where theoretical and empirical studies fuse" (p. xiv).

12

Changing the Subject:
Rorty and Contemporary
Rhetorical Theory[1]

<E> <E>

Janet S. Horne

The reawakening of interest in rhetorical theory begun by Robert Scott in 1967 has branched into a number of identifiable themes.[2] One can hardly find a rhetorical theory article in the speech communication literature does not contain either a reference to Scott's seminal article, or to *descendants*[3] that can be traced to it. Richard Rorty's *The Linguistic Turn* also was published in 1967, and his ongoing rethinking of philosophy's aims, purposes, and goals to some degree parallels that of rhetorical theorists.[4] Although responses to Scott and to Rorty are far from unified, their effect upon rhetoric and philosophy is much the same: each has succeeded at stirring up the waters of formerly complacent pools.

The purpose of this essay is to consider Rorty's proposals for changing the subject of inquiry within philosophy, in relation to a variety of proposals for rebuilding rhetoric's reputation, which can be traced back to Scott. While Rorty has succeeded in reawakening interest in pragmatism among scholars in numerous disciplines, including rhetoric, his *recovery* of pragmatism is seen by many as seriously incomplete, and therefore *flawed*.[5] I will suggest here that these criticisms are understandable but misguided. First, some background on the issues is necessary.

Background: The Context of Rhetoric and Inquiry

That a rhetorical *turn*[6] in inquiry has been occurring in recent years cannot be denied. From Robert Scott's declaration almost twenty-five years ago that rhetoric is epistemic, to Calvin Schrag's 1985 pronouncement situating rhetoric at the *end of philosophy*,[7] to Nelson, Megill, and McCloskey's[8] compendium of the *rhetoric of the human sciences*, the evidence for a reawakening of interest in rhetoric is plentiful. This renaissance includes a diversity of opinion as to the direction and meaning of the rhetorical turn, although all points of view have in common an interest in reassessing the nature and function of rhetoric in both academic discourse and popular culture. Contemporary rhetorical scholars unanimously deplore the image of rhetoric popularized in the mass media and the status of rhetoric in the academic community.

Along with this common interest, however, there is divergence as well. Bineham[9] for instance, indicates that while many scholars agree on rhetoric as an important contemporary area of study, few agree on the nature and function of that rhetoric, or on the ontological and epistemological issues surrounding it. In this essay I focus on three dimensions in the contemporary resurgence of interest in rhetorical theory: (1) *rhetoric of inquiry*, as instantiated by the Project on Rhetoric of Inquiry (POROI);(2) *epistemic rhetoric*, as initiated by Robert Scott, and (3) *critical rhetoric*, as introduced by Raymie McKerrow.[10]

My thesis is that in spite of this rejuvenation in rhetorical studies, we have had little success in actually "chang[ing] the subject"[11] from traditional epistemological issues to newer, more *edifying ones*.[12] Thus, I will consider the extent to which the rhetoric of inquiry, epistemic rhetoric, and critical rhetoric have *changed the subject* of rhetoric. In order to accomplish this, I will examine how each of these respecifications of rhetoric understand the purposes and ends of inquiry. I will compare their proposals to Richard Rorty's position on the purpose of inquiry and will also consider Rorty's debt to and reinterpretation of the classical American pragmatists.

I maintain that if rhetoric truly is to take its place at the end of philosophy, it must succeed in changing the subject of inquiry. Rorty's work has done much to call attention to the need for traditional philosophy to take a critical and historical turn. I wish to examine the value of that work for the study of inquiry in general, and for the study of rhetorical inquiry—the place of rhetoric in inquiry—in particular. First, a brief sketch of Rorty's position on the purposes of inquiry is needed.

Rorty on the Purposes of Inquiry

Rorty changes the subject from the *normal* discourse of *constructive* and *systematic* philosophy traced in *Philosophy and the Mirror of Nature*[13] to conversation,[14] edification,[15] and circumvention.[16] This amounts to a change in the aims for inquiry that are embedded in the Western intellectual tradition. In Rorty's version of the history of philosophy, the unitary vision of convergence favored by the foundationalist should be replaced by a divergent, *reformist*[17] vision favored by the edifier.[18]

To be sure, if Platonists had never existed, Rortys would not be necessary; likewise, if a unitary vision were possible, it seems likely that we would be closer to it by now. Briefly stated, Rorty proposes a divergence of inquiry into new directions and new problems, which replaces the hope for convergence at the end of inquiry. One commentator summarizes many of the implications of Rorty's strategies in this way:

> Fundamental to Rorty's project is the hope that problems about realism and antirealism, for so long central to English-speaking philosophy, will become obsolete. He wants questions about mind-independent and language—independent reality to be replaced by political questions: How free and open is our community? Are we sufficiently sensitive to outsiders who are suffering or who have new ideas?[19]

Rorty's response to the "dream at the heart of philosophy"—that "hope for just the sort of unique, total, closed vocabulary which Heidegger and Derrida rightly say we are not going to get"[20]—is to set that dream aside; to change the subject; to *recontextualize*[21] it; to *circumvent* it. He proposes that giving up the idea of convergence, of being able to rest ultimately within our "metaphysical comfort,"[22] leads us to stress *praxis* over theory-building and problem solving over ideology. This view presents a classically *heuristic* and experimental approach to inquiry that is quite consistent with the American pragmatist tradition. John McDermott's remarks on the openness of inquiry as seen by James and Dewey would apply equally to Rorty. These pragmatists, McDermott says:

> Bequeath to us a doubt about the possibility of finality, closure, and any effort to designate decisions and values in a way which precludes the press of experience. For Dewey, the ontology of our human situation is that it is problematic. . . . [To] be human is to be in an irresolute situation in so far as ultimate meaning is sought but never realized. For James, the world can never be grasped as whole or as finished. . . . James joins with C. S. Peirce in the belief that all experience is riven with chance and novelty as a permanent condition.[23]

Knowledge and inquiry are self-correcting in the sense of being perpetually open to revision and change.

Another facet of the pragmatist approach to inquiry is the emphasis upon newness or *novelty* as a goal. Diversity, growth, development of new ideas and approaches to problems are all principles rooted in the classical pragmatic tradition. The ability to adapt to changing conditions and transform them, to *redescribe* things in new vocabularies (as Rorty puts it[24]) is crucial for avoiding potential complacency and stultification. While inquiry progresses day to day within what Kuhn calls *normal* discourse, the eruption of *abnormal* discourse pushes the investigator's imagination toward new problems—or toward new ways of solving old ones.[25] Thus, Rorty explictly suggests replacing the "logocentrist's unveiling-reality model of inquiry [with the] pragmatist's invention-of-new-tools model."[26]

Rorty even goes so far as to redefine inquiry itself. He holds that from within a foundationalist perspective, inquiry is merely *an exchange of views*.[27] Kolenda sees Rorty's "campaign against metaphysics" as:

> The other side of his wish to avoid what Peirce called "blocking the road to inquiry." But he goes beyond Peirce by suggesting that what he calls "conversation" should not *degenerate* into inquiry, indicating thereby that "inquiry" is more at home in "normal" discourse, where things are settled by appeal to criteria. In contrast, conversation includes revolutionary ventures, where we struggle with anomalies and with other situations with which we don't know how to cope. Here the appeal to criteria or truth will not help us.[28]

Rorty's position on inquiry, in contrast, utilizes the concepts McDermott identifies in classical pragmatist ethics: transience, pluralism, and melioration. "Science as solidarity," for instance, clearly employs these concepts. Rorty cites Peirce's "contrite fallibilism" in support of an "alternative account of the nature of intellectual and moral responsibility."

> Theoretical questions would thus be replaced with practical questions about whether we ought to keep our present values, theories, and practices or try to replace them with others. Given such a replacement, there would be nothing to be responsible to except ourselves.[29]

Furthermore, since there is no longer any God's-eye view to tell us how to answer such questions, the "best way to find out what to believe is to listen to as many suggestions and arguments as you can."[30] The choices one makes on the basis of such principles do not have the "transcultural validity" sought by many philosophers.[31] But they do show us ways in which "we might be better than we presently are . . . [by means of] the actual or imagined existence of other human beings who were already better (utopian fantasies, or actual experience, of superior individuals or societies)."[32]

The trouble this position has gotten Rorty into is most evident in discussions and exchanges concerning his implied or explicit political views.[33] The central metaphor of the *conversation of mankind* in *Philosophy and the Mirror of Nature*,[34] and his insistence upon the continuation of inquiry within "free and open encounter[s]"[35] have drawn criticism. Whether seen as imperialistic, elitist, or naive by earlier critics, these ideas take on additional meaning when seen from within the framework of a pragmatist notion of the purpose of inquiry as it has been more recently illuminated by Rorty himself.[36] Also, Rorty's assertion in *Contingency, Irony, and Solidarity* that "if we take care of freedom, truth can take care of itself"[37] has taken on more flesh and substance in essays that sketch out specific political implications of his *social democratic utopia*.[38]

Rorty's *conversation of mankind* prescription for philosophy's future can be taken as less a return to Oakeshott's cordial collegiality of the *universitas*[39] than as an echo of James's prescription in the campfire conversation anecdote in "What Pragmatism Means."[40] James there tells a story about a "ferocious metaphysical dispute" concerning a human being observing a squirrel on a tree trunk:

> The human witness tries to get sight of the squirrel by moving rapidly round the tree, but no matter how fast he goes, the squirrel moves as fast in the opposite direction, and always keeps the tree between himself and the man, so that never a glimpse of him is caught. The resultant metaphysical problem now is this: *Does the man go round the squirrel or not?*[41]

James uses this story to emphasize the determining feature of pragmatism, the pragmatic method: "to try to interpret each notion by tracing its respective practical consequences."[42] He points out the use of this method on questions such as the one under discussion around the campfire:

> What difference would it practically make to any one if this notion rather than that notion were true? If no practical difference whatever can be traced, then the alternatives mean practically the same thing, and all dispute is idle. Whenever a dispute is serious, we ought to be able to show some practical difference that must follow from one side or the other's being right.[43]

James reminds us here of pragmatism's persistent demand that we change the subject of inquiry from metaphysical argument to pragmatic concern.

Rorty's position amounts to a corollary of James's (and Peirce's) notion that the purpose of inquiry is production of a means of determining conduct, or Peircean "rules for action."[44] More specifically, Rorty's correlative purpose is to engender means of preserving and enlarging freedom:

> Concrete suggestions are a necessary condition of intellectual and moral progress, but not, of course, sufficient. Good luck is another necessary condition, *and political and cultural freedom are others.* . . [My own hope] is that our culture is gradually coming to be structured around the idea of freedom—of leaving people alone to dream and think and live as they please, so long as they do not hurt other people[45]

Rorty's emphasis is on the priority of concrete political guarantees of freedom to philosophical quests for truth. He specifically opposes processes of inquiry that pursue philosophical questions of definition, correspondence, and justification, and which argue that certain positions (i.e., those of the *cultural left*) are better grounded *ideologically* than pragmatically.[46] While Rorty expresses considerable agreement with the goals of academics who wish to promote multicultural perspectives in education, he holds that the positive aspects of that program have no need for philosophical or ideological grounding. Multicultural perspectives are needed in our educational systems because we are a multicultural society in a mass media age.[47] We may well have a private need to better understand members of other cultures because of our religious beliefs, or our beliefs in Enlightenment ideals, or simply because of our liberal leanings. But we as a society have a public imperative to do so because of the way the world is now, and because of the kinds of things we have learned from the past.[48]

Within the framework of inquiry as recontextualization, Rorty posits the self as a "web of beliefs,"[49] and proposes that beliefs are compared with other beliefs in terms of how they fit together, rather than by comparison with something outside and *other*. The latter comparison is necessary for *realism*, understood as "the idea that inquiry is a matter of finding out the nature of something which lies outside the web of beliefs and desires."[50] Rejecting the realist/antirealist dualism is the first step toward changing the subject of inquiry to "reweaving a web of beliefs" rather than continuing to seek correspondence of our beliefs with something outside ourselves. Beliefs relate to each other as "central, difficult-to- imagine-revising" beliefs in contrast to more marginal, loosely held beliefs, which we view as more open to revision.[51]

I may speculate further on this issue and propose that by setting inquiry into the framework of a *free and open encounter*, Rorty is indicating his awareness of the *certainty* that individuals and groups may *encounter* topics of conversation that are offensive, distasteful, perverse, stupid, or naive. He sees, however, that our society can maintain itself only on a basis of "unforced agreement"[52] by allowing such encounters to continue, and by developing solidarity with those who share our goals.

In summary, Rorty's position regarding the aims, goals, and purposes of inquiry shares many characteristics with classical American pragmatism. In spite of the fact that Rorty has not adopted *whole cloth* the pragmatism of Dewey, or of James, or of Peirce, he implicitly emphasizes the need they saw for philosophers to speak to human problems and human needs. One way of doing this is to radically *change the subject* of philosophical inquiry from epistemological arguments concerning the nature and justification of truth claims, to a more rhetorical project of proposing interpretations and courses of action in public debate. This project includes "disempowering and disillusioning all those who hold to a correspondence theory of truth or conscience,"[53] and thus "undermining"[54] their claims to privileged philosophical foundations.

Changing the subject does not allow compromise, and Rorty is especially adept at ferreting out closet foundationalism. He chides Hilary Putnam, for instance, for claiming to give up the idea of a "God's eye view" while continuing to search for an "idea of 'truth' [charged with] what he [Putnam] calls 'normative' meaning. He had better look elsewhere for regulation and criticism—away from traditional topics of philosophical reflection.[55]

Ideally, pragmatic debate occurs both in academic journals and in more widely distributed media. Nonetheless, the debate reflects decidedly pragmatic ends. While Rorty unabashedly favors continuing the Western social-democratic "experiment," he bases that preference on a clearly defined but ungrounded (in a foundational sense) criterion of freedom, rather than on an unresolvable debate about truth. For Rorty, when we take a pragmatic perspective on the process of inquiry:

> [The] question, "What is the truth of our society?" fades out in favor
> of questions like "What would let more people in this society get more
> freedom?" . . . The question 'How can you be sure your values are
> unconditionally valid?" fades out in favor of the question "How can
> we be sure that discussion of alternative values is as free, open, and
> imaginative as possible?"[56]

From *Philosophy and the Mirror of Nature's* introduction of edification, to *Consequences of Pragmatism's* philosophy with a lower-case p,[57] through the critical emphasis of *Contingency, Irony, and Solidarity* and recent essays on politics in American and European culture,[58] Rorty continually pushes philosophy toward pragmatic, rhetorical ends.

The Rhetoric of Inquiry

The *rhetoric of inquiry* is used here as an umbrella term, encompassing those academic endeavors included in the Nelson, Megill, and McCloskey anthology. It is explored in the rhetoric of science[59] and the rhetoric of technology.[60]

A common concern of scholars in this area is to place the purpose of inquiry into the realm of communication. In other words, aside from the specific disciplinary content of the physical and social sciences, the rhetoric of inquiry studies ways in which research results are presented and have their impact on disciplinary content. Rhetoric of inquiry proposes that writing about, speaking about, and otherwise disseminating knowledge are important *purposes* of inquiry itself, and important *subjects* of inquiry.[61] In short, this endeavor stresses the process of communicating knowledge over the process of defining it.

The pragmatic implications of such a perspective are obvious. Unless research is communicated, it fails to advance understanding and knowledge. Furthermore, unless it is communicated *effectively*, either to other members of a sphere of inquiry or to the public as a whole, it languishes in impotent obscurity. Rhetoric of inquiry also posits that knowledge and inquiry depend upon the persuasiveness of the arguments presented rather than upon the correspondence of the arguments to objective truth or reality. This emphasis is similar to Rorty's move toward edification in contrast to systematic philosophy, since, for edification, "the way things are said is more important than the possession of truths.[62]

The more subtle but also pragmatic implications of the rhetoric of inquiry position include the unmasking of methodology and pretensions to objectivity and the study of how research *really* gets done in libraries, laboratories, and field studies. To the extent that one aim of the rhetoric of inquiry school is to uncover the rhetorical *foundations* of various areas of inquiry, this aim coincides with Rorty's exposure of the rhetoric of philosophy[63]

Yet Rorty's notion of contingency is more radical than is suggested by Nelson et al. Nelson still wants foundations of some sort, even if they are *rhetorical* ones.[64] Rorty warned, at the 1984 Iowa conference, that "rhetoric might bid to become the new unifier of the academy, methodism with a new face.[65] Where Nelson et al. come closest to Rorty is in their interest in rhetoric within various disciplines.[66] This concern directly parallels Rorty's desire to "expand the horizons of philosophy beyond the limits artificially imposed by restricting it to 'officially' sanctioned channels and by the professionalization of the subject.[67]

Nelson wants rhetoric to "form the *grounds* of postmodern episte-mology,"[68] while Rorty is content with a contingent view of knowledge congruent with Lyotard's noncumulative, incommensurate view of the progress of inquiry.[69] Rorty's emphasis on contingency recognizes the limitation of our knowledge to what we have had access to through communication, and celebrates our ability to *cope* in spite of that limi-tation. From an activist pragmatic perspective, the problems we face require action in the face of incomplete or uncertain knowledge. This emphasis on contengency gives us a more radical sense of *epistemic rhetoric* than we find in contemporary rhetorical theory.

Epistemic Rhetoric

The positions generally categorized as *epistemic rhetoric* are even more diverse than those of the *rhetoric of inquiry*. Leff[70] and Bineham[71] have surveyed two decades of scholarship resulting from Robert Scott's 1967 article. From the point of view of the *ends* of inquiry, the differ-ences in perspectives between the rhetoric of inquiry and most of the scholarship in epistemic rhetoric are quite clear.[72]

Despite the diversity of *positions* within epistemic rhetoric, there is consistency with regard to the purposes and ends of inquiry: inquiry is the attempt to reach consensus on disputed correlations between rhetoric and the *real world*. The sides of the debate have coalesced around the Scott-Brummett[73] intersubjectivist position and the Cherwitz et al. objectivist-realist position.[74] I will refer to the sides in the debate as the intersubjectivist group and the objectivist-realist group. The objectivist-realist group takes what Rorty calls a "corre-spondence theory" position.[75] Quite unambiguously, the objectivist-realist seeks to be able to evaluate rhetorical discourse on the basis of how well the truth of the discourse matches up with the way things really are.[76]

The intersubjectivists present a more problematic view. Brummett clearly follows Scott in taking the position that *the truth* of how things really are is created, *intersubjectively*, through communication.[77] What matters about our discourse is the degree to which we can reach inter-subjective agreement about the world, rather than questions as to the way things really are, apart from our discourse about them. While Rorty's position is more in line with that of the intersubjectivists, those scholars are still caught up in the desire for truth. Thus their evaluation of rhetorical discourse is based upon the ability of inquirers to reach consensus (intersubjective agreement) on a *picture* of how things really are.[78] This consensus approach, however, remains within the correspondence position as described by Rorty.

The difference between the objectivist-realist and intersubjectivist positions rests, then, on the difference between truth as correspondence with reality, and truth as correspondence of (intersubjectively affirmed) meanings with each other. While Rorty would clearly prefer the latter to the former, significant differences remain between his program and that of the intersubjectivists.

First, Rorty proposes that certain philosophical problems, such as the nature of truth, should be "set aside."[79] Rorty owes a tremendous debt here to Dewey, as he acknowledges by quoting Dewey's "The Influence of Darwin on Philosophy":

> Intellectual progress usually occurs through sheer abandonment of questions together with both of the alternatives they assume [reality/ideality; materiality/essence; sense/reference, e.g.]—an abandonment that results from their decreasing vitality and a change of urgent interest. We do not solve them; we get over them.[80]

Rhetorical discourse can be quite effectively evaluated on the basis of *accuracy*—that is, with respect to how well the discourse matches up with historical events as we know them, the *facts of the case*, as it were—without worrying too much about philosophical questions. Questions of accuracy are, by and large, historical rather than philosophical questions. The aim of inquiry with respect to accuracy, and the aim of inquiry with respect to *truth*, are quite different. Neopragmatism proposes that the latter aim should be set aside, and the former should be couched in terms of *contingency* with respect to what we *have* consensus on at the present time. In other words, in the most radical pragmatic interpretation of epistemic rhetoric, the issue is quite simple: rhetoric is epistemic because our knowledge is limited to information available in our culture at any given time.[81] The fact that such data are subject to political and ideological filters simply reinforces the Rortyean privilege of freedom over truth.

A second difference between intersubjectivism and Rorty's pragmatism results from the intersubjectivists' involvement in arguments presented by the objectivist-realists. Insofar as they do so, the intersubjectivists have failed to change the subject. Rorty reminds us that Wittgenstein, Heidegger, and Dewey avoided proposing "'alternative theories of knowledge' or 'philosophies of mind.' They set aside epistemology and metaphysics as possible disciplines.[82] By participating in a set of ends and purposes of inquiry indistinguishable from those of the objectivist-realist perspective, the intersubjectivists attempt to change the game while playing by the same rules. The old questions reemerge: "How do we evaluate whether or not a particular piece of rhetorical discourse matches up with what *we have agreed upon* as the truth?" Thus, despite obvious disagreements with regard to the nature and source of *truth*, the *question* of what truth is and the need for rhetoric to match up to it remains crucial to epistemic rhetoric.

In contrast, Rorty's pragmatism proposes:

> If we could ever become reconciled to the idea that most of reality is indifferent to our descriptions of it, and that the human self is created by the use of a vocabulary rather than being adequately or inadequately expressed in a vocabulary, then we should at last have assimilated . . . the Romantic idea that truth is made rather than found.[83]

This point is reiterated by Prado: "What needs to be emphasized . . . is that the dispute [about what counts as knowledge] is not about the world but about what we say and believe about it.[84] To assert this position, furthermore, is not to claim that no material reality exists outside language, or that all reality is constituted in language, or that language *creates* the world.[85] To a neopragmatist, these positions retain an idealist metaphysics. But since what we say and believe about the world is not *about* it, in a referential sense, what we say and believe can be changed without engaging in metaphysical debates.

Finally, both objectivists and intersubjectivists stress the importance of closure and consensus in spite of their differences with respect to the grounds for agreement. From the objectivist-realist perspective, closure is desirable and possible and can be reached by demonstrable proof, at which point one's disputant has no recourse but to capitulate. From the neopragmatist perspective, closure cannot be distinguished in a serious way from intersubjective agreement, based on what Rorty calls contingency and what McDermott summarizes as transiency. What we think of as settled matters, according to Rorty, are less accurate descriptions than they are language games. Since the world is largely "indifferent" to our descriptions of it, "the fact that Newton's vocabulary lets us predict the world more easily than Aristotle's does not mean that the world speaks Newtonian."[86] Significant scientific and cultural changes throughout history are a matter of cultures having "gradually lost the habit of using certain words and gradually acquired the habit of using others.[87] For Rorty, the process of reaching closure on any description is less a process of demonstrable proof than it is a process of reaching intersubjective agreement about descriptions of an *indifferent* reality. Hence, our agreement is always contingent.

But Rorty goes even further and rejects the ideal of consensus and intersubjective agreement important to Scott and Brummett, in favor of difference, of disagreement, of what Lyotard calls *paralogy*.[88] The bankruptcy of foundationalist, correspondence theories of truth leads as well to what Rorty calls the "contingency of conscience."[89] It obligates us to question claims to truth—regardless of the grounds upon which they are based—and to continually redescribe them. Rorty's contingency of objectivity and of conscience bears a striking resemblance to what McDermott calls the pragmatists' notion of transiency:

> [The evidence for] a rescue from the snares of time does not exist. [For the pragmatist], for whom the everyday is constitutive of all that we have and is the only reality with which we can communicate, the doctrine of transiency turns out to be the bottom line of authenticity. Relegating the disasters of the present to the potential redemption of an unknown, uncharted and nonempirical future is the height of self-deception.[90]

For Rorty, we should read "unknown, uncharted, and nonempirical" as any extrahuman or ahistorical criteria—any criteria that are somehow *found* rather than *made*.[91] Since the only criteria we have for evaluating inquiry are those that we make ourselves, we all have an obligation of conscience to not only find areas of agreement with others, but to point out areas of divergence as well. Pragmatists, in short, modestly posit the "goal of inquiry (in any sphere of culture) as the attainment of an appropriate mixture of unforced agreement with tolerant disagreement.[92]

I would propose that a thoroughly pragmatist response to these disputes is much like James's response to the dispute about the squirrel. James relates that his companions accused him of a "shuffling evasion"[93] when he proposed that both sides in the dispute were both right *and* wrong, depending upon one's interpretation of what it meant to *go round*. He suggested that such questions be set aside in favor of more consequential matters. Directing inquiry into a new direction—*changing the subject*—requires putting aside those *fundamental* disagreements that no discourse can resolve. The pragmatists, including Rorty, direct us instead toward the arena of *praxis*—an arena that is more prominent in rhetoric of inquiry and in McKerrow's critical rhetoric than in epistemic rhetoric.

Critical Rhetoric

The final theme in contemporary rhetorical studies to be considered in relation to Rortyean pragmatism's view of the aims of inquiry is the *critical rhetoric* of Raymie McKerrow.[94] The purpose of inquiry for critical rhetoric, according to McKerrow, is to "unmask or demystify the discourse of power."[95] Although he relies primarily upon Foucault, critical rhetoric is compatible with pragmatism's sense of the purposes of inquiry. This compatibility emerges from McKerrow's key conception of criticism as act, or praxis, and *performance*.[96] Critical rhetoric's central definitions conform to important concepts in pragmatism: rhetoric as contingent; knowledge as doxastic; language as nominalist; the critic as inventor; criticism as invention. McKerrow's version of *changing the subject* occurs in his

> attempts to rescue rhetoric from its subservient role . . . dependent on universal standards of reason as a means of responding to Plato's critique. . . . If we are to escape from the trivializing influence of universalist approaches, the task is not to rehabilitate rhetoric, but to *announce* it in terms of a critical practice."[97]

McKerrow eschews *arguing* for any ontological or epistemological status for critical rhetoric.[98] Instead, he offers a redescription of the background of the practice of criticism—a background that creates a pragmatic rather than a philosophical imperative. This refusal to argue echoes Rorty's announcement: "conforming to my own precepts, I am not going to offer arguments against the vocabulary I want to replace, . . . I am going to try to make the vocabulary I favor look attractive by showing how it may be used to describe a variety of topics."[99]

Two other dimensions of McKerrow's conceptualization of critical rhetoric congruent with the aims of inquiry as formulated by pragmatism are the *transformative* power of critical practice, and the importance of the *consequences* of critical practice. McDermott refers to a related theme, classical American pragmatism as *melioration*: the transformative power of new linguistic relations to create insights otherwise locked into our assumptions may help us devise ways to make things better.[100]

Moreover, McKerrow's insistence that "a critical practice must have consequences,"[101] repeats the central feature of pragmatism. His *critique of domination* aims at uncovering and (in Rorty's terms) *empowering*[102] hidden aspects of social relations. The consequences of his *critique of freedom* would be (in Rorty's terms) *constraints*,[103] which remind us that no critique can be immune to redescription or be considered complete and final.

McKerrow's more recent work refines a key distinction between *criticism* and *critique*.[104] Rorty's radical pragmatism enables us to appreciate the sharp divergence between critical rhetoric and other contemporary rhetorics. By identifying critical rhetoric with *critique*, McKerrow forces rhetoric beyond the criteriological frame of discourse grounded in rationalism, since he understands critique "as a 'transformative practice rather than as a 'method' of inquiry."[105] In Rorty's vocabulary, McKerrow's *criticism* conforms to *normal* discourse, where standards *other than* and *outside of* the critical object prevail. *Critique*, however, breaks out into *abnormal* or revolutionary discourse:[106] "Criticism operates from an acceptance of the tenets of rational democracy, while critique offers the possibility of challenging those tenets."[107] "The *idea*," as Rorty puts it, "is to get a vocabulary which is (at the moment) incommensurable with the old in order to draw attention away from the issues stated in the old."[108]

Critical rhetoric examines the relationship of inquiry to its context which is always understood as embedded within power relations. Once we do this, our attention is called to the ways political structures, including reward systems, influence the processes of inquiry. As an example: when we apply the power/knowledge relationship invoked by McKerrow to academic discourse, we can see how that ability to ground knowledge claims upon epistemological foundations carries with it the promise of greater *cash value* than is accorded to critique that resists closure.

Conclusion

We can now return to our original theme of the purposes of inquiry in order to consider the mutual implications of diverse rhetorical studies and contemporary pragmatism. If we look at contemporary rhetorical studies from the point of view of what kinds of questions rhetoric of inquiry, epistemic rhetoric and critical rhetoric ask, we can discern certain compatibilities with pragmatism. The rhetoric of inquiry asks: What are the distinctive and common features of academic discourse? How much of the sociology of knowledge depends upon discovering truth and how much depends on inventing it? Epistemic rhetoric asks: What is the relation between rhetoric and truth? What is the nature of truth and how is it accessible to us? Critical rhetoric asks: What is there about this situation that informs my chances of having some kind of *effect* upon in? What are the constraints on what I can say and how I can say it?

This pattern of questions is revealing: the questions asked by epistemic rhetoric are identifiable in Rortyean terms as classic *Philosophical* questions, while those asked by rhetoric of inquiry and critical rhetoric are *philosophical* questions,[109] even, I would suggest, *rhetorical* questions.

Critical rhetoric differs from the rhetoric of inquiry, however, in that it sets aside questions of truth and objectivity. It understands knowledge as doxastic and understands *itself* as nonfoundational. It rejects "distinctions between discursive and non-discursive practices,"[110] and asserts that theorizing itself is not a *constructive* activity but a form of critical practice.[111] It thus conforms to Rorty's sense of the purpose of inquiry as edification. As self-reflexive critique, critical rhetoric demonstrates that in any postfoundational system, the notion of inherent, essential privilege is undermined.

Each of the contemporary rhetorics discussed in this essay succeeds in changing the subject of inquiry in some way: the logic of inquiry becomes the rhetoric of inquiry; philosophy as the purveyor of epistemology gives way to rhetoric as epistemic; rhetorical theory and criticism to criticism and theory as rhetoric; all consist of a *redescription* of the role of rhetoric in inquiry. Rorty and McKerrow seem to stand alone, however, in changing the subject to rhetoric without foundations.

Earlier in this essay, I referred to some rhetoricians' aversion to Rorty's philosophy. The implications of Rorty's thought about the status of academic disciplines, which becomes more explicit in some of his later essays, should dissolve that hostility to Rorty's philosophy. What Rorty calls the "antiessentialist philosopher" might also be called the *postmodern rhetorician*:

> [who] looks forward to the day when all the pseudo-problems created by the essentialist tradition—problems about the relation of appearance to reality, of mind to body, of language to fact—will be dissolved . . . [who] sees the distinction between reality and appearance as a way of suggesting that some set of relations, some context, is intrinsically privileged.[112]

Read rhetorically, this understanding of philosophy suggests that *rhetoric*—not philosophy, or epistemology, or ontology—is ultimately *honest* in the pursuit of knowledge, since rhetoric historically acknowledges not only the contingency of language but also the contingency of truth. Placing contingency at the center of inquiry undermines the hierarchy that Plato created and rhetoric inherited. Rorty encourages us to set aside rhetoric's obeisance to Plato, to let philosophy be philosophy and rhetoric be rhetoric—an ongoing critique and quite serious play of language.

13

Icons, Fragments, and Ironists: Richard Rorty and Contemporary Rhetorical Criticism

❧ ❧

Mick Presnell

The study of public address in the United States began its odyssey by identifying its object (public oratory delivered to a specific audience by a speaker) and method (the analysis of the speaker's method of influencing the audience).[1] In the last three decades or so, this traditional view of the discipline has altered significantly. The object of study has been expanded such that *public address* now includes virtually any communicative expression directed to an audience, including media messages, public events, and architecture. Studies of public address employ the full array of social science and humanities approaches such as historical research, discourse analysis, narrative theories, genre theories, structuralism, deconstructionist strategies, and ideological criticism.[2] Recent debates about the impact of postmodern social conditions on the nature and function of public address have raised new questions regarding how we might locate and understand an object of critical analysis. The reexamination of the tradition of public address criticism has led to a shift from a focus on speech as an event to speech as a text.[3]

One philosopher whose work has drawn the attention of those struggling with contemporary debates about the nature and function of rhetoric is Richard Rorty. Not only is Rorty's work often cited among rhetoricians, he has participated in conferences devoted to expanding the scope of rhetorical inquiry. For instance, in a report on a 1984 conference on the Rhetoric of Human Sciences held at the University of Iowa, Simons remarks that "no one was more persuasive at the conference than Richard Rorty."[4] I argue that Rorty's pragmatism offers an important response to issues of public address criticism by providing an alternative approach to contemporary debates about the nature of the epistemology and ontology of human communication.

I will explore Rorty's contributions to public address criticism by arguing that (1) debates among scholars of rhetoric in the United States have centered in part around the tension between conceptions of public address as an event and as a text, (2) these debates strive to resolve the event-text tension by treating the relationship as a dialectic in which one term is favored over the other, and (3) Rorty's neopragmatism provides a useful way of conceptualizing this supposed dialectical tension. Finally, I will remark on some of the contributions and limitations of Rorty's view regarding our understanding of public address as a mechanism for promoting a tolerant and just society.[5]

Public Address: Event or Text?

Philosophers from Plato to Husserl have tended to characterize spontaneous speech as an inherently pure expression of the immediacy of thought. In this view, spontaneous speech is a perfect union of intention and expression. To speak is to simultaneously know and express one's mind. For the Stoics and later for the Judeo-Christian tradition, speaking is the manifestation of *logos*—that is, spirit as the expression of an ordered universe.[6] These ancient traditions that have played key roles in Western civilization consider speech more than just a tool that we use to link otherwise disjunctive experiences. Speech is itself the expression of the integrity of the human spirit participating in divine integrity. The definition of the loss of the integrity of a speaker is the speaker's failure to match his or her intentions with their expressions. Writing poses a danger to this unity. In the *Phaedrus*, Plato warned that writing would lead to the conceit that we have learned something by reading. According to Plato, the best that writing can do is to remind us of that which we already know and can speak about. Once the immediacy of the speaking event is lost through its mediation by writing, truth and integrity are lost.

The contemporary practice of rhetorical criticism has in part been informed by the tension between treating speech as an event and as a text. Many scholars have developed their critical approaches through an exploration of this tension. For instance, in an essay celebrating the seventy-fifth anniversary of the Speech Communication Association, Iltis and Browne describe public speaking as both an event that is ephemeral and a text that endures.

Speech considered as an *event* is experienced as an immediate presentation of an intentional act to an audience that strives to interpret the message of the speaker. As an event, speech is ephemeral.[7] Following Ricoeur's theory of textual hermeneutics, Iltis and Browne argue that the study of speech is made possible by considering the speech event as a text, that is, as an object of criticism freed from ostensive reference in the situation, the immediate intentions of the author, and the interests of a particular audience.

For Iltis and Browne, speech considered as a *text* has the permanence and repeatability that speech as an event does not. The public speaking event exists as a totality, a holistic presence that stands in contrast to devitalized fragmented texts. The speech as a text, as Plato suggested in the *Phaedrus*, is treated as a fundamentally truncated communicative phenomenon compared to the richness of the speech event. Iltis and Browne assert that "there can be no overlooking the flawed nature of the situation offered in the text of a public speech."[8]

Even though rhetorical theorists and critics commonly credit speech as the original event of meaning, most researchers assume that the study of rhetoric must acknowledge that communication is always a dynamic process that is both eventful and textual. *Text* and *speech* are often abbreviations for communication as, respectively, the memory or inscription of a communicative event and a situated response to messages. Thus, communication is variously treated as a text that displays the dynamics and sense of presence of a performance or as an event that has some of the permanence and objectivity of a text.

Two recent research projects that have been understood as paradigmatic of this general trend in contemporary research are the close reading of texts as developed by Leff, and McGee's emphasis on the fragmented eventfulness of speech as part of the ideological struggle of audiences.[9] Leff privileges the text as object and focuses attention on the text's internal dynamics as engaging the reader in an eventful process of reading. McGee privileges the event of an audience's interpretation of messages and considers texts to be the product of this event. I will briefly summarize and compare the projects of Leff and McGee, and evaluate both positions from Rorty's neopragmatist perspective.

Text as Eventful

Leff and Sachs describe the history of modern rhetorical criticism from the neo-Aristotelian focus on content and argument to the contemporary emphasis on style. Style, they say, is displacing content and argument as the center of rhetorical criticism. "We are reaching the point where manner of expression, the generation and use of symbols, has become the substance of our study, and argument appears as a supplement."[10] Thus, Leff and Sachs describe a historical dichotomy of form as stylistic effect, and content as topic and argument. They wish to resolve this dichotomy, suggesting that emphasizing either form or content "deflect[s] attention from the complex, variegated texture of specific rhetorical products." Reducing rhetoric to either form or content misleadingly results in a "focus upon abstract, essentialized conceptions of the rhetorical process."[11]

Leff and Sachs propose a *close reading* of texts as a solution to the tension between form and content. Such a reading aims to disclose how rhetorical style interacts with representational content, especially through the use of iconicity.[12] Some stylistic choices are understood as iconically representing experiences and events—that is, as representing content of the speech. As an example of the close reading of iconicity, Leff and Sachs analyze a speech by Edmund Burke regarding the British Parliament. In his speech, Burke describes the gamelike process of the Parliament passing anti-Catholic legislation. He criticizes the Parliament for becoming so engaged in the self-contained competitive sport of political maneuvering that not only was unjust legislation passed, but it was legislation that neither political bloc intended to actually approve. Burke employs a complex syntax and an ambiguous use of pronouns that Leff and Sachs argue "iconically represents the resulting confusion."[13] These *iconic* dimensions of discourse call upon the reader to consider the text as a perceptual object with mimetic characteristics that reinforce arguments and propositions.

Leff and Sachs argue that "Burke's example shows us something that abstract theory disguises — the power of discourse to blend form and meaning into local unities that 'textualize' the public world and invite audiences to experience that world as the text represents it."[14] Interpretation is informed in part by reading as an *enactment* of meaning. The text is treated as demanding a kind of interpretive performance by the reader—that is, as a speechlike event. Textual evidence for the rhetorical excellence of Burke's speech is provided by reading the text as an expressive intertwining of stylistic choice and meaning.

Leff and Sachs seek to ground interpretation in the presence of the relation between text and reader. The phenomenon of iconicity draws attention to reading as an embodied process. The text is treated as a perceptual object, not just a transparent representation of content. Thus, reading takes on characteristics usually associated with speech—namely, the richness and dynamics of the immediate percep-

tion of an expression. Texts are described as "inviting audiences to experience [the] world as the text represents it."[15]

Events as Textual

Contrasting in some important respects with Leff's strategy of *close reading*, McGee is concerned with the relationship between the cultural and social context of public address and how discourse is taken up by audiences. He promotes the evaluation of public discourse as supporting, resisting, or articulating ideologies. One difference between the work of Leff and McGee is, respectively, the difference between a micro and macro perspective on the rhetorical function of public address.[16] For Leff, a close reading of a text reveals how it negotiates various historical tensions and contradictions that may have been salient for its audience. For McGee, the location and meaning of a text is understood partly through an examination of the historical and ideological context.

McGee, along with a number of researchers within the communication discipline, characterizes our contemporary historical period as "postmodern."[17] Definitions of *postmodern* are plentiful. Two inter-related characteristics of the *postmodern era* are particularly relevant for McGee: (1) the fragmentation of community interests, and (2) the fragmentation of audience member identity as an interpreter of messages.

According to McGee, populations always have been fragmented by geography, ethnicity, class, gender, or race. The *apparent* coherence of national cultures was the product of the homogeneity of ruling classes that produced and controlled the public discourse within a society as a whole. McGee, describing premodern Western European culture, remarks that "except for everyday conversation, all discourse within a particular language community was produced from the same resources. Further, all discourse found its influence on the same small class of people who comprised the political nation."[18] Diversity among those not in power was either ignored or repressed.[19]

In the beginning of the industrial revolution and early electronic age, hopes were expressed for a global unity or *totalization* of interests. But the global village has failed to materialize. Instead, society is increasingly fragmented by the extension of specialized and symbolically defined criteria. Marketing, advertising, and political analysis of audiences provide research data about a wide range of target population attributes. Group identity among members is fostered through their common characteristics that are reflected to them through the use of this research. A single individual becomes a member of a number of special interest groups, depending on the person's role as a consumer of different product types[20] or as a voter with different political agendas. Mass consumer society both requires and creates increasingly specific target audiences. In short, one effect of mass media is the increased fragmentation of the public into special interest groups that can serve as target audiences. McGee suggests that "we stand now in the middle . . . of a seventy-year movement which has fractured and fragmented American culture. Contemporary discourse practices this fragmentation."[21] The specificity of interest groups results in the diffusion of cultural beliefs and undermines the ability of these groups to find a common ground to resolve conflicts and reach a consensus about community issues.

The fragmentation of individual interests is a counterpart to the fragmentation of community interests. The bureaucratization of modernism has spread beyond the work place and has become accepted as a natural form of reason. Role divisions and the resulting sense of having *multiple selves* is no longer experienced as a condition of alienation (as in modernism's nostalgia for a lost integrity) but is accepted as a reasonable adaptive response of the person who faces numerous different discourse contexts. Social divisions between public and private, strict task differentiations, hierarchies of command and control, and spheres of interests are no longer seen as carved out of the homogeneity of the life-activity of individuals. The agrarian rhythms of early modern life were experienced as violated and disrupted by the timetables of the industrial work environment. Now these segmentations are taken for granted.

In contemporary society the formation of texts out of fragments of available discourse is happening at an increasingly rapid pace. One media image barely has time to become common usage when it is replaced by another. The multitude of public messages throws the interpretation of specific texts into a crisis simply because it is increasingly difficult to isolate a specific text from its context. Following suggestions by Said, McGee remarks that "the solution is to look for formations of texts rather than 'the text' as a place to begin analysis. . . . From one angle . . . I would want to explore the sense in which 'texts' have disappeared altogether, leaving us with nothing but discursive fragments of context."[22]

McGee doubts the feasibility of locating the origin of interpretation in a coherent, locatable unity. Instead, rhetorical criticism must assume an interested position within discourse and piece together a response from fragments of context. Instead of texts "inviting audiences to interpret experiences as texts represent them" (Leff and Sachs's view), McGee suggests that textual fragments invite productive and critical reflection. Texts are the product of a simultaneous process of rhetorical invention and situated interpretation.

Both Leff and McGee reconceptualize the role of the audience/reader. However, even though Leff and Sachs set for themselves the goal of exploring the eventful use of public speaking, the authors discuss audiences as only *implied* by the play of discourse within the text. The motives and strategies of audiences as *users* of discourse are not described as playing a role in the constitution of rhetorical texts. McGee reverses the usual role of speaker and audience, emphasizing that audiences must construct coherent texts out of fragments of discourse.[23] McGee sees the audience's process of constructing a rhetorical event/text as "a dense reconstruction of all the bits of other discourses from which it was made." The location of any fragment of that discourse, what Leff would consider a text, is but one voice in the conversation. The dramatizations, debates, parodies, excerpts, and paraphrases that contextualize these fragments are also part of the discourse that can be articulated as a response by an audience—that is, that can be fused into a text by the circumstantial interests of audiences.

Leff and Sachs treat the solitary experience of reading like an audience's encounter with a speaker. Texts are treated as eventful. McGee reverses the role of rhetor and audience, placing the audience in the role of inventor of texts. Leff and Sachs want to refer to objective characteristics of inscription to provide evidence for interpretation, but also want to retain the concept that communication is an eventful process. McGee gives up attempting to locate texts at the beginning of criticism and instead asserts that identifying texts should be the first *goal* of criticism. The audience's interpretive activity is a condition for the emergence of texts.

Leff and Sachs still theorize within the assumption of modernism, seeking a resolution to one of modernism's most pernicious dualisms, style and content. McGee breaks with the modernist assumption that texts are perceptual objects that can be located unproblematically, but retains modernism's nostalgia for the text as a possible nodal point of meaning. Although he problematizes audiences as a stable position from which texts might be constructed, McGee retains some of modernism's vocabulary and epistemology. For instance, McGee's proposals for a postmodern construction of texts are presented as responses to objective changes in our communication environment.

Rorty's Attempt to Change the Topic

From Richard Rorty's neopragmatist perspective, the debates over the nature of public address as first of all textual or eventful would be better understood as part of a language-game rather than a search for essential traits of discourse. Rorty thinks that how we speak and write about things and events constitutes what they mean. Language, according to Rorty, can be more usefully thought about in relation to what kinds of conversations we have about language use than about any supposed represented or revealed truth.

The notion that we could characterize discourse in general as essentially more like an event than a text, or vice versa, is foreign to Rorty's postmodern pragmatism. Neither does Rorty wish to argue against ontologies or epistemologies that assume extradiscursive foundations. He would prefer to simply change the subject and try out a different sort of vocabulary, one descriptive of the way we talk about things rather than about the supposed essential characteristics of things.

Rorty's NeoPragmatism and Leff's Iconicity

Rorty and Leff share some opinions about discourse. Both argue against the rational world paradigm of objectivism, both are unhappy with dualisms such as style/content, and both reject materialist and idealistic reductionism. Leff and Sachs accept that reductionism has played a positive role in the development of rhetoric but complain that the benefits of reductionism risks masking "the situated character of rhetorical discourse and its function as a practical mode of encompassing concrete social and political issues."[24] However, there are important points of contention between the close reading approach of Leff and Rorty's neopragmatism.

From Rorty's perspective, Leff's claim that the phenomenon of iconicity resolves the tension between style and content is unsatisfactory for two reasons. First, Leff's effort is an attempt to resolve a tension that Rorty would rather avoid by simply adopting a different vocabulary. The concept of *iconicity* is, from Rorty's view, yet another theoretical concept that is indebted to a metaphysic that should be abandoned. The modern dualism of style and content is a reverberation of the ideal/material, subject/object, emotion/reason dualisms with which Western philosophy has been preoccupied. It has led to the modern debasement of rhetoric until the relatively recent influence of antifoundationalist philosophers such as Nietzsche, Heidegger, Dewey, Gadamer, and Derrida.

Second, Rorty would reject Leff's focus on the iconic dimensions of texts because Leff treats iconicity as though it is an objective perceptual given. Iconic structures are treated as having the same validity as empirical objects in traditional science even though Leff and Sachs claim to reject rhetorical texts as a *mirror of reality*.[25] Leff and Sachs compare icons to metaphors and characterize both as drawing on our natural ability to perceive similarities of reference.[26] They claim that the phenomenon of icons "outstrip[s] our capacity to describe them in theoretical terms."[27]

The ineffability of icons is derived from their nature as nonsymbolic representations of our sensuous experience of the world. An icon is not a symbol (not conventional) but rather "is a representational mark (signifier) bearing an actual resemblance to whatever it signifies."[28] Its origin is assumed to be causal rather than symbolic, but it functions, according to Leff and Sachs, to add content to discourse and to further argument. Thus icons serve as a link between the material inscriptions of language (style) and the world to which language refers (content).

Rorty responds to similar attempts to ground knowledge in theories of causality by arguing that an iconic theory "of language will only be possible if physical relationships are substituted for conventional ones in explaining how words hook up with the world."[29] The problem for Rorty is that such physicalist accounts of perception themselves rely on language-games. Even though the account pretends to have bypassed the influence of language by providing evidence that the relationship between signs and an extratextual reality is natural rather than conventional, it still depends on a certain way of talking about the sign-world relationship.

In other words, for Rorty, the meaning of iconic dimensions of texts remains the product of how we talk about what we experience and cannot be justified by claims that its meaning is an ineffable, true representation of sensuous experience. Rorty would presumably be comfortable with Leff's notion of iconicity if Leff limited his investigation to how we talk about terms like style and content in relation to other terms such as metaphor and analogy. What Rorty would reject is the claim that these terms derive their validity from their origin in natural perception.

Rorty has developed an unusual approach to the nature of metaphor and uses iconic signs as examples of how metaphors function. However, Rorty does not believe that metaphor is a comparison based on the perception of similarity, the link that Leff thinks it has with icons. Rather, Rorty claims that metaphor is the use of language in an abnormal, irrational way. For Rorty, metaphor is one way that we acquire new beliefs. The other two avenues for change of belief are perception and inference, which do not alter our language. Rorty considers the affect of metaphor to explain why language is an open rather than a closed system.[30]

Metaphor introduces change in language similar to how random variation in genetic structure introduces evolutionary change in organisms.[31] Rorty argues that metaphor functions as a means of language change precisely because it adds expressions into conversation that are not already part of the current system of meaning. Hence, metaphor cannot be understood as having a literal and a figurative meaning that are juxtaposed or compared, but rather must be understood as "like suddenly breaking off conversation long enough to make a face, or pulling a photograph out of your pocket and displaying it, or pointing at a feature of the surroundings."[32] Metaphor is the intrusion into language of what Freud called unconscious impulses, motivated but not yet articulated. Rorty takes the perspective that whoever we might consider ourselves to be, we are through language. However, the phenomenon of metaphor suggests to Rorty that who we are is partly influenced by that which we are not, most importantly the urges and motivations that we have not yet named and consequently have not yet identified as part of us. Metaphors, like impulsive gestures, are the product of nonarticulate emotions and desires. They create the possibility of change precisely because they are powerful but ambiguous intrusions that demand our attention but evade our capacity to completely draw them into our existing web of meaning. Consequently we are motivated to seek new configurations of meaning that accommodate these evocative expressions.

Rorty and Leff do agree that metaphoric and iconic expressions are important aspects of language, and both emphasize the nonsymbolic nature of icons. However, Rorty's postmodern pragmatism emphasizes the situated and implicitly political nature of Leff's notion of iconicity by drawing attention to who would read and construct texts in the way a close reading would suggest. From Rorty's perspective, the question of who uses the vocabulary of close reading and why, is more interesting than the attempt to resolve the style/content dualism or to ground the origin of icons and metaphors in an empirical theory of perception.

McGee, Rorty, and Inventing Texts

Rorty and McGee are in agreement on many but not all issues. McGee sees *Rorty and his allies* creating the possibility that rhetoric will be taken seriously as a contingent but constitutive praxis.[33] Both Rorty and McGee reject the idea that truth can be founded on essential characteristics of either subjective or objective reality, and both want to understand critical reflection as a practical, contextual activity of users of discourse. Rorty's description of the activity of the pragmatist is similar to McGee's description of audiences assembling fragments of discourse in contemporary society. Rorty, like McGee, understands interpretation to be an ad hoc inventive task that audiences accomplish in response to particular circumstances. McGee suggests that the commonly used phrase *rhetorical criticism* indicates that we have turned the object of study (rhetoric) into a mere qualifier of what has become the main focus of attention in recent decades—namely, criticism as the study of methodology.[34] Both Rorty and McGee reject that methodology, in the sense of preestablished algorithms, rules, or logical procedures, can adequately found the interpretive process.

Rorty compares the invention of new interpretive strategies to the invention of a new tool. He qualifies his analogy by noting that, although the use of a tool usually implies that the person inventing a tool knows in advance what the tool will be used for, the inventor of a new vocabulary does not know precisely what new uses we may discover for a new vocabulary.[35] In the face of problems of interpretation, people try out new strategies to see what advantages they may have. Each critical approach we invent implies a certain kind of object of analysis that corresponds to the method.[36] In short, the method (not grand theories, pregiven methodologies, or deterministic ideologies) creates the object (topic) of discourse. Similarly, McGee is led to the proposal that "our first job as professional consumers of discourse is *inventing a text suitable for criticism.*"[37] The objects of critical rhetoric are determined by taking a position within discourse, rather than the critic's position being determined by the pregiven position of the objects of criticism.

According to both Rorty and McGee, the interpretation of an already constituted text as the origin of meaning does not constitute a justifiable response to discourse. For Rorty, considering texts to be the origin of interpretation is another misguided attempt to ground interpretation in an epistemology that we are better off without. For McGee, the unquestioned acceptance of an apparently coherent, identifiable object of discourse is a recipe for the unwitting perpetuation of ideology. Neither can the presence of speech as an event provide such a foundation by claiming that the immediacy of experience provides authority for one interpretation over another. Speech events enter into the diverse play of interests of communities who take up these *fragments* by inventing ways to use them.

Postmodern rhetorical criticism is *first of all* a process of rhetorical invention. If traditional metaphysical categories are to be retained at all, rhetoric is not so much epistemological as ontological. In fact, if we insist on thinking of rhetoric as epistemological—that is, as a methodology for understanding meaning that already exists in discourse—we miss the opportunity for a self-creative movement of language. Rhetorical criticism is a movement through which we are able to invent new contexts of interpretation that are not prefigured or predicted. As Rorty remarks, our "new vocabulary makes possible, for the first time, a formulation of its own purpose. It is a tool for doing something which could not have been envisaged prior to the development of a particular set of descriptions, those which [the vocabulary] itself helps to provide."[38] Like McGee, Rorty does not despair that meaning is contingent upon social constructions. He wants to turn to language as the site of the production of our human Being, not as a self-conscious process of assertion and hypostatization, but as the process of discovering who we are from what we can say about ourselves.

There are also some key differences between the perspectives of McGee and Rorty. First of all, Rorty would not accept McGee's treatment of the dualism between speech as text and event. Although McGee reverses the usual priority of text and event by treating the event of audience response as the moment of possible textual invention, McGee does not question the traditional categories themselves. Like Leff's use of iconicity as a link between style and content, McGee wants to use the concept of a fragment of discourse to collapse the distinction between text and context. McGee argues that "all of culture is implicated in every instance of discourse," that is, in every fragment. Rorty wants to leave behind these dualisms and holistic assumptions. For Rorty, the mediating role of the fragment of discourse in postmodern society is itself an artifact of the prior assumption that there has been a text/context dialectic that has collapsed.

Mentioning Habermas favorably, McGee promotes treating speech as the "regulative ideal of discourse" and asserts that rhetoricians "are concerned more with speech than writing."[39] Rorty explicitly rejects the transcendental character of Habermas's Ideal Speech Situation, even though he accepts Habermas's political agenda of democracy and social equality.[40] In other words, Rorty rejects the use of speech as a regulative principle except as a strategic move in response to particular circumstances.

When McGee shifts attention to speaking he also emphasizes the rhetor's process of inventing discourse from "scraps and pieces." The fragments of postmodern discourse, according to McGee, no longer have a discoverable coherent context within which they make sense. We are faced with fragments that might cluster or have some themes in common, but they can no longer be considered texts in the traditional sense.[41] Our interests in the outcome of discourse leads us as audience members to literally make sense out of the fragments. Thus, rhetoric is guided by the desire for *"empowerment,* seeking to discover how and with what consequence *doxa* can be used to authorize a redress of human grievances."[42]

Rorty would reject McGee's implication that our current cultural condition can be objectively described as *postmodern*. Whereas McGee compares contemporary postmodern society with agrarian society as two objective social conditions, Rorty insists that history amounts to the conversations we have about our past. Rorty calls himself a *postmodernist bourgeois liberal*, by which he means a bourgeois liberal that has given up the Enlightenment vision of a transcultural justification of liberalism, and yet maintains that liberalism is nonetheless the political position he wants to assert.[43] He does not mean by *postmodern* the emergence of qualitatively different historical circumstances that provide objective conditions for the abandonment of Enlightenment metaphysics.

There are many similarities between the projects of McGee and Rorty. From Rorty's point of view, most of their differences do not amount to much, since they mostly consist of metaphysical assumptions made by McGee that Rorty believes are irrelevant. What Rorty can contribute to McGee's perspective is the suggestion that the contemporary turn to speech as a regulative principle of discourse by McGee, Habermas, Karl-Otto Apel, and others should be understood as a strategic move rather than the discovery or rediscovery of the truth of discourse.[44] I believe that furthering our understanding of the speaking subject is an important strategy for coping with the effects of new technology and a mass society saturated with media images. Being reminded of the historically contingent nature of this strategy can lessen the tendency to project logocentric assumptions about discourse into historical periods and social contexts that might be better understood from other perspectives.

Rorty and Public Address Criticism

One shared concern of many public address critics and Rorty is the relationship between language use and liberal democracy. Although Rorty rejects any version of foundationalism and asserts that all that we might call Truth is the product of language-games, he has a clear political and moral agenda. Not only does Rorty defend liberal democracy in general, he suggests what sorts of moral agents are appropriate to maintain a liberal democracy, details what characteristics the heroes of such a society might have, and how such heroes could fail in their roles and become totalitarian thinkers.

The study of public address in the West has emphasized its role in the process of both maintaining and embodying liberal democratic values. The study of public argument and persuasion has generally assumed that such expressions should help support democratic decision-making by giving free voice to interested parties of deliberation and consensus formation. Likewise, Rorty's philosophy emphasizes the freeing of different vocabularies from dogmas and prejudices for the sake of a liberal democracy defined as a society that not only accepts but values difference. Such a society promotes open discussion, accepts that private and public arenas are different spheres of discourse, and is bound together by participation in a common public vocabulary.[45]

Rorty suggests two important and complementary moral tasks within liberal democracy. One is the role of *agents of love* also called by him *connoisseurs of diversity*. The role of the agents of love is to expand society's imagination, appreciation, tolerance, and compassion for those who are not currently afforded the protection of procedural justice within liberal society. The second moral role Rorty calls *agents of justice* who ensure that those who are included within liberal society are treated according to a procedural justice that is fair and impartial regarding matters of race, ethnicity, religion, lifestyle, and so forth. Rorty promotes open conversation between these two moral roles as one of the key features of liberal democracy.[46]

One task for a public address critic accepting Rorty's views might be to investigate the adequacy of the roles played by agents of love and agents of justice, and how well they complement one another. Such criticism could examine a number of different parts of the conversation about a specific issue. For instance, the public address critic might assess how successful a social movement has been in introducing a vocabulary that includes previously muted groups, and how fairly liberal institutions protect their interests once they are brought into public conversation.

Rorty describes the sort of person who can effectively serve as an agent of love. He describes the self-creative, inventive, and ironic poet as the hero of liberal democracy and the *vanguard of the species*.[47] By "poet" Rorty means someone who invents new vocabularies, not just someone who participates in the literary tradition of writing poetry. Rorty does not believe that such a person is likely to bring about cultural change directly through his or her personal action. The function of the ironic poet is to invent new possibilities of language. Inventions such as metaphors are bound to be initially rejected, because language is a conventional system. Expressions that do not fit current conventions tend to be ignored or denounced. But the ironic poet introduces an element of change, and therefore plays an important role.

Rorty does not wish to promote a romantic version of the ironic poet as expressing an authentic or essential self.[48] Rorty spends as much time describing the importance of irony as he does the importance of poetic invention. Ironists doubt their own vocabulary because they have been impressed by other *final* vocabularies—that is, vocabularies that constitute a person's sense of their everyday life and world. Ironists realize that argument cannot settle disputes between *final* vocabularies, and they do not think that their vocabulary is any closer to *reality* than any other.[49] Thus, the ironist believes that "anything can be made to look good or bad by being redescribed," consequently they are "never able to quite take themselves seriously."[50] "The opposite of irony is common sense" because common sense supposes that a *final* vocabulary is sufficient for making claims of truth.[51]

The critic of public address might provide an account of the social impact of the ironic poet. Because this impact can be accomplished only by understanding how their inventiveness is incorporated into wider spheres of discourse, part of the analysis would include a look at the relationship between idiosyncratic aesthetic inventions and the way in which conventional discourses are gradually changed by the incorporation of these inventions. The analysis would have to be a close reading in the sense that particular textual inventiveness would need to be identified. However, unlike Leff's close reading the assessment of the discourse would also have to include an investigation of its influence on other texts through time. Thus, a concern for individual creation would be combined with a look at subsequent historical influence and the ways in which this dynamic relationship expands or contracts social freedom and justice. The analysis would focus on neither the uniqueness of individual expression nor broad changes in the history of ideas. Rather, the investigation would focus on how what *was* said influences what *can* be said, by whom, and under what circumstances.

Rorty's ironist can make the mistake of becoming an *ironist theorist*, a mistake made when an ironist "wants the kind of power which comes from a close relation to somebody very large."[52] Rorty characterizes Hegel as an ironist theorist, because Hegel not only asked us to understand knowledge as historical, but also proposed that history could eventually complete itself and come to an end. Nietzsche becomes an ironist theorist when he supposes the Antichrist to be a prototype for a new vision of humanity. Heidegger gets the nomination when he promotes the end of metaphysics and points to the ontological difference between Being and being. Rorty admires some of the contributions of all these thinkers, yet attempts to show how they are led to propose foundationalist responses instead of remaining ironists.

A public address critic might show how a shift in vocabulary or other discursive choices lead the ironist poet in the direction of an ironic theorist, thus potentially abdicating their role as the vanguard of liberal democracy. Perhaps certain strategies of reading lead a particular discourse to be assimilated by traditional metaphysics, turning an ironic discourse into one of an ironic theorist. Or an old turn of phrase might be drawn into contemporary conversation in a way that treats it as an expansion of possibilities and a challenge to foundationalism. These concerns are not entirely new, sharing as they do some similarities with other deconstructive strategies. However, because of locating the discourse of agents of love and justice, the possibility of linking such an analysis to a social movement perspective, and the lack of the necessity to use an elaborate technical vocabulary for accomplishing the criticism, the criticism would be very different than the deconstruction promoted by, for instance, Derrida or de Man.

Rorty's views have not escaped criticism by those interested in the political role of public address. Even though Rorty asserts a number of strong positions regarding the nature of discourse, reflection, ethics, and politics, his emphasis on the contingency of language and meaning has earned him the reputation of being a relativist. For instance, Lyne calls Rorty an *arch-relativist*,[53] McGee and Lyne argue that Rorty's approach is consistent with the *anarchism* of other postmodern views.[54] Geertz has attacked Rorty's suggestion that we accept a certain version of ethnocentrism.[55]

Rorty wants us to suspend judgment about the assumed link between foundations and the possibility of living a moral and ethical life. He suggests that instead we will discover we do not need foundationalist arguments after all, and that a great deal of human suffering and wasted resources could be avoided by giving up defenses of metaphysical groundings for what we want to accomplish or how we want to live. In other words, Rorty asks us to try out his view, rather than offering an argument for why foundationalist metaphysics are false. Rorty "urges liberals to take with full seriousness the fact that the ideals of procedural justice and human equality are parochial, recent, eccentric cultural developments, and then to recognize that this does not mean they are any the less worth fighting for."[56] Rorty could be accused of being self-contradictory because he advocates both the contingency of meaning and promotes particular values and goals. He attempts to sidestep this criticism by denying that the assertion of values requires a foundationalist grounding.

The problem for those of us who have been steeped in the rhetorical tradition is that Rorty not only sidesteps a logical contradiction, but also side-steps the importance of logical argument about foundations. Whatever the outcome, we are used to thinking that sustained, well-informed logical argument can improve our understanding about anything, at least anything that is important and not obvious. Professional philosophers may be upset by Rorty's suggestion that philosophers have a lot less to talk or argue *about* than they have thought. Rhetoricians, on the other hand, might be more upset with Rorty's proposal that the usefulness of *argument* is much more limited than we have supposed. Nothing can be more frustrating to someone raised in an intellectual tradition informed and inspired by public debate than the dismissal of a controversial and apparently important topic by someone saying "It's not worth arguing about. Let's just change the subject."

Ideology criticism may have another objection to Rorty's work. Rorty sometimes gives the impression that he advocates an *end of ideology* view similar to that of Daniel Bell. For instance, Burrows argues that Rorty's views are similar to pragmatists who rely on functionalism.[57] However, Rorty's *postmodern* pragmatism cannot be reduced to modernist versions of functionalist pragmatism. Functionalism assumes that goals of social systems are objectively discoverable and explain how and why systems work. Rorty considers the vocabulary of empirical observations to be just as contingent as any other vocabulary. In other words, such observations are not based on the perception of the way the world is independent of the vocabulary we use to describe it. Thus, Rorty's neopragmatism has no place for the kind of ideology criticism that treats ideology as a distortion of social truths that are grounded in material relations, dialectical or otherwise. But if ideology is taken to be a discursive phenomenon through which power and authority are legitimized, Rorty's political agenda does allow for ideology critique when the mechanisms of ideology interfere with liberal democracy.

Some Cautions about Rorty's View of Communication

Although I do not believe that Rorty's view is open to the usual criticism of functionalism as ideological, Rorty's version of language does raise some serious ideological concerns. First, Rorty's linguistic behaviorism inhibits the rhetorical critic's ability to discuss how ideology might be embedded in discourse through implicatures and associations. Even though Rorty discusses how Freud's theory of the unconscious contributes to our understanding of the contingency of the self, he fails to account for how Freud also provides a model of ideology other than that stemming from manipulative intent or mystification about real conditions.

The relationship between consciousness and the unconscious can be considered the relationship between two dimensions of one (not necessarily coherent) system of discourse, rather than between a true and a distorted apprehension of the world. Symptoms such as hallucinations and obsessions can then be understood as the product of structures of discourse that are not different in kind from other more salient or acceptable apprehensions of the world. Their abnormality can be understood as attempts to adapt to circumstances of emotional stress and systemic contradictions rather than as distortions of perception. In the same way, social expressions can be understood to further oppression and implicitly express vested interests without assuming that ideology is a false consciousness that could be dispersed by the light of reason. Rorty's behaviorism makes this sort of semiotic or hermeneutic interpretation of Freud difficult.

Second, Rorty insists that one of the central features of liberal democracy is the separation of private and public spheres of discourse. However, not only is this distinction saturated with political significance that Rorty does not work through, but asserting a topic of conversation as public or private is one way that political struggles are advanced. For instance, child labor, spouse abuse, and the disposal of industrial waste have all been considered private matters. It was only when these issues became matters of public debate that liberal society provided some protection of children, spouses in abusive relationships, and public health. Likewise, abortion rights advocates attempt to secure the right of women to control their own bodies by arguing that the decision to have an abortion is not a public concern but a private one. Rorty's insistence that the two spheres should be kept separate can obscure the importance of the fluidity of the relationship between public and private. Struggles between these spheres have typified liberal democratic efforts to gain rights and protection from exploitation. They are the kind of struggles that public address scholars find especially interesting. Speeches that assert that people should not be considered private property but rather pubic citizens, or speeches that describe the private frustration and alienation felt when taxes are imposed without public representation, are important examples for how rhetoric functions to support liberal democracy.

Finally, Rorty speaks about the ideal of a liberal democratic society as if it is a coherent model of how an actual society could function. It is more likely that societies will continue to be mixtures of democratic, socialist, monarchical, and authoritarian institutions and values. Many of the characteristics of a just and free society that Rorty wants are probably only possible through varying combinations of institutional forms that are capable of responding to constantly changing national, international, and environmental circumstances.

Keeping Rorty's Conversation Going

Rorty's style of writing is often disarmingly casual and conversational. It has a plain-speaking tone that can invite dialogue, but also can stifle reflection through its commonsense appeal. His work is contradictory if we insist that all the positions he takes should logically flow into one another. His work is relativist if we demand that any vision of life must ground itself in some sort of first principle. And his politics are ideological if we expect that social values must be justified through an argument for the political utopia they are designed to support. Nonetheless, Rorty's approach to language, personal identity, social solidarity, and the traditional issues with which philosophers have been concerned, is sophisticated and rich in its implications for those of us concerned with public address and communication in general.

I have proposed some strengths and weaknesses of Rorty's work. Accepting what I take to be Rorty's main purpose in writing anything at all, I suggest that my own or other accounts of his contributions should keep the conversation going rather than pretending to be definitive statements or final. If we can treat Rorty's work as in some sense the discourse of an agent of love, perhaps some of his contradictions can become an inspiration for inventing our own vocabulary.

Notes

⟨⟨≋⟩⟩ ⟨⟨≋⟩⟩

Chapter 2

1. Richard Rorty, *Consequences of Pragmatism* (Minneapolis: University of Minnesota Press, 1982), 160.

2. See, e.g., Richard Rorty, *Objectivity, Relativism, and Truth: Philosophical Papers Volume 1* (New York: Cambridge University Press, 1991), 156–58.

3. Rorty, *Objectivity*, 35–45, 197–202.

4. Ibid., 166.

5. Ibid., p. xxx.

6. Ibid., 160. That Peirce himself is, pace Rorty, a critic of foundationalism has been persuasively argued by C. F. Delaney and Richard J. Bernstein. See C. F. Delaney, "Peirce's Critique of Foundationalism," *The Monist* (April 1973): 240–251; and Richard J. Bernstein, "Peirce's Theory of Perception" in *Studies in the Philosophy of Charles Sanders Peirce*, Second Series, ed. Edward C. Moore and Richard S. Robin (Amherst: University of Massachusetts Press, 1964), 165–89, and *Praxis and Action: Contemporary Philosophies of Human Activity* (Philadelphia: University of Pennsylvania Press, 1971), 174.

7. Rorty, *Consequences*, 161.

8. Ibid.

9. The possibility of overcoming tradition or (to alter the metaphor) of razing rather than renovating our inheritance is problematic, even for deconstructionists and those (like Rorty) who have been influenced by this form of critique.

10. Rorty, Consequences, 161; see Richard J. Bernstein, *Beyond Objectivism and Relativism* (Philadelphia: University of Pennsylvania Press, 1983), 8.

11. Rorty, *Consequences*, 161.

12. In 1905, Peirce confessed that, "finding his bantling 'pragmatism' so promoted, feels that it is time to kiss his child good-by and relinquish it to its higher destiny; while to serve the precise purpose of expressing the original

271

definition, he begs to announce the birth of the word 'pragmaticism,' which is ugly enough to be safe from kidnappers" (CP 5.415). (For an explanation of the system used in citing Peirce's writings, see note 14, below.) One distinctive feature of pragmaticism (i.e., Peircean pragmatism) is precisely its connection with semeiotic or a theory of signs in general. In MS 322, Peirce explains this connection in this manner: pragmaticism "must be founded exclusively upon our understandings of signs, without drawing support from any principle either of metaphysics or psychology" (12).

13. Rorty, *Objectivity*, 218.

14. In this note, I will, first, explain my system of citing the writings of Charles S. Peirce and, then, elaborate the point in the text. In accord with the established practice of Peirce scholarship, all references to Peirce's writings will be given in the body of this paper. "CP" refers to the *Collected Papers of Charles Sanders Peirce* (Cambridge: Belknap Press of Harvard University Press, 1931–58). Volumes 1–6 were edited by Charles Hartshorne and Paul Weiss, volumes 7 and 8 by Arthur W. Burks. The passages are cited in accord with what has long been the standardized convention among Peirce scholars, e.g., CP 5. 500 (where the number preceding the decimal point designates the volume of the *Collected Papers* and the one following the decimal indicates the paragraph). "W" refers to the available volumes of *Writings of Charles S. Peirce: A Chronological Edition* being published by Indiana University Press; "W 1: 300," e.g., refers to volume 1, page 300, of this edition. "SS" refers to *Semiotic and Significs: The Correspondence between Charles S. Peirce and Victoria Lady Welby*, ed. Charles S. Hardwick (Bloomington: Indiana University Press, 1977). "MS" refers to one of Peirce's unpublished manuscripts in the Houghton Library at Harvard University. For data regarding the mss. cited in this paper, see Richard S. Robin's *Annotated Catalogue of the Papers of Charles S. Peirce* (Amherst: The University of Massachusetts Press, 1967). Let me turn from this to an elaboration of the point in my paper concerning how Peirce himself explains the articulation of a general theory of signs. "The most important operation of the mind is," according to Peirce, "that of generalization" (CP 1.82). According to Peirce, "generalization refuses to limit itself to the past, but involves virtual prediction" (CP 8.155). "Another operation closely allied to generalization is abstraction. . . . This consists of seizing upon something which has been conceived as . . . a meaning not dwelt upon but through which something else is discerned, and converting it into . . . a meaning upon which we rest as the principal subject of discourse" (CP 1.83). In one place, Peirce describes semeiotic as "the quasi-necessary, or formal doctrine of signs" (CP 2.227). He then goes on to explain what he intends by this: "I mean that we observe the characters of such signs as we know [through our utterance or interpretation of these signs], and from such an observation, by a process I will not object to naming Abstraction, we are led to statements, eminently fallible, and therefore in one sense by no means necessary, as to what must be the characters of all signs used by 'scientific intelligence,' that is to say, by an intelligence capable of learning by experience. As to that process of abstraction, it is itself a sort of observation. The

faculty which I call abstractive observation is one which ordinary people perfectly recognize, but for which the theories of philosophers sometimes hardly leave room" (CP 2.227).

15. Max H. Fisch, *Peirce, Semeiotic, and Pragmatism*, ed. Kenneth Laine Ketner and Christian J. W. Kloesel (Bloomington: Indiana University Press, 1986), 357.

16. Rorty, *Objectivity*, 154-59. Also see Vincent Colapietro, "Purpose, Power, and Agency" in a forthcoming issue of *The Monist* devoted to "Pragmatism—A Second Look."

17. Peirce went so far as to claim that pragmatism "is merely a method of ascertaining the meanings of hard words and of abstract concepts" (CP 5.464).

18. In MS 602 ("On the Classifications of the Sciences"), Peirce explicitly makes this point, asserting that "inquiry is only a particular kind of conduct" (8).

19. John Dewey, *Lectures in China*, 1919-1920, trans. and ed. Robert W. Clopton and Tsuin-Chen Ou (Honolulu: University of Hawaii Press, 1973), 45.

20. "To speak summarily and use a symbol of abbreviation, rather than an analytical and iconical idea, we may say that the purpose of signs—which is the purpose of thought—is to bring truth to expression. The law under which a sign must be true is the law of inference; and the signs of a scientific intelligence [i.e., an intelligence capable of learning from experience] must, above all other conditions, be such as to lend themselves to inference. Hence, the illative relation is the primary and paramount semiotic relation" (CP 2.444n1). The illative relation is the relationship between or among signs in an inferential pattern or process.

21. Vincent M. Colapietro, *Peirce's Approach to the Self: A Semiotic Perspective on Human Subjectivity* (Albany: SUNY Press, 1989) 69ff.

22. For the opposite emphasis, see Sandra B. Rosenthal, *Speculative Pragmatism* (Amherst: University of Massachusetts Press, 1986), 4.

23. In fact, Peirce's theory of signs will *not* be the resource upon which I either exclusively or primarily draw. That is, I shall in this paper leave unopened the toolbox of Peirce's semeiotic. Thus, this paper is a series of prolegomena.

24. Peirce did not, of course, entirely ignore questions of communication. Far from it. But he did not investigate them in a systematic and sustained way or, more accurately, he did not articulate the results of his investigation into such questions in a systematic and developed manner. Nor did Peirce develop his general theory of signs primarily in reference to the communicative practices of humans. In *The Message in the Bottle* (New York: Farrar, Straus and Giroux, 1954), Walker Percy articulates what is arguably a distinctively Peircean approach to human communication.

25. See Fisch, *Peirce*, 356–61; also see chapter 1 of my book on *Peirce's Approach*.

26. The *explicit* model of Peirce's semeiotic theory appears to have been conversation or dialogue. See Fisch, *Peirce*, 357. But the sort of conversation that Peirce seems to have had in mind is one in which the discourse is controlled by reference to a commonly accessible domain of perceivable objects and empirical events. (For Peirce's distinction between objects and events, see CP 1.336.) Such conversation is the form of discourse in which we are most likely to arrive at a rational and uncoerced consensus (uncoerced, that is, by any force other than the *majeur* force of our cumulative, communal experience). For Rorty, such coercion—such submission to the force of experience—entails an abdication of our creativity. It is, in short, servile. See, e.g., Richard Rorty, *Philosophy and the Mirror of Nature* (Princeton: Princeton University Press,1979), 373-79, esp. 378.

27. On this point, see Joel Weinsheimer, "The Realism of C. S. Peirce; or How Homer and Nature Can Be the Same" in *American Journal of Semiotics*, 2, no. 1–2 (1983):1 225–263; and John Sheriff, *The Fate of Meaning: Charles Peirce Structuralism, and Literature* (Princeton: Princeton University Press, 1989). Rorty himself has at least recently been making a similar, if not identical, point. For example, in "Texts and Lumps"—a paper included in *Objectivity, Relativism, and Truth*, 78–92— he urges that "we avoid Dilthey's suggestion that we set up distinct parallel metavocabularies, one for the Geist- and one for the Naturwissenschaften. We should instead assume that if a philosophical doctrine is not plausible with respect to the analysis of lumps by chemists, it probably does not apply to the analysis of texts by literary critics either" (79).

28. The capacity of Peirce's semeiotic to cast an ever-wider net of an ever-finer mesh—the capacity of this theory to do justice to, say, comunication in all its complexity—results primarily from the way the recursive categories of firstness, secondness, and thirdness function within semeiotic inquiry.

29. On this point, see David Savan, *An Introduction to Charles Peirce's Full System of Semeiotic* (Toronto Semiotic Circle, Monograph Series #1); also Michael Shapiro, *The Sense of Grammar: Language as Semeiotic* (Bloomington: Indiana University Press, 1983).

30. Those who have been schooled in a hermeneutic of suspicion are likely to hear any reference to revelation as a vestige of onto(theo)logical discourse, a discourse shaped by (among other factors) a commitment to the "metaphysics of presence." If by such a metaphysics is meant the doctrine that being is that which can, in principle, be fully and infallibly present to consciousness, Peirce anticipated the contemporary repudiation of this doctrine. However, if the rejection of the metaphysics of presence is intended to foster a total skepticism about both the character of beings and that of Being, Peirce did not anticipate this trend; rather he strenuously opposed what were its counterparts in his own day (positions he tended to subsume under the rubric of "nominalism").

31. Justus Buchler, *Metaphysics of Natural Complexes,* second expanded edition (Albany: SUNY Press, 1990), 1.

32. Paul Weiss, "Common Sense and Beyond" in *Determinism and Freedom in the Modern Age,* edited by Sidney Hook (New York: New York University Press), 232. The connection between pragmatism and commonsensism should be stressed here. In one place (MS 280), Peirce asks "[What are to be the definite ideas into which the vague notions of instinct, tradition, and uncontrolled intellection are to be translated?" To this, he responds that "Pragmaticism is an attempt to answer a part of this question." In other words, pragmaticism provides the means for at least a partial "translation" of our commonsensical ideas and beliefs. In another place, he contends that: "This [pragmatic] maxim once accepted . . . speedily sweeps all metaphysical rubbish out of one's house. Each abstraction is either pronounced gibberish or is provided with a plain, practical definition. The general leaning of the results is toward what the idealists call the naive, toward common sense, toward anthropomorphism" (CP 8.192).

33. Here it is worthwhile to recall one of Peirce's explicit pronouncement regarding common sense: "I do not think there can be any *direct* profit in going behind common sense—meaning by common sense those ideas and beliefs that man's situation absolutely forces upon him. But the difficulty is to determine what really is and what is not the authoritative decision of common sense and what is merely *obiter dictum*. In short, there is no escape from the need of a critical examination of 'first principles'" (CP 1.129).

34. For an excellent study of this hierarchy, see Beverley Kent, *Charles S. Peirce: Logic and the Classification of the Sciences* (Kingston and Montreal: McGill-Queen's University Press, 1987).

35. For suggestive comments by a pragmatist on this omnipresent tendency toward overgeneralization, see John Dewey, *Experience and Nature* (Carbondale: Southern Illinois University Press, 1988), 147. For a good discussion by a postmodernist of play, see John Caputo, *Radical Hermeneutics* (Bloomington: Indiana University Press, 1989), 227ff.

36. In one sense, the *ultimate* root of all scientific inquiry is not phenomenology but mathematics. (In another, it is the cosmos itself or perhaps the divinity creating itself in and through the cosmos.) The ultimate fruits are specific scientific investigations of an evermore precise and narrow scope. Taken as coextensive with logic in the most inclusive sense (i.e., the sense in which logic includes speculative grammar, critic, and speculative rhetoric or methodeutic), semeiotic itself is one of the three normative sciences. The other two are esthetics and ethics.

37. For an excellent account of Peirce's classification of the sciences, see Beverley Kent's *Charles S. Peirce: Logic and the Classification of the Sciences.*

38. In the interest of clarity, it might be helpful to distinguish between a *transcendental justification* and a *pragmatic explication* of norms and ideals.

Whereas the former justifies norms and ideals by an appeal to what altogether transcends our historical practices, the latter explicates these in terms of the exigencies and possibilities of these very practices. In MSS 892 and 893, Peirce makes several highly suggestive comments about the nature of morality. In MS 893, he notes that "ethical research begins only after we are already committed to moral positions." It is always as already committed agents that we reflect on our moral commitments.

39. The "fallacy of misplaced concreteness" is, of course, an expression devised by Alfred North Whitehead. In the context of our concerns, Hugh Joswick's "The Object of Semiosis," an as yet unpublished paper presented at the Peirce Sesquicentennial Congress (Harvard University, September 7, 1989), presents a strong case for seeing Peirce's own general theory of signs as a project (in effect) illustrative of this fallacy; for the very possibility of specifying an object of semiosis requires the presence of a sign-user, in particular, an interpreter.

40. In *The Public and Its Problems* (Carbondale: Southern Illinois University Press, 1988), Dewey makes this point in a forceful and eloquent way: "To learn to be human is to develop through the give-and-take of communication an effective sense of being an individually distinctive member of a community; one who understands and appreciates its beliefs, desires and methods, and who contributes to a further conversion of organic powers into human resources and values. But this translation is never finished" (332).

41. For a fine recent study of the degenerate forms of secondness and thirdness, see Felicia E. Kruse, "Genuineness and Degeneracy in Peirce's Categories" in *Transactions of the Charles S. Peirce Society* 27, no. 3 (summer 1991): 267–98.

42. Fisch, *Peirce*, 268–69; 371–72.

43. "A sign, or *representamen*, is something which stands to somebody for something in some respect or capacity" (CP 2.228). "It seems to me that one of the first useful steps toward a science of semeiotic . . . or the cenoscopic science of signs, must be the accurate definition, or logical analysis, of the concepts of the science. I define a *Sign* as anything which on the one hand is so determined by an Object and on the other so determines an idea in a person's mind, that this latter determination, which I term the *Interpretant* of the sign, is thereby mediately determined by that Object" (CP 8.343). However, since both of these definitions include a reference to mind, they are not sufficiently general. Thus, the following definition more adequately defines the formal object of semiotic inquiry: "A sign is . . . an object which is in relation to its object on the one hand and to an interpretant on the other, in such a way as to bring the interpretant into a relation to the object, corresponding to its own relation to the object" (CP 8.332). Even so, Peirce in a letter written near the end of his life made this confession: "It is clearly indispensable to start with an accurate and broad analysis of the nature of a Sign. I define a Sign as anything which is so determined by

something else, called its Object, and so determines an effect upon a person, which effect I call its Interpretant, that the latter [or Interpretant] is thereby mediately determined by the former [or Object of the Sign]. My insertion of 'upon a person' is a sop to Cerberus, because I despair of making my own broader conception understood" (SS 80–81). For a detailed and illuminating discussion of Peirce's "despair" in this regard, see George A. Benedict, "What Are Representamens?," *Transactions of the Charles S. Peirce Society* 21, no. 2 (spring 1985): 241-70.

44. John Dewey, *Theory of the Moral Life* (New York: Holt, Rinehart, and Winston, 1960), viii.

45. Dewey, *Experience and Nature*, 132.

46. In *The Public and Its Problems,* Dewey asserts that "Combined activity happens among human beings; but when nothing else happens it passes as inevitably into some other mode of interconnected activity as does the interplay of iron and the oxygen of water. What takes place is wholly describable in terms of energy, or, as we say in the case of human interactions, of force. Only when there exist signs and symbols of activities and of their outcome can the flux be viewed as from without, be arrested for consideration and esteem, and be regulated. Lightning strikes and rives a tree or rock, and the resulting fragments take up and continue the process of interaction, and so on and on. But when the phases of the process are represented by signs, a new medium is interposed. As symbols are related to one another, the important relations of a course of events are recorded and are preserved as meanings. Recollection and foresight are possible; the new medium facilitates calculation, planning, and a new kind of action which intervenes in what happens to direct its course in the interest of what is foreseen and desired.Symbols in turn depend upon and promote communication" (1927 [1988], 330–331).

47. Winfried Noth, *Handbook of Semiotics* (Bloomington: Indiana University Press, 1990), 168.

48. Ibid., 167.

49. Ibid., 67–68; Dewey, *Experience and Nature*, 141.

50. Vincent M. Colapietro, "The Vanishing Subject of Contemporary Discourse: A Pragmatic Response," *Journal of Philosophy*, 87, no. 11 (November 1990): 644–55.

51. Colapietro, *Peirce's Approach*, 114.

52. See, e.g., Roland Barthes, *Elements of Semiology* (New York: Hill and Wang, 1985) and *S/Z* (New York: Hill and Wang, 1974); Umberto Eco, *A Theory of Semiotics* (Bloomington: Indiana University Press, 1976); and Thomas Sebeok, *Contributions to the Doctrine of Signs* (Lanham, Maryland: University Press of America, 1976).

53. Jacques Derrida, *Of Grammatology*, trans. Gayatri Chakravorty Spivak (Baltimore: Johns Hopkins University Press, 1974), 158.

54. Ibid., 157.

55. Ibid., 157; see 296.

56. Ibid., 158

57. Jacques Derrida, "Deconstruction and the Other" (an interview with Richard Kearney), in *Dialogues with Contemporary Continental Thinkers: The Phenomenological Heritage,* ed. Richard Kearney (Manchester: Manchester University Press, 1984), 123.

58. Derrida, "Deconstruction," 12–24.

59. Richard Rorty, *Philosophy and the Mirror of Nature* (Princeton: Princeton University Press, 1979), 161.

Chapter 3

1. Richard Rorty, *Consequences of Pragmaticism* (Minneapolis: University of Minnesota Press, 1982) 165. Patrick Sullivan, "Pragmatics and Pragmatism," *Philosophy Today* 35, no. 2 (summer 1991), applies this argument directly to current research on discourse in the discipline of communication: "A 'pragmatism' of communication would be, therefore, specifically concerned with the analysis of the inferential structure of communication as a process of thought, directed towards a 'conception of the real,' and governed by the 'experimental logic' of abduction, deduction, and induction. A 'pragmatism' of communication would be concerned, in other words, with the *discovery of continuity* expressed as a law or habit, and not with the invention of contextual 'rules' expressed as 'conventions' or 'conversational maxims" (p. 182; my emphasis).

2. Charles S. Peirce, *Collected Papers of Charles Sanders Peirce*, 8 vols., ed. Charles Hartshorne and Paul Weiss, vols. 1–6; ed. Arthur W. Burks, vols. 7–8 (Cambridge: Harvard University Press, 1963), 5.506. Following the practice of Peircian scholarship, codex citations to volume and paragraph number are used.

3. Peirce, *Collected Papers*, 2:229.

4. Rorty, *Consequences*, 165.

5. Ibid., 166.

6. Peirce, *Collected Papers*, 5:171.

7. Ibid., 5:590.

8. Ibid., 2:105; 2:623.

9. Ibid., 3:621.

10. Rorty, *Consequences*, 166.

11. Ibid.

12. Anthony Wilden, *The Rules Are No Game: The Strategy of Communication* (New York: Routledge & Kegan Paul, 1987), 67, 303–321.

13. Maurice Apprey and Anne Eckman, "Toward a Complicit System of Mutual Implications in the Study of Science and Gender," *New Literary History: Journal of Theory and Interpretation* 23, no. 4 (November 1992) in press; ms. 10.

14. Richard L. Lanigan, *The Human Science of Communicology: A Phenomenology of Discourse in Foucault and Merleau-Ponty* (Pittsburgh: Duquesne University Press, 1992).

15. Peirce, *Collected Papers*, 1:564.

16. Edith W. Schipper and Edward Schuh, *A First Course in Modern Logic* (New York: Henry Holt, 1960), 238.

17. Trudy Govier, *A Practical Study of Argument*, 3rd ed. (Belmont, Calif.: Wadsworth, 1992), 308.

18. Richard L. Lanigan, "Enthymeme: The Rhetorical Species of Aristotle's Syllogism," *Southern Speech Communication Journal* 39 (spring 1974): 207–222.

19. Aristotle, *Posterior Analytics* in *The Complete Works of Aristotle*, revised Oxford trans., ed. Jonathan Barnes (Bollingen Series 71) 2 vols. (Princeton: Princeton University Press, 1984), 71b.16–24.

20. Peirce, *Collected Papers*, 2:582.

21. Ibid., 4.537.

22. Lanigan, *Enthymeme*, 209.

23. Peirce, *Collected Papers*, 2:449n.1; 2:451; 2:582 on Kant's use of enthymeme; 3:167; 4:52.

24. Ibid., 5:144; 7:249; 8:209.

25. Ibid., 6:66.

26. Ibid., 2: 619–635. This citation is to a simple explication of the three logics including the simplified terminology of rule, result, and case to distinguish propositions in the syllogisms of abduction, induction, and deduction.

27. A very readable account of this technical point is Nicholas Rescher, *Peirce's Philosophy of Science: Critical Studies in His Theory of Induction and Scientific Method* (Notre Dame: Notre Dame University Press, 1978), 41 ff. See Christopher Hookway, *Peirce* (Boston: Routledge & Kegan Paul, 1985).

28. Maurice Merleau-Ponty, *Phenomenology of Perception*, trans. Colin Smith; corrections by Forrest Williams and David Guerrière (Atlantic Highlands, N.J.: Humanities Press) 209, 213. See Sandra B. Rosenthal and Patrick L. Bourgeois, *Pragmaticism and Phenomenology: A Philosophic Encounter* (Amsterdam: B. R. Grüner; Philadelphia: John Benjamins North America, 1980); and Patrick L. Bourgeois and Sandra B. Rosenthal, *Thematic Studies in Phenomenology and Pragmaticism* (Amsterdam: B. R. Grüner Philadelphia: John Benjamins North America, 1983).

29. Arthur W. Burks, "Peirce's Theory of Abduction," *Philosophy of Science* 13 (1946): 305. For a comprehensive review of key issues, see K. T. Fann, *Peirce's Theory of Abduction* (The Hague: Martinus Nijhoff, 1970).

30. Richard A. Shweder, *Thinking Through Cultures: Expeditions in Cultural Psychology* (Cambridge: Harvard University Press, 1991), 361. I am indebted to Andrew Smith for referring me to this source. A similar suggestion occurs in Michael D. Bybee, "Abduction and Rhetorical Theory," *Philosophy and Rhetoric* 24:4 (1991): 281–300. Caveat: Bybee correctly interprets (a la Aristotle) the place of enthymeme as a *structure* in argument, but he fails to note that Peirce also takes the material form of *abduction* from Aristotle as well. More to the point, Bybee assumes uncritically that the theory of logic (abduction) and the practice of rhetoric (enthymeme) are synonymous, thereby mistakenly attributing the discovery of abduction to C. S. Pierce.

31. Ru Michael Sabre, "Peirce's Abductive Argument and the Enthymeme," *Transactions of the Charles S. Peirce Society* 36, :no. 3 (fall 1990): 363, 370.

32. Sabre's citation is to John T. Gage, "An Adequate Epistemology for Composition: Classical and Modern Perspectives" in *Essays on Classical Rhetoric and Modern Discourse*, ed. Robert J. Conners, Lisa S. Ede, and Andrea Lunsford (Carbondale: Southern Illinois University Press, 1984).

33. Sabre, "Peirce's Abductive," 368.

34. See Stephen Toulmin, Richard Rieke, and Allan Janik, *An Introduction to Reasoning*, 2nd ed. (New York: Macmillan, 1984).

35. Sabre's citation is Lawrence D. Green, "Enthymemic Invention and Structure Prediction," *College English* 41, no. 6 (1980) [no pages given].

36. Schutz's notions of *because-motive* and *in-order-to motive* in the communication process are discussed in Richard L. Lanigan, *Phenomenology of Communication: Merleau-Ponty's Thematics in Communicology and Semiology* (Pittsburgh: Duquesne University Press, 1988), 218.

37. Aristotle, *Rhetoric* in *The Complete Works of Aristotle*, 1355b.26

38. Patricia A. Turrsi, "Peirce's Logic of Discovery: Abduction and the Universal Categories," *Transactions of the Charles S. Peirce Society* 26.4 (fall 1990): 481. The same point in the context of Peirce's view "that abductive inference

shades into perceptual judgment without any sharp line between them" is suggested in Patrick F. Sullivan, "On Falsificationist Interpretations of Peirce," *Transactions of the Charles S. Peirce Society* 27.2 (spring 1990): 207.

39. Roman Jakobson, "Language in Relation to Other Communication Systems" in *Selected Writings, Vol II: Word and Language* (The Hague: Mouton, 1971), 703. For a comprehensive account of Jakobson's phenomenological communication theory, see Elmar Holenstein, *Roman Jakobson's Approach to Language: Phenomenological Structuralism*, trans. Catherine and Tarcisius Schelbert (Bloomington: Indiana University Press, 1976).

40. Plato, *Phaedrus* in *Plato: The Collected Dialogues including the Letters*, ed. Edith Hamilton and Huntington Cairns (Bollingen Series 71) (New York: Pantheon Books; Random House, 1961), 275a.

41. Julian Jaynes, *The Origin of Consciousness in the Breakdown of the Bicameral Mind* (Boston: Houghton Mifflin, 1976), 27.

42. Stephen Toulmin, *The Uses of Argument* (Cambridge: Cambridge University Press, 1969).

43. Sabre, "Peirce's Abductive," 365.

44. Ibid., 366. Line adjustment and use of arrows to visually clarify the confusing original are mine. The relevant Peirce citation is *Collected Papers*, 2:511.

45. Sabre, "Peirce's Abductive," 369.

46. Peirce, *Collected Papers*, 8:297. See William L. Rosensohn, *The Phenomenology of Charles S. Peirce: From the Doctrine of Categories to Phanerscopy* (Amsterdam: B. R. Grüner, 1974); Alan Brinkley, "The Phenomenology of C. S. Peirce," (Ph.D. diss., Tulane University, 1960 [UMI no. 60–5943]); Catharine W. Hantzis, "Peirce on Logic: Phenomenology as the Basis for Normative Science," (Ph.D. diss., University of California, Berkeley, 1981 [UMI no. 8211951]).

47. Lanigan, *The Human Science of Communicology*, Appendix B.

48. Sabre, "Peirce's Abductive,"366.

49. Gregory Bateson and Mary C. Bateson, *Angels Fear: Towards an Epistemology of the Sacred* (New York: Macmillan, 1987), 206.

50. Ibid., 37.

51. Peirce, *Collected Papers*, 1:187–90; 1:280.

52. Ibid., 2:634.

53. Gaston Bachelard, *The New Scientific Spirit*, trans. Arthur Goldhammer (Boston: Beacon Press, 1984), 6 (original work published 1934). I am indebted to Professor Maurice Apprey, dept. of behavioral medicine and psychiatry, University of Virginia School of Medicine, for this reference.

54. Lanigan, *Enthymeme*, 222.

55. John Searle, *Intentionality: An Essay in the Philosophy of Mind* (New York: Cambridge University Press, 1983), 141. I should note that while a post-doctoral research associate in the department of philosophy, I participated in the "Seminar on the Explanation of Human Behavior" conducted by Hubert L. Dreyfus and John Searle during the winter quarter 1982 at the University of California at Berkeley where this book, in manuscript form, was debated. At that time I introduced the complications of considering the actuality of realized human communication in place of the standard model of the ideal speech act situation used by Anglo-American analytic philosophy or German critical philosophy. The background of the discussion was Searle's *Speech Acts: An Essay in the Philosophy of Language* (Cambridge: Cambridge University Press, 1969) and my critique offered in Lanigan, *Speech Act Phenomenology* (The Hague: Martinus Nijhoff, 1977).

56. Searle, *Intentionality*, 165.

57. Ibid., 166.

58. Peirce, *Collected Papers*, 3.641.

59. Ibid., 6:469.

60. Sabre, "Peirce's Abductive,"367.

61. Lanigan, *Enthymeme*, 213.

62. Sabre, "Peirce's Abductive," 366.

63. Lanigan, *The Human Science of Communicology*, Figure 8. See Yuri M. Lotman, *Universe of the Mind: A Semiotic Theory of Culture*, trans. Ann Shukman (Bloomington: Indiana University Press, 1990) for a general discussion of "rhetoric as a mechanism for meaning-generation" where a tropic logic is discussed from the perspective that "a trope is a semantic transposition from a sign *in praesentia* to a sign *in absentia*, 1) based on the perception of a connection between one or more semantic features of the signified; 2) marked by the semantic incompatibility of the micro- and macro-contexts; 3) conditioned by a referential connection by similarity, or casuality, or inclusiveness, or opposition" (40).

64. Peirce, *Collected Papers*, 2:96.

65. Ibid., 2:276–277; my insertions.

66. Ibid., 5:181; my insertions.

67. Shweder, *Thinking Through Cultures*, 2. My insertions are to show the enthymematic conjunction of the because-motive as belonging to abduction and the in-order-to-motive as belonging to deduction.

68. An introductory discussion is offered by Hubert G. Alexander, *The Language and Logic of Philosophy* (Lanham, M.: University Press of America,

1988), 236, 247.

69. G. W. F. Hegel, *The Phenomenology of Mind*, trans. J. B. Baille (New York: Harper & Row, 1967), 131–145; 789–808, et passim.

70. Franz Brentano, *The Theory of Categories*, trans. Roderick Chisholm and Norbert Guterman (Boston: Martinus Nijhoff, 1981), 40–45, 134–135, et passim. (original work published 1933). Franz Brentano, *Sensory and Noetic Consciousness: Psychology from an Empirical Standpoint III*, trans. Maragarete Schättle and Linda McAlister (New York: Humanities Press, 1981), 81–89, et passim. (original work published 1929).

71. Peirce, *Collected Papers*, 4.537–38.

72. Sabre, "Peirce's Abductive," 370, n. 4.

73. Richard L. Lanigan, "The Contingency of the Flesh: Merleau-Ponty's Discourse on the Esoteric and Foucault's Discourse on the Exoteric," *Sozialphilosophie und Lebenswelt; Maurice Merleau-Ponty*, (Seminar paper at the Inter-University Centre of Dubrovnik, Yugoslavia, 25 March- 5 April, 1991).

74. Peirce, *Collected Papers*, 8:209.

75. Ibid., 5:76; my emphasis.

76. Ibid., 7:585; my insertion. A current application in communication research of this Peircian theorem is Klaus Bruhn Jensen, "When is Meaning? Communication Theory, Pragmaticism, and Mass Media Reception," in *Communication Yearbook 14*, ed. James A. Anderson (Newbury Park, Calif.: Sage Publications; International Communication Association, 1991), 3–32.

Chapter 4

1. For a lucid discussion of the paradoxical aporias of justice, see Jacques Derrida, "Force of Law: The Mystical Foundation of Authority," in *Deconstruction and the Possibility of Justice*, ed. Drucilla Cornell, Michel Rosenfeld, and David Gray Carlson (New York and London: Routledge, 1992), 3–29. We are indebted to John Caputo for bringing this source to our attention. For a discussion of the surprising relation between Derrida and C.S. Peirce, see Vincent Colapietro's essay in this volume.

2. For elaborations of these positions, see Richard Rorty., *Contingency, Irony, and Solidarity* (Cambridge: Cambridge University Press, 1989), and *Objectivity, Relativism and Truth: Philosophical Papers Volume 1* (Cambridge: Cambridge University Press, 1991).

3. See Jean-Francois Lyotard, *The Differend: Phrases in Dispute* (Minneapolis: University of Minnesota Press, 1988), 28, 30, 38–39. References are to paragraph numbers rather than pages. Allusions to *The Differend* and

Lyotard appear throughout this essay. Contrary to what one might expect,. Lyotard extends pragmatism in ways that, we believe, Peirce and Dewey would approve of.

4. Thomas Kochman, *Black and White Styles in Conflict* (Chicago: University of Chicago Press, 1981), 61–62.

5. In classical rhetorical theory stasis disputes develop, first, by agreeing that a problem exists and that time should be stopped (stasis) in order to seek resolution; second, that the problem can—or cannot—be defined as a case of, e.g., harassment (definitive stasis); third, that the type of harassment committed was—or was not—e.g., sexual harassment (constitutive stasis); and fourth, that the body adjudicating the dispute is—or is not—competent to render judgment, e.g., there is no conflict of interest (translative stasis). For a discussion, see George Kennedy, *The Art of Persuasion in Greece* (Princeton: Princeton University Press, 1963), 303–26. It is interesting that the four modes of stasis developed by Hermagoras, Hemogenes, Cicero, and others cohere nicely with Lyotard's discussion of the "four silences" that constitute a "wrong." See *The Differend*, 21–27.

6. One notable exception is Cornel West, *The American Evasion of Philosophy: A Genealogy of Pragmatism* (Madison: University of Wisconsin Press, 1989).

7. Rorty, *Objectivity*, 23. For a discussion of the distinction between relativism and ethnocentrism, see 29–31 and 38–39.

8. See "Pragmatism, Davidson and Truth," in *Objectivity*, 126–50. Originally published in *Truth and Interpretation: Perspectives on the Philosophy of Donald Davidson*, ed. Ernest LePore (Oxford: Blackwell, 1986), 333–68. For a critical discussion of Rorty's appropriation of Davidson's positions for pragmatism, see C.G. Prado, *The Limits of Pragmatism* (Atlantic Highlands, N.J.: Humanities Press International, 1987). See also Robert Kraut, "Vagaries of Pragmatism," *Mind* 99 (1990): 157–83. One of Rorty's interpretations of Davidson's theory is as follows: "[Davidson's] argument that coherence yields correspondence comes down to saying the following: From the field linguist's point of view, none of the notions which might suggest that there was more to truth than the meaning of words and the way the world is are needed; if you are willing to assume this point of view you will have no more skeptical doubts about the intrinsic veridicality of belief" (*Objectivity*, 139). See also Donald Davidson, "On the Very Idea of a Conceptual Scheme," in *Inquiries into Truth and Interpretation* (Oxford, Clarendon Press, 1984), 183–98.

9. Davidson's theory of truth can be found in *Inquiries*; see especially "Truth and Meaning," 34: "We could take truth to be a property, not of sentences, but of utterances, or speech acts, or ordered triples of sentences, times, and persons; but it is simplest just to view truth as a relation between a sentence, a person, and a time." Original publication in *Synthese* 17 (1967): 304–23.

10. Richard Shweder, *Thinking Through Cultures: Expeditions in Cultural Psychology* (Cambridge: Harvard University Press, 1991).

11. I am taking the term quasitranscendental from John Caputo, "On Not Circumventing the Quasi-Transcendental: The Case of Rorty and Derrida," *Working Through Derrida*, ed. Gary Madison (Evanston: Northwestern University Press, 1992). Shweder and Caputo would agree that Derrida does not completely abandon transcendental concerns—with provisions. See also note 14.

12. In Lyotard's terms, this is the risk and commitment involved when people engage in a "differend" collaboratively outside formal procedures, e.g., litigation.

13. See Shweder, Thinking, 108–10.

14. This argument engages the problematics of deconstruction. See Richard Rorty,. "From Ironist Theory to Private Allusions: Derrida," in *Contingency*, 122–37. Rorty follows Derrida's criticism of context as delimiting the generation of meaning; see Jacques Derrida, "Signature Event Context," in *Margins of Philosophy*, trans. Alan Bass (Chicago: University of Chicago Press, 1982), 310: "But are the prerequisites of a context ever absolutely determinable? . . . I would like to demonstrate why a context is never absolutely determinable, or rather in what way its determination is never certain or saturated." See also *Writing and Difference*, trans. Alan Bass (Chicago: University of Chicago Press, 1972). In this context Rorty takes issue with John Caputo concerning the Heideggarian notion that language functions both primordially and poetically. For a discussion, see *Contingency*, 122n4; For Caputo's argument, see "The Thought of Being and the Conversation of Mankind: The Case of Heidegger and Rorty," *Review of Methaphysics* 36 (1983): 661–85; and *Radical Hermeneutics* (Bloomington: Indiana University Press, 1988), 130–32 and 192–97. See John Ellis, *Against Deconstruction* (Princeton: Princeton University Press, 1989), 52–53.

15. He extends this particular argument in "On Ethnocentrism: A Reply to Clifford Geertz," *Objectivity*, 203–10. Rorty defends the "anti anti-ethnocentrism" movement which "should be seen neither as putting forward a large philosophical view about the nature of culture nor as recommending a social policy. Rather, it should be seen as an attempt to resolve a small, local, psychological problem . . . found only within the souls of bourgeois liberals who have not yet gone postmodern, the ones who are still using the rationalistic rhetoric of the Enlightenment to back up their liberal ideas. These liberals hold on to the Enlightenment notion that there is something called a common human nature, a metaphysical substrate in which things called rights are embedded, and that this substrate takes moral precedence over all merely cultural superstructures. Preserving this idea produces self-referential paradox as soon as liberals begin to ask themselves whether their belief in such a substrate is itself a cultural bias" (207).

16. See especially Shweder's discussion of an Orissan man's response to Kohlberg's Heinze dilemma, in *Thinking*, 186 passim. See Peter Winch, "Understanding a Primitive Society," in *Understanding and Social Inquiry*, ed. Fred Dallmayr and Thomas McCarthy (Notre Dame: University of Notre Dame Press, 1977, 159–88.

17. Shweder *Thinking*, 360n4. For elaborations of abduction as a poetic modality of cultural and intercultural communication, see James Clifford, *The Predicament of Culture: Twentieth Century Ethnography, Literature and Art* (Cambridge: Harvard University Press, 1988), 37; Gregory Bateson and Mary Catherine Bateson, *Angels Fear: Toward an Epistemology of the Sacred* (New York: Macmillan, 1987), 37; Richard L. Lanigan, *Phenomenology of Communication: Merleau-Ponty's Thematics in Communicology and Semiology* (Pittsburgh: Duquesne University Press, 1988), 22, 158. See also Lanigan's essay in this volume; Umberto Eco, A Theory of Semiotics (Bloomington: Indiana University Press, 1979), 131–33; and Donald Polkinghorne, *Methodology for the Human Sciences: Systems of Inquiry* (Albany: State University of New York Press, 1983).

18. See Lyotard, *The Differend*, 22.

19. For a superb discussion of the stakes of this debate, see Seyla Benhabib, *Critique, Norm, and Utopia: A Study of the Foundations of Critical Theory* (New York: Columbia University Press, 1986).

20. As Richard Bernstein discusses in *The New Constellation: The Ethical-Political Horizons of Modernity/Postmodernity* (Cambridge: MIT Press, 1992), 323–40.

21. See Colapietro's essay in this volume.

22. Charles Sanders Peirce, *Collected Papers of Charles Sanders Peirce*, ed. Charles Hartshorne, Paul Weiss, and Arthur W. Burks (Cambridge: Harvard University Press, 1966), 5:181. All references are to volume and paragraph numbers rather than pages. All subsequent references to the *Collected Papers* will be indicated as, e.g., CP 5:181.

23. Julia Kristeva takes up this issue, among other places, in *Revolution in Poetic Language*, trans. Margaret Walker (New York: Columbia University Press, 1984). For a discussion of stasis theory and the representamen (in post-Peircean sense), see 171–77.

24. See CP 5:151–212; 2:100–104.

25. This is Husserl's term, not Peirce's or Dewey's, but it is apt usage for designating precisely how temporality is linked to postulating truth and rendering justice. To protend is to extend into the future from a present point and to imbue the present with this future protention. For a discussion of Husserl's notion of time as a network of intentionalities, see Maurice Merleau-Ponty, *The Phenomenology of Perception*, trans. Colin Smith; trans. rev. Forrest Williams

(London: Routledge & Kegan Paul, 1986), 416–17. See also Andrew Smith, "Phenomenology of Intercultural Communication," *Japanese and Western Phenomenology*, ed. Philip Blosser et al. (Boston: Kluwer Academic Publishers, 1993), 235–47.

26. For a discussion of these levels of communication, see Jurgen Reusch and Gregory Bateson, *Communication: The Social Matrix of Psychiatry* (New York: W.W. Norton, 1968), 273–89.

27. John Dewey, *The Later Works:*, vol. 12, ed. Jo Ann Boydston (Carbondale: Southern Illinois University Press, 1986), 494–95.

28. Dewey, "The Development of American Pragmatism," *The Later Works* 2:12.

29. Rorty would probably agree with this view, but not take consequents as far as the end of inquiry; see "Texts and Lumps," in *Objectivity*, 78–92.

30. See Rorty, *Objectivity*, 131. The questions Rorty poses with regard to ends arise in his critique of the "ideal speech situation," defined by Habermas, in which a postulation of a universal criterion is used to evaluate particular conversations, outcomes, inquiries, and so on. Rorty suggests an analogical relation between the Peircean notion of "ideal end" and Habermas's "ideally free community" and "ideal speech situation." See "Habermas," in *Essays*, 166–67. We are arguing implicitly in this essay that Habermas's conception is not what Peirce had in mind.

31. Throughout the *Collected Papers* Peirce struggles to articulate what he means by pragmaticism, or "pragmatism," in terms of possible consequence. Here is one example: "About forty years ago . . . my studies led me, after convincing myself that all thinking is performed in Signs, and that meditation takes the form of a dialogue, so that it is proper to speak of the meaning of a concept, to conclude that to acquire full mastery of that meaning it is requisite, in the first place, to learn to recognize the concept under every disguise, through extensive familiarity with instances of it. But this, after all, does not imply any true understanding of it; so that it is further requisite that we should make an abstract logical analysis of it into its ultimate elements, or as complete an analysis as we can compass. But, even so, we may still be without any living comprehension of it; and the only way to complete our knowledge of its nature is to discover and recognize just what general habits of conduct a belief in the truth of the concept (of any conceivable subject, and under any conceivable circumstances) would reasonably develop; that is to say, what habits would ultimately result from a sufficient consideration of such truth. It is necessary to understand the word conduct, here, in the broadest sense. If, for example, the predication of a given concept were to lead to our admitting that a given form of reasoning concerning the subject of which it was affirmed was valid, when it would not otherwise be valid, the recognition of that effect in our reasoning would decidedly be a habit of conduct" (C.P. 6:481).

32. See his *Logic: The Theory of Inquiry* (New York: Henry Holt, 1938), 345: "The best definition of truth . . . known to me is that of Peirce: The opinion which is fated to be ultimately agreed to by all who investigate is what we mean by the truth." But Dewey does not "follow" Peirce in the sense of setting out to develop specific Peircean ideas. He arrives at his conclusions about truth and consequences independently and finds in Peirce's *Collected Papers* support and corroboration for his views. This is made clear in a letter Dewey wrote to Haskell Fain, dated 26 April 1949, where he discusses the "influence of Peirce and James" on his thinking. See *The Dewey Collection*, 14, Special Collections, Morris Library, Southern Illinois University at Carbondale. See also John Dewey, "The Pragmatism of Peirce," in *The Middle Works:* vol. 10, ed. JoAnn Boydston (Carbondale: Southern Illinois University Press, 1976), 71–75; "Peirces's Theory of Quality," in *The Later Works* 2:86–94. "The Development of American Pragmatism," in *The Later Works* 2:3–17; and "Peirce's Theory of Linguistic Signs, Thought, and Meaning," in *The Later Works* 15:142–52.

33. See *Experience and Nature* , vol.1 of *The Later Workss*, 361–64.

34. Dewey, "The Problem of Truth," in*The Middle Works* 6:12–63. The three lectures are entitled, respectively, "Why is Truth a Problem?," "Truth and Consequences," and "Objective Truths."

35. "The Problem of Truth," 45n8.

36. Ibid., 57.

37. Ibid., 42–3.

38. See ibid., 40–41: "But since the way the ship goes—and all the consequences that flow from this—is influenced by the needle's record, its position gets an entirely new type of value. It is no longer a mere effect of its past, but the effect is a sign of a possible future belonging to something else beside and beyond itself, namely: the ship. It is the sign of the progress of events toward their termination, their fulfillment, their consequences. . . . When a question of further use, or reference to future consequences enters in, we are inevitably concerned with the fitness, the adaptability, of the thing for the use intended. It stands for a result to be attained; and since the *way* it stands for the result affects the result finally attained, its worth as representative is a genuine matter" (emphasis in original).

39. "The Problem of Truth," 60–61.

40. Ibid., 68.

41. See "Reality Without Reference," in *Inquiries*, 215–26.

42. "On the Very Idea," in *Inquiries*, 196-97.

Chapter 5

1. I wish to thank Deborah L. Eicher for her research assistance in the preparation of this manuscript.

2. As H. S. Thayer indicates: "It was James who launched pragmatism as a new philosophy in a lecture 'Philosophical' Conceptions in 1898; it was under his leadership that pragmatism came to be famous; and it was primarily his exposition that was received and read by the world at large." Paul Edwards, gen. ed., *The Encyclopedia of Philosophy*, vol. 5 and 6 (New York: Macmillan, 1967), 433.

3. William James, "What Pragmatism Means," in *Essays in Pragmatism* (New York: Hafner, 1948), 145.

4. Daniel Canary and Brian Spitzberg, "Attribution Biases and Associations Between Conflict Strategies and Competence Outcomes," *Communication Monographs* 57 (1990): 139.

5. Brian Spitzberg and William Cupach, *Interpersonal Communication* Competence (Beverly Hills: Sage, 1984). Also, by the same authors: *Handbook of Interpersonal Competence Research* (New York: Springer-Verlag, 1989).

6. Spitzberg and Cupach, *Handbook*, 17–24.

7. Canary and Spitzberg, "Attribution," 139, and Spitzberg and Cupach, *Handbook*, 25–49.

8. William James, "The Thing and Its Relations," James succinctly commented that: "Experience in its immediacy seems perfectly fluent" *Essays in Radical Empiricism*, ed. Frederick Burkhardt and Fredson Bowers, [*The Works of William James* Cambridge: Harvard University Press, 1977], 45.

9. Richard J. Bernstein, *The New Constellation* (Cambridge: MIT Press, 1991), 325.

10. Thomas Kuhn, *The Structure of Scientific Revolutions*, 2nd ed. rev. (Chicago: Chicago University Press, 1970).

11. Jacques Derrida, "Structure, Sign, and Play in the Discourse of the Human Sciences," in *Writing and Difference*, trans. Alan Bass (Chicago: Chicago University Press, 1978), 277–8. Caputo reminds us that "the critique of the 'metaphysics of presence' was launched by Kierkegaard, although he had to wait for philosophy professors like Heidegger and Derrida to give his project conceptual formulation and thematic development." See John D. Caputo, *Radical Hermeneutics* (Bloomington: Indiana University Press, 1987), 17–18.

12. No attempt is made here to provide a comprehensive examination of postmodern theoretical perspectives on competence, communication, and the human sciences. This essay has a restricted focus on American (USA) pragmatism and communicology.

13. This point could not possibly be better exemplified than by Illinois Governor James Edgar who has supported a plan to "guarantee" the skills of community college graduates in his state. According to Edgar: "Guarantees send a powerful message that community colleges can provide employers with a quality product. Businesses need to know that hiring a graduate of the community college system will benefit them in both quality and productivity" (Brandi Tipps, "State to ensure college skills," *Daily Egyptian* [Southern Illinois University at Carbondale] 22 Apr. 1992: 1).

14. Marc Rosenberg, "Performance Technology: Working the System," *Training* (February 1990): 43.

15. Several sources emphasize this theme: Rosenberg, "Performance," 1990. Barry Reece, "Developing Those Critical Human Relations Skills," *Vocational Education Journal* 63 (1988): 44–45. Thomas Inman, "Communication and the Entrepreneur," *Business Education Forum* (April 1990): 29–31. George Klemp, "The Meaning of Success: A View from Outside the Academy," *Liberal Education* 74 (1988): 37–41. Patricia K. Cross, "Making Students Successful: The Search for Solutions Continues," *Change* (November-December, 1985): 48–51. Susan Aranoff, "Teaching Business Communication Skills at Community Colleges," Journal of Education for Business 65 (1989): 53–55.

16. Rosenberg, "Performance," 43.

17. Ibid., 45.

18. Ibid., 46–48.

19. Inman, "Communication," 29.

20. Reece, "Developing," 45.

21. Inman, "Communication," 30.

22. Charles M. Stanton, "A View from the Portico: Lessons from the Greeks" (Paper deliverd at the Annual Meeting of the Association for the Study of Higher Education, San Antonio, February 1986); Spitzberg and Cupach, 1984.

23. Everett M. Rogers and Steven H. Chaffee, "Communication as an Academic Discipline: A Dialogue," *Journal of Communication* 33 (1983): 18–30.

24. Philip Backlund, Kenneth Brown, Joanne Gurry, and Fred Jandt, "Recommendations for Assessing Speaking and Listening Skills," *Communication Education* 31 (1982): 9–17; Rebecca Rubin, "Assessing Speaking and Listening Competence at the College Level: The Communication Competency Assessment Instrument," *Communication Education* 31 (1982): 19–31; Brian Spitzberg and H. Hurt, "The Measurement of Interpersonal Skills in Instructional Contexts," *Communication Education* 36 (1987): 28–45.

25. Rubin, "Assessing," 19.

26. Peter White, "A Model of the Layperson as Pragmatist," *Personality and Social Psychology Bulletin* 10 (1984): 333–48.

27. Vincent Hazleton and William Cupach, "An Exploration of Ontological Knowledge: Communication Competence as a Function of the Ability to Describe, Predict, and Explain," *Western Journal of Speech Communication* 50 (1986): 119–32.

28. Quoted in Rebecca Rubin's essay, "Communication Competence,"in *Speech Communication: Essays to Commemorate the 75th Anniversary of the Speech Communication Association*, ed. G. Phillips and J. Wood (Carbondale: Southern Illinois University Press, 1990), 94.

29. Dean Hewes, Michael Roloff, Sally Planalp, and David Seibold, "Interpersonal Communication Research: What Should We Know?" in *Speech Communication: Essays to Commemorate the 75th Anniversary of the Speech Communication Association*, ed. G. Phillips and J. Wood (Carbondale: Southern Illinois University Press, 1990), 130.

30. Rubin, "Communication," 95.

31. Hewes, "Interpersonal," 132.

32. William James, "The Sentiment of Rationality," *Essays in Pragmatism* (New York: Hafner, 1948), 3–36.

33. White, "A Model," 344.

34. Ibid.

35. Rubin, "Communication," 94–129.

36. William James, *The Varieties of Religious Experience* (New York: Modern Library, 1929), 478.

37. John Wild, "William James and Existential Authenticity," *Journal of Existentialism* 5 (1965): 243–56. William Gavin, "Regional Ontologies, Types of Meaning, and the Will to Believe in the Philosophy of William James," *Journal of the British Society for Phenomenology* 15 (1984): 262–70. James Edie, *William James and Phenomenology* (Bloomington: Indiana University Press, 1987). Charlene Seigfried, "William James' Phenomenological Methodology," *Journal of the British Society for Phenomenology* 20 (1989): 62–76.

38. Fred Dallmayr, "Pragmatism and Hermeneutics [review of *Beyond Objectivism and Relativism*]," *Review of Politics* 47 (1985): 411.

39. James, "Sentiment," 1948.

40. Ibid., 14.

41. Ibid., 8.

42. Quoted in Seigfried, "William James," 65.

43. Ibid., 63.

44. Edie, *William James*, 72.

45. Seigfried, "William James," 64.

46. Quoted in Seigfried, "William James," 64.

47. Wild, "William James,"

48. William James, *The Will to Believe* (New York: Dover, 1956) 1-31.

49. William Barrett, *The Illusion of Technique: A Search for Meaning in a Technological Civilization* (Garden City, NY: Anchor, 1979), 251–345.

50. Wild, "William James," 255.

51. Dallmayr, "Pragmatism," 421.

52. Stanley Deetz, "Reclaiming the Subject Matter as a Guide to Mutual Understanding: Effectiveness and Ethics in Interpersonal Interaction," *Communication Quarterly* 38 (1990): 226–43.

53. Seigfried, "William James," 70.

54. Ibid., 71.

55. Ibid., 74.

56. Ibid., 75.

57. Arthur Bochner, "Perspectives on Inquiry: Representation, Conversation, and Reflection," in *Handbook of Interpersonal Communication*, ed. M. Knapp and G. Miller (Newbury Park, Calif.: Sage, 1985), 28–58.

58. Richard Lanigan, *Phenomenology of Communication* (Pittsburg: Duquesne UP, 1988).

59. Deetz, "Reclaiming," 226–43.

60. Bochner, "Perspectives," 39.

61. Ibid., 39.

62. Isaac E. Catt, "Im Namen des Pragmatismus oder philosophische Reflexion ist keine Untugend [In the name of pragmatism, or philosophic reflection is no vice]," *Kann man Kommunikation Lehren? Sprache und Sprechen* (Frankfurt: Scriptor Press, 1988). A further example of this is my "Rhetoric and Narcissism: A Critique of Ideological Selfism," *Western Journal of Speech Communication* 50 (1986): 242–53.

63. Donald Hook and Lothar Kahn, "The Liberal Arts and Career Education," *Liberal Education* 72 (1986): 47.

64. Rubin, "Communication," 96.

65. Ibid., 97.

66. Bernard Murchland, "The Eclipse of the Liberal Arts," *Change* (November 1976): 24.

67. Ibid., 62.

68. Richard Lanigan, "Semiotic Phenomenology: A Theory of Human Communication Praxis," *Journal of Applied Communication* Research 10 (1982): 62–73.

69. James, "Sentiment," 8.

70. Ibid., 13.

71. Isaac E. Catt, "Textual Fidelity as a Problem of Communication," (Paper presented at the Western Speech Communication Association, Fresno, Calif., Feb. 1987).

72. Edie, *William James*, 71.

73. Richard Bernstein quoted in Dallmayr, "Pragmatism," 421–22.

74. Ibid., 422.

75. Deetz, "Reclaiming," 228.

76. Ibid.

77. Ibid., 229.

78. Ibid., 228.

79. Ibid., 230.

80. Anthony Wilden, *The Rules are No Game: The Strategy of Communication* (New York: Routledge & Kegan Paul, 1987).

81. Calvin Schrag, *Communicative Praxis and the Space of Subjectivity* (Bloomington: Indiana University Press, 1986).

82. Lanigan, *Phenomenology of Communication* , 1988.

83. William James, *The Principles of Psychology* (Cambridge: Harvard University Press, 1890), 188–91.

Chapter 6

1. John Dewey, *Experience and Nature,* vol. 1 of *The Later Works,* ed. Jo Ann Boydston (Carbondale: Southern Illinois University Press, 1981), 12 (subsequent references will be to Dewey, *Experience,The Later Works*).

2. Dewey, *Experience, The Later Works,* 23.

3. See Thomas M. Alexander, *John Dewey's Theory of Art, Experience, and Nature* (Albany: State University of New York Press, 1987), 26.

4. See Seigfried, "Vagueness and the Adequacy of Concepts: In Defense of William James's Picturesque Style," *Philosophy Today* 26 (winter 1982): 357–67, reprinted in *Twentieth Century Literary Criticism* vol. 32 (Detroit: Gale Research, 1989), 337–41.

5. William James, "Truth—Reality, etc., 1907–1910," in *Manuscript Essays and Notes*, eds. Frederick H. Burkhardt, F. Bowers, and I.K. Skrupskelis (Cambridge: Harvard University Press, 1988), 238 (*The Works of William James*) (subsequent references will be to James, *Manuscript Essays*).

6. James, "Idealism [I] 1880-1884," *Manuscript Essays,* 182.

7. See William James, *"The Meaning of Truth,"* in *The Works of William James,* ed. Frederick H. Burkhardt, F. Bowers, and I.K. Skrupskelis, (Cambridge: Harvard University Press, 1975), 79–86 (subsequent references will be to James, *Meaning*).

8. James, *Meaning,* 115–16.

9. Ibid., 23n6; see also 14.

10. John Dewey, "Context and Thought,"in vol. 6 of *The Later Works, 1931–1932* (Carbondale: Southern Ilinois University Press, 1985), 11.

11. William James, *"Some Problems of Philosophy,"* in *The Works of William James,* eds. Frederick H. Burkhardt, F. Bowers, and I.K. Skrupskelis, *Some Problems of Philosophy,* by William James (Cambridge: Harvard University Press, 1979), 206 (subsequent references will be to James, *Some Problems*).

12. James, *Some Problems,* 206–7.

13. Seigfried, "Like Bridges Without Piers: Beyond the Foundationalist Metaphor, in *Anti-Foundationalism Old and New,* ed. Tom Rockmore and Beth J. Singer (Philadelphia: Temple University Press, 1992), 143–64.

14. For James's natural history methodology, see Seigfried, *William James's Radical Reconstruction of Philosophy* (Albany: State University of New York Press, 1990) 139–70. (Subsequent references will be to Seigfried, *William James's Radical*).

15. William James, *"A Pluralistic Universe,"* in *The Works of William James,* ed. Frederick H. Burkhardt, F. Bowers, and I.K. Skrupskelis (Cambridge: Harvard University Press, 1977), 10 (subsequent references will be to James, *Pluralistic*).

16. John Dewey, *Art as Experience,* vol. 1 of *The Later Works,* ed. Jo Ann Boydston, (Carbondale: Southern Illinois University Press, 1987), 47 (subsequent references will be to Dewey, *Art, The Later Works*).

17. William James, *Essays in Psychology,* ed. Frederick H. Burkhardt, F. Bowers, and I.K. Skrupskelis, (Cambridge: Harvard University Press, 1983), 271-73, (in *The Works of William James*) (subsequent references will be to James, *Essays in Psychology*). See also Seigfried, *William James's Radical,* 30–32, 53ff., and 60. For his last crisis, see James, *Pluralistic,* 94ff.

18. For his first crisis, see John J. McDermott, ed., *The Writings of William James* (New York: Modern Library, 1968), 6–8. For the three crises, see Seigfried, *William James's Radical,* 10–15. See also Richard J. Bernstein's Introduction to James, *Pluralistic,* xxii, ff.

19. Ralph Barton Perry, *The Thought and Character of William James,* vol. 1 (Boston: Little, Brown, 1935), 322ff.

20. Nietzsche says, for instance, that "all experiences are moral experiences, even in the realm of sense perception." *The Gay Science,* ed. Walter Kaufmann (New York: Vintage Books, 1974), section 114.

21. James, *Pluralistic,* 118.

22. Frederick H. Burkhardt, F. Bowers, and I.K. Skrupskelis, ed., *Essays in Philosophy,* by William James (Cambridge: Harvard University Press, 1978), 189, in *The Works of William James* (subsequent references will be to James, *Essays in Philosophy*).

23. James, *Essays in Psychology,* 7 n3.

24. In the following articles I argue that James never rethought his phenomenological claims in light of his hermeneutical insights: "The Pragmatist Sieve of Concepts: Description vs. Interpretation," *The Journal of Philosophy,* 87:11 (Nov., 1990): 585–592; "The World We Practically Live In," *Reinterpreting the Legacy of William James,* ed. Margaret E. Donnelly (Washington, D.C.: American Psychological Association Press, 1992), 77–89; and "William James's Concrete Analysis of Experience," *Monist,* 75:4 (Oct, 1992): 538–550.

25. Frederick H. Burkhardt, F. Bowers, and I.K. Skrupskelis, ed., The *Principles of Psychology,* vol. 2, by William James (Cambridge: Harvard University Press, 1981), 960, in *The Works of William James* (subsequent references will be to James, *Principles*).

26. James, *Principles,* 962–63n11.

27. James, *Some Problems,* 106.

28. Dewey, *Experience, The Later Works,* 190 and 180.

29. For an explanation of pragmatic rationality in terms of the dynamic relation between aesthetic and practical rationality, see Seigfried, *William James's Radical,* 29–38, 117–38, and 373–89.

30. Frederick H. Burkhardt, F. Bowers, and I.K. Skrupskelis, ed., *Pragmatism,* by William James (Cambridge: Harvard University Press, 1975),

70, in *The Works of William James* (Subsequent references will be to James, *Pragmatism*).

31. James, *Pragmatism*, 71.

32. Ibid.

33. Frederick H. Burkhardt, F. Bowers, and I.K. Skrupskelis, ed., "Emerson," *Essays in Religion and Morality*, by William James (Cambridge: Harvard University Press, 1982), 111, in *The Works of William James*.

34. See Frederick H. Burkhardt, F. Bowers, and I.K. Skrupskelis, ed., "The Moral Philosopher and the Moral Life," *The Will to Believe*, by William James (Cambridge: Harvard University Press, 1979), 141–59 (subsequent references will be to James, *Will*), and "On a Certain Blindness in Human Beings," *Talks to Teachers on Psychology*, by William James (Cambridge: Harvard University Press, 1983), 132–38.

35. James, *Pluralistic*, 27.

36. See James, "The Sentiment of Rationality," *Will*, 57–89.

37. See James, *Will*, 98. The following two paragraphs are partially from Seigfried, *William James's Radical*, 382. Dewey adopted the same revised reflex arc model. See Alexander, 128–135.

38. James, *Will*, 106.

39. Ibid., 100.

40. Ibid., 99.

41. Ibid., 95.

42. Dewey, *The Later Works*, 109.

43. James, *Pluralistic*, 27.

44. Dewey, *Experience, The Later Works* , 1:104.

45. James, *Principles*, 1181.

46. James, *Pluralistic*, 19.

47. James, *Pragmatism*, 131.

48. John Dewey, *Democracy and Education*, vol. 9 of *The MIddle Works*, ed. Jo Ann Boydston (Carbondale and Edwardsville: Southern Illinois University Press, 1980), 93.

49. James, *Meaning*, 23–24.

50. Frederick H. Burkhardt, F. Bowers, and I.K. Skrupskelis, ed., *The Varieties of Religious Experience*, by William James (Cambridge: Harvard University Press, 1985), 359, in *The Works of William James*.

51. Dewey, "A Resume of Four Lectures on Common Sense, Science and Philosophy," *The Later Works*, 6:431.

Chapter 7

1. For examples of works in the so-called Anglo-American or Analytic tradition, see Steven Toulmin's *The Place of Reason in Ethics* (Chicago: University of Chicago Press, 1986) or R.M. Hare's *The Language of Morals* (Oxford: Clarendon Press, 1952), and *Freedom and Reason* (Oxford: Clarendon Press, 1963); for the continental tradition, see Jean-Paul Sartre, *The Critique of Dialectical Reason* (London: NLB, 1976), Maurice Merleau-Ponty, *Humanism and Terror*, trans. John O'Neill (Boston: Beacon Press, 1969), and *Adventures of the Dialectic* (Evanston, Ill.: Northwestern University Press, 1973).

2. Both Rawls and Habermas resurrect different features of Enlightenment rationality. Rawls claims that he has tried to "carry to a higher order of abstraction the traditional theory of the social contract carried out by Locke, Rousseau, and Kant." His model, though influenced by game theory, is thoroughly in this tradition. The basic principles of justice are determined by the contextless, self-interested, calculative individuals who are given the task of constructing a game in which they do not know which parts they will play: "each person must decide by rational reflections what constitutes his good, the system of ends which it is rational for him to pursue," and "the choice which rational men would make in this hypothetical situation of equal liberty . . . determines the principles of justice" (*A Theory of Justice* [Cambridge: Belknap Press, 1973], 11–12). Habermas is highly critical of the way the Enlightenment developed its side of "subjective rationality," the kind exhibited in Rawls's approach, but seeks to go back, "revising the Enlightenment with the very tools of the Enlightenment," to arrive at an intersubjective or communicative model of rationality (*The Philosophical Discourse of Modernity* [Cambridge: MIT Press, 1987], Lecture XI, 30; this whole chapter is a lucid synopsis of Habermas's position). While I think this position has much to recommend it, Habermas still wants all contextual, historical, "located" discourse to be critiqued by a universal, ahistorical, "transcendental" rationality much along the lines of Peirce's final opinion of the ideal "community of inquiry." He also clearly accepts the project of determining meaning and truth in terms of the tradition from Frege to Davidson (and Husserl)—that is, of "truth condition semantics" (312). The aim is to determine the exact truth of the sentence, the basic *unit of meaning*, in light of what it would take for rational beings to affirm that it was true. This itself I find to be a questionable commitment stemming ultimately from the Enlightenment, to reduce meaning to epistemology, if not to the atomic unit of the term, then to the indicative sentence. Sentences only gain meaning within larger dynamic processes of human action, many of which are not cognitive or epistemological projects at all. The humanism of E.M. Adams, especially his recent work, *The Metaphysics of Self and World* (Philadelphia: Temple University Press, 1991), should also be mentioned here.

For a powerful critique of the Enlightenment approach, see Roberto Mangabeira Unger, *Knowledge and Politics* (New York: Free Press, 1975) and *Passion* (New York: Free Press, 1984).

3. See Herbert Marcuse, *One Dimensional Man* (Boston: Beacon Press, 1964), Theodore Adorno, *Negative Dialectics*, Jean Francois Lyotard, *The Post-Modern Condition* (Minneapolis: Minnesota University Press, 1984), Michel Foucault, *The Order of Things* (New York: Pantheon Books, 1971), C.B. MacPherson, *The Real World of Democracy* (Oxford: Clarendon Press, 1966), Richard Rorty, *Contingency, Irony and Solidarity* (New York: Cambridge University Press, 1989).

4. Voltaire says, "What is toleration? It is the endowment of humanity. We are all steeped in weaknesses and errors; let us forgive each other our follies; that is the first law of nature." *Philosophical Dictionary*, "Tolerance," trans. Peter Gay (New York: Harcourt, Brace and World, 1962), 482.

5. This study continues the discussion initiated by Bellah et al. in *Habits of the Heart* (New York: Harper and Row, 1986); see also Thomas Alexander, "The Human Eros" and Raymond Boisvert "Heteronomous Freedom," in *Philosophy and the Reconstruction of Culture: Pragmatic Essays after Dewey*, ed. John Stuhr (Albany: State University of New York Press, 1993).

6. Donna Haraway, "Situated Knowledges: The Science Question in Feminism and the Privilege of Partial Perspective," in *Simians, Cyborgs, and Women* (New York: Routledge, 1991), 196. See also the important essays by Lisa Heldke, "John Dewey and Evelyn Fox Keller: A Shared Epistemological Tradition," *Hypatia* 2, no. 3 (1987), and Eugenie Gatens- Robinson, "Dewey and the Feminist Successor Science Project," *Transactions of the Charles S. Peirce Society* 27, no. 4, 1991. A special 1993 volume of *Hypatia* is devoted to the relationship between pragmatism and feminism.

7. See Peter Gay, *The Enlightenment: An Interpretation* (New York: W.W. Norton, 1966) as well as his anthology, *The Enlightenment: A Comprehensive Anthology* (New York: Simon and Schuster, 1973), Ernst Cassirer, *The Philosophy of the Enlightenment* (Princeton: Princeton University Press, 1951), and Henry May, *The Enlightenment in America* (New York: Oxford University Press, 1976).

8. See Locke's *Essay Concerning Human Understanding*, Book II: vi, 2, "The two great and principal actions of the mind . . . are these two: *perception or thinking* and *volition or willing*. The power of thinking is called the *Understanding*, and the power of volition is called the *Will*, and these two powers or abilities of the mind are denominated *faculties*." At II:21, 5, he adds "Perception, which we make the act of the understanding, is of three sorts: (1) The perception of ideas in our minds, (2) The perception of the signification of signs, (3) The perception of the connection or repugnancy, agreement, or disagreement, that there is any between any of our ideas."

9. See *Essay* III: i-ii.

10. David Hume, Thomas Reid, Etienne Bonnot de Condillac, and Immanuel Kant, each in his own way but following Locke, tried to be a "Newton of the mind." See, for example, Robert Hahn, *Kant's Newtonian Revolution* (Carbondale: Southern Illinois University Press, 1988).

11. See, for example, Lev Vygotsky, *Thought and Language* (Cambridge: MIT Press, 1986), Jean Piaget, *Thought and Language of the Child* (New York: Harcourt, Brace, 1932), Jerome Bruner, *Actual Minds, Possible Worlds* (Cambridge: Harvard University Press, 1986), and Diane Gillespie, *The Mind's We: Contextualism in Cognitive Psychology* (Carbondale, Ill.: Southern Illinois University Press, 1992).

12. See George Lakoff, *Women, Fire, and Dangerous Things* (Chicago: University of Chicago Press, 1987), Mark L. Johnson, *The Body in the Mind* (Chicago: University of Chicago Press, 1989), and Eve Sweerser, *From Etymology to Pragmatics* (New York: Cambridge University Press, 1990).

13. This is discussed at length in my book, *John Dewey's Theory of Art, Experience and Nature: The Horizons of Feeling* (Albany: State University of New York Press, 1987); see especially chapter 4.

14. Though in the *Investigations*, Wittgenstein points to the diversity of language games and different *forms of life*, he says virtually nothing about how one form of life transforms into another; this, no doubt, fell outside philosophy's therapeutic mission for him (if meaning lies in use, in *following a rule*, what kind of meaning would there be to describe the transformation of the rules of a language game within which it was played?). This led to the views of language change we see in the accounts of Davidson and Rorty, in which metaphoric transformations are meaningless, nonlinguistic events that somehow disrupt and change language games. See Rorty's *Contingency, Irony, and Solidarity*, chap. 1. This view of language has been powerfully challenged by the works mentioned in note 12, above.

15. See Alasdair MacIntyre, *Whose Justice? Which Rationality?* (Notre Dame: University of Notre Dame Press, 1988), Allan Bloom , *The Closing of the American Mind* (New York: Simon and Schuster, 1987), E.D. Hirsch, *Cultural Literacy* (Boston: Houghton Mifflin, 1987). For a defense of cultural pluralism in education, see Thomas Alexander, "The Moral Imagination and the Aesthetics of Human Existence," in *Moral Education and the Liberal Arts*, ed. Michael Mitias (New York: Greenwood Press, 1992).

16. John Dewey, "The Reflex Arc Concept in Psychology," in *The Early Works*, vol. 5, ed. Jo Ann Boydston (Carbondale: Southern Illinois University Press, 1975), 97.

17. John Dewey, *Ethics*, vol. 7 of *The Later Works*, ed. Jo Ann Boydston (Carbondale: Southern Illinois University Press, 1975), 289.

18. John Dewey, "The Reflex Arc Concept in Psychology," 97.

19. Ibid., 98.

20. James J. Gibson, "Notes on Action," in *Reasons for Realism*, ed. Edward Reed and Rebecca Johns (Hillsdale, N.J.: Erlbaum, 1982), 385–92. As Eleanor J. Gibson, his wife, explains in the foreword: "A careful description of the information for perception, even as it approaches elegance in the form of mathematical statement, does not convey sufficiently the reciprocity of a creature and the environment, especially in its own niche or habitat. This mutuality of creature and environment is the basis of the need for an ecological optics, one that is meaningful for a living creature. The surfaces and substances of the environment provide opportunities of diverse kinds for the creature's activities, offering it support for living successfully in the world. These opportunities are its 'afforance' (a made-up word)" xiii. See also the essays "Ecological Optics," "Perceptual Learning: Differentiation or Enrichment?," and "The Concept of the Stimulus in Psychology" as well as Gibson's major book, *The Ecological Approach to Visual Perception* (Boston: Houghton Mifflin, 1979).

21. See Mark L. Johnson, *The Body in the Mind*.

22. John Dewey, *Experience and Nature*; vol. 1 of *The Later Works*, ed. Jo Ann Boydston (Carbondale: Southern Illinois University Press, 1981), 139.

23. See *Democracy and Education*, vol. 9 of *The Middle Works*, ed. Jo Ann Boydston (Carbondale: Southern Illinois University Press, 1983), 40.

24. John Dewey, *Experience and Nature*, 141.

25. Ibid., 143.

26. See my expanded discussion of this in my paper, "The Human Eros," cited in note 5, above.

27. See Clifford Geertz, "Found in Translation: On the Social History of the Moral Imagination," in *Local Knowledge* (New York: Basic Books, 1983).

28. John Dewey, *Democracy and Education*, 7.

29. Ibid., 7–8.

30. Ibid., 8.

31. Ibid., 18.

32. Ibid., 8–9.

33. See *Art as Experience*, vol. 10 of *The Later Works* , ed. Jo Ann Boydstron (Carbondale: Southern Illinois University Press, 1987), 248–249.

34. John Dewey, *The Public and Its Problems*, vol. 3 of *The Later Works* , ed. Jo Ann Boydston (Carbondale: Southern Illinois University Press, 1981), 328.

35. Ibid., 330.

36. Ibid., 332.

37. For Dewey's discussion of democracy as primarily a cultural idea rather than merely a political one, in addition to *The Public and Its Problems*, see *Freedom and Culture* (in *Later Works* 13).

38. For an important application of the role of difference in perspective in ethical thinking, see Carol Gilligan, *In a Different Voice* (Cambridge: Harvard University Press, 1982).

Chapter 8

1. See Janet Horne, "Rhetoric after Rorty," *Western Journal of Speech Communication* 53 (Summer 1989), pp. 247–59. See also Arthur P. Bochner, "Perspectives on Inquiry: Representation, Conversation, and Reflection," in *Handbook of Interpersonal Communication,* ed. M. L. Knapp and G. R. Miller (Beverly Hills, Calif.: Sage, 1985), 27–58.

2. The clearest articulation of Rorty's most recent position can be found in *Contingency, Irony, and Solidarity*. See also *Consequences of Pragmatism (Essays: 1972–1980)* (Minneapolis: University of Minnesota Press, 1982).

3. Rorty, throughout *Consequences of Pragmatism,* is never particularly clear about what he means by pragmatism. He often uses the concept, generally, as a kind of Occam's razor to dismiss confusing (in other words, *useless*) lines of inquiry, as he does with Peirce (*Consequences*, 160–61): "For all his genius, however, Peirce never made up his mind what he wanted a general theory of signs *for*. . . ." Bochner, closely following Rorty's work, equates pragmatism with *methodological pluralism*—a sort of live-and-let-live approach to theory and research in the communication discipline. ("Perspectives", 27–58).

4. It may be argued that Rorty is, in *Contingency, Irony, and Solidarity,* guilty of this particular practice, attempting to balance the emancipatory interests of Derrida against the conservative, reformist tendencies of liberalism.

5. Thomas Alexander, *John Dewey's Theory of Art, Experience, and Nature: The Horizons of Feeling* (Albany: SUNY Press, 1987).

6. For an excellent discussion of the thematic bases of French critical theory, see Vincent Descombes, *Modern French Philosophy*, trans. L. Scott-Fox and J. M. Harding (New York: Cambridge University Press, 1980).

7. See Bochner, ""Perspectives,". 50–52.

8. See Michel Foucault, *Death and the Labyrinth: The World of Raymond Roussel,* trans. Charles Ruas (New York: Doubleday, 1986).

9. See H. S. Thayer, *Meaning and Action: A Critical History of Pragmatism* (New York: Bobbs Merrill, 1968).

10. A number of outstanding works outlining the issues guiding the school of thought known as American (U.S.A.) pragmatism have endeavored

to make this very point. In addition to Alexander's fine work, see Victor Kestenbaum, *The Phenomenological Sense of John Dewey: Habit and Meaning.* (Atlantic Highlands, N.J.: Humanities Press, 1977); John E. Smith (1978) *Purpose and Thought: The Meaning of Pragmatism.* (Chicago: University of Chicago Press, 1978); and Thayer, *Meaning and Action.*

11. See Michel Foucault, *The Archæology of Knowledge, and the Discourse on Language,* trans. A. M. Sheridan Smith (New York: Pantheon Books, 1972).

12. See Gilles Deleuze and Felix Guattari, *The Anti-oedipus: Capitalism and Schizophrenia,* trans. Robert Hurley, Mark Seem, and Helen R. Lane (New York: Viking Press, 1977).

13. Michel Foucault, *The Order of Things: An Archaeology of the Human Sciences,* trans. anon. (New York: Pantheon Books).

14. Alexander, *Dewey's Theory,* 277.

15. John Dewey, *Art as Experience,* vol. 10 of *The Later Works,* ed. JoAnn Boydston (Carbondale: Southern Illinois University Press, 1987), 43. Originally published at *Art as Experience* (New York: Putnam's Sons, 1958) (subsequent references will be to Dewey, *The Later Works*).

16. In most respects, Alexander does not posit a qualitatively different argument from that made by Kestenbaum—although Alexander does not choose to come out and state, with Kestenbaum, that Dewey's concept of experience is both existential and phenomenological, but neither does he substantially disagree at any point with the Heideggerian and Merleau-Pontyan reading of Dewey supplied by Kestenbaum. Alexander, moreover, cites Kestenbaum frequently, making many of the same comparisons between Dewey and Merleau-Ponty.

17. Smith, *Purpose,* 145.

18. The most thorough (and original) discussion of the *lived body* as a central metaphor of French existential and semiotic phenomenology can be found in Maurice Merleau-Ponty, *Phenomenology of Perception,* trans. Colin Smith (New York: Routledge & Kegan Paul, 1962). See also Richard L. Lanigan, *Speaking and Semiology: Maurice Merleau-Ponty's Phenomenological Theory of Existential Communication* (The Hague: Mouton, 1972), and *Phenomenology of Communication: Merleau Ponty's Thematics in Communicology and Semiology* (Pittsburgh: Duquesne University Press, 1988).

19. Alexander, *Dewey's Theory,* 144.

20. Ibid., 143.

21. Dewey, *The Later Works 10:* 295.

22. See Michel Foucault, "A Preface to Transgression," in *Language, Counter-Memory, Practice: Selected Essays and Interviews,* ed. Donald F. Bouchard,

trans. Donald F. Bouchard and Sherry Simon (Ithaca, N.Y.: Cornell University Press, 1977). See also Deborah Cook, "Nietzsche, Foucault, Tragedy," in *Philosophy and Literature* 13 (1989): 140–150.

23. Foucault, *Archaeology*, 79–125.

24. Foucault, *Language, Counter-Memory, Practice*, 52.

25. For fuller development of this judgment, see Giles Gunn, *Thinking Across the American Grain: Ideology, Intellect, and the New Pragmatism* (Chicago: University of Chicago Press, 1992).

26. The three mentioned here are listed because of their interest in connecting primary strains of Dewey's work to the contemporary thematics of existentialism, phenomenology, and postmodern criticism. It is important to note that other contemporary writers on the revival of interest in pragmatism have produced different lists. See Gunn, *Thinking*, 1992, p. 72

27. Ibid.

28. Since he did not follow up on Peirce's semiotics (or explicitly develop one of his own), nor did he actively maintain his interest in James's psychology, he has tended to be relegated to "third place" by contemporary thinkers currently reinvestigating the work of the "big three" pragmatists.

29. Foucault, *Language, Counter-Memory Practive*, 51.

30. Michel Leiris, *Manhood*, trans. Richard Howard (London: Jonathan Cape, 1968). Cited in Foucault, *Language, Counter-Memory, Practice*, 51.

31. This statement captures Merleau-Ponty's notion of speech as the lived embodiment of authentic choice. See Merleau-Ponty, Phenomenology, 148–206. See also Georges Gusdorf, *Speaking (La Parole)* Trans. Paul T. Brockelman (Evanston: Northwestern University. Press, 1965). In identifying *another way* for expression, the person first encounters the inherent ambiguity of lived existence.

32. Foucault, *Death and the Labyrinth*, 14.

33. John Ashbery, "Introduction: On Raymond Roussel," in Foucault, *Death and the Labyrinth*.

34. Ibid., xix.

35. Foucault, *Order of Things*, xvi.

36. Foucault, *Death and Labyrinth*, 45.

37. Ibid., 23.

38. Gunn, *Thinking*, 72.

39. Rorty, *Philosophy and the Mirror of Nature* (Princeton, Princeton University Press, 1979). See also Rorty, *Contingency*.

40. See Alexander, *Dewey's Theory*.

41. Rorty, *Consequences of Pragmatism*, 175.

42. Rorty, *Contingency*, 64.

43. Foucault, *Politics, Philosophy, Culture: Interviews and Other Writings, 1977–1984*, ed. Lawrence D. Kritzman, trans. Alan Sheridan and others (New York: Routledge, 1988), 265.

44. It is important to underscore the distinction Foucault draws between the Kantian, anthropological interests of the social sciences (as practiced in the last century) and the postmodern interests of the human sciences. See Foucault, *Order of Things*, 344–87.

45. See Alexander, *Dewey's Theory*, 183–267.

46. Ibid., 188.

47. See Dewey, *The Later Works* 10.

48. Georges Bataille, "The Reasons for Writing a Book . . ."*Oeuvres complètes, Ecrits Posthumes 1922–1940*, vol. 2, trans. Elizabeth Rottenberg (Paris: Gallimard, 1988), 143. Cited in *Yale French Studies 79: Literature and the Ethical Question*, ed. Claire Nouvet (New Haven: Yale University Press, 1991), p. 11.

49. See Rollo May, *The Cry for Myth*. (New York: W. W. Norton, 1991).

50. See Deleuze and Guattari, *Anti-Oedipus*.

51. Jean-François Lyotard, *Tombeau de l'Intellectuel* (Paris: Galilee, 1984), pp. 15-16.

52. Foucault, *Politics, Philosophy, Culture*, 125–151.

53. See Dewey, *The Later Works* 10.

54. Lyotard, *The Postmodern Condition: A Report on Knowledge*, trans. Geoff Bennington, Brian Massumi, and Régis Durand (Minneapolis: University of Minnesota Press, 1984), 80.

55. Dewey, *The Later Works* 10:41

56. Lyotard, *The Postmodern Condition*, 26–27.

57. See Rorty, *Philosophy* and *Consequences of Pragmatism*.

58. I am using the word "altar" in a special sense. In modern pronunciation, there is virtually no difference between the pronunciation of 'alter' and 'altar.' Altar denotes a place of worship, or more specifically, it is a surface used as a center of a ritual on which sacrifices are offered or incense is burned. Alter, as noun, denotes both "other" and "second." As a verb, it means "to change." So, altar becomes a familiar ritual surface on which changes occur; a surface that has, thus, two sides and two possibilities.

Chapter 9

1. "The obligation which the charitable individual feels is the demand that these restrictions [economic, feudal, and cultural class distinctions] should be removed. It is not a demand which society as it is now organized can enforce against him. It is a part of the growing consciousness that society is responsible for the ordering of its own processes and structure so that what are common goods in their very nature should be accessible to common enjoyment. We vaguely call it 'progress'." George Herbert Mead, "Philanthropy from the Point of View of Ethics," in *Selected Writings: George Herbert Mead,* ed. Andrew J. Reck (Chicago: University of Chicago Press, 1964), 406–07; hereafter referred to as *Selected Writings.*

2. John Dewey, *Individualism Old and New* (New York: Minton, Balch, 1930), 154, 156.

3. Mead, "Scientific Method and the Moral Sciences," *Selected Writings,* 257.

4. George Herbert Mead, *Mind, Self, and Society: from the Standpoint of a Social Behaviorist,* ed. Charles W. Morris (Chicago: University of Chicago Press, 1934), 265; hereafter referred to as *MSS.*

5. Mead, cited in Dimitri Shalin, "G. H. Mead, Socialism, and the Progressive Agenda," *American Journal of Sociology* 93, no.4 (1988): 920–21. Reprinted in *Philosophy, Social Theory, and the Thought of George Herbert Mead,* ed. M. Aboulafia (Albany: SUNY Press,1991), 21–56. Earlier in the same year he had written to his friend, "Nothing could meet the wants of mankind as Christianity, and why not have a little deception if need be?" In Shalin, "Progressive Agenda," 921.

6. Mead, "Scientific Method and the Moral Sciences," *Selected Writings,* 258. See also "Philanthropy from the Point of View of Ethics," *Selected Writings,* 397.

7. Shalin, "Progressive Agenda," 918–19.

8. "Oberlin College was at the center of the new currents of theological, political, and social thought. In the 1880s and 1890s, it was the site of several conferences in which the Rev. Washington Gladden, Walter Rauschenbusch, Lyman Abbot, Richard T. Ely, Carroll D. Wright, and scores of other liberal theologians and reformers debated topics." Shalin, "Progressive Agenda," 919. Walter Rauschenbusch was Richard Rorty's maternal grandfather.

9. See Jean-François Lyotard and Jean-Loup Thébaud, *Just Gaming,* trans. Wlad Godzich (Minneapolis: University of Minnesota Press, 1985).

10. See Jean François Lyotard, *The Postmodern Condition: A Report on Knowledge,* trans. G. Bennington and B. Massumi (Minneapolis: University of Minnesota Press, 1984). It would perhaps be stretching terms a bit to place

Emmanuel Levinas in the postmodern camp, but his attack on all totalizing movements in the name of the other can be used to buttress certain antiuniversalist claims. He has left his mark on Lyotard. See Lyotard's *Just Gaming*.

11. Perhaps Mead's struggle is a strength at a time, our time, when, on the one hand, uncritical universalistic claims often make the rounds in influential circles, while, on the other, particularity is sanctified at the seeming price of dismissing universality and its alleged attendant totalizing ghosts.

12. For all their differences, there are some interesting connections to be drawn between Gadamer's notion of effective history and Mead's claims regarding sociality and the relation of the past to the present. See Hans Georg-Gadamer, *Truth and Method* (2nd revised edition), revised by Joel Weinsheimer and Donald G. Marshall (New York: Crossroad, 1989), 300–307.

13. Mead, I believe, would suggest that in the desire to defend those who have been marginalized by hegemonic forces, we may become seduced by our own rhetoric into forgetting the universalist assumptions that stand behind many of our ethical impulses. See Jürgen Habermas, *The Philosophical Discourse of Modernity*, trans. Frederick Lawrence (Cambridge: MIT Press, 1987).

14. See Brook Thomas, *The New Historicism* (Princeton: Princeton University Press, 1991), chapter 4.

15. Mead, "Scientific Method and the Moral Sciences," *Selected Writings*, 263–64.

16. Mead, *MSS*, 47.

17. Ibid., 69.

18. See J. David Lewis, "A Social Behaviorist Interpretation of the Meadian 'I'," *American Journal of Sociology* 85, no. 2 (1979): 261–87. Reprinted in Aboulafia, *Philosophy*, 109–33.

19. Jürgen Habermas, *The Theory of Communicative Action, Vol. II*, trans. Thomas McCarthy (Boston: Beacon Press, 1987), 15–22.

20. Habermas, *Theory*, 23.

21. Mead, *MSS*, 132–33.

22. Ibid., 151.

23. Ibid., 154.

24. The implications of these terms, as well as the issue of how one might reconcile the *I* and *me* aspects of the individual, are unfortunately beyond the scope of this paper. See Mitchell Aboulafia, *The Mediating Self: Mead, Sartre, and Self-Determination* (New Haven: Yale University Press, 1986); Sandra B. Rosenthal and Patrick L. Bourgeois, *Mead and Merleau-Ponty: Toward a Common Vision* (Albany: SUNY Press, 1991).

25. Mead, *MSS*, 157.

26. Ibid., 260–61.

27· Ibid., 262.

28. "If, with George Herbert Mead, we understand the process of social-ization itself as one of individuation, the sought-for mediation between indi-vidual and society is less 'puzzling'. Then, of course, the structuralist concept of language, restricted to the logical-semantic dimension, has to be expanded; language has to be conceived of as a medium that both draws each participant in interaction into a community of communication, as one of its members, and at the same time subjects him to an unrelenting compulsion toward individu-ation." Habermas, *Philosophical Discourse*, 334.

29. Mead, *MSS*, 326.

30. In addition, each is also capable of novel responses in terms of the *I*, which is an avenue I have already committed myself to refrain from exploring in this paper.

31. While Mead would argue for the irreducible individuality of each person, he would not have thought, contra Levinas, that irreducible otherness was the source of the ethical. Otherness *and* universality are the grounds of the ethical.

32. "But society is the interaction of these selves, and an interaction that is only possible if out of their diversity unity arises. We are indefinitely differ-ent from each other, but our differences make interaction possible. Society is unity in diversity. . . . There are two sources of its unity—the unity arising from the interconnection of all the different selves in their self-conscious diversity and that arising from the identity of common impulses." Mead, "National-Mindedness and International-Mindedness," in *Selected Writings*, 359. The danger for Mead of the latter alternative—unity through identity of impulse—is that it can lead to war in a post World War I world, a world in which war is clearly unacceptable.

33. Mead, *MSS*, 325.

34. Ibid., 265

35. Mead, "Scientific Method and the Moral Sciences," *Selected Writings*, 258.

36. Walter Watson, *The Architectonics of Meaning: Foundations of the New Pluralism* (Albany: SUNY Press, 1985; Chicago: University of Chicago Press, 1993) and David A. Dilworth, *Philosophy in World Perspective: A Comparative Hermeneutic of the Major Theories* (New Haven: Yale University Press, 1989).

37. Examples may be worth a thousand words here. The following fig-ures have an affinity for the respective voices: personal—Protagoras,

Nietzsche, W. James, Sartre; objective—Democritus, Hume, Peirce, Russell; diaphanic—Plato, Augustine, Heidegger, Levinas; disciplinary—Aristotle, Aquinas, Kant, Dewey. No doubt Mead's texts present certain problems if we are going to attempt to arrive at a common voice for the author behind the texts, in part because much of what we know as his texts were not published by him, but were student notes or unpublished notes. But I will argue that there is a preferred voice for Mead.

38. Dilworth, *World Perspective,* 27. In a private correspondence, Dilworth suggested that Mead has a disciplinary perspective and he gave as evidence the generalized other. I obviously think that he is correct and appreciate the suggestion.

39. See J. David Lewis and Richard L. Smith, *American Sociology and Pragmatism: Mead, Chicago Sociology, and Symbolic Interaction* (Chicago: University of Chicago Press, 1980). See also *Symbolic Interaction* 6 (spring 1983) for an exchange on this book.

40. The issue is actually complicated by the fact that if one brings in other levels of analysis, other connections become apparent. Those familiar with this approach will find, I believe, that Mead's method is by and large similar to that of James and Peirce, a problematic method, while his governing principle is that of James, not Peirce. All of this is further complicated by the fact that Mead often drew on a dialectical method, and this is apparent in the manner he discusses self and other; it is also, I would argue, related to certain Christian sensibilities that he never left behind.

41. George Herbert Mead, *Philosophy of the Present* (Chicago and London: University of Chicago Press, 1980), 35.

42. Mead, "The Teaching of Science in College," *Selected Writings,* 62.

43. Mead, "A Behavioristic Account of the Significant Symbol," *Selected Writings,* 245.

44. "And our disciplinary perspectives do not by their limitations limit the degree of truth we can attain, but rather it is through these limitations that it is possible to attain a truth appropriate to each perspective." Watson, *Architectonics,* 34.

45. Mead would have agreed with Kant that war will eventually become an unacceptable option in the modern world. However, this did not lead him to believe that warfare had already become impossible. In "National-Mindedness and International-Mindedness," published in 1929, he wrote, "The Great War has presented not a theory but a condition . . . . Every war if allowed to go the accustomed way of wars will become a world war, and every war pursued uncompromisingly and intelligently must take as its objective the destruction not of hostile forces but of enemy nations in their entirety. It has become unthinkable as a policy for adjudicating national differences. It

has become logically impossible. This is not to say that it may not arise. Another catastrophe may be necessary before we have cast off the cult of warfare, but we cannot any longer *think* our international life in terms of warfare." *Selected Writings,* 362–63.

46. See Mead, "Mindedness," *Selected Writings,* 355–70.

47· Mead, "Mindedness," *Selected Writings,* 368–69

Chapter 10

1. John Dewey, *Experience and Nature,* vol.1 of *The Later Works,* ed. Jo Ann Boydston (Carbondale: Southern Illinois University Press, 1988), 132; Gustav Bergmann, *Logic and Reality* (Madison: University of Wisconsin Press, 1964), 177, quoted by Richard Rorty, "Introduction," in *The Linguistic Turn,* ed. Richard Rorty (Chicago: University of Chicago Press, 1967), 8; George Herbert Mead, *Mind, Self, and Society,* ed. Charles W. Morris (Chicago: University of Chicago Press, 1934), 50; Charles Sanders Peirce, *Collected Papers of Charles Sanders Peirce,* ed. Charles Hartshorne and Paul Weiss (Cambridge: Harvard University Press, 1935), 5.18.

2. It has become common to use "praxis" in English without translation or marking as a Greek term—often, with warnings against any easy translation as "practice." I adopt that custom here in regard to "poiesis," with correlative cautions again any easy translation with variations of "poetic" in a purely aesthetic sense.

3. This may seem an odd division of labor, given Rorty's well-known advice to philosophers about joining in "the conversation of mankind." It is congruent, however, with my thesis in this chapter: despite his more recent references to conversation, Rorty's neopragmatism retains language philosophy's basis in praxis; in the use of a product (language) that is already made, rather than in the innovative, insightful connection of elements that is basic to the doing of communication and articulated most thoroughly in Peirce's concept of abduction. In other words, this division of labor is another way of speaking of what I explicate throughout the chapter as the differences between the poetic and praxial (doing and making) functions of communication.

4. In citing Aristotle's definition, I am not suggesting that we accept its implied instrumental sense of rhetoric. To the contrary, I find in the impetus pragmatism gives for a philosophy of communication rooted in the primacy of poiesis, an impetus also for reconceptualizing rhetoric's breadth. An instrumental view of rhetoric—more generally stated, a view of communication as mere means for transmission of messages—is a forced separation of philosophy from rhetoric that relies on some rather thoroughly discredited representationalist epistemological and ontological assumptions, which maintain poiesis,

praxis, and episteme in the hierarchy set by Plato's Divided Line. Several strands of contemporary rhetoric echo what I present here as classical pragmatism's alternative sense of the relationship among poetic, praxial, and epistemic functions of communication, by connecting philosophy's traditional concern for what is, what is good, and knowing to rhetoric's focus on actual communication. Michael Hyde's exposition of rhetoric's ontological function (rooted in a Heideggerean, rather than pragmatist, philosophy of communication) emphasizes the closeness of (in my terms) the praxial and poetic functions of communication: "Heidegger understood poetry as a mode of thinking and communicative practice wherein Being (i.e. the presencing of what is) is made-known through an act of creativity" that "functions to liberate present understanding from the determinacy of the past"("Rhetorically, Man Dwells: On the Making-Known Function of Discourse," *Communication* 7 [1983], 207–8). That "creating" function, he goes on to say, "does maintain a primacy over rhetoric with respect to the initiating and fostering . . . wherein Being is revealed. Yet, once Being is revealed in a moment of truth, in a poetic disclosure, it becomes the task of rhetoric to 'preserve' the meaning of this revelation" (ibid., 213–14). A critical rhetoric focused, as in Raymie McKerrow's project, on the pervasive presence of power in communication challenges a might-makes-right conception of the good. "Power," in his analysis, "is not a possession or a content—it is instead an integral part of social relations," which discourse "creates and perpetuates" ("Critical Rhetoric: Theory and Praxis," *Communication Monographs* 56 [1989] 99). Rather than proposing a positive, static standard against which "the discourse of power" is to be assessed, McKerrow argues that a "critique of domination" with an "emancipatory purpose" must be joined to a "critique of freedom" requiring "permanent criticism—a self reflexive critique that turns back on itself even as it promotes a realignment in the forces of power that construct social relations" (ibid., 91). His rejection of critical theories, which presume a standard of abstract reason as the good, is intensified in Michael Huspek's criticism of Habermas's theory of communicative action for "its top-heaviness and its insensitivity to practice-based meanings" ("Taking Aim on Habermas's Critical Theory," *Communication Monographs* 58 [1991] 232). Huspek argues instead for identifying intrinsic values informing actual struggles against oppressive power as the basis for critique that "proves itself critical and emancipatory by grounding itself in the realm of practice, tapping into the lifeworld meanings that inform speakers' everyday discursive struggles, and then going on to search out . . . actualized or implicit instances of ideology critique and emergent communicative competencies" (ibid.). John Lyne, in presenting several functions of rhetoric as seen by the contemporary rhetoric of inquiry project, notes that "the constitutive function of rhetoric is one that should probably get more attention in our literature than it does." Rhetoric, he goes on to say, "serves to constitute parts of our world" ("Rhetorics of Inquiry," *Quarterly Journal of Speech* 71 (1985) 68). The definition of rhetoric in another presentation of the rhetoric of inquiry project is especially reminiscent of classical pragmatism's union of epistemic and melioristic interests: "Traditionally, rhetoric includes how and what is communicated, what happens then, and what improvements are possible. To this, rhetoric of inquiry adds the interaction of communication with inquiry" (John Nelson and Allan Megill, "Rhetoric of Inquiry: Projects and Prospects," *Quarterly Journal of Speech* 72 [1986] 35). Reconceptualizing "knowing" as this sort of "inquiring" certainly is congenial to classical pragmatism's focus on actual process in contrast to theoretically formed method.

5. This account of Dewey's portrayal of the history of science as moving from an empirical to an experimental orientation is a gloss on his discussion at the beginning of "Experience and Nature: A Re-Introduction," which Dewey wrote in 1949–1951 for a proposed revision of *Experience and Nature*. As edited by Joseph Ratner, it is published as "Appendix 1: The Unfinished Introduction" in John Dewey, *Experience and Nature, The Later Works*, 1:329–64.

6. "A Re-Introduction," 343 (see note 5). Further quotations from this appendix will be identified by page numbers following the quotations.

7. For extended discussion of the presence and absence of this sort of reasoning in diverse communicative media, see my *Reasoning Across the Media: Verbal, Visual, and Televisual Literacies* (Montclair (N.J.) State College: Institute for Critical Thinking Resource Publication, Series Three, Number Two), 1989. A more extensive treatment is in preparation: *Media as Embodiment of Rationality: An Essay in the Praxiology of Communication*.

8. For a detailed discussion, see Thomas M. Alexander, *John Dewey's Theory of Art, Experience and Nature* (Albany: SUNY Press, 1987), especially 213–32.

9. Medical practice as illustrative of this sense of art evokes Kant's example of "pragmatic belief" in the *Critique of Pure Reason* (B 851–52).

10. For detailed discussions of praxis and poiesis in the context of the philosophy of communication, see Calvin O. Schrag, *Communicative Praxis and the Space of Subjectivity* (Bloomington: Indiana University Press, 1986) and Andrew R. Smith, "A Theory of Transcultural Rhetoric: Poiesis and Mishima Yukio's Textuality" (Ph.D. dissertation, Southern Illinois University, 1990).

11. Peirce's investigation of the conditions of possibility of what is—that is, with "conditions for" in contrast to "products of"; of the constitution of categories, as well as their use—is central to his general revisioning of Kant. That goal is evident throughout Peirce's work and is especially present in his discussions of pragmatism (as "practical ethics") in volume five of the *Collected Papers*.

12. *The Later Works* 1:135.

Chapter 11

We would like to thank Carolyn Ellis, Bruce Silver, and Butler Waugh for reading and commenting on this chapter.

1. Usually, meeting the standards of science is what it takes for a theory to count as knowledge, since in the English-language tradition, epistemology has been identified more often than not with the philosophy of science. Before Kantianism gave rise to the notion that philosophy was *the* discipline which had as its core the *theory of knowledge,* and that as such it dealt with the foundations of the empirical sciences and was thus distinct from them, philosophy was not clearly demarcated from science, though conceptions of *science* were, of course, different at different points in the Western intellectual tradition; see Richard Rorty, *Philosophy and the Mirror of Nature* (Princeton: Princeton University Press, 1979), 131 ff. Recently philosophers like Quine have argued once again that philosophy cannot be clearly demarcated from science; see W.V.O. Quine, *From A Logical Point of View* (Cambridge: Harvard University Press, 1953) and *Ontological Relativity and Other Essays* (New York: Columbia University Press, 1969).

2. See Humberto Maturana, "The Ontology of Scientific Explanation," in *Research on Reflexivity,* ed. Fred Steier (Beverly Hills, Calif.: Sage, 1991). All further references to this volume will be noted in parentheses following the citation.

3. Richard Rorty, *Objectivity, Relativism, and Truth: Philosophical Papers,* *Vol. I* (New York: Cambridge University Press, 1991), 96. All further references to this volume will be noted in parentheses following the citation. The idea that to be on the *frontiers of knowledge* one must study everything *scientifically* is to conceive of the *frontiers of knowledge* as they were conceived of in the eighteenth century. This is not modern, let alone innovative thinking, unless one is using *modern* in the sense in which historians of philosophy refer to the thought of the seventeenth and eighteenth-centuries. As Rorty points out, it is an eighteenth century notion that "the access to Nature which physical science had provided should now be followed by the establishment of social, political, and economic institutions which were in accordance with Nature" and that by applying the methods of the physical sciences to the study of society, politics, and economics, that such institutions will come to be established (p. 22).

4. This view of the relation of the external world to the mind via language was the subject of Rorty's *Philosophy and the Mirror of Nature,* and continues to be contested in his more recent works. For references and detailed discussions of the unweaving done by these other thinkers, see, in addition to this work and *Objectivity, Relativism, and Truth* (n. 2, above): Richard Rorty, *Consequences of Pragmatism* (Minneapolis: University of Minnesota Press, 1982); *Contingency, Irony, and Solidarity* (New York: Cambridge University Press, 1989); and *Essays on Heidegger and Others: Philosophical Papers,* vol. 2 (New York: Cambridge University Press, 1991).

5. *Contingency, Irony, and Solidarity*, 5–6.

6. *Mirror of Nature*, 155–60.

7. Ibid., 157.

8. Ibid. According to Liddell-Scott, the earliest usages of the Greek *theoria* from which *theory* are translated into English as "a looking at, viewing, beholding" as well as "the being a spectator at the theatre or the public games," *Liddell and Scott's Greek-English Lexicon* (Oxford: Clarendon Press, 1975).

9. Jacques Derrida's works, taken as a whole, may be seen as a sustained inquiry into how philosophical writing as a genre disguises that it is a genre of writing; see, for example, *Dissemination* (translated with an Introduction and Additional Notes, by Barbara Johnson, [Chicago: University of Chicago Press, 1981]. The claim that the evolution of philosophical writing as a genre is tied to the emergence of alphabetic writing in early Greece is the major focus of the late Eric Havelock in his writings on early Greek society. Havelock's argument, first made in *Preface to Plato* (Cambridge: Harvard University Press, 1963) is that the pre- Socratics and Plato were an integral part of the transition in Greece from a traditional society in which oral poetic performance functioned as the primary vehicle for preserving and transmitting culturally significant communication to a society in which those charged with cultural preservation were literate—that is, were able to read and write their language and employed these techniques in storing and retrieving information. For further discussion of how Havelock's argument about the how and when of the emergence of philosophical writing can be combined with Derrida's inquiry into how philosophical writing as a genre disguises that it is a genre of writing, as well as a discussion of the alternative for "philosophical writing" that Heraclitus presented, see Joanne B. Waugh, "Heraclitus: The Postmodern Presocratic?" in *The Monist*, 74, no. 4 (1991): 605–23. A list of Havelock's other works dealing with Greek literacy and philosophy is found in notes 3 and 4 of this chapter. The suggestion that Havelock's argument about the effects of writing on the development of philosophical writing be combined with Derrida's insight into how philosophical writing represents speech and rhetoric is also made by Thomas Cole in *The Origins of Rhetoric in Ancient Greece* (Baltimore: Johns Hopkins University Press, 1991). The shift from the oral and aural to the visual in Greek cultural communication on which Havelock and Cole focus makes their work of particular interest here, since this shift may have something to do with Plato's choice of ocular metaphors, and with the fact that the position of *describing or writing-about* that is developed out of this metaphor leads to a *theory* of theory that has serious shortcomings, especially when it serves a model for a theory of communication, which is, after all, not an instance of describing but of talking with.

10. This may account for some of the hostility that Havelock's work provoked when it was first published, for the suggestion that philosophy awaits something so historical and contingent as alphabetic writing undermines some

central assumptions in the Western intellectual tradition. For further discussion of this point see Waugh, "Heraclitus: The Postmodern Presocratic?"

11. *Mirror of Nature*, 157–58.

12. Thomas Cole, *The Origins of Rhetoric in Ancient Greece*, 44.

13. *Mirror of Nature*, 141 ff.

14. See Rorty, *Contingency, Irony, and Solidarity*, 23–43; and Donald Davidson, "The Myth of the Subjective," in *Relativism: Interpretation and Confrontation*, ed. Michael Krausz (Notre Dame: University of Notre Dame Press, 1989), 159–72.

15. *Mirror of Nature*, 257 ff.

16. Ibid., 316–17.

17. Wilfrid Sellars, *Science, Perception and Reality* (New York: Routledge, 1963), 160. Rorty cites this passage in *Mirror*, 182.

18. *Science, Perception, Reality*, 169. This discriminative behavior in response to stimuli is "simply reliable signaling"; Rorty, *Mirror*, 182.

19. *Mirror of Nature*, 183.

20. See n. 1.

21. Thomas Kuhn, *The Structure of Scientific Revolutions* (Chicago: University of Chicago Press, 1970).

22. Thomas Kuhn, *The Essential Tension* (Chicago: University of Chicago Press, 1978).

23. Rorty, *Mirror of Nature*, 316. It is not that the virtues of science are denied. They are seen as belonging to science as a kind of community, rather than to science as a natural kind.

24. *Mirror of Nature*, 315–16.

25. Ibid., 315–16 and 316 n1.

26. See n. 14, above.

27. Donald Davidson, *Inquiries into Truth and Interpretation* (Oxford: Clarendon Press, 1984).

28. Donald Davidson, "A Nice Derangement of Epitaphs," in *Truth and Interpretation: Perspectives on the Philosophy of Donald Davidson*, ed. Ernest LePore (New York: Basil Blackwell, 1986), 445. Further references to this article will be notes in parentheses after the citation. Davidson notes that "the theory we actually use is geared to the occasion. We may decide later we could have done better by the occasion, but this does not mean necessarily that we now have a better theory for the next occasion. The reason for this is . . . perfectly obvious:

a speaker may provide us with information relevant to interpreting an utterance in the course of making an utterance (441–42).

29. Gregory Bateson, "Cybernetic Explanation," in *Steps to an Ecology of Mind*, ed. G. Bateson (New York: Ballantine Books, 1972), 399–410.

30. Robert Bostrom and Lewis Donohew, "The Case for Empiricism: Clarifying Fundamental Issues in Communication Theory," *Communication Monographs*, 59, no. 2 (June 1992): 109–129.

31. John Dewey, *The Quest for Certainty: A Study of the Relation of Knowledge and Action* (New York: Putnam, 1960). For a broad discussion of the alienating effects of the visualist metaphors associated with the orthodox canons of social science, see Michael Jackson, *Paths Toward a Clearing: Radical Empiricism and Ethnographic Inquiry* (Bloomington: Indiana University Press, 1989), esp. 5–12. All further references to this volume will be noted in parentheses following the citation.

32. Rorty, *Contingency, Irony, and Solidarity*, 4.

33. Of course, within a certain "final vocabulary," to use Rorty's phrase, the world may "decide" whether a particular sentence is true or false. But the world cannot propose a language for us to speak; *Contingency, Irony, and Solidarity*, 5.

34. Hayden White, "The Value of Narrativity in the Representation of Reality," *Critical Inquiry*, 7, no. 1 (1980): 5–27.

35. Richard Rorty, *Consequences of Pragmatism*, 197.

36. Kuhn, *Structure of Scientific Revolutions*.

37. See, e.g., Richard A. Schweder, *Thinking Through Cultures: Expeditions in Cultural Psychology* (Cambridge: Harvard University Press, 1991) where he advances the hopeful argument "that it is our prejudices and partialities that make it possible for us to see, if not everything, then at least something" (66). Also see Schweder's brilliant account of multiple objective worlds, "Divergent Rationalities," in *Metatheory in Social Science* eds., D. W. Fiske and R. A. Schweder (Chicago: University of Chicago Press, 1986).

38. See James Clifford, "Introduction: Partial Truths," in *Writing Culture: The Poetics and Politics of Ethnography,* eds. James Clifford and George E. Marcus (Berkeley: University of California Press, 1986), 1–26.

39. Laurel Richardson, "The Consequences of Poetic Representation: Writing the Other, Rewriting the Self," in *Investigating Subjectivity: Research on Lived Experience,* eds. C. Ellis and M. Flaherty (Newbury Park, Calif.: Sage Publications, 1992), 125–37.

40. See Rorty's discussion of this contrast in *Consequences of Pragmatism*, 191–210, esp. 195.

41. See David R. Maines, "Narrative's Moment and Sociology's Phenomena: Toward a Narrative Sociology," *The Sociological Quarterly*, 1993 (in press).

42. Rorty, *Consequences of Pragmatism*, 202.

43. Rorty, *Contingency, irony, solidarity*, esp. 3–22.

44. Robert Coles, *The Call of Stories: Teaching and the Moral Imagination* (Boston: Houghton Mifflin, 1989).

45. See Renato Rosaldo, *Culture and Truth: The Remaking of Social Analysis* (Boston: Beacon Press, 1989).

46. Henry Glassie, *Passing the Time in Ballymenone: Culture and History of an Ulster Community* (Philadelphia: University of Pennsylvania Press, 1982), xiv. All further references to this volume will be noted in parentheses following the citation.

47. Heinz von Foerster, "Through the Eyes of the Other," in *Research and Reflexivity*. eds. C. Ellis and M. Flaherty (Newbury Park, Calif.: Sage Publications, 1991), 63–75.

48. Barbara Myerhoff, *Number Our Days* (New York: Simon and Schuster, 1978), 19.

49. Dan Rose, *Black American Street Life: South Philadelphia, 1969-1971* (Philadelphia: University of Pennsylvania Press, 1987) esp. "Knowing Ourselves," 1–29.

50. Victor Turner, "Foreword," *Number Our Days*, xvii.

51. Rorty, *Contingency, Irony, Solidarity*, 189–98. In Rorty's view of solidarity, narrative inquiry is a means for achieving solidarity. As he says, "detailed descriptions of particular varieties of pain and humiliation (in e.g., novels or ethnographies), rather than philosophical or religious treatises, [are] the modern intellectual's principal contributions to moral progress" (192).

52. Jackson, *Paths Toward a Clearing*, 2.

53. Nelson Goodman, *Languages of Art* (New York: Bobs-Merrill, 1968), 6.

54. Arthur P. Bochner, "Recovering the Moral Imperatives of Social Science" (Keynote Address delivered at the International Conference on Personal Relationships, Oxford University, Oxford, England, July 1990).

55. Philip Roth, *Patrimony: A True Story* (New York: Simon and Schuster, 1991).

56. Sandra Butler and Barbara Rosenblum, *Cancer in Two Voices* (San Francisco: Spinsters Book Company, 1991).

57. Mark Neumann, "Living on Tortoise Time: Alternative Travel as the Pursuit of Lifestyle," *Symbolic Interaction*, 16 (1993): 201–35.

Chapter 12

1. I would like to acknowledge the support of the National Endowment for the Humanities during the preparation of this essay, and thank Raymie McKerrow for his helpful comments.

2. Robert L. Scott, "On Viewing Rhetoric as Epistemic," *Central States Speech Journal* 18 (1967): 9–17.

3. Barry Brummett, "Some Implications of 'Process' or 'Intersubjectivity': Postmodern Rhetoric," *Philosophy and Rhetoric* 9 (1976): 21–51; Richard A. Cherwitz and James W. Hikins, "Toward a Rhetorical Epistemology," *Southern Speech Communication Journal* 47 (1982): 135–52; Earl Croasmun and Richard A. Cherwitz, "Beyond Rhetorical Relativism," *Quarterly Journal of Speech* 68 (1982): 1–16; Richard A. Cherwitz and James W. Hikins, "Rhetorical Perspectivism," *Quarterly Journal of Speech* 69 (1983): 249–66; Barry Brummett, "A Eulogy for Epistemic Rhetoric," *Quarterly Journal of Speech* 76 (1990): 69–72; Richard A. Cherwitz and James W. Hikins, "Burying the Undertaker: A Eulogy for the Eulogists of Rhetorical Epistemology," *Quarterly Journal of Speech* 76 (1990): 73–77; see also Robert L. Scott, "On Viewing Rhetoric as Epistemic: Ten Years Later," *Central States Speech Journal* 27 (1976): 258–66.

4. Richard Rorty, ed., *The Linguistic Turn: Recent Essays in Philosophical Method* (Chicago: University of Chicago Press, 1967).

5. Typical of these responses are Robert Westbrook, Cornel West, and John Gouinlock. See *Westbrook, John Dewey and American Democracy* (Ithaca, N. Y.: Cornell University Press, 1991), 537–42, for his assessment of what Rorty leaves out of his Deweyan pragmatism. West's *The American Evasion of Philosophy: A Genealogy of Pragmatism* (Madison: University of Wisconsin Press, 1989) credits Rorty's influence on the reawakening of interest in pragmatism, citing "a widespread disenchantment with the traditional image of philosophy as a transcendental mode of inquiry" (3) as a contributing factor to this interest. West's chapter on Quine and Rorty provides an impressive summary of the influence of Dewey on Rorty, as well as another account of his misreadings (see Dewey's philosophical professionalism, 199). West isolates Rorty's truncated historicism painted with the broad brush, his "distrust of theory and . . . preoccupation with transient vocabularies" (208-9) as the major flaws in Rorty's neopragmatism. West would prefer a more politically radicalized neopragmatism. James Gouinlock, in "What is the Legacy of Instrumentalism? Rorty's Interpretation of Dewey," *Journal of the History of Philosophy* 28 (1990): 251–69, takes Rorty to task for rejecting Dewey's metaphysics, the bad Dewey. All of these critics seem to overlook the point that Rorty might be interested in doing something other than being a footnote to Dewey. See C. G. Prado, *The Limits of Pragmatism* (Atlantic Highlands, N.J.: Humanities Press International, 1987), 47: "there was Dewey. Now there is also Rorty's Dewey. The only issue is which we find most productive in our own projects."

6. I am borrowing here from Herbert W. Simons, ed., *The Rhetorical Turn: Invention and Persuasion in the Conduct of Inquiry* (Chicago: University of Chicago Press, 1990).

7. Calvin O. Schrag, "Rhetoric Resituated at the End of Philosophy," *Quarterly Journal of Speech* 71 (1985): 164–74.

8. John S. Nelson, Allan Megill, and Donald N. McCloskey, ed., *The Rhetoric of the Human Sciences: Language and Argument in Scholarship and Public Affairs* (Madison: University of Wisconsin Press, 1987).

9. Jeffrey L. Bineham, "The Cartesian Anxiety in Epistemic Rhetoric: An Assessment of the Literature," *Philosophy and Rhetoric* 23 (1990): 43–61.

10. Raymie E. McKerrow, "Critical Rhetoric: Theory and Praxis," *Communication Monographs* 56 (1989): 91–111.

11. Rorty, "A Reply to Six Critics," *Analyze & Kritik* 6 (1984): 85.

12. Rorty, *Philosophy and the Mirror of Nature* (Princeton: Princeton University Press, 1979), chap 8.

13. Ibid.

14. Ibid., 315ff.

15. Ibid., 357ff.

16. Rorty, "Deconstruction and Circumvention," *Critical Inquiry* 11 (1984): 1–23.

17. Rorty, "Two Cheers for the Cultural Left," *South Atlantic Quarterly* 89 (1990): 227–34.

18. Kolenda rightly corrects the assumption that Rorty views the constructive and the systematic as dispensable with a toss of the head [see James W. Hikins and Kenneth S. Zagacki, "An Attenuation of the Claims of the Rhetoric of Inquiry," *Quarterly Journal of Speech* 74 (1988):201–28]. Kolenda reminds Rorty's readers that constructive philosophy, just as normal discourse of normal science, consists of a backdrop against which the edifier plays his role. See Konstantin Kolenda, *Rorty's Humanistic Pragmatism: Philosophy Democratized* (Tampa: University of South Florida Press, 1990), 97–98.

19. Cover notes. Richard Rorty, *Objectivity, Relativism, and Truth: Philosophical Papers*, vol. 1 (Cambridge: Cambridge University Press, 1991), 93–110.

20. Rorty, "Deconstruction," 20.

21. Rorty, "Inquiry as Recontextualization."

22. Rorty, "Solidarity or Objectivity?" in *Objectivity*, 31.

23. John J. McDermott, "The Pragmatists," in *Reading Philosophy for the XXIst Century*, ed. George F McLean (Latham: University Press of America, 1989), 251.

24. The importance of redescription is developed at length in *Contingency, Irony,* and *Solidarity* (New York: Cambridge University Press, 1989); see also further applications of it discussed in "Truth and Freedom: A Reply to Thomas McCarthy," *Critical Inquiry* 16 (1990): 633–43. McCarthy's article is "Private Irony and Public Decency," *Critical Inquiry* 16 (1990): 355–70.

25. See esp. Rorty, *Mirror,* 377; also see Thomas S. Kuhn, *The Structure of Scientific Revolutions,* 2nd ed. (Chicago: University of Chicago Press, 1970).

26. Rorty, "Truth and Freedom," 643.

27. Rorty, *Mirror,* 372.

28. Kolenda, *Rorty's Pragmatism,* 100.

29. Rorty, "Science as Solidarity," in *Objectivity,* 41.

30. Ibid., 39.

31. Rorty, "Truth and Freedom," 635; the major focus of the exchange with McCarthy in *Critical Inquiry* is the notion of transcultural validity.

32. See in addition to the exchange with McCarthy already cited, Richard Bernstein, "One Step Forward, Two Steps Backward: Richard Rorty on Liberal Democracy and Philosophy, "*Political Theory* 15 (1987): 538–63; Rorty, "Thugs and Theorists: A Reply to Bernstein," *Political Theory* 15 (1987): 564–80; and Guadalajara, Mexico, November 10–15, 1985, in *Proceedings and Addresses of the American Philosophical Association* 59 (1986): 747–59.

34. Ibid., 264.

35. See Rorty, *Mirror,* esp. 389-94; Rorty, "Truth and Freedom, 634, and elsewhere; also "Special Reports," cited above. Rebecca Comay, in "Interrupting the Conversation: Notes on Rorty," *Telos* 67: 119–30, is especially critical of Rorty's perception of the freedom of inquiry.

36. Rorty, "Truth and Freedom." In this essay, Rorty *backed off* the somewhat strident tone (he calls it his *perhaps overblown rhetoric* of the controversial remarks made at the Inter-American congress of Philosophy in Guadalajara, but he continues to stress his belief in the inability—or perhaps a better word is uselessness—of philosophy to serve as the foundations of politics. His point in "Truth and Freedom" is that critical *redescriptions* of his work have shown him points where he does *look pretty bad* (635).

37. Rorty, *Contingency,* 176; the same point is also made in "The Priority of Democracy to Philosophy," in *Objectivity,* 175–96.

38. Rorty, "Thugs and Theorists," 571.

39. Rorty, *Mirror,* 318; Rorty's critics have tended to minimize the move he makes here from Oakeshott's *universitas* dominated by epistemology to societas dominated by hermeneutics as a model of inquiry: "For epistemology, conversation is implicit inquiry. For hermeneutics, inquiry is routine conversation."

40. William James, "What Pragmatism Means," *Pragmatism and American Culture*, ed. Gail Kennedy (Boston: D.C. Heath, 1950), 1–22.

41. Ibid., 12.

42. Ibid.

43. Ibid., 12–13

44. Ibid., 13

45. Rorty, "Truth and Freedom," 635; emphasis added.

46. Rorty, "Two Cheers."

47. Rorty differs programmatically with multiculturalists on one important aspect: he suggests the need for *socialization* into the traditions of our society to remain a primary emphasis, especially among younger children. Multicultural perspectives should gradually increase as children advance into secondary and postsecondary education, which will most likely result in gradual expansion of such perspectives into lower levels—just as *new math*, computers, and structural linguistics have. See "Two Cheers."

48. This is of course a reference to the controversial division made in *Contingency* between philosophy that affects our private hopes and that which can be useful in a public way. The reference to learning from the past comes from Rorty's embrace of fallibilism discussed in "Truth and Freedom"; see McDermott, "Pragmatism," on the fallibilism of the tradition.

49. Rorty, "Inquiry as Recontextualization," 93. Also see "The Contingency of Selfhood" in *Contingency*.

50. Rorty, "Inquiry as Recontextualization," 96.

51. Ibid., 101; see Hikins and Zagacki, "An Attentuation."

52. Rorty, "Science as Solidarity," 38.

53. W. Barnett Pearce, *Review of Contingency, Irony, and Solidarity, Communication Theory* 1 (1991): 70.

54. Rorty, *Mirror*, 7.

55. Rorty, "Truth and Freedom," 634. In this same article, Rorty again takes up the charge that the *relativist* philosopher cannot provide an *answer* to Hitler: "But I have always . . . been puzzled about what was supposed to count as the knockdown answer to Hitler. Would it answer him to tell him that there was a God in Heaven who was on our side? How do we reply to him when he asks for evidence for this claim? Would it answer him to say that his views are incompatible with the construction of a society in which communication is undistorted . . . ?" (636). Rorty indicates that questions such as these led him to give up on the idea of *demonstration* as the goal of philosophy, "that demonstration was just not available in this area, that a theoretically sophisticated

bully and I would always reach an argumentative standoff" (637). Of interest to scholars of rhetoric is that given the task of *answering* the Nazi, but of *converting* him, Rorty says he "would have some idea of how to set to work" (637). The hope of reweaving the Nazi's web of beliefs and desires is borne by rhetoric; not philosophy.

56. Rorty, "Truth and Freedom," 643.

57. See Rorty, "Introduction: Pragmatism and Philosophy," in *Consequences of Pragmatism* (Minneapolis: University of Minnesota Press, 1982), xiii–xlvii; Janet S. Horne, "Rhetoric after Rorty," *Western Journal of Speech Communication* 53 (1989): 247–53.

58. Rorty, "The Intellectuals at the End of Socialism," *Yale Review* 80 (1992): 1-16; 1 Rorty, "Feminism and Pragmatism" (Tanner Lecture, University of Michigan, December 7, 1990).

59. See James B. McOmber, "An Annotated Bibliography on the Rhetoric of Inquiry" (paper given to Speech Communication Association, April 1990); also see Lawrence J. Prelli, *A Rhetoric of Science: Inventing Scientific Discourse* (Columbia: University of South Carolina Press, 1989).

60. See Martin J. Medhurst, Alberto Gonzalez, and Tarla Rai Peterson, ed., *Communication and the Culture of Technology* (Pullman; Washington State University Press, 1990).

61. See Nelson *et al.,* "Rhetoric of Inquiry," 5: "rhetoric of inquiry does not seek to be a subject unto itself or an authority over other investigations." Nevertheless, the importance of the study of rhetoric within various disciplines is demonstrated in the volume that follows the essay cited.

62. Rorty, *Mirror*, 359.

63. See Horne, "Rhetoric After Rorty."

64. See John S. Nelson, "Seven Rhetorics of Inquiry," in the *Rhetoric of the Human Sciences*, 407–14.

65. John Lyne, "Rhetorics of Inquiry," *Quarterly Journal of Speech* 71 (1985): 65.

66. John S. Nelson et al., "Rhetoric of Inquiry," *The Rhetoric of the Human Sciences*, 3–18.

67. Kolenda, *Rorty's Pragmatism*, xii.

68. Nelson, "Seven Rhetorics of Inquiry," 413, emphasis added.

69. See Rorty, "Deconstruction and Circumvention," 4; and Jean-Francois Lyotard, *The Postmodern Condition: A Report on Knowledge,* trans. Geoff Bennington and Brian Massumi (Minneapolis: University of Minnesota Press, 1984).

70. Michael J. Leff, "In Search of Ariadne's Thread: A Review of the Recent Literature on Rhetorical Theory," *Central States Speech Journal* 29 (1978): 73–91.

71. Bineham, "Cartesian Anxiety."

72. The recent exchange between Brummett and Scott in *The Quarterly Journal of Speech* may illustrate the extent to which the two schools of thought overlap. See Barry Brummett, "Eulogy," and Robert L. Scott, "Epistemic Rhetoric and Criticism: Where Barry Brummett Goes Wrong," *Quarterly Journal of Speech* 73 (1990): 300–303.

73. Regardless of the issues raised by the recent exchange in the *Quarterly Journal of Speech* between Brummett and Scott, their basic agreement on inter-subjectivity is not in question.

74. See n. 2, above

75. Rorty, *Mirror*, chapter 7. Also see Cornel West, *The American Evasion of Philosophy*, for an excellent analysis of Rorty's radical turn toward postfoundationalism in 1972, when he wrote "The World Well Lost," found in *Consequences*, 3–18.

76. See Richard Cherwitz and James Hikins, "Toward a Rhetorical Epistemology," *Southern Speech Communication Journal* 47 (1982): 135–62; Earl Croasmun and Richard A. Cherwitz, "Beyond Rhetorical Relativism," *Quarterly Journal of Speech* 68 (1982): 1–16; Richard Cherwitz and James Hikins, "Rhetorical Perspectivism," *Quarterly Journal of Speech* 69 (1983): 249–66; Hikins and Zagacki, "An Attentuation," and "Rhetoric, Objectivism, and the Doctrine of Tolerance," in *The Critical Turn: Rhetoric and Philosophy in Postmodern Discourse*, eds. Ian Angus and Lenore Langsdorf (Carbondale: Southern University Illinois Press, 1993), 100–125.

77. Barry Brummett, "Some Implications of Process."

78. See Bineham, "Cartesian Anxiety," 52–55.

79. Rorty, *Mirror*, 6.

80. Rorty, "Inquiry as Recontextualization," 96, n. 2.

81. As this essay was being prepared, for instance, the controversy surrounding the death of President Zachary Taylor was settled. This trivial but pointed example serves to illustrate that, had it been demonstrated conclusively that Taylor was poisoned, the contingency of our knowledge up to the present would have been made apparent. The pragmatist would submit that all our knowledge is thus historically, culturally, and rhetorically bound.

82. Rorty, *Mirror*, 6.

83. Rorty, *Contingency*, 7.

84. Prado, *The Limits of Pragmatism*, 10.

85. See note 51, above.

86. Rorty, *Contingency*, 6–7.

87. Ibid., 6.

88. Lyotard, *The Postmodern Condition*, 60.

89. Rorty, *Contingency*, 9.

90. McDermott, "The Pragmatists," 254. Prado, The Limits of Pragmatism, 9, discusses transiency as *temporality of reality*," following Philip Wiener, "Pragmatism," in *Dictionary of the History of Ideas*, ed. Philip Wiener (New York: Charles Scribner's Sons, 1973), 551–70.

91. Rorty, *Contingency*, 6–7.

92. Rorty, "Science as Solidarity," 41.

93. James, "What Pragmatism Means," 12.

94. See n. 10, above; also McKerrow, "Critical Rhetoric and Propaganda Studies," *Communication Yearbook* 14: 249–55; "Critical Rhetoric and the Possibility of the Subject," in *The Critical Turn*.

95. McKerrow, "Critical Rhetoric: *Theory and Praxis*," 91.

96. Ibid., 91, 108.

97. Ibid., 91; emphasis added.

98. See Richard A Cherwitz and James W. Hikins, "Burying the Undertaker," for their criticisms of Horne and McKerrow for not engaging in philosophical argument. In "Rorty's Circumvention of Argument: Redescribing Rhetoric," *Southern Communication Journal* 58: 169–181, I sketch out possible reasons why, from the pragmatist's view, rhetoric needs no philosophical support. For Rorty's position, see "Pragmatism, Relativism, and Irrationalism," in *Consequences* and "Truth and Freedom."

99. Rorty, *Contingency*, 9.

100. McDermott, "The Pragmatists," 257–59.

101. McKerrow, "Critical Rhetoric: Theory and Praxis," 92.

102. Rorty, "Private Irony and Liberal Hope," in *Contingency*. Empowerment is also discussed by Horne in "Rhetoric after Rorty."

103. See Rorty, "Pragmatism, Relativism, and Irrationalism," in *Consequences*, 167, for a discussion of the function of conversational constraints and conversational support: "the real issue is not between people who think one view as good as another and people who do not. It is between those who

think our culture, or purpose, or institutions cannot be supported except conversationally, and people who still hope for other sorts of support."

104. McKerrow, "Critical Rhetoric and Propaganda Studies."

105. Ibid., 250.

106. For discussion of the categories of normal and abnormal discourse, see Rorty, *Mirror*, 322ff.; see also Kuhn, *The Structure of Scientific Revolutions*.

107. McKerrow, "Critical Rhetoric and Propaganda Studies," 250.

108. Richard Rorty, "Beyond Realism and Anti-Realism," in *Wo steht die sprachanlytische Philosophie heute* eds., Herta Nagl-Docekal et al. (Vienna: Oldenbourg, 1986), 114; emphasis added.

109. This distinction is discussed by Rorty in "Introduction: Pragmatism and Philosophy," *Consequences*, xii-xlvii.

110. McKerrow, "Critical Rhetoric: Theory and Praxis," 103.

111. Ibid.

112. Rorty, "Inquiry as Recontextualization," 99.

Chapter 13

1. Herbert A. Wichelns, "The Literary Criticism of Oratory," *Studies in Rhetoric and Public Speaking in Honor of James Albert Winans*, ed. A Drummond (New York: Century, 1925), 181–216; Michael C. Leff and Margaret Organ Procario, "Rhetorical Theory in Speech Communication," *Speech Communication in the 20th Century*, ed. Thomas W. Benson (Carbondale: Southern Illinois University Press, 1985), 3–27; David Zarefsky, "The State of the Art in Public Address Scholarship," in *Texts in Context: Critical Dialogues on Significant Episodes in American Political Rhetoric*, ed. Michael C. Leff and Fred J. Kauffeld (Davis, Calif.: Hermagoras Press, 1988), 13–27; Robert S. Iltis and Stephen H. Browne, "Tradition and Resurgence in Public Address Studies," *Speech Communication: Essays to Commemorate the 75th Anniversary of the Speech Communication Association*, ed. Gerald M. Phillips and Julia T. Wood (Carbondale: Southern Illinois University Press, 1990), 81–93.

2. W. Barnett Pearce, "Scientific Research Methods in Communication Studies and their Implications for Theory and Research," *Speech Communication in the 20th Century*, ed. Thomas W. Benson (Carbondale: Southern Illinois University Press), 255–81. The diversity of contemporary approaches is evident in popular textbooks, such as Malcom O. Sillars, *Messages, Meanings, and Culture: Approaches to Communication Criticism* (New York: Harper Collins, 1991) and Karyn Rybacki and Donald Rybacki, *Communication Criticism: Approaches and Genres* (Belmont, Calif.: Wadsworth, 1991).

3. Leff and Kauffeld, *Texts in Context;* John Angus Campbell, ed., *Special Issue on Rhetorical Criticism, Western Journal of Speech Communication,* 54, no. 3 (1990). Martha Solomon, "The Things We Study: Texts and Their Interactions," *Communication Monographs* 60 (1993): 62–68.

4. Herbert Simons, "Chronicle and Critique of a Conference," *Quarterly Journal of Speech* 71 (1985): 58. Simons's remark should not be taken to indicate that Rorty was entirely successful in his persuasion. Simons also reports that most participants at the conference responded to Rorty as a relativist and ultimately rejected much of his view. For the most sustained response to Rorty in a Speech Communication Association journal, see Janet Horne, "Rhetoric after Rorty," *Western Journal of Speech Communication* 53 (1989): 247–59.

5. Although Rorty has engaged in some public dialogue with scholars of rhetoric, and his work is referenced and discussed in our journals and books, Rorty has not yet written a detailed response to the debates occurring among rhetoricians. Nonetheless, for reasons of convenience I will sometimes refer to positions that I believe are consistent with Rorty's published work as "Rorty's position" or "Rorty's view" and the like, of course citing appropriate passages from Rorty as evidence.

6. F. E. Peters, *Greek Philosophical Terms: A Historical Lexicon* (New York: New York University Press, 1967); David J. Wolpe, *In Speech and in Silence: The Jewish Quest for God* (New York: Henry Holt, 1992).

7. Iltis and Browne "Tradition," 84.

8. Ibid., 85.

9. Michael Leff and Andrew Sachs, "Words the Most Like Things: Iconicity and the Rhetorical Text," *Western Journal of Speech Communication* 54 (1990): 252–73; Michael Calvin McGee, "Text, Context, and the Fragmentation of Contemporary Culture," *Western Journal of Speech Communication* 54 (1990): 274-289. Both Leff and McGee have produced an influential body of scholarship. The special issue of the *Western Journal of Speech Communication* in volume 54 is devoted to their projects and critical responses by other major contemporary rhetorical critics. I will refer to the Leff and Sachs article as an important expression of Leff's general project. The available works of Leff suggests that the article is consistent with Leff's earlier views. I do not intend to minimize Sachs' contributions to the article, but merely wish to focus on its relationship to earlier works by Leff.

10. Leff and Sachs, "Words," 253.

11. Ibid., 253.

12. Ibid., 257.

13. Ibid., 266.

14. Ibid., 270.

15. Ibid., 270.

16. This is part of Campbell's assessment of the difference between the two research trends that McGee and Leff represent. See John Angus Campbell, "Between the Fragment and the Icon: Prospect for a Rhetorical House of the Middle Way," *Western Journal of Speech Communication* 54 (1990): 346–76. McGee seems to accept this characterization. See Michael Calvin McGee, "An Interview with Michael C. McGee," *The Iowa Gazette* (spring 1993): 3.

17. Some researchers limit the definition of *postmodern* to name an approach to criticism rather than historical period. But even those who promote the definition of *postmodern* as a critical tendency claim that our contemporary period seems to be engaged in this mode of criticism more than other periods. For the purposes of this paper, I will assume that *postmodern* names certain historical conditions. For discussions about the definition of postmodern, see Jean-François Lyotard, *The Postmodern Condition: A Report of Knowledge* (Minneapolis: University of Minnesota Press, 1984); Ihab Hassan, *The Postmodern Turn: Essays in Postmodern Theory and Culture* (Columbus: Ohio State University Press, 1987); E. Ann Kaplan, ed., *Postmodernism and Its Discontents* (New York: Verso, 1988; Charles Jencks, *What is Post-Modernism?* (New York: St. Martin's Press, 1989); and Scott Lash, *Sociology of Postmodernism* (New York: Routledge, 1990).

18. McGee, "Text, Context," 284.

19. Carole Spitzack and Kathryn Carter, "Women in Communication Studies: A Typology for Revision," *Quarterly Journal of Speech* 73 (1987): 401–23 describe how this exclusionary tendency has obscured the contributions of women to society, and how traditional definitions of *public address* tend to perpetuate this exclusion.

20. Mark Fenster, "The Problem of Taste within the Problematic of Culture," *Communication Theory* 1 (1991): 87–105, reviews and critiques research about how consumer preferences form *cultures of taste*. Popular media consumption of music, film, and television entertainment provide some examples of how group identity can be formed through audience member interactions. Mary Ellen Brown, "Soap Opera and Women's Culture: Politics and the Popular," in *Doing Research on Women's Communication: Perspectives on Theory and Method*, ed. Kathryn Carter and Carole Spitzack (Norwood, N.J.: Ablex, 1989), 161–90, describes how soap operas allow for a collective *oppositional reading* among women struggling against sexism. Also see Jim Collins, *Uncommon Cultures: Popular Culture and Post-Modernism* (New York: Routledge, 1989), and Alan Tomlinson, ed., *Consumption, Identity, and Style: Marketing, Meanings, and the Packaging of Pleasure* (New York: Routledge, 1990) for postmodern accounts of subcultures generated by consumerism.

21. McGee, "Text, Context," 286.

22. Ibid., 287.

23. Ibid., 274.

24. Leff and Sachs, "Words," 255.

25. Ibid.

26. Ibid., 259.

27. Ibid.

28. Ibid., 258.

29. Rorty, *Consequences of Pragmatism*, 133.

30. Rorty, *Essays : Volume 2*, 14.

31. Rorty, *Contingency*, 14.

32. Ibid., 18.

33. McGee, "Text, Context," 276.

34. Ibid., 275.

35. Rorty, *Contingency*, 12.

36. Here, I am distinguishing between *methodology* as the logic or science of investigative strategies, and *methods* as particular strategies of investigation. Thus, to say that an object of investigation "corresponds" to its method is merely to acknowledge that every method picks out what it considers its object of investigation. I do not intend to imply a correspondence theory of truth in which a method might be construed as picking out objective characteristics of the world that have an ontological status independent of our means of inquiring about them.

37. McGee, "Text, Context," 288, emphasis in the original.

38. Rorty, *Contingency*, 13.

39. McGee, "Text, Context," 279.

40. Rorty, *Contingency*, 67.

41. McGee, "Text, Context," 287.

42. Ibid., 281.

43. Richard Rorty, *Objectivity, Relativism, and Truth: Philosophical Papers Volume I* (Cambridge: Cambridge University Press, 1991), 207–8. Also see Richard Rorty, "Postmodern Bourgeois Liberalism," *Journal of Philosophy* 80/10 (1983): 583–89.

44. McGee suggests that Habermas and Karl-Otto Apel "are virtually alone in their attempt to theorize speaking as the regulative ideal of discourse" (278). This statement curiously excludes the work of a wide range of scholars who have been influenced by Heidegger, Merleau-Ponty, Kristeva, and Bakhtin, to mention a few of the most important figures who treat speaking as the richest and most salient model for understanding human communication.

45. Rorty's views on these issues are expressed most forcefully in *Contingency, Irony, and Solidarity,* and in the final chapter of *Objectivism, Relativism, and Truth.*

46. Richard Rorty, "On Ethnocentrism: A Reply to Clifford Geertz," *Michigan Quarterly Review* 25 (1986): 525–34. Reprinted in Rorty, *Objectivity, Relativism, and Truth,* 203–10.

47. Rorty, *Contingency,* 20.

48. Ibid., 19.

49. Ibid., 73.

50. Ibid.

51. Ibid., 74.

52. Ibid., 102.

53. John Lyne, "Rhetorics of Inquiry," *Quarterly Journal of Speech* 71 (1985): 67.

54. Michael Calvin McGee and John R. Lyne, "What are Nice Folks Like You Doing in a Place Like This?: Some Entailments of Treating Knowledge Claims Rhetorically," *The Rhetoric of the Human Sciences: Language and Argument in Scholarship and Public Affairs,* ed. John S. Nelson, Allan Megill, and Donald N. McCloskey (Madison: University of Wisconsin Press, 1987), 398.

55. See Rorty's response to a paper presentation by Geertz in Rorty, *Objectivity, Relativism, and Truth,* 203–10. Also see "Science and Solidarity" in the same volume for arguments pertinent to Rorty's claim that ethnocentrism is not necessarily in conflict with liberal democratic values.

56. Rorty, *Objectivity, Relativism, and Truth,* 208.

57. Jo Burrows, "Conversational Politics: Rorty's Pragmatist Apology for Liberalism," *Reading Rorty,* ed. Alan Malachowski (Cambridge, Mass.: Basil Blackwell, 1990), 322–38.

Contributors

⟨⟩ ⟨⟩

Thomas M. Alexander is associate professor in the department of philosophy at Southern Illinois University at Carbondale. He is the author of *John Dewey's Theory of Art, Experience, and Nature: The Horizons of Feeling* (SUNY Press, 1987) and several articles on American as well as classical philosophy, political philosophy, and aesthetics. Most recently, he has published "The Human Eros," in *Philosophy and the Reconstruction of Culture*, edited by John Stuhr (SUNY Press, 1993).

Mitchell Aboulafia is professor of philosophy and the humanities at the University of Houston–Clear Lake. He is the author of *The Mediating Self: Mead, Sartre, and Self-Determination* (Yale University Press, 1986) and *The Self-Winding Circle: A Study of Hegel's System* (W.H. Green, 1982). He edited *Philosophy, Social Theory, and the Thought of George Herbert Mead* (SUNY Press, 1992), and he is writing a book that is tentatively entitled *Mead, Pragmatism, and Modernity*. He publishes in the areas of social theory, continental theory, and pragmatism and is a member of the executive committee of the Society for the Advancement of American Philosophy.

Arthur P. Bochner is professor of communication and co-director of the Institute for Interpretive Human Studies at the University of South Florida. He has written numerous articles on family communication. His most recent published work focuses on narrative as social inquiry and the impact of research involvement on the lives of researchers. He is advisory editor for *Communication Theory* and associate editor of *Text and Performance Quarterly*.

Isaac E. Catt is professor and chair of the department of communication and theater at Millersville University of Pennsylvania. His research focuses on issues in the phenomenology of communication and has been published in *Communication and Social Control*, *Communication as Performance*, the *Western Journal of Speech Communication*, *Journal of Communication Therapy*, *Literature as Performance*, and (in translation) in *Sprache und Sprechen*.

Vincent M. Colapietro is professor in the philosophy department at the Rose Hill campus of Fordham University. He is the author of *Peirce's Approach to the Self* (SUNY Press, 1989) and *Glossary of Semiotics* (Paragon House, 1993). His research, which focuses on classical American pragmatism, the general theory of signs, and contemporary approaches to subjectivity, has appeared in *The Journal of Philosophy*, *The Monist*, *The Journal of Speculative Philosophy*, and *International Philosophical Quarterly*.

Janet S. Horne is assistant professor in the department of communication arts at Salisbury State University in Maryland. Her research, which focuses on rhetorical theory and criticism, philosophy of communication, and religious communication, has been published in the *Western Journal of Communication*, the *Southern Communication Journal*, and the *Journal of Communication and Religion*. She is completing a book on Richard Rorty that is tentatively entitled *Conversation, Contingency, and Civil Society: The Rhetoric of Richard Rorty*.

Lenore Langsdorf is professor of the philosophy of communication in the speech communication department of Southern Illinois University at Carbondale. Her research primarily uses hermeneutic phenomenology to explore issues in the communicative constitution of social life, the rationality of lived experience, and rhetorical and philosophical ways of inquiry. She has been published in several edited volumes and in *Human Studies*, *Informal Logic*, and the *Review of Metaphysics*. She is co-editor (with Ian Angus) and a contributor to *The Critical Turn: Rhetoric and Philosophy in Postmodern Discourse* (Southern Illinois University Press, 1993), editor of a 1994 special issue of *Human Studies* on phenomenology in communication research, co-director of the Society for Phenomenology and Existential Philosophy, member of the executive committee of the Society for the Advancement of American Philosophy, and general editor of the Philosophy of the Social Sciences series at SUNY Press.

Richard L. Lanigan is professor of the philosophy of communication in the speech communication department of Southern Illinois University at Carbondale. He has been a postdoctoral fellow in philosophy at the University of Dundee (Scotland) and at the University of California at Berkeley. He has served four terms as the chair of philosophy of communication division of the International Communication Association, is a founding member of the commission on semiotics and communication of the Speech Communication Association, and is president of the Semiotic Society of America. He has written numerous articles and five books on semiotic phenomenology, the most recent of which is *The Human Science of Communicology: The Phenomenology of Discourse in Foucault and Merleau-Ponty* (Duquesne University Press, 1992), and is editor of and a contributor to a special four-number issue of *Semiotica* (1982) entitled "Semiotics and Phenomenology."

Frank J. Macke is assistant professor in the department of communication and theatre arts at Mercer University. His most recent research employs Foucault's genealogical method in examining the problematic relationship of eloquence to institutional discourse. He has published in *Communication Education* and the *Journal of Communication Studies*, as well as in several edited volumes.

Mick Presnell is assistant professor in the department of human communication studies at California State University, Chico. His research has been published in *Quarterly Journal of Speech*, *Text and Performance Quarterly*, *Journal of Broadcasting and Electronic Media*, and several edited volumes. He is co-editor (with Kathryn Carter) and a contributor to *Interpretive Approaches to Interpersonal Communication*, and is completing a book entitled *Postmodern Strategies for Communication Research*.

Charlene Haddock Seigfried is professor in the philosophy department at Purdue University. She is the author of two books on William James: *Chaos and Context* (Ohio University Press, 1980) and *William James's Radical Reconstruction of Philosophy* (SUNY Press, 1990) and has published numerous book chapters, articles, and dictionary entries on classical American philosophy. Central to her research are issues of antifoundationalism, scientific methodology and hermeneutics, aesthetics, rhetoric, and philosophical psychology. She is editor of a special 1992 issue of *Hypatia* on feminism and pragmatism, and received a Center for Humanistic Studies grant for a book on the same topic. She is a past national fellow of the W.K. Kellogg Foundation and has directed faculty seminars at several universities on the individual and community.

Leonard Shyles is associate professor in the department of communication arts at Villanova University. His essays on political communication and propaganda analysis have appeared in *Political Communication, Armed Forces and Society,* and *The Journal of Broadcasting,* and his research on televised political advertising in political campaigns has appeared in edited volumes. He is co-editor (with Thomas A. McCain) and a contributor to *The Thousand Hour War: Communication in the Gulf* (Greenwood Press, 1994).

Andrew R. Smith is assistant professor in the speech and communication studies department at Edinboro University of Pennsylvania. His research on intercultural rhetoric and critical phenomenology has been published in *Human Studies, Japanese and Western Phenomenology,* and *Text and Performance Quarterly.* He is a founding member of the commission on semiotics and communication in the Speech Communication Association, an associate editor of *Text and Performance Quarterly,* and is completing a book (with Jacqueline Martinez) entitled *Signifying Harassment: Communication, Ambiguity and Power.*

Joanne B. Waugh is associate professor in the department of philosophy at the University of South Florida. Her research, which focuses on ancient philosophy and contemporary aesthetics, has been published in *The Monist, The Journal of Aesthetics and Art Criticism, The Journal of Aesthetic Education,* and *Art Criticism.* She is co-editing (with Francisco Gonzalez) and is a contributor to *The Third Way: A New Approach to Platonic Studies.*

Name Index

⪻⪼

Aboulafia, Mitchell, 15–16
Alexander, Thomas M., 12–13, 156, 161, 163, 170–71
Apel, Karl-Otto, 263, 327
Aristotle, 49, 51, 52–56, 61–65, 73, 180, 192, 199, 200
Austin, J. L., 4, 199

Barthes, Roland, 41
Bateson, Gregory, 60, 68, 223
Bergmann, Gustav, 195–96, 199–200
Berkeley, Bishop George, 217
Bernstein, Richard, 105
Bineham, Jeffrey L., 236, 243
Bochner, Arthur P., 16–17, 106–07, 157, 230, 301 n. 3
Brummett, Barry, 243, 245

Catt, Isaac E., 11–12
Colapietro, Vincent M., 8–9
Derrida, Jacques, 9, 33, 41, 44–46, 160, 215
Dewey, John, 2, 5, 6, 7, 10, 12–15, 17, 24–25, 34, 72, 75, 81, 86, 88–90, 94, 115–16, 117, 126–28, 132–34, 136, 138–54, 155–76, 180–81, 195–208, 244
Davidson, Donald, 16, 76, 91, 93, 221–22
Descartes, Rene, 2, 7, 26, 86, 148, 199, 203, 214–15, 217

Foucault, Michel, 13–14, 52, 65, 67, 155, 157, 159–61, 163–71, 247
Freud, Sigmund, 172, 260, 268

Gadamer, Hans-Georg, 145, 306 n. 12
Galileo Galilei, 200–03
Gibson, James J., 141–42, 148

Glassie, Henry, 227–28, 233

Habermas, Jurgen, 16, 131–32, 149, 153, 184–86, 262–63, 287, 310 n. 4
Hegel, G. W. F., 67, 81, 83, 118, 156–57, 162–63, 182–83, 266
Heidegger, Martin, 104–05, 164, 266, 310 n. 4
Horne, Janet S., 17–18
Hume, David, 217

Jakobson, Roman, 57, 59, 62, 68
James, William, 2, 5, 7, 10–12, 17, 24–45, 97, 99, 102–07, 110, 113–14, 116–28, 239

Kant, Immanuel, 24, 136, 217, 311 n. 11
Kuhn, Thomas S., 1, 7, 16, 219–20, 225

Langsdorf, Lenore, 14–15
Lanigan, Richard L., 9–10, 109–10
Leff, Michael, 18–19, 243, 253–55, 257–60, 265
Locke, John, 4, 135–37, 139, 141, 146, 217
Lyotard, Jean-Francois, 25, 74, 80, 160, 172, 174, 176, 243, 245

MacIntyre, Alasdair, 138
Macke, Frank J., 13–14
McDermott, John J., 237, 245–47
McGee, Michael Calvin, 18–19, 253, 255–57, 261–63, 266
McKerrow, Raymie E., 236, 246–49, 310 n. 4
Mead, George Herbert, 2, 5, 13–16, 132, 138, 142, 179–94, 195–96, 199, 204–05, 208
Merleau-Ponty, Maurice, 40, 54, 65, 67–69, 157, 163–64, 173

Subject Index

❧ ❧

abduction, 9, 10, 29, 50, 52–55, 58–69, 76, 78–80, 82–88, 93, 196, 202, 207
aesthetic experience, 11, 13–14, 32, 85–90, 124–26, 133, 148, 150, 157, 162–64
agency, 27, 30, 32, 37–39
art, 152, 167–68, 170–73, 205–06
axiology, 4, 5, 6, 10, 73–74, 76, 79–82, 85, 93, 110, 198

being, 44–45, 101, 249
belief, 2, 27, 30, 120-21, 240
body, 14, 143, 157, 163

cash-value, 11–12, 97–114, 248
categories, 5, 8, 30, 33, 42–44, 45–46, 82
common sense, 27, 30, 38–39, 42, 47, 97, 117, 201, 265
communication, philosophy of, 1–5, 11–12, 14, 19, 196, 203–04, 265
communication theory, 51–52, 211, 223–24
community, 3, 7, 12, 47, 71–72, 88, 92, 148–50, 153, 183–84, 187–90, 192–93
competence, 11–12, 97, 103
conversation, 9, 17, 195–96, 206–07, 224–25
coping, 47, 224, 227, 243, 263
creativity, 14–15, 157, 159, 161–62, 203, 206–07
culture, 2, 5, 88–89, 136, 149
cultural psychology, 10, 55, 62–64, 67, 79

deconstruction, 16, 45–46, 198, 266
deduction. See Inference
democracy, 12, 74–76, 128, 131–33, 137–39, 142, 149–54, 189, 197, 264, 268
dialogue, 36, 51–53, 64, 77–78
difference, 33, 44, 82, 182, 264
dispute, 75, 80, 92

emergence, 2, 8, 25, 184, 257
empiricism, 2, 101, 103–07, 112–13, 159–60, 200-02, 205, 217, 228
ends, 10-11, 81, 85–87, 119, 158
Enlightenment, the, 12, 131–37, 153, 160, 183, 212, 263, 297 n. 2
epistemology, 4, 5, 17, 45, 47, 81, 116–17, 127–28, 198, 218, 224, 236, 262
ethics, 11, 14, 32, 85–88, 90, 107–08, 110-12, 181
ethnocentrism, 7, 73–76, 78, 84, 87, 89, 91, 266
ethnography, 228, 231–33
experimentalism, 14, 15, 200-02, 204

fallibilism, 2, 4, 7, 10, 33, 47, 81, 91, 238
firstness. See Categories
foundationalism, 2, 23, 182, 241, 249, 263, 266–67
fragmentation, 18, 125–26, 255–56

generalized other, 179, 183, 187, 192–94

habits, 6, 26, 30, 32, 36, 41–42, 127, 163–64

iconicity, 18–19, 254, 258–60, 262
idealism, 46–47, 138, 160
ideology, 98, 240, 255, 262, 267–68
imagination, 6, 8, 10, 13, 38, 43, 79, 91, 132, 144, 146–49, 151, 154, 171
induction. See Inference
inference, 27, 50, 54, 58–60, 62, 65, 68, 82, 202, 218
inquiry, 2, 4, 5–6, 10, 13–14, 17, 25, 29, 43, 236–37
intercultural contexts, 10, 72, 74, 78–81
interdependence, 16, 184, 193

335